COMPUTATIONS FROM THE ENGLISH

A PROCEDURAL LOGIC APPROACH FOR REPRESENTING AND UNDERSTANDING ENGLISH TEXTS

ROBERT F. SIMMONS

University of Texas, Austin

INCLUDING HCPRVR
AND ITS DOCUMENTATION
BY DANIEL L. CHESTER

Prentice-Hall, Inc., Englewood Cliffs, New Jersey 07632

Library of Congress Cataloging in Publication Data

Simmons, Robert F. (date)
  Computations from the English.

  Bibliography: p.
  Includes index.
  1. English language—Data processing. 2. Linguistics
—Data processing. I. Chester, Daniel L. Using
HCPRVR. 1984. II. Title.
PE1074.5.S5 1984   420'.72   83-6693
ISBN 0-13-164640-0

Editorial/production supervision
  and interior design: LYNN S. FRANKEL
Cover Design: BEN SANTORA
Manufacturing buyer: GORDON OSBOURNE

©1984 by Prentice-Hall, Inc., Englewood Cliffs, New Jersey 07632

All rights reserved. No part of this book
may be reproduced, in any form or by any means,
without permission in writing from the publisher.

Printed in the United States of America

10 9 8 7 6 5 4 3 2 1

ISBN 0-13-164640-0

Prentice-Hall International, Inc., *London*
Prentice-Hall of Australia Pty. Limited, *Sydney*
Editora Prentice-Hall do Brasil, Ltda., *Rio de Janeiro*
Prentice-Hall Canada Inc., *Toronto*
Prentice-Hall of India Private Limited, *New Delhi*
Prentice-Hall of Japan, Inc., *Tokyo*
Prentice-Hall of Southeast Asia Pte. Ltd., *Singapore*
Whitehall Books Limited, *Wellington, New Zealand*

Computations
 So Like Poems
  Limn the Mind
   In Truth

CONTENTS

1 NOW AND THEN   1

    1.1   Today: An Advertisement   1
    1.2   Yesterday: A Historical Review   4
         1.2.1   Goals   4
         1.2.2   Mechanical translation   5
         1.2.3   Text management   6
         1.2.4   Question answering   6
         1.2.5   Understanding text   7
         1.2.6   Theoretical developments   9
         1.2.7   Logic and language   10
    1.3   This Book   12
    1.4   Selected Readings   13

2 KNOWLEDGE AND COMMUNICATION   14

    2.1   Knowing and Knowledge   14
    2.2   Knowing Something   16
    2.3   Representing Knowledge   17
    2.4   Defining Communication   19
         2.4.1   Thoughts, images, and concepts   19
    2.5   An Introspective Protocol   20

2.6	Symbolizing Concepts 23	
2.7	Semantic Processing 26	
2.8	Semantic Networks 28	
2.9	Selected Readings 29	

3 THE PLACE OF LOGIC   31

    3.1   Propositional Logic   31
    3.2   Predicate Logic   35
    3.3   Procedural Logic   39
    3.4   Definite Clause Grammars   48
    3.5   Exercises   52

4 REPRESENTING CONSTITUENTS OF ENGLISH TEXT   53

    4.1   Levels of English   53
    4.2   Constituents   55
    4.3   Inflectional Constituents   60
    4.4   Clausal Constituents   62
    4.5   Adjectival and Adverbial Constituents   65
    4.6   Determiners, Negations, and Conjunctions   66
    4.7   Sentential Constituents   68
    4.8   Theory of Semantic Relations   72
    4.9   Logic of Case Relations   73
    4.10 Exercises   75

5 TRANSLATING SENTENCES TO SEMANTIC RELATIONS   76

    5.1   Parsing and Translation   76
    5.2   Dependency Trees   78
    5.3   Computing Semantic Relations   81
    5.4   Semantic Translation   85
    5.5   Procedural Grammar for a Sentence   88
    5.6   Exercises   96

6 COMMANDING A ROBOT BLOCK-STACKER   99

    6.1   Background   99
         6.1.1 Simulating hand and blocks   100
         6.1.2 Defining the blocks   103

Contents   vii

    6.2   The English Command Subset   104
    6.3   Analyzing Commands   109
    6.4   Conjunction of Arguments and Commands   112
    6.5   Procedural Semantics   113
    6.6   Exercises   115

7   QUERYING A DOCUMENT DATA BASE   119

    7.1   A Shelving Robot   119
    7.2   Background   120
    7.3   A Document Data Management System   123
    7.4   A Formal Query Language   128
            *7.4.1   Program description of the formal
                      language interpreter   130*
    7.5   The English Query Language   134
            7.5.1   Program description of procedural logic grammar   136
    7.6   Protocol of System Behavior   140
    7.7   Extending the System   147
    7.8   Exercises: 150

8   CASE STUDIES OF A NARRATIVE SCHEMA   151

    8.1   Studies of Discourse   151
    8.2   The V-2 Rocket Story   153
    8.3   A Flight Schema   155
            8.3.1   Computing the schema instantiation   159
    8.4   Bottom-Up Control of Schema Instantiation   162
            8.4.1   Bottom-up program description   166
    8.5   Schema Analysis   170
    8.6   Exercises   172

9   QUESTIONING AND SUMMARIZING THE TEXT   174

    9.1   Background of Research   174
    9.2   Asserting an Instantiated Schema as a Text Data Base   175
    9.3   Analysis of English Questions   177
    9.4   Retrieving Answers with Fuzzy Matching   181
    9.5   Questions and Answers   184
    9.6   Generating English Answers   186
    9.7   Computing Summaries   188
    9.8   Exercises   193

10 PARSING AND PARAPHRASE — 194

    10.1   Parsing Procedures   194
           10.1.1   Top-down and bottom-up parsing   195
    10.2   A Strictly Top-Down Parser   197
    10.3   Bottom-Up Parsing   200
    10.4   Chart Parsing   202
    10.5   Translation and Paraphrase   207
    10.6   Paraphrasing Sentences   208
    10.7   Translation Examples   212
    10.8   Context Sensitive Translation from English to Japanese   214
    10.9   Summary   222
   10.10 Exercises   223

11 KNOWLEDGE SYSTEMS — 224

    11.1   Introduction   224
    11.2   An Example Expert Mechanic   225
    11.3   Applications to Teaching   233
    11.4   Knowledge Systems for Understanding Language   234
    11.5   Knowledge Schemas   239
    11.6   Constructing Knowledge Schemas   243
    11.7   The Knowledge Paradigm   246
    11.8   Closure   247
    11.9   Exercises   248

APPENDIX A   USING HCPRVR, by Daniel Chester — 249

APPENDIX B   FURTHER ANALYSIS OF THE ROCKET STORY OF CHAPTER 8 — 272

REFERENCES AND BIBLIOGRAPHY — 289

INDEX — 299

AUTHOR INDEX — 305

PREFACE

The purpose of this book is to describe a procedural logic approach to the representation of English for various computational uses. Such uses include parsing and translating sentences and texts, transforming English commands into robot actions, translating English questions into formal-language queries to data bases, transforming text into knowledge bases that support questioning and summarizing, and communicating in general with specialized knowledge systems. Some tasks, such as translating robot commands or data base queries from the English, are well understood; others, such as transforming English text into a knowledge system, questioning and summarizing it, and translating it into other languages remain at the level of experimental research. Procedural logic systems are described to accomplish each of these tasks for example texts; the reader who masters these techniques will be in an excellent position to use these experimental procedures in wider applications and so gradually promote them to well-understood methods.

    A general perspective of thirty years of computational research devoted to understanding natural language is given in Chapter 1. A commonsense philosophy and phenomenology of what it means to "know," "understand," and "communicate" is offered in Chapter 2. Procedural logic is introduced and informally presented in the third chapter. The fourth provides an outline of linguistic case analysis and a system for representing sentences as semantic relations. The fifth chapter develops a procedural logic grammar for translating sentences into semantic relations. Chapters 6 and 7 describe canonical-form logic programs for commanding a robot and questioning a document data base. Chapters 8 and 9 present experimental systems for transforming narrative text into a knowledge system, and questioning and summarizing. The next chapter analyzes and compares various logic implementations of parsing algorithms, then applies the techniques to paraphrasing and translating natural language. Chapter 11 offers an example of an expert knowledge system and explores some possible approaches to text knowledge bases. The procedural logic interpreter HCPRVR is documented in Appendix A and Appendix B includes grammars and programs related to Chapter 8.

I have used the book as a text for advanced undergraduates in computer sciences for courses in artificial intelligence and natural-language processing, and as a programming manual in a graduate seminar in computational linguistics. It can be read at several levels. The first level is an evening's "read"—ignoring anything that is difficult; at this level the reader gains a sense of what kinds of understanding of language computers can be expected to exhibit. The next level is one of verbal understanding of the techniques that can be used to enable computer applications with language; in this reading the sections that offer detailed descriptions of procedures are skipped. The third level includes understanding the algorithms and procedures in a manner that convinces the reader that he or she could make such programs. The fourth level includes careful study of the text description and accomplishment of the exercises and suggested readings; this is the level of mastery. A fifth level will be achieved by some minority of readers who perceive more elegant and effective procedures for computing with English. I look forward to hearing from them.

Some of the questions that underlie the preparation of this book—most of which still need answers—are the following.

- What is a language that we can communicate with it, and what can be expected from inserting a computer into the communication process?
- In what sense does a computer "understand" English?
- Is there some positive world where computers send each other technical documentation in an English untouched by human hands, and where, if everything goes well, humans never have to read it?
- Can computers describe pictures in English and provide drawings to illustrate a text?
- Can computers accumulate knowledge systems automatically from reading text?
- Are we ready to undertake the mammoth task of describing natural languages in sufficient detail to support automatic translation of technical documents?
- Are these procedural logic descriptions for understanding fragments of language a partial theory of human understanding?
- When we ascribe knowledge, goals, and intentions to a computer to ease our process of prediction and understanding, should we believe it?
- When we describe human knowledge, goals, and intentions as computational processes, should we believe that our minds are computers?

ROBERT F. SIMMONS

1
NOW AND THEN

1.1 TODAY: AN ADVERTISEMENT

You can purchase a natural-language interface for your favorite data base—going price, $40,000. You may not find it as friendly as the advertisements led you to believe, but you will at least be able to add to its vocabulary.

You can subscribe to a legal text searching service and for a few hundred dollars an hour browse on your console with Boolean logic combinations of terms through a complete collection of state and federal lawbooks.

You can join a library network or a news story retrieval service, and using key words—words describing titles, names, places, and events—find a large set of documents relevant to your interests. Or you might enlist an automatic dissemination service to keep you abreast of documents in your own special field.

Even translating systems for words, phrases, and sentences can be bought—*caveat emptor*.

But the real excitement is found in the natural-language laboratories and in the past several years of dissertations, monographs, and research reports. Starting about 1975, an imaginary "Optimistic News Service" might have published the following bulletins:

> (*ONS 1975*) Scripts and Frames Combine Atomic Meanings. Roger Schank at Yale and Marvin Minsky at MIT show that understanding of implicit meanings is possible if sentences or perceptions are fitted into models of larger ideas. Wendy Lehnert demonstrates that scripts answer questions, and uses "ghost paths" to show what might have been.

(*ONS 1976*) Knowledge Representation Language Announced. Daniel Bobrow and Terry Winograd announce KRL as a frame-based system for high-level computations. Their GUS system simulates a travel agent.

(*ONS 1976*) Meehan's Computer Composes Stories. James Meehan at Yale demonstrates that a story is derived by simulated characters satisfying their motivations in cooperation and conflict with others in a simulated world. Problems, attempts, failures, and successes form the plot. Translating to English used a simple procedure.

(*ONS 1977*) Yale Natural Language System Scans News Stories. Yale computer connected to news service scans news stories for automobile accidents and terrorist attacks, providing gists of content.

(*ONS 1979*) Carbonell's Program Interprets Meanings. A new language-processing program developed by Jaime Carbonel for his Yale dissertation makes widely differing conservative and liberal interpretations of the political significance of the Panama Canal Treaty.

(*ONS 1978*) Epistemology of Language Outlined. Brachman, in the tradition of his professor Wm. Woods, shows the finest grain of conceptual representation for English. Fahlman and Shapiro claim precedence in fine-grain network computations.

(*ONS 1978*) Cooperative Question Answering Possible. Jerry Kaplan in his University of Pennsylvania dissertation shows that computers can explain why they fail to find answers to questions.

(*ONS 1979*) Palo Alto Proliferates Expert Knowledge Systems. Professors Feigenbaum and Buchanan at Stanford announce several new knowledge systems for applications to medical diagnosis. SRI's expert, Prospector, makes mineral discoveries. Knowledge acquisition systems query experts to obtain inference rules.

(*ONS 1980*) Sager, Petrick, Robinson, and R. Bobrow report grammars for "significant" subsets of English. Large computational grammars for automatic analysis of English sentences are available in several laboratories.

(*ONS 1981*) Automatic Translation of German Technical Text. A new report by J. Slocum gives translation of 200 pages of technical German to good quality English.

(*ONS 1981*) Taxonomy for English Dictionary. R. A. Amsler presents taxonomic structure of thousands of nouns and verbs from the *Merriam-Webster Pocket Dictionary*.

(*ONS 1981*) Computers to Understand Intentions. Tennant, Cohen, Perrault, and Allen agree that computer users expect natural language data retrieval systems to understand their users' intentions, speech acts, and goals. Allen's dissertation program in Toronto computes the intention of "Can you reach the salt" to be "Please pass the salt."

(*ONS 1981*) SRI Scientists Report Principles of Dialogue. Task Dialogue Understanding System developed for instructing an apprentice to assemble an air compressor.

(*ONS 1981*) Procedural Logic Closes Procedural-Declarative Gap. A high-level programming language, PROLOG, long familiar to Europeans is used by Warren and Perreira to describe and apply grammars. Kowalski argues that from one viewpoint it is a logical description, while from another, that of the PROLOG compiler, it is a procedural programming language. McDermott expresses friendly skepticism.

(*ONS 1982*) Newest Grammar Learning Systems. Berwick at MIT and H. Smith at the University of Texas induce natural-language grammars from previously analyzed sentences.

(*ONS 1982*) Insightful Books Published for Natural Language Buffs. New books became available over the past few years: Sager, Tennant, Findler, Barr and Feigenbaum, Winograd, Schank and Riesbeck, Schank, and Simmons. (See Selected Readings at the end of this chapter.)

So much for public relations. But...

If we faced some great urgency to construct the most general and intelligent natural-language computing system that today's understandings of linguistics, logic, and computer science could support, the result would at best be comparable to an *idiot savant*, age ten.

It would include marvelous, inhuman abilities for verbatim storage and word-oriented retrieval of dictionaries and printed text in hundreds of millions of words. It would contain fairly general grammars for syntactically analyzing wide ranges of sentence structures. It would have systems for semantic analysis—translation of sentences into formally defined languages—for a fairly small range of sentence structures. For some of these it could respond by manipulating appendages such as robot arms; for some requests it could return answers from a database; for others it could create new entries.

Its farthest reach would be fairly limited abilities to participate intelligently in highly specialized dialogues. At the conceptual level, only the beginnings of representation for interlocking, embedded concepts—in terms of such schemas as scripts and frames—could be included. Only the crudest representations of how concepts actually interrelate in texts could be provided. Multiply embedded belief spaces for understanding interactive plans and interpreting speech acts are only dimly understood.

It would surely be able to translate sentences from one natural language to another—albeit with marginal accuracy. It could learn the grammars it requires for analyzing sentences by deducing them from example translation pairs, but it would be notably stupid in resolving pronouns and ellipsis, or recognizing references to concepts used in previous sentences, and it would misunderstand most metaphors. It would be largely at a loss to understand and cooperate with human intentions and goals as they are implied—not expressed—in natural language and the situation of its use. It would be quite shaky in its causal representations for events and states described in language. And of course it would be largely deaf to spoken language and blind to the meaning of pictures.

Fortunately no urgency calls to build this poor creature; rather it should first evolve at least to a "teenage savant" in its present environment—a hundred laboratories across the world. Its computational organs grow in widely dispersed locations, and its organization evolves in many minds and many books. Predictions of when this evolution will culminate in general, cooperative, sensible language knowledge systems are hazardous; but I dare assert that the reader who, appreciating the history that led to this point, masters the logical structures and computations currently understood will stand comfortably at the threshold ready to assist and receive this new creature's birth.

1.2 YESTERDAY: A HISTORICAL REVIEW

1.2.1 Goals

Among the earliest and most enduring goals of computer science is the expectation that digital computers will be programmed to read and communicate in natural human languages. In 1950, Turing's [1963] design to test the difference between a computer and a human intelligence assumed the development of systems that could maintain a dialogue in English. By 1947, Andrew Booth and Warren Weaver confidently expected that mechanical translation between natural languages would be among the early important accomplishments of nonnumeric computation [Locke and Booth, 1955]. Vannevar Bush [1955] was concerned with automated indexing and access to a library of books and documents; he outlined a system called Memex to allow a researcher to browse through an automated library of ultra-microfilm, marking associative trails to record his comments and cross-references to related texts, as he studied a particular topic. The Memex library would gradually accumulate associative references to related materials as an aid for future uses of the system.

These ideas were current in the 1940–1950 decade, and as mathematical theories of computation were realized in vacuum tubes and wire during the same period, nonnumeric computations for translating computer languages (i.e., compiling), for task scheduling in operating systems, and for accessing libraries of subroutines were among the first notable successes beyond the numerical calculations that were the obvious motivation for computer development. And research on actual systems for processing natural languages began. Attempts at mechanical translation, automatic indexing, abstracting, dissemination, and retrieval of printed documents became common in the 1950s decade, and initial attempts at natural-language dialogues began to appear in the literature.

1.2.2 Mechanical Translation

The first approaches to mechanical translation (MT) were based on the assumption that word-for-word substitutions from a computer-accessible dictionary would result in usable translations. It was soon apparent that words had so many different meanings, depending on their uses in various contexts, that purely lexical translation could not provide a satisfactory result. Emphasis shifted to study of the syntactic structure of natural language, and the development of automatic syntactic analysis procedures to produce tree structures within which the substitution of lexical translations would be more limited and better controlled. Some improvements of translation resulted, but the vast scope of the problem of understanding the content of natural-language texts became increasingly apparent. Attempts at classifying words into finer distribution categories became an important part of the MT effort and, gradually, some notable successes in terms of high quality translation for small texts, and gross but usable translations of books were reported by the early part of the 1960s. By then, however, several of the early workers had become thoroughly disillusioned and U.S. funding agencies became convinced that high quality automatic translation was simply not a practical goal for the immediate future. At that time, dozens of translation projects existed in the United States and in Europe, several of which were accomplishing excellent research. By 1970 only a trickle of funds was devoted to MT in the United States and research continued in only two or three of the centers.

A notable irony was that the government agencies that had procured crude MT systems were able to use them effectively for preliminary examination of literature to decide what deserved high-quality human translation effort. Survivors of one of the more successful projects at Georgetown University created a corporation to sell automated translation services and continue to provide them at less than high-quality levels to this day. The Europeans continued their research which has finally achieved a level sufficient to seek significantly large funding from the Common Market organization for a multilanguage system to support translations of technical communications among participating countries. Japan, also, has assigned MT research a significant national priority. In the United States, only one of the original translation efforts survived; that at the Linguistic Research Center of the University of Texas, concerned with German-English translation of specialized technical literature. That project has recently reported good quality translation for a few hundred pages of text. In Canada at least one project at the University of Montreal maintained some funding until recently. European work was surveyed in English by Vauquois [1979] and in a German paper by Bruderer [1978]. An early survey Machine Translation edited by Booth [1967] is still an excellent grounding in the MT area.

At this writing, there is one NSF-funded project in MT research at Yale and two or three others supported by industrial funding in the United States. The outlook for practical applications to technical documentation is increasingly good as a result of improved computers, high-level languages, sophisticated operating systems, and most important, increased understanding of the structure of natural language.

1.2.3 Text Management

Research on information management of natural-language text fared better. By the late fifties and early sixties techniques had been developed to characterize text by content terms, and systems for retrieving documents related to a user's key word request became common. Attempts at automatic extracting were published, and systems for automatically characterizing a text by its most frequent content terms were studied. Experimental systems for automatically disseminating documents to users on the basis of key word profile matching were to be found in several organizations. These lines of research resulted in commercial systems for document management that have become widely used by business, industry and libraries throughout the world. The success of these efforts derives from the fact that the words of a text do represent the nature of its content on a statistical basis. Full text searching systems that are queried by a Boolean combination of content words have proved to be a most excellent way of browsing through large collections of documents; these are particularly useful if they are supported by methods for truncating inflectional endings of words and recognizing synonyms. Borko [1967] surveys various key word approaches among early studies of natural-language understanding.

Such systems are limited by the fact that they do not have capabilities for recognizing differing meanings of words depending on the contexts in which they occur. Nor can they focus the meaning of a question to distinguish "what," "where," "when," "how," and "why" types of answers; they only find the contexts in which a given set of words are used. The general problem of natural-language understanding requires far more than these capabilities. Artificial intelligence (AI) research aimed early toward the problems of understanding questions and computing intelligent answers from structured data sometimes derived from the analysis of natural-language texts.

1.2.4 Question Answering

The canonical form of most research in question answering is a system for translating natural-language questions into statements in a formal query language. These are interpreted as programs to access a highly structured data base—usually hand-constructed. One of the earliest of these systems was a conversationalist that could carry through a discussion about the weather, supported by data that included relevant information about the past, current, and forecasted weather reports. This was succeeded by systems to answer questions about family trees and to query baseball records. These were immediately followed by programs to understand and solve algebra problems, and one that asserted simple statements to a data base and answered questions about it. All these systems, and many others of the same type, were accomplished by 1965, and each contributed some understandings about computational analysis of natural-language questions. By the early 1970s this work reached fruition in Lunar, a large prototype system for natural-language queries to a moon rocks data base that led to today's beginnings of commercial applications—natural-language interfaces for data management systems. Several of these systems are described in the *Handbook of Artificial Intelligence* by Barr and Feigenbaum [1981].

1.2.5 Understanding Text

The general problem of transforming a text to a well-structured data base received much attention during the same period. Methods for representing the content of the text as network structures of words or concepts were introduced by Quillian [1969], and these *semantic networks* found successful applications as a viable alternative structural form for general data bases. Yet, the meaning structures that could be computed from sentences of text were obviously much shallower than a human's understanding. Finding terms to which pronouns referred was a frustrating problem for which no general solution emerged; relating a sentence at hand to a preceding context of sentences led to numerous difficulties; and representing the organization of a narrative or an exposition required an understanding of the author's intentions that remained largely beyond the capabilities of researchers in the 1970s.

Problems of representation of natural-language meanings became a dominant theme of the 1970s. At MIT Winograd's remarkable SHRDLU program could command a robot hand and answer questions in English about a microworld of blocks. This program represented its world as theorems in Microplanner—a procedural form of logic—and provided a version of Halliday's Systemic Grammar for a small but complex subset of English statements and questions. Shortly thereafter, Charniak reported a rather significant failure in attempting to use similar methods to understand text from a second-grade reader. He found that he could construct procedures to assert implications of any text statement (e.g., "Tim saw that it was raining" implies "Tim may take his umbrella," etc.) and procedures to use those implications to understand an otherwise disconnected event in text. But he noticed that in such an apparently simple example as

> "Don't get Tim a top. He already has one.
> He'll make you take it back."

finding the correct antecedent for "it" requires much understanding of human shopping behavior patterns, and no simple semantic rules are sufficiently general to work in all cases. He was also distinctly dissatisfied with the ad hoc nature of procedures for making and using text implications. His dissertation demonstrated that there is a vast distance between successful understanding of sentences and questions in a microworld, and the understanding of the simplest texts for children.

At Stanford, Roger Schank and his associates had invented an approach to understanding language that involved translating sentences into networks of verbal concepts—conceptual dependency structures. As each sentence was so translated, it would automatically generate a large set of implications. For example, "John hit Mary" might generate,

> John was angry with Mary.
> Mary might be hurt.
> Mary might hit John.
> Mary might be angry with John.
> etc.

The obvious problem of choking the system with inferences ensued.

Schank's solution, as he joined Abelson at Yale, was to embark on the study of prepackaged inference schemas—called scripts and plans. The now classic Restaurant Script included roles for the customer, waitpersons, and cashier and provided expected sequences of events: for example, the customer is hungry, he enters a restaurant, a waitperson comes to take his order, a meal is brought, the customer eats, pays the cashier, and exits. A script applier recognizes patterns of key words in a parsed sentence and selects the scripts it matches. The events specified by the script serve as amplifying information that can be used to understand omitted events: for example, John went to a restaurant and got a plate of wonton. In this example, the restaurant script makes explicit the events of entering, ordering, being served, eating, and paying, all of which are inferred by the ordinary reader of the sentence.

The script approach was augmented by introducing plans and relatively standardized methods of accomplishing them with planboxes. For example, if "John was hungry" is encountered, the hunger goal is aroused associated with a planbox that might include "go to the kitchen and prepare food," "go to a restaurant," and so on. These plans may refer to the "cooking" or "restaurant" scripts to provide further details for the understanding process.

Recent results of this approach include moderately successful programs for scanning newspaper stories to select those concerning particular classes of events (e.g., automobile accidents and terrorist activities have been studied in detail). As a result of the scriptal analysis, texts are enriched and structured to provide very good question answering, and summarizing capabilities. Supporting the systems with a generation grammar in another language has provided the capability to translate by summarizing the event in the new language. The work of the Yale group has been widely publicized in books by Schank and Abelson [1977], Lehnert [1978], and Schank and Riesbeck [1980]. These texts cite several Yale dissertations, each of which takes a step in applying plans and scripts to one or another area, or in studying plan and goal taxonomies. If this approach is to be faulted, its weakness may lie in the absence of any apparent intention of accumulating and communicating sufficient lexicon, grammar, and higher-level schemas for broad understanding of English texts.

At New York University, Naomi Sager and Ralph Grishman have developed large lexicons and grammars for the analysis of pharmacological texts. In this work they observed that within a discipline there are *content sublanguages*. "Pharmacological agents affect organs," "people test drugs," and so on, show acceptable forms of content statements, whereas "drugs test people" and "organs affect drugs" do not. A book by Sager [1981] provides detailed descriptions of the lexical and grammar forms and the methods of text analysis. The linguistic system has been under development for more than a decade and these researchers appear to have accumulated one of the largest and most general English grammars in the country.

Natural-language research at Stanford Research Institute (SRI) has also resulted in a large grammar prepared mainly by Jane Robinson [1982]. Although the research problems concerned speech understanding during a pump assembly task, the syntactic portion of the grammar needed little revision to analyze a large set of queries to a naval data base. At IBM Yorktown, Petrick and his colleagues also developed a significantly large grammar for understanding English queries to a data base. It may be hoped that the grammars accumulated in these laboratories can be augmented with appropriate schema structures to apply to the understanding of narrative and expository texts.

1.2.6 Theoretical Developments

Contemporary with Woods' successful development of Lunar at Bolt Beranek and Newman, other BBN workers were concerned with applying semantic networks to tasks of computer-assisted instruction. Carbonell's early work with Scholar [1970] was followed by a most sophisticated teaching system by J. S. Brown and others [1975]. These teaching systems used networks of verbal concepts to represent their knowledge and incorporated parsing systems similar to those developed on the Lunar project. A notable paper, "What's in a Link" [Woods, 1975] raised important theoretical issues concerning the formal structure of semantic networks that were largely answered in subsequent research. Hendrix [1975] at Texas developed a mathematical basis for one form of semantic networks; Schubert [1976] and others in Canada developed them as predicate logic structures, and Shapiro [1979] further advanced the graph-theoretic basis for his network processing system. A collection of papers encompassing these developments under the title *Associative Networks* appeared in 1979, [Findler 1979], providing both a history and various applications of the ideas.

The decade of the 1970s also saw the introduction of the philosophical problem of speech acts; a series of works beginning with Perrault and Cohen [Cohen, 1978] was augmented most recently by James Allen [1979] showing the application of speech act theory to the analysis of dialogue. Two conferences concerning Theoretical Issues in Natural Language Processing, [Tinlap, 1975, 1978] included psychological and philosophical contributions in addition to the usual experimental programming papers. Enough work has been published in the area of speech acts to offer convincing evidence that such philosophical formulations as Searle's [1969] and Grice [1975] have definite practical implications for natural-language processing programs.

In a more theoretical vein, cognitive psychologists and text linguists have been concerned to understand methods by which humans comprehend texts. Beaugrande [1980,1981] surveyed the various text linguistic approaches to language as well as those developed in computational linguistics and AI. His work is rich with example analyses of various multisentence texts. Norman and Rumelhart [1975] considered semantic networks as a model of human cognitive representation, and Miller and Johnson-Laird present detailed semantic analyses for a wide range of vocabulary items in their book *Language and Perception* [1976].

1.2.7 Logic and Language

Various theorem provers were among the first successful AI programs. Wang's algorithm and Newell and Simon's Logic Theorist and General Problem Solver (GPS) were among early notably successful AI programs. Raphael's initial procedural question answerer led him to a series of logic-based natural-language systems that eventually culminated in QA-4, a high-level computer language for computing AI and natural-language problems. Black's implementation of a backward chaining logic as a realization of GPS was a concise theorem prover that showed how English-like questions could be answered by logic. Except for a lack of efficiency in binding variables, this system anticipated later developments in resolution theorem proving that led to the construction of the procedural logic compiler PROLOG.

Soon thereafter, Alan Robinson [1965] described a resolution proof procedure, and a whole school of theorem-proving studies developed offering numerous improvements to the basic resolution algorithm. To this school it was apparent that most AI problems could be expressed in first order logic and solved with a resolution theorem prover. This was the declarative position in contrast to a procedural viewpoint that held that problems could best be solved with procedures tailored to fit the special needs of particular situations. Two criticisms of the declarative position were common: first, not all problems could be expressed in first-order logic, and second, resolution theorem proving was not particularly efficient, so problems requiring dozens of axioms could not in practice be proved in any reasonable length of time. Of course, the procedural position was subject to the major criticism that if a new procedure were written for every problem variation, AI would not be a science, as much as a bag of tricks.

The situation was thus set for new developments. The procedurally oriented MIT laboratory developed advanced procedural languages, PLANNER and CONNIVER, in which procedures were invoked by pattern, and problem solving by backward and forward chaining was incorporated. SRI provided the high-level language, QA4—a logic based descendent of Raphael's work on question answering—that offered comparable capabilities. The chief problem with early implementations of these languages was that they were excessively expensive and slow to use. Large problems could not in fact be solved in these systems in any reasonable length of time.

But at the same time, the realization grew in the theorem-proving community that an axiom system and a theorem prover were analogous to a program and its interpreter. A monograph by Kowalski [1974] developed this idea of logic as procedures and showed that suitably ordered axiom systems could be interpreted by a resolution theorem prover as effective procedures for computing numerical operations such as addition, multiplication, and factorials; for solving problems in the microworld of blocks; for accomplishing list operations; and for parsing sentences. Contributing importantly to these ideas was work by Colmerauer [1978], who had collaborated in the development of PROLOG, a first procedural logic interpreter reported by Roussell [1975]. Colmerauer's interest was in parsing and translating natural French, and PROLOG was designed to provide a programming language that could deal with nondeterministic natural-language translation systems. PROLOG evolved as a general system for interpreting sets of logical axioms expressed in a form called Horn clauses. Warren, Pereira, and Pereira [1977] further developed the language and Warren [1977] introduced a compiler. Most recently, Pereira and Warren [1982] have reviewed and developed Colmerauer's theories of grammar and showed the nature of grammars for parsing sentences and for translating English sentences to quantified first-order logic statements.

Procedural logic was also introduced into the LISP language by Komorowski [1982], Chester [1980], and by Robinson and Sibert [1980]. A series of logic programming workshops communicated the efficacy of PROLOG throughout much of Europe, and applications to natural language control of data bases and expert knowledge systems became very common in Europe during the seventies. A book by Gallaire and Minker [1978] reports several such systems as well as other applications, and Clark and Tarnlund's *Logic Programming* [1982] shows further theory and applications. A detailed description of procedural logic is provided in Chapter 3 of this book. In fact, this book came into being following a series of experiments by the author and Dan Chester in using procedural logic to accomplish the parsing, translation, generation, and question-answering tasks we were concerned with. We found the approach remarkably effective and efficient for concisely expressing and interpreting complicated language processing tasks.

The developments of computational logic with respect to natural language provide a most encouraging history of small steps followed by significant insights such as the resolution algorithm, again followed by a series of improvements and the sudden realization that axiom systems could be interpreted as procedures, resulting in a powerful new high-level programming language, PROLOG. Along the way, the procedural-declarative controversy dissolved into a realization that in procedural logic, a few ordering constraints on a logical description ensures that the description can be interpreted as a procedure. As in physics with waves and particles, a system of procedural logic axioms may be viewed in two alternative ways—as declarative or procedural, depending on the researcher's purpose.

1.3 THIS BOOK

Today, approximately 40 years since the first efforts at natural-language research on computers, thousands of scientific papers and dozens of books record successes, algorithms, truths, and half-truths of the computational structure of natural language. Large commercial applications are based on word searching of texts or of document titles, using little more than an alphabetically ordered index of words. In the last 10 years, formal languages for computer search of data bases have approximated the convenience of natural human language and, most recently, several firms offer "natural-language interfaces" as a general customizing service for particular data management systems. Only two or three firms offer automated translation, however, and reports of users suggest that their service is less than satisfactory.

It is the case that much practical understanding is available for some aspects of the task of using natural language for various computing applications. Commanding a robot to accomplish simple tasks, asking questions of a data base, applying a grammar to the analysis of sentences, representing a sentence as a formal language data structure, and generating sentences from such data structures are all examples of computations that are well understood for significantly large classes of natural-language sentences. Transforming a narrative or an expository argument into a data structure, answering questions from it, creating summaries, and translating into other natural languages or pictures, are all examples of tasks that have been demonstrated in the literature, but which are certainly not understood in sufficient generality for practical applications. It is the purpose of this book to describe a uniform approach to all of these tasks both at the sentence and at the narrative level.

It is still too early in the history of computational linguistics to suppose that the techniques described here are anything but an initial approximation to a computational practicum for natural language. Nevertheless, the book offers a consistent system of representation for the meanings it deals with, a general system for applying procedural logic to the analysis and synthesis of natural language, and a range of techniques for accomplishing (at least on a small scale) such tasks as parsing, generation, questioning, summarizing, and translating from English to formal languages for simple texts, commands, and data base queries. It is hoped that this book will have the heuristic effect of challenging the reader to extend and improve the formalisms and so to advance the science of computational linguistics.

1.4 SELECTED READINGS

Barr, A., and Feigenbaum, E., *The Handbook of Artificial Intelligence,* Vols. 1 and 2, William Kaufman, Los Altos, Calif., 1981.

Findler, N. V., (ed.) Associative Networks, Academic Press, New York, 1979.

Lehnert, W. C., *The Process of Question Answering: A Computer Simulation of Cognition,* Lawrence Erlbaum Associates, Hillsdale, N.J., 1978.

Sager, N., *Natural Language Information Processing,* Addison-Wesley, Reading, Mass., 1981.

Schank, R., *Dynamic Memory,* Cambridge University Press, New York, 1983.

Schank, R. and Riesbeck, C., *Inside Natural Language Understanding,* Lawrence Erlbaum Associates, Hillsdale, N.J., 1980.

Tennant, H., *Natural Language Processing,* Petrocelli, Princeton, N.J., 1981.

Winograd, T., *Language as a Cognitive Process, Vol. 1: Syntax,* Addison-Wesley, Reading, Mass., 1983.

2
KNOWLEDGE AND COMMUNICATION

At the base of human uses of language is some human's knowledge and an intention to accomplish something by expressing or understanding a communication. In the simplest computations with language, a program has built into it both "intentions" (e.g., to translate a sentence into a structure or vice versa) and a capability, representing some human's knowledge, of how to accomplish the task. If the machine is a data base robot it includes abilities for recognizing questions and assertions of fact and varies its behavior accordingly. Its data base is a representation of factual knowledge provided by people for use by people. We often use English loosely to say "The system *knows* about documents... and *understands* questions and assertions." The italicized terms in that sentence are philosophically disturbing, and although there is nothing particularly wrong about extending the meanings of words such as "intelligence," "understanding," "intending," and "knowing" so that they apply to computations, it is certainly desirable to establish a philosophical and linguistic foundation for such extensions of meaning.

2.1 KNOWING AND KNOWLEDGE

Knowing, experiencing, awareness of happening—the dynamic of consciousness—is common to all humans and presumably to many other animals as well. Experience can be apprehended directly by the experiencer, described in language, and inferred by an observer about some other person. Usually, experience has a content, the perception of happenings; but there is also the null experience of deep sleep, the null perception of nonhappening. The great bulk of language is about happenings and from people's description of events, we infer their awareness while we consciously experience the descriptions they utter.

A robot computer with tactile, visual, auditory, and other sensors, which computes symbolic representations corresponding to happenings, is a very close analog to an experiencing being. The robot may have a model of the world it moves in, a model of its body moving in that world, and a memory of a long succession of such representations and their correlations with subsequent or antecedent happenings. It might talk sensibly and pass the Turing test (i.e., leave us unable to distinguish its answers to questions from those of humans), do well on intelligence tests, create new ideas, and even be classified by some personality traits common to it and humans. As Asimov suggested many years ago, a court of law might declare that it had all the rights of a person. We might also imagine that like a human, such a system could be subject to various cognitive disorders resulting in behavior counter to its own interests.

We could go further and give it subtle sensors to determine the levels of fuel, lubrication, temperature of its surroundings, and so on, and program these values to influence its decisions and particularly its model of its "feeling state." Yet with all this analogical structure of experience, I know of no reason to infer that the robot is aware or conscious in the sense that I am and that I infer that the reader is. Nor is there any test (applicable to either the robot or the reader) that can clarify the question. My own awareness is an organic given, and while I happily watch the newest baby in the family awake to consciousness of the world, I never doubted her essential awareness from the time of her birth. Her awareness is my assumption, essential to recognition of her human existence.

The argument above concerns the dualistic position that distinguishes consciousness as a transcendent phenomenon different from the objects of the "real" world. From that viewpoint it seems inconceivable that rocks, streams, or robots could be conscious. Yet, if the robot is organic, genetically engineered living protoplasm, programmed as above, I would naturally, as with people, cats, and dogs, assume that it was conscious. But I have more difficulty assuming consciousness in microbes, genes, viruses, and so on, and I would look with scepticism at any argument that extolled the virtues of large conglomerations of organic molecules as the source of such a transcendent phenomenon. The position that consciousness is an epiphenomenon emergent from any sufficiently complex information-processing system is equally unattractive, Heinlein notwithstanding.

Since I cannot deny my own consciousness nor define it within the dualistic system, let us abandon dualism. Modern psychology and physics recognize that physical objects in the "real" world are in the final analysis, highly reliable (and probable) perceptions of some experiencer. Our world certainly exists as experience; there is no ultimate assurance that there is anything but experience. If we abandon dualism and assume only that our world is part of human experience, then mountains, streams, rocks, and robots are all part of our conscious experience. Similarly, other people and organisms are part of my conscious experience, which in its turn is a tiny part of an infinity of possible human experience. So the world as I know it is part of my consciousness and partakes of consciousness. The rocks, mountains, streams, robots, and other people are all the same stuff of conscious experience and may be categorized as conscious or unconscious for personal or scientific convenience.

Is this solipcism? No; consciousness is taken as the world. My experience is a viewpoint and the other people in my experience are other viewpoints. Together, we—these viewpoints—interact with each other to construct a social consensus called "reality"—the emphasis on some experiences as public and sharable and others as unique and perhaps "unreal." The world of conscious experience is just as reliable as the "real" world of the dualistic standpoint. The people and objects are just as real. Instead of being isolated minds in a dualistic, mind-body world, we are interrelated human viewpoints of experience. Why is there reliability between two persons looking at the world of experience? Because the world of conscious experience is a reliable reality; there is no need to hypothesize physical objects beyond our perceptions. Gravity, light, and vibrations of air resulting in sounds are all reliable perceptions, and the fact that a charging tiger is only a perception does not change the "fact" that it may be a terminal experience. The fact that a fellow human may be part of my conscious experience does not make her any more predictable than if she were part of the dualistic "real" world.

This position is sometimes called phenomenalist or monist in that it disposes of the distinction between objects and awareness of objects. In practice it has little effect beyond providing an answer to "What is consciousness?" The theories of physics remain as valid as ever, bridges still carry traffic, and robots continue to carry out intelligent operations exhibiting their own quirky personality traits. That the physicists are really doing psychology by exploring the nature and limits of experiences of the world does not mean that they do the same things as academic psychologists; in effect, they remain physicists. Mathematicians, musicians, and poets continue exploring realms of abstract experience as they always have. The distinctions among imagination, perception, and action remain as useful as ever. Engineers can continue to use a dualistic interpretration of the world and to transform "unreal" thoughts into "real" bridges. Only the theory of knowledge is affected, and the result is a system of thought that can accept human and robot minds as (potentially) equal conscious entities.

2.2 KNOWING SOMETHING

The discussion above emphasizes the *act* of knowing apart from the content that is known. Knowing something can be visualized as the illumination of some portion of some possible world of human experience. Experience is introspected as a state of awareness composed of perceptions of continuous phenomena in a space-time framework usually with reference to the self as an observer, an actor and/or an affected entity. Together with direct perceptual experience, there are also remembered experiences that are similar or contrasting to the current one, and fragments of language. It is possible to be completely absorbed in the experience of the moment and to have no thoughts about it or its meaning; in states of delirium, ecstasy, or advanced drunkenness, for example, a person may go consciously from event to event but not remember the previous event and may have no recollection whatever of any of the series of events when he wakes the following day. More usually, experience includes some appreciation of associated experiences and meanings. This meta-experience is probably our perception of forming a knowledge representation that integrates the present experience with our previous history.

Forming knowledge representations from direct experience is the first stage of cognition and communication. In this stage, the continuous events of experience appear to be mapped into a discrete space of concepts that relate experiences in terms of similarity and difference. This mapping must discard a great deal of information in order to abstract significant commonalities from successive experiences. Presumably, the process of relating abstracted experience to remembered concepts is the process of understanding.

When a robot transforms the continuous electrical signal from a sensor first into digital time segments, and eventually into concepts, it is processing a communication from its environment. That the process *is* communication is obvious in the case that the signal is a voiced command that the robot is attempting to understand, but recognizing a corridor or a stairwell is also to communicate the state of the environment to the robot's knowledge representation. In the human, the first stage of communication is to transmute the stuff of experience into a conceptual representation. The resulting conceptual representation is inevitably associated with additional stuff of experience, and this experience combines with the perceptual experience of the next instant in a continuing process. The experience may give rise to an action which itself is an experience and which may change the world, thus leading to a new experience of the world, in a lifetime succession that pauses only in deep sleep.

2.3 REPRESENTING KNOWLEDGE

At the periphery of the organism, sense organs are specialized to olfaction, taste, vision, touch, hearing, and kinesthesis. Artificial intelligence has studied some aspects of these processes. Common to all these senses is the problem of transforming a continuous signal in several dimensions into some ordered sequence of symbols that are a well-formed statement in some formal language. The task is known to be horrendously difficult, requiring computations that are almost unmanageable in realtime for a sequential computer.

Great ambiguities among possible local translations are only to be resolved by the introduction of larger contexts and higher-level interpretations, and the optimal organization of these contextualizing processes is still in question. On the motor side, control of robot movements requires a coordination of perceptual computations of what the machine is doing with what its goal is. Translating from sensory information into conceptual meaning, then into action, is the continuous process of perceiving and interacting with the world. How well it is accomplished is one basic measure of intelligence. Yet in the nineteenth century, psychologists were greatly disappointed that such measures simply did not distinguish between bright and dull people. At the level of dealing successfully with sensory input, physiologically normal people are uniformly good.

Useful measures of intelligence were found to depend on some method for estimating the conceptual structures available to people. The younger child is sharply limited in understanding vocabulary, search strategies, analogies, and hidden spatial figures. As the child matures these abilities grow. Measurement of these abilities with paper and pencil tests has been the province of psychometricians from the time of Binet at the turn of the century. For some purposes, a 30 minute test of vocabulary, spatial, and numeric understanding reliably distinguishes among people as fast and slow learners of academic or clerical skills. Despite our present considerable difficulties in transforming from sensory inputs to conceptual structures, evidence is already accumulating that computer intelligence depends vastly more on the richness of the conceptual lexicon for decoding the sensory data, than on the effectiveness of the sensory apparatus.

The computational study of natural language understanding avoids the difficulties of translating from continuous speech sounds into words and concepts when it works with printed text that has already completed that level of process. Yet it, too, is characterized by dependence on context and on the requirement of interacting levels.

Understanding of single sentences independent of context is a reasonably well understood computation, but integrating sentences into narrative and expository contexts introduces new orders of difficulty. The size of a natural language also forms a significant barrier in that an ordinary person recognizes a vocabulary on the order of tens of thousands of words and is able to use at least thousands in speaking and writing. It is still unclear how large a grammar is required to account for the syntax of English, and the amount of semantic information needed to understand a book is simply unknown. The most crucial problem is certainly that of crossing levels, syntactic to semantic, clausal to narrative, statement to intention, and so on. The task of finding an appropriate knowledge content and representation for lexical, syntactic, and semantic information is not completed. The task of finding an appropriate representation for sentences, arguments, narratives, and other text forms is only well begun.

2.4 DEFINING COMMUNICATION

A general definition from Merriam-Webster's dictionary states that to communicate is "to make known." A more complete pattern for the definition is, "someone makes something known to someone by some means." The means of communication vary widely with the situation, ranging from speech and written text to gesture, facial expression, dance, music, and the visual arts. The "something" communicated is usually taken to be a thought or a conception, but the notion generalizes to a physical sharing as of a disease, or the blessing of communion as well. One simplified model of this idea is that a person has a thought which is translated into some kind of utterance that a second person can perceive. The receiver of the utterance in turn translates it into thoughts and feelings and thereby understands the communication. The communication may fail for any number of reasons; the sender may inadequately translate his thought into language, there may be too much noise for the language to be perceived, or the listener may not be attending or may not understand the language that he receives.

2.4.1 Thoughts, Images, and Concepts

A key aspect of the model is the translation from thought to utterance. The utterances that this book is concerned with are natural-language statements and texts. What is meant by "thoughts" deserves much discussion. The content of thought may include visual, tactile, and auditory images, fragments of speech or of mathematics, feelings, and intentions. Intuitively, the world of thought is sometimes continuous as in the case of an inner melody, or the image of a ball rolling down a hill, and sometimes discontinuous as with the idea that "tang" rhymes with "fang" or that 144 is the product of 3 and 48. There is a level of direct, remembered, or imagined perceptual experience in which events unfold in time and space, and another level where such events are described in some form of symbol system. These two levels, although almost always intermixed, suggest a distinction between perceptual and conceptual thought. They are necessarily intermixed in that the remembered perceptual experience may be associated with some symbolic representation that refers to it and similar experiences. The perceptual experience may include visual, auditory, and kinesthetic images, and intended actions, and be richly associated with emotional coloring. The conceptual thought, in contrast, although also associated with characteristic feelings and images, can be abstracted as purely a system of symbols.

There seems to be no simple way to say that one thought has ended and another begun; thoughts flow, enclosing, interpenetrating, and succeeding one another. Yet there is no difficulty in selecting one visual image or one part of an image among others. At the conceptual level, we are easily able to extract one formula or principle from memory and distinguish it from the cloud of associated facts and symbols. Presumably this is a nonarbitrary truncating operation that is called into play by the process of attentive thinking.

These ideas about thoughts can be abstracted into the following definitions:

A *thought* is an image or a concept optionally followed by a thought;
An *image* is a perception of an act, an event, or a memory;
A *concept* is a name associated with a thought.

In this definition "perception" is extended to include remembered and imagined continuous events and actions, as well as those happening at a given moment. It may include associated feelings as well. The words "perceptualization" and "conceptualization" will occasionally be used to emphasize the idea of sequential systems of thought.

These definitions suggest that if a perception is to be communicated in English, to another person, it must first be translated into concepts associated with it, which are then ordered, translated into English, and expressed. The receiver receives the English and translates it into concepts and then into his own perceptual structure. Common experience suggests that these stages of translation may be highly abbreviated in the case of familiar communications; that is, the words of the communication may be treated as simple signals that release highly practiced behaviors without the need for detailed thought. Or they may be remarkably complicated in the case of evaluating persuasive discourse, requiring conscious examination of multiple belief spaces: the listener's, the listener's belief of the speaker's belief, the listener's belief about the speaker's belief of the listener's belief about the speaker's belief about ...

2.5 AN INTROSPECTIVE PROTOCOL

If conceptualizations are largely symbolic, in what kind of symbols might they be expressed? Our reported introspections will agree in showing us that our thought is composed of one or another type of imagery and fragments of one or another language. If I think of Cornwallis sending troops to Castlebar to quell an Irish rebellion, I have a mixture of images of the man in his headquarters with his staff, marching redcoats, a waiting army of French troops supporting the Irish rebels, a camp outside the town, and so on. These images are faint and come into focus only as I attend to them closely. But they led almost instantaneously to the natural language expression of which the fragments seem to have been something like the following list:

Sec. 2.5   An Introspective Protocol

    L1.   Irish rebellion of 1798
          Lord Cornwallis at his headquarters
          Cornwallis with his staff
          French and Irish troops at Castlebar
          Cornwallis to attack
          Military camps for the two sides
          Marching redcoated soldiers

Then I utter the sentence,

    Cornwallis sent an army to attack the French troops and Irish rebels at Castlebar.

In the process of knitting conceptions into that sentence, an explicit army is added as the means of attack. The staff, headquarters, military camps, and redcoated soldiers were left unexpressed. Also unexpressed is the situational context of the reader of this book attending to the argument for which the example sentence is adduced. And as a communicator I have intentions and purposes which are left to be inferred from the larger context of natural language research.

    Now imagining myself as the reader, I am forming a conceptualization of the author's argument, probably testing for consistency and correspondence to my own thoughts about communication as I read along. As reader I am being asked to consider what happens in my mind as I read the example sentence, and I find the following concepts:

    L2.   [Example of communication]
          [Introspect process of understanding]
          Cornwallis the general
          Cornwallis sends an army
          English army marching to Castlebar
          Where is Castlebar?
          Irish rebels and French troops at Castlebar
          Cornwallis to attack

The bracketed phrases indicate the context and intention that direct my attention to the task of observing my understanding of the sentence as an example of communication. The rest of the phrases are an ordered representation of the main ideas of the sentence augmented with a question about Castlebar. The "marching" of the English army is a consequence of "sent" (as signaled by a completed past form). Since Cornwallis sent an army, the consequence is that the army is moving in its customary eighteenth-century manner. With these concepts in mind, I, as reader, can answer various questions or form various perceptual images. Here, the example of communication is completed. If the actual reader will examine the concepts aroused by the sentence, it is expected that something similar to the phrases of L2 will be observed, but the images should vary among individuals.

The images of the sender and the receiver of a communication are highly idiosyncratic, depending on their respectively unique histories, and therefore at least as different as two paintings of the same scene. Nor are the detailed conceptualizations the same.

The words of each phrase in the list, L1, easily expand into larger conceptualizations partly corresponding to dictionary definitions, but largely containing my own idiosyncratic world knowledge. For example,

> L3. Irish rebellion := the catholics of Ireland have been fighting their English invaders since the the times of Cromwell and consistently failing to gain independence or any resolution of their situation.
>
> 1798 := the year the French, shortly after their own revolution, landed an army in Ireland to support the rebels as part of Napoleon's war with England.
>
> Lord Cornwallis := an English general who commanded the British troops during the American Revolution, and surrendered to Washington. He commanded the British forces in southern Ireland.

These expansions could go on indefinitely, but as I write them I have only fleeting fragments of images; instead, the key phrases "Irish Catholics," "English invaders," "time of Cromwell," "French Revolution," and "Napoleon" all appear in appropriate sequences together with relational conceptions such as invading, time, failed revolts, marching, sailing, fighting, commanding, planning, and so on. Other relational ideas include the limiting of the Catholics to those in Ireland, and specifying the time as coincident with that of Cromwell, and the British forces as those in Ireland. Although my imagined reader's conceptualizations from the sentence show appreciable overlap with the author's, the lexicons of world knowledge could hardly correspond so well—unless the reader is also involved in Thomas Flanagan's novel *The Year of the French*.

The result of this introspection showed mainly fragments of natural language, although with a definite impression of images lying around if needed or desired. The language fragments are mainly noun phrases associated with images of the setting, the events, and the actors involved in the initial recollection. The prepositions and modifiers of these noun phrases provide relational information to limit the concept, and to place it in time, space, and dynamic event contexts. But what did we see of process? Just that a fragment of knowledge was suddenly realized as thought by a series of concepts, which could be combined into a sentence or a series of images, or whose elements could be individually expanded into more detailed concepts. I never sensed any detailed process of change from knowledge to thought; just an initial state of knowing that I knew—ZAP—and a subsequent state in which concepts were present—two successive states of a cognitive computation. This reveals an obvious and well-known limitation of introspection; we must deduce the process from the state-changes we can observe. Nor should we suppose that what we observed were really the English phrases we reported. The very process of introspection probably translated from uniquely conceptual symbols—whatever they may be—into language. From this example, however, we can notice that verbal communication must result from partial correspondence of conceptual structures between sender and receiver, and that the effectiveness of communication depends on a shared repertory of concepts with some basis of shared definitions and world knowledge.

2.6 SYMBOLIZING CONCEPTS

A few paragraphs ago a thought was defined recursively as a concept name or an image possibly followed by a thought. "Cornwallis commanding English soldiers" is an English representation of a concept. "Cornwallis," "commanding," "English," and "soldiers" are also representations of concepts. Each of the terms of these representations is an English word and a concept name; "commanding" is one example of a relational concept in that it describes an action or state with at least the two participants, a commander and those commanded. "English soldiers" combines two concept names to describe a subset of soldiers in the English army. The nominals include "Cornwallis," "English," and "soldiers." Although "Cornwallis" can be expanded using our world knowledge to include the fact that his full title is "Lord Charles Cornwallis" (as well as additional items of his biography), it is a primary concept name. In contrast, "English" is a combination of two primary concepts in a relation (i.e., "entity of England"); while "soldiers" combines the primary concept "soldier" with the relation of "quantity greater than one," signified by the plural "s." This analysis may suggest that our skill with natural language is so much a part of our conceptual thought processes that even our fragmentary conceptualizations tend to use natural language syntax as part of the coding of concepts.

At least reports of our introspections do so. Alternatively, we might suppose that the conceptualization process uses abstract, nonverbal symbols—pointers to verbalizable concepts which when uttered must follow the rules of language. In my introspections there is a sense of concepts beyond those in focus and this vague sensing may be suitably modeled by pointers. In accord with this interpretation, when I speak or write without introspection there is also a hazy sense of what might be added to what is being uttered, without any particular knowledge of what it is until selected. This phenomenon, too, might be modeled by supposing that the concept in focus has pointers to related concepts which are experienced as vague potentialities.

But considerations of economy argue that what introspection shows as "Ireland" and "Irish," or "rebel" and "rebels," should share conceptual definitions, as should all the forms, "attack," "attacks," "attacking," "attacked" and so on. So I hypothesize that below the level of my introspections there is a more explicit language than the English fragments I sense floating through my mind. Most natural-language researchers agree with this hypothesis and assume that underlying the English constructions are certain deeper representations that can best be expressed in one or another form of logic. The choice in this book is a form called semantic relations, but some researchers prefer standard quantified predicate logic, and others a system called conceptual dependencies. Whatever system is finally found to be most appropriate, all current approaches include many natural-language elements as terms in the formalism.

For the example communication about Cornwallis sending an army, we can now look again at the reader's conceptualizations given in L2, by drawing a graph showing concepts connected by named semantic relations.

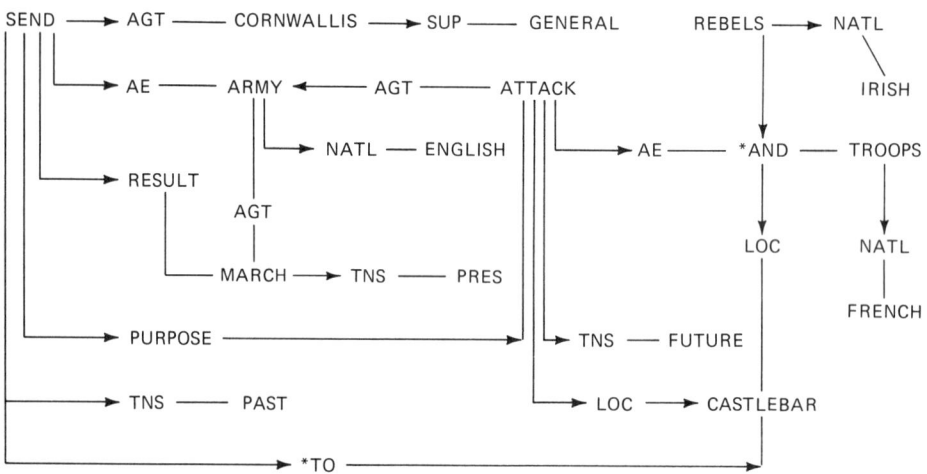

The relation names used in this graph are: AGT for agent of an action, AE for the affected entity—that which was immediately affected by the act or event, SUP for assigning a class, NATL for nationality, *AND for a conjunction of concepts, LOC for location, *TO for entering a location, TNS for tense of the verb, and RESULT and PURPOSE in their usual meanings.

The graph could be expanded by augmenting each concept with the definitional and world knowledge associated with it, but it would soon become so large and so interwoven with crossing lines as to be unreadable. For the

Sec. 2.6 Symbolizing Concepts

present example, however, it explicates several important connectivities. The result of Cornwallis sending troops is that they march; the purpose is a future attack on Castlebar where the French and Irish are located; the army sent by Cornwallis is English; the English army is to do the attacking; and the army is sent to Castlebar. Each of these connectivities goes beyond what is explicitly stated in the sentence, given again below:

> Cornwallis sent an army to attack the Irish rebels and the French troops at Castlebar.

They are derived from additional lexical understandings such as:

> English generals usually command English armies.
> If a general sends an army, the result is that the army marches.
> If an army is to attack at a place, it must go to that place.

If someone sends someone to do x, doing x is a purpose. This kind of information must be represented as general rules that can be applied in the process of understanding a sentence or a text.

Graphs of concept interrelations such as that shown above have generally been called *semantic networks*. The network property is connectivity, shown by labeled lines in the graph; the epithet, semantic, is traditional, reflecting the facts that the nodes of the graph are natural-language word forms connected by explicitly named semantic relations derived from the syntactic orderings of words in text. Networks have proved most useful in understanding computations and many algorithms and procedures have been developed for computing various connected sets from them. Networks are also useful for representing procedures and their control flow as they operate, provided that there is an appropriate interpreting program. Any program can be drawn as a transition network showing conditions, operations, and procedure or function calls as arcs leading to various alternative paths of computation.

But when the graph of a network becomes larger than a page or two, it becomes most difficult to read. For semantic relations, there is a linear notation that is easily learned and much more concise to print. It uses parentheses so that the embedding of one conceptualization within another can easily be noted. The graph given earlier is approximated linearly as follows:

```
(SEND AGT (CORNWALLIS ISA GENERAL)
     AE (ARMY NATL ENGLISH)
     PURPOSE (ATTACK AGT ARMY
                     AE (REBELS NATL IRISH
                           *AND (TROOPS NATL FRENCH))
                     LOC CASTLEBAR)
     RESULT (MARCH AE ARMY TNS PRES )
     *TO CASTLEBAR
     TNS PAST)
```

With certain conventions to be given in later chapters, the graph may be exactly represented in linear form so that all connections are shown, but such complexity is beyond the present purpose of showing roughly how conceptualizations can be represented as data structures for computation.

The language of semantic relations is discussed in detail in a subsequent chapter. Here, it is introduced as a representation of the conceptual thought that underlies our introspections. Like our reported introspections, it contains ordinary English words and terms, but in order to minimize redundancy in the dictionary and to simplify the logic of procedures that consult these expressions, it uses root forms for each English term and arranges them in explicit semantic relations with each other and with such primitive syntactic notions as PRESENT, PAST, SINGULAR, PLURAL, and so on.

2.7 SEMANTIC PROCESSING

Given a representation for concepts, we now need to introduce some mechanism to go from one to another or from concept strings to language, and vice versa. If we associate a term such as "Cornwallis" with an (abbreviated) definition as follows:

Cornwallis := (title Lord, firstname Charles, profession General, nationality English)

then surely it is a simple computer program that will expand the concept into the following form,

(CORNWALLIS TITLE LORD FIRSTNAME CHARLES
PROFESSION GENERAL
NATIONALITY ENGLISH)

One of the simplest ways to translate the definition to English would use a *rule* such as the following:

(X TITLE Y FIRSTNAME Z PROFESSION W NATIONALITY V)
→ Y Z X WAS A(N) V W.

The definition matches the left half of the rule under the convention that X, Y, Z, W, and V are *variables* that match any term, and the right half of the rule provides a *reordering* of the values that the variables matched to produce

LORD CHARLES CORNWALLIS WAS A(N) ENGLISH GENERAL.

We notice that this rule does not work backwards very well, since "Mickey's dog Pluto was a long-eared hound" would result in,

(PLUTO TITLE MICKEY'S FIRSTNAME DOG PROFESSION HOUND
NATIONALITY LONGEARED)

Sec. 2.7   Semantic Processing   27

But the right-pointing arrow of implication does not imply that the rule is symmetric. Actually, the process of translating in either direction between semantic relations and English sentences is very complex, requiring cascades of grammar rules supported by semantic tests and transformations. One saving aspect in all this complexity, though, is the fact that the translation rules can be symmetric, with the result that one set of such rules is sufficient for translating in both directions. Chapter 5 is devoted to describing such systems of translation rules.

A crucial test for the success of communication is to question the receiver. We might ask such questions as:

   Who sent an army?
   Where was the army sent?
   Why was the army sent?

These question the literal text, so when translated into semantic relations,

   (SEND AGT ?WHO AE (ARMY DET A NBR SING) TNS PAST)
   (SEND AE ARMY LOC ?WHERE)
   (SEND AE ARMY PURPOSE ?WHY)

they can be answered simply by matching the assertions in the network of semantic relations, and returning the value that matches the special variable ?WH... Other questions are more difficult if they use words not given in the communication, or question things implied but not stated. For example,

   Where was the English army going?
   Why was the army marching?
   What color were their uniforms?
   Where is Castlebar?
   Who is Cornwallis?

The latter set of questions test the correspondence of the receiver's world knowledge and rules for understanding English. In later chapters we will study methods for using world knowledge both in transforming text into semantic relations and in inferring answers to questions.

Generally the process depends on rules of the type shown earlier. For example, the following is a rule to relate "going" and "marching":

   (GO.X) ← (MARCH.X)

This rule simply states that a semantic relation headed by MARCH implies the same statement headed by GO, so if it is desired to establish that someone went somewhere, ask if he marched. The X in these terms is a variable that stands for the rest of the semantic relation, against which the other constraints of the question must be satisfied. The program that models conceptual processing uses rules of the type sketched in this section. It is a procedural logic theorem prover for which the rules are generalizations and the semantic relations given in the world knowledge lexicon and recorded from text are assertions. The rules show how to transform one set of assertions into another to accomplish such tasks as translating sentences into semantic relations, paraphrasing relations, and answering questions. The theorem prover itself is remarkable in its simplicity; it recursively compares hypotheses with assertions and rules that match, and uses just one inference rule, *modus ponens*, to accomplish its task. The complexities of the processes for communicating with English are not in the theorem proving algorithm, but are instead provided in the lexicon and rule systems that the prover applies in its task of proving a hypothesis. The theorem prover and its logic are discussed in detail in Chapter 3.

2.8 SEMANTIC NETWORKS

Theories of semantic networks have evolved over the past decade to provide a formalism in which conceptual thought may be represented. The requirements imposed on each such theory are that it provide a means for representing any conception that can be expressed in natural language, and that it include a system that can translate from natural language texts into the formalism, and back into natural language. It must also represent conceptions so as to enhance such operations as paraphrasing, question answering, and translation to other languages. Since natural language can be used effectively to make general statements in predicate logic and mathematics, the theory is required to represent such statements also. Eventually, the theory must be developed to include perceptual descriptions as well as those at the conceptual level, but at this time it is still limited to conceptual symbols, and such applications as translating language into pictures or speech into conceptualizations require auxiliary systems to work within the continuous perceptual spaces.

A semantic network represents a concept as an isolated named node, or as a node connected by semantic relation names to other nodes.

> A concept is a named node,
> or a named node connected by semantic
> relation names to other concepts.

The names of nodes are lexical entries and the semantic relations are names selected from an inventory of 100 or so that represent the relations holding between constituents of texts. The lexical entry that describes a name may itself be a complex concept or it may be a terminal name and thus a primitive in the system.

In using semantic networks to represent the conceptual structure theorized to underlie English texts, no claim need be made that the network represents the meaning of the text. Even when the network is used to answer questions or to translate from English into commands to a robot, it is not the network, nor the semantic relations, nor the lexical nodes that represent meaning; in these cases there is a system of paraphrase rules that claim that two structures represent the same meaning. The meaning itself is in the mind of the writer and the reader, not in the text or its representation. In the event that a system were provided with rules that would allow it to generate well-formed sentences correctly describing elements of its lexicon, or its own procedures for inference, it would still be working at a level of translation from one conceptual representation to another. In humans meaning appears to accompany the process of relating conceptual representations to experience, but it must be admitted that there is much uncertainty here, and it may be more convenient to suggest that the computational system is dealing with meanings despite the fact that it is limited to a conceptual representational level.

In any event, we stand on secure foundations if we consider the computational system as a highly specialized communication device, which can represent and preserve the information content of a text. Given texts as input, it produces conceptual representations in the form of networks of semantic relations; given questions it responds with answers; given English commands to a robot, it translates to the robot's order code, and perhaps carries out the command. All these accomplishments are enabled by its conceptual representation of lexical elements and their semantic relations, and of course by its procedures for processing. Finally, these structures and procedures are provided by a person who describes formalized subsets of natural language as high-level programs for a computer.

The concepts of interest in understanding natural language are primarily those concerned with words and their orderings to form communications. But perceptions and acts have their parts to play in such a theory. Some communications are commands that must be translated into order codes for a robot, and others may describe scenes to an image construction system. In systems that are designed to understand human speech, or to describe images from a television camera, the perceptual level of communication requires massive computations to translate from continuous auditory or visual signals into conceptual form. But the perceptual aspects of language go far beyond the scope of this book, which limits itself to describing conceptual structures as semantic relations and computing with them in procedural logic.

2.9 SELECTED READINGS

Dennett, D. C., *Brainstorms: Philosophic Essays on Mind and Psychology*, MIT Press, Cambridge, Mass., 1981.

Mascaro, J., *The Upanishads*, Penguin Books, Baltimore, Md., 1965.

Mascaro, J., *The Bhagavad Gita*, Penguin Books, Baltimore, Md., 1962.

Norman, D. A., and Rumelhart, D. E., *Explorations in Cognition*, W. H. Freeman, San Francisco, 1975.

Suzuki, S., *Zen Mind, Beginners Mind,* Weatherhill, New York, 1970.

Whitehead, A. N. *Process and Reality*, Harper and Row, New York, 1929.

Wittgenstein, L., *Philosophical Investigations*, Third Edition, Transl., Anscombe, G. E. M., The Macmillan Co., New York, 1953.

3

THE PLACE OF LOGIC

Chapter 2 closed with the argument that although computers can represent text in a formal language that supports questioning and paraphrase operations, the language is not the meaning. Meaning happens in the mind of the writer and reader, and the computer with its program can communicate from one to the other, adding to a given text new information generally available in dictionaries, encyclopedias, or grammars. Nor is logic concerned directly with the meanings people take from language; rather it is a study of how statements, whatever they mean, can be combined by the connectives "and," "or," and "not." In logic there are truth values of "True" and "False"—sharply circumscribed meanings—that can be assigned to ordinary statements. Of course, there are statements such as "This sentence is false" that elude this classification because they are inherently contradictory, and a consistent set of statements must exclude them. When a set of sentences has been assigned truth values, logic provides rules for computing the truth values of their combinations.

3.1 PROPOSITIONAL LOGIC

The statements used in propositional logic denote propositions and it is the propositions rather than the statements that are in fact true or false. Thus logicians recognize that it is not meaningful to say that a linguistic string is true or false; only its propositional meaning can be classified in that fashion. A statement such as "grass is green" asserts a corresponding proposition that relates two human experiences. The proposition is true insofar as the human experiences are consistent with the asserted relation. Except in mathematical statements, absolute truth escapes us and the truth of propositions is generally an empirical relation derived from fallible observations. But logic is not, in fact, concerned with absolute truth; instead, it is a calculus that derives new truth values from combinations of statements that have been assigned truth values. "New lamps for old" was the magician's cry as he sought Aladdin's magical lamp; "new truth values for old" is the magic of logic.

A logical system is composed of a set of statements—axioms—composed of assertions that represent what are believed to be true propositions, and rules for deriving new statements by combining and operating on the assertions in certain limited ways. Logical systems are used to determine if a new statement—called a theorem—is consistent with a given set of assertions and derivation rules. Although intuitively less obvious than proving consistency, it is often easier to show that a theorem is inconsistent with at least one axiom of the system. This approach leads to a proof method—called resolution [Robinson, 1965]—in which the falsification of a theorem is shown to be inconsistent with one or more axioms. Since there are only two truth values, if the negation of the theorem is inconsistent, the theorem must be consistent with the system, and therefore True. Such a proof procedure applies only to closed mathematical and logical systems where the sole truths are those given by the axioms. Ordinary life is not as simple; our knowledge bases are open and incomplete, our "true facts" often subject to revision, and our rules for drawing conclusions are often fallible.

Variables are essential elements in logic. They are usually signified by single letters, $a \ldots z$, occasionally adorned with subscripts and primes. A variable is a universal pronoun; it can stand for any one set of symbols in the system, but once assigned such a value, its value remains the same during a proof. The variables, p, q, r, and s are often used in logic texts to represent propositions. The propositional variables p and q might represent statements, as follows:

p rain falls
q the streets are wet.

Thenceforth, p stands for the statement, "rain falls," and $\sim p$, read "not p," stands for its negation. If we take "rain falls" to represent a true proposition, p is True and $\sim p$ is False. In a similar fashion the statement labeled q represents a proposition. If the streets are actually wet, the proposition q is True and $\sim q$ is False. If the streets are actually dry, then q is False and $\sim q$, its negation, is True. The operator $\sim$, not, inverts truth values. The evaluation of a proposition results in a truth value, either True or False, and $\sim$True = False while $\sim$False = True.

Sec. 3.1   Propositional Logic

The connectives "and" and "or" also operate on truth values. The compound statement, $p \wedge q$, read as "p and q," is true only if both p and q represent true statements. In contrast, $p \vee q$, read as "p or q" is true either if p is true or if q is true. Assuming both p and q to be true propositions,

$\sim p \wedge p$ is False $p \wedge \sim p$ is False
$\sim p \vee p$ is True $p \vee \sim p$ is True
$\sim p \wedge q$ is False $\sim q \wedge \sim p$ is False
$\sim p \vee q$ is True $\sim q \vee \sim p$ is True

Using propositional variables with the truth functions "not," "and," and "or," with parentheses to eliminate ambiguities, compound formulas—called well-formed formulas or wffs—can be constructed. Every such formula can be reduced to a truth value.

The connective of implication is usually used in propositional logic, signified by a right-pointing arrow, $\rightarrow$. The sentence "If it rains, then the streets are wet," or using the propositional variables assigned above, "If p, then q," is represented by

$$p \rightarrow q$$

Intuitively, we understand the implication statement to mean that if it is raining we expect the streets to be wet. If it is not raining we make no prediction. But if it is raining and the streets remain dry, we must recognize that the implication statement is false. Logically identical ideas are expressed by the formula $\sim p \vee q$: "It is not raining or the streets are wet."

p = rain	q = wet streets	Truth Value of $\sim p \vee q$
True	True	True
True	False	False
False	True	True
False	False	True

The first line of the table shows both p and q to be True; consequently $\sim p \vee q$ is True—because q is True. The second line shows the case where p is True and q is False; thus $\sim p \vee q$ evaluates to "False $\vee$ False," and the truth value for the whole expression is False. This line shows that the implication rule will be False if it happens that it is raining and the streets are dry. The remaining two lines appear at first glance to be counterintuitive in that they allow the rule to hold whether or not the streets are wet if it is not raining. But clarification results if we focus on the fact that we are talking about conditions under which we can accept or reject the rule. If it is not raining, the rule is irrelevant, so no condition of the streets can be used as evidence to support or disprove the rule. If it rains and the streets are wet, that is support; if it rains and the streets are dry, the rule is False.

We can now accomplish an inference using just the axioms, p and $\sim p \lor q$. We wish to prove the theorem, q. This is accomplished by tentatively adding the negation of q, $\sim q$, to the axioms to give

$$\sim q \land p \land (\sim p \lor q)$$

This formula is in conjunctive normal form, which means that there are no negations of parenthesized expressions and there are no disjunction symbols except within parentheses. Each element separated by a conjunction symbol is called a *clause*. The method of resolution [Robinson, 1965, 1980] is a proof method that asserts the negation of the theorem to be proved, then attempts to show that the negation of the theorem is inconsistent with the axioms of the system. If the theorem's negation is inconsistent, then the theorem must be consistent and it is thereby proved. The actual proof can be constructed as a tree.

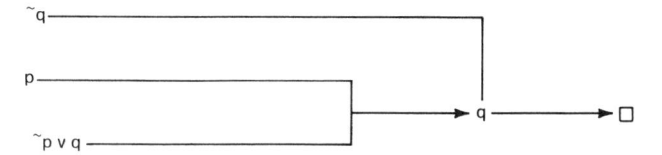

We can think of resolution as a cancellation operation. The proposition p is compared with the clause $\sim p \lor q$, resulting in q, since p and $\sim p$ form a contradiction. Then $\sim q$ is found to contradict q and there is nothing left, as symbolized by $\square$, called "box." Box is also called the empty clause which is immutably False. Since a logical system is a conjunction of True formulas (e.g., "snow is white" is True, "snow is not green" is True) any system of axioms that contains $\square$ or False is necessarily inconsistent. Since every clause canceled, the system of axioms that includes the negation of the theorem has been shown to be inconsistent; therefore, the theorem must be true.

The resolution proof method is an algorithm that results in a short effective computer program for proving theorems. A comparable procedural method for accomplishing a proof by cancellation was given in 1964 by Black [1968]. Each axiom was represented as a list composed of a conclusion and premises, if any; each conclusion and each premise was a list, a factual statement was a list containing that one element as a conclusion with no premises, and an implication was a list whose first element was the conclusion and whose remaining elements were the premises. For example (using a slightly simpler structure than the one Black actually computed with), the factual statement "rain falls" is represented as the list,

((RAIN FALLS))

The implication statement "If rain falls, then the streets are wet," is reversed to give "The streets are wet if rain falls," presenting the conclusion first, then the premise.

((STREETS ARE WET)(RAIN FALLS))

The theorem to prove is (STREETS ARE WET). The theorem is matched against the axioms to discover if it is the first element of any axiom. It matches the conclusion of the implication statement.

(STREETS ARE WET)
(STREETS ARE WET)(RAIN FALLS))

The element matched is then canceled leaving the new question (RAIN FALLS), which in its turn matches the first and only element of,

((RAIN FALLS))

This new question cancels, leaving no more questions. Since all subquestions were answered, the theorem, (STREETS ARE WET) is consistent with the axiom system.

Although Black's work preceded the discovery of the resolution principle, his method can be interpreted in resolution terms; when a theorem (i.e., question) matches a conclusion, the two cancel, showing a contradiction between the negation of the theorem and the conclusion part of an axiom. The premises of a conclusion are taken as new questions and each is matched against the axioms. When all questions have been canceled with axioms and no questions remain, the negated theorem is shown to be inconsistent with the axioms, leading to the conclusion that the theorem is true.

Black's proof procedure has been sketched here as an easily understood precursor of the advanced resolution proof procedures developed since. Although this procedure applies to both propositional and predicate logic, improved resolution procedures include a very sophisticated approach to the treatment of variables and the indexing of axioms. These improvements have made the theorem-proving programs efficient enough to be useful for moderate-to-large computations.

3.2 PREDICATE LOGIC

So far we have restricted our discussion to propositional logic in which variables must stand for complete statements. In predicate logic, variables may stand for elements that occur within statements. In programming languages we are quite accustomed to expressions such as Greater(x, y) or Between(x, y, z). In logical formulas, the variables x, y, and z can take on any values whatever. If we assign the values $x = 20$, $y = 10$, $z = 0$, then the instantiations of the formulas are:

$$\text{Greater}(20,10)$$
$$\text{Between}(20,10,0)$$

In these instantiations, the first formula is True, and the second False, (assuming that the first argument is supposed to be between the second and third). We might assign the values differently:

$$x = \text{apple}, \quad y = a, \quad z = 2000,$$

to give,

$$\text{Greater}(\text{apple}, a)$$
$$\text{Between}(\text{apple}, a, 2000)$$

If we do so, the definitions of Greater and Between might be expected to return False, although if they are realized as computer procedures, they are more likely to halt the program with some kind of error message. In these examples, Greater and Between are called predicate symbols, and x, y and z are referred to as argument terms.

Predicate logic also permits the use of functions as arguments for predicate symbols. A statement such as:

Didmarry(Mother(John), Father(Mary), Father-Donahue)

might stand for the sentence, "Father Donahue married John's mother to Mary's father." Mother(John) and Father(Mary) are functions that serve as unique names for John's mother and Mary's father, respectively. More complex mathematical functions, such as $\text{Sqr}(\text{Sum}(x, y))$ and $\text{Product}(u, \text{Sum}(v, w))$, which specify unique numerical values, frequently occur in uses of predicate logic. When evaluated, some functions, such as Sum and Product, return unique numerical values; others, such as Mother-of(w, John), may return a unique name, say Rebecca, as the value of w. But often in logical proofs the functions need not be evaluated, serving instead as complex names. While Mother(w, John) contains less information than the evaluated form Mother(Rebecca, John), it can nevertheless be treated as a constant in any proof. In addition to variables and functions, argument terms include constants (i.e., numbers and words) and lists, which are described later.

A predicate name associated with its argument terms—constants, numbers, and functions—is called an atomic clause or literal. Atomic clauses can be combined with the connectors $\land$, $\lor$, and $\sim$ just as propositional statements were to construct non-atomic clauses (i.e. well-formed formulas).

The presence of variables in clauses complicates matters considerably. If we form the atomic clause, DidMarry(x, y, z), the variables x, y, and z, are in no way restricted in the values they can assume, so for some combinations of values the statement is true, for others false. Some statements such as ~Integer $(x) \lor$ Successor$(x,$ Sum$(x, 1))$—"Every integer has a successor that is the sum of that integer and 1"—are universally true for all values assigned to x. If x is not an integer, the statement remains true; if it is, it must have a successor since every integer does. Other statements, for example, Mother-of(x, y) are overgeneralized; every person has a mother, but everything is not the mother of everything. This statement asserts that y is the mother of x, and obviously not every value of y is the mother of every value of x. Unless some method is introduced to restrict the values of variables, clauses containing variables will often be overgeneralized.

Quantifiers are introduced into predicate logic to distinguish whether a variable refers to every value or to at least one. The convention is that ALL means every possible value, and SOME means at least one. When quantifiers are added as in the following examples, the variables are appropriately restricted to result in complete sentences of predicate logic.

SOME x, y, z Didmarry(x, y, z)
ALL x ~Integer$(x) \lor$ Successor$(x,$ Sum$(x, 1))$
ALL y SOME x ~Human$(y) \lor ($Mother-of$(x, y) \land$ Human$(x))$

The result is that all three statements are now true for every possible value assigned to their variables. There is at least one case where some person x was married to some person y by some person z. The statement about successors does not change its meaning, since ALL does not restrict the variable; ~Integer(x) does. The statement about motherhood required additional constraints on its variables to ensure exclusion of rocks and rocket ships; it states that for every y there is an x, and either y is not human or there is a mother x, and x is also human.

Quantifiers control the generality of the statements made in predicate logic. Specific statements such as Mother-of(Rebecca, James), more general statements such as, SOME y Mother-of$(y,$ Richard$)$, and completely general statements such as ALL $x y$ ~Married$(x, y) \lor$ Married(y, x)—"if x is married to y then y is married to x"—are expressible.

Clausal logic is a notational form in which the precision of quantification is obtained without explicitly stating the quantifiers. The key to this result is the fact that any formula containing existential variables can be rewritten as an equivalent one with only universal quantification. If we wish to represent the statement "Every tree has roots," an explicitly quantified form is,

ALL X SOME Y ~tree$(x) \lor$ haspart$(x, y) \land$ roots(y)

the contrasting clausal form is

~tree$(x) \lor$ haspart$(x,$ roots$(x))$

Similarly, "Every person has a mother" is represented as,

$$\sim\text{person}(x) \lor \text{mother-of}(\text{mother}(x), x)$$

Substituting a function that asserts the existence of a particular set of roots associated with each tree, or which names the unique mother of each person, causes the statements to become universally true with no need for the existential quantifier. Since clausal logic assumes that all variables are universally quantified, there is also no need to redundantly state the ALL. The result is a quantifier-free, conjunctive-normal form of logic in which the precision of quantified logic is retained in a syntactic structure only slightly more complex than that of the propositional calculus.

For proving theorems in clausal logic the resolution procedure is generalized to substitute values from the theorem for variables in the axiom set—and vice versa. If we wanted to prove that John had a parent, parent(x, John), from the following axiom set

$$\sim\text{mother-of}(x, y) \lor \text{parent}(x, y)$$
$$\text{mother-of}(\text{Rebecca}, \text{John})$$

the first step would be to negate the hypothesis, parent(x, John) and add it as a third axiom. Resolution can then be used to show that the negation of the hypothesis is inconsistent with the other axioms. The following tree shows that ~parent(x, John) matches an element of the first axiom shown above.

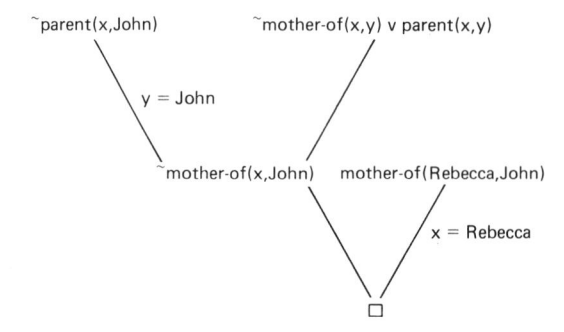

In this tree, the theorem ~parent(x, John) matched as an instance of parent(x, y) by assigning the value John to the variable y wherever it occurred in the clause ~mother-of(x, y) $\lor$ parent(x, y), giving ~mother-of(x, John) $\lor$ parent(x, John). Parent(x, John) cancels with ~parent(x, John), leaving the remainder of the disjunctive clause, ~mother-of(x, John), which then matched and canceled with the literal mother-of(Rebecca, John) to result in box □, showing an inconsistency in the set of axioms when the negated hypothesis was added. In the process x was assigned the value Rebecca. If we now substitute for variables in the theorem, parent(x, John), the result is parent(Rebecca, John), showing that it is not the case that for every x, x is *not* the parent of

John because Rebecca is an x who forms a counterexample. Thus parent(Rebecca, John) is True.

The procedure of matching formulas and substituting variables is called *unification*, and computer procedures for accomplishing this process as rapidly as possible have received much study and achieved a state of great efficiency (see Boyer and Moore [1979]). A theorem unifies with a formula if the predicate name of the theorem matches that of the formula, and if each argument term of the theorem matches a corresponding term of the formula. Two terms match if,

> they are identical,
>
> one is a variable, or
>
> they are composed of elements that match.

When a variable matches a term, then wherever else the variable occurs in the theorem and the clause, the term is substituted as the value of the variable. If, initially, any variable symbols occur both in the theorem and the clause, they must be renamed to avoid confusion. If after renaming variables, it happens that a variable is compared to a term that already contains that variable, the match fails.

Resolution with unification is a logically complete procedure for proving any true theorem from a set of axioms, but not necessarily in a reasonable length of time. Originally, linear resolution required comparisons of all pairs of clauses in the system, and the computations approached n factorial comparisons for n clauses. Much research was devoted to organizing the theorems and axioms to reduce this combinatorial space by resolving only clauses that could be relevant to a proof. An important result of this research was the development of procedural logic. Although there are well-known methods for translating explicitly quantified logic into quantifier-free, conjunctive-normal form (e.g., Nilsson [1980]), an attractive alternative approach is to express logical descriptions directly in a quantifier-free, clausal form. This is the approach illustrated earlier in applying Black's proof procedure to propositional logic. This is also the approach adopted for logic programming in procedural logic languages such as PROLOG.

3.3 PROCEDURAL LOGIC

In the early 1970s several researchers, including Kowalski [1974], van Emden [1977], Colmerauer [1978], and Roussell [1975], recognized that a theorem prover could be viewed as an interpreter of programs prepared in the form of clausal logic axiom systems. The result of this insight was the development of the procedural logic program interpreter PROLOG [Roussell, 1975], and its DEC10 compiler [Warren, 1977]. PROLOG has been made available as of this writing for IBM, CDC, and DEC computers and for several microcomputers as well.

Following the successful PROLOG implementations, comparable procedural logic systems were developed for the LISP environment: QLOG by Komorowski [1982], HCPRVR by Chester [1980a], and LOGLISP by Robinson and Sibert [1980]. Kowalski's book, *Logic for Problem Solving* [1979] provides detailed treatment of the logic and methods for using clausal logic to express programs that range from brief standard algorithms for factorials, set operations, and sorting, to quite complex procedures for solving classical AI problems and parsing natural language. The following paragraphs show how the logic ideas previously developed are to be interpreted in procedural logic and applied to programming tasks including our central interest, tasks in natural language computation.

Every sentence (i.e., well-formed formula) in procedural logic is represented as a quantifier-free sequence of atomic formulas or literals that state a conclusion followed by its necessary conditions or premises. The interpretation of such a sentence is that conclusion C1 or C2 or ... Cn is True, if premises, P1 and P2 and ... Pn are True.

$$C1 \vee C2 \vee \ldots Cn \leftarrow P1 \wedge P2 \wedge \ldots Pn$$

or alternatively,

$$C1 \vee C2 \vee \ldots Cn \vee \sim(P1 \wedge P2 \wedge \ldots Pn)$$
$$C1 \vee C2 \vee \ldots Cn \vee \sim P1 \vee \sim P2 \ldots \sim Pn$$

It is actually the last form, further abbreviated by gathering the conclusions and the premises into separate lists and dropping the connective and negation symbols, that is used by a resolution algorithm to interpret procedural logic sentences.

$$((C1,C2,\ldots,Cn)(P1,P2,\ldots,Pn))$$

This structure of a clause is further simplified by restricting the left half of the rule to a single literal or formula—a form called a Horn clause.

$$((C1)(P1,P2,\ldots,Pn))$$

The notation is thus simplified to that used by Black's early question-answering system—a list of lists of query clauses. The explicit representations of quantification, disjunction, negation, and implication have all vanished, embedded in the resolution procedure.

These changes in notation do not in any way reduce the completeness or the power of predicate logic as a deductive system. (See Robinson [1980] and Kowalski [1979] for detailed discussions of this matter). Kowalski's syntactic description of these clauses provides the basis for the following explanation.

Sec. 3.3 Procedural Logic

A procedural logic sentence has the form

$$(C_1, C_2, \ldots, C_m)(P_1, P_2, \ldots, P_n)$$

where,

$C_1 \cdots C_m$ and $P_1 \cdots P_n$ are atomic clauses,
m and n are greater or equal to zero,
the C_i are Conclusions, and the P_i are Premises.

If the clauses contain variables, $X_1, \ldots, X_k$, they are taken as universally quantified and the clause may be stated in English as: "For all $X_1, \ldots, X_k$, C1 or C2 or $\cdots$ Cn is True if P1 and P2 and $\cdots$ Pn are True."

Case 1: If m = 1 and n = 0, i.e., a Horn clause of the form (C1) without premises, then it states, "For all $X_1, \ldots, X_k$, C1 is True."

Case 2: If m = 1 and n > 0, e.g., (C1)(P1, ..., Pn), then it states, "For all $X_1, \ldots, X_k$, C1 is True if P1 and ..., Pn are True."

Case 3: If m = 0 and n > 0, e.g., (P1, ..., Pn), then it states, "For all $X_1, \ldots X_k$, it is not the case that P1 and ..., Pn are all True."

Case 4: If m = 0 and n = 0, then □, meaning False.

For clarity in discussing the use of procedural logic it will prove convenient to retain the implication sign as a separator of *Conclusion* and *Premises*, even though it is redundant to the formal-language definition.

Case 1 is an assertion of a factual axiom:

e.g. Human(Socrates) ←

Case 2 is the assertion of a rule—also called a procedure:

e.g. Fallible(x) ← Human(x)

Case 3 is a theorem to be proved:

e.g. ← Fallible(Socrates)

in procedural terms, it is a goal or problem to be solved.

Case 4 results from a contradiction;

e.g. Human(Rocket) → □,

means that if □ follows from ← Human(Rocket), then ~Human(Rocket) contradicts the axiom set.

The semantics of evaluating Horn clauses is a simpler version of resolution—called LUSH resolution. Robinson [1980, p. 9] explains that in LUSH resolution the theorem resolves with the consequent of one clause in the axiom set. The resolvent includes any antecedent formulas which are then resolved in turn until box is achieved or resolution fails or is terminated. Robinson describes LUSH resolution as

> a logical computation whose successive states are the successive query clauses and of which the driving program is the list of assertion clauses. A total proof search then becomes a tree of such logical computations, branching non-deterministically at the states corresponding to sequents [i.e. clauses] for which there is more than one LUSH-resolvent. The tips of such a tree correspond to successful computations exactly when the query clause is empty. An unsuccessful computation, or failure, corresponds to a state whose query clause is not empty but for which there are no LUSH-resolvents.

The method of LUSH resolvents completes a spiraling evolution from Black's cancellation proof method, through linear resolution and its many improvements, to LUSH resolution and procedural logic for programming. A procedural logic program is a system of axioms—assertions and rules. Input to such a program is in the form of a theorem or goal with particular variables or constants as values for its arguments. Evaluating the theorem is a matter of chaining through successive subquestions until either all subquestions are canceled, or the proof fails.

An example program to decide relative sizes of some planets will serve as a first demonstration of procedural logic. For this and subsequent demonstrations, we will shift to LISP list notation conventions. Each assertion or rule is a list of lists, but for convenience, the outer parentheses will be dropped. Each atomic clause is a list whose first element is a predicate name with subsequent elements as argument terms. The abbreviated arrow of implication, <, is used to distinguish conclusion and premises, but frequently it is omitted if there is no loss in clarity. Variables are chosen from the letters M through Z with or without attached numbers.

```
(LARGER SUN JUPITER)
(LARGER JUPITER SATURN)
(LARGER SATURN NEPTUNE)
(LARGER NEPTUNE EARTH)
(LARGER EARTH VENUS)
(LARGER VENUS MARS)
(LARGER MARS MERCURY)

(LARGER X Z) < (LARGER X Y)(LARGER Y Z)
```

The program is called with the theorem

```
<(LARGER SUN V)
```

The first answer is given by the immediate match with (LARGER SUN JUPITER). Other answers are also available, since the question matches a rule:

```
            (LARGER SUN V)
            (LARGER X Z) < (LARGER X Y)(LARGER Y Z)
```

whose variables take on the following values:

```
            X := SUN, V := Z
            (LARGER SUN Z) < (LARGER SUN Y)(LARGER Y Z)
```

The subquestion, (LARGER SUN Y) matches (LARGER SUN JUPITER), binding JUPITER as the value of Y in the next subquestion,

```
            (LARGER JUPITER Z)
```

which matches,

```
            (LARGER JUPITER SATURN)
```

giving the binding Z := SATURN. Since the variable V in the original question was bound to Z, V := Z := SATURN, Therefore, (LARGER SUN SATURN), and if all answers are returned, the list continues with NEPTUNE, EARTH, VENUS, MARS, and MERCURY as successive answers. [Note though, that when all the literal clauses have been exhausted, this particular axiom set causes an endless recursion, (LARGER SUN Z) < (LARGER SUN Y)...(LARGER SUN Z) < (LARGER SUN Y)..., by continuing to match the rule. This endless recursion can be avoided by changing the form of the rule to (BIGGER X Z) < (LARGER X Y)(BIGGER Y Z)].

A theorem could be presented in two other ways: (LARGER X Y), (LARGER X MERCURY). Each of these questions has a first answer, and all answers for each form result eventually in the entire list of LARGER relations between planets and the sun.

Procedural logic interpreters generally follow a strategy of finding a first answer by a top-down exploration of the resolution proof space. By requesting further answers, the user causes the procedure to reject its current answer and seek another; when no further answers are discovered, the procedure has found all answers to the query. Although the program shown above will answer relative size questions, it is not yet a convincing demonstration of the generality of procedural logic as a complete programming language.

To move in that direction we must define another form of term, the list. So far terms have included constants, variables, and functions; the inclusion of lists adds an important dimension to logical notation, in that lists introduce multiple values as terms. A function identifies a single value for a term; a list identifies one or several values. Structurally, a list is an assemblage of values in the form of a tree. The list (A B) actually refers to the tree (A.(B.NIL)), where each dot represents the operation of constructing a list by adding (i.e., CONSing) an element to the front of a list.

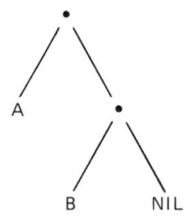

There is a reserved constant, NIL, equivalent to ( ), the empty list. A list is always either NIL or a pair of elements, a head, h, and a tail, t, in the form (h.t). The tail of a nonempty list may be NIL or it may itself be a list. The structures below are lists with the full dot notation shown on the left, contrasted with an equivalent abbreviated notation on the right.

```
NIL                  NIL
()                   ()
(A.NIL)              (A)
(A.(B.NIL))          (A B)
(A.(B.(C.NIL)))      (A B C)
((A.(B.NIL)).(C.NIL))  ((A B) C)
```

These conventions were given by McCarthy [1960] for LISP notation of lists. In LISP, the first element of a list, L, is given by the function, Car(L); the tail is given by Cdr(L), and the constructor function, Cons(Car(L),Cdr(L)), restores the list. In LISP the parenthesis preceding the first argument is moved to the immediate left of the function to give (CAR L),(CDR L), and (CONS(CAR L) (CDR L)). The use of capital letters in most LISP notation is merely a habit inherited from earlier times when computers were limited to uppercase type fonts.

Given a list containing constants and a list

(A B C (D E))

the topmost elements are A, B, C, and (D E). In complete dot notation, the list is given as

(A.(B.(C.((D.(E.NIL)).NIL)

Any LISP system takes exactly the same meaning from the two alternative forms, but the first is much easier for a human user to read and write. The values of list notation for procedural logic derive principally from the way in which variables and lists of variables are bound to lists containing constants. Suppose that the list above is an argument of some atomic clause with predicate name Pred.

(PRED (A B C (D E)))

Sec. 3.3 Procedural Logic

Then in matching the theorem (PRED X), X := (A B C (D E)). Following is shown the correspondence to various lists of variables in the theorem and their bindings when matched to the assertion.

```
(PRED X)          X := (A B C (D E))
(PRED (X.Y) )     X := A  Y:= (B C (D E))
(PRED (X Y.Z) )   X := A  Y:= B  Z := (C (D E))
(PRED (X.Y Z) )   ILL-FORMED
(PRED (X Y Z W) ) X := A  Y:= B  Z:= C
                  W:= (D E)
(PRED (X Y Z (U V)) X := A  Y:= B  Z:= C
                  U := D  V:= E
```

The correspondence between variables and lists derives from the manner in which the unification algorithm incorporated in procedural logic compares the elements of a theorem with the corresponding elements of a matching clause. The practical result is that list manipulations become an integral part of procedural logic. Such list operations as CAR, CADR, CDR, CONS, and often, APPEND are accomplished by designation. Another example of designation is seen in the way LISP accepts a list, (A B C), to stand for the operations

(CONS A(CONS B(CONS C NIL))).

Let us define an operation to split a list into its head and tail portions.

(SPLIT (X.Y) X Y) <

Then the theorem

<(SPLIT (A B C (D E)) U V

returns

(SPLIT (A B C (D E)) A (B C (D E)))

with variable bindings as follows:

```
(X.Y) := (A B C (D E))
U := X := A
V := Y := (B C (D E))
```

No special rules were needed to obtain the car and cdr; the unification algorithm automatically accomplished it according to the way we organized variables in defining the rule.

The operation of discovering whether one list is a subset of another will further illuminate list manipulations in logic. In English, x is a subset of y if for all *z*, if *z* is a member of *x*, *z* is a member of *y*. In procedural logic the definition is as follows:

    (SUBSET NIL X)
    (SUBSET (X.Y) W) < (MEMBER X W)(SUBSET Y W)
    (MEMBER U (U.V))
    (MEMBER U (W.V)) < (MEMBER U V)

Translating back to English, these clauses read:

> NIL, the empty list, is a subset of any list, *x*;
> Any list with head *x* and tail *y* is a subset of the list *w* if *x* is a member of *w*, and *y* is a subset of *w*;
> An object, *u*, is a member of any list whose head is *u*;
> An object, *u*, is a member of any list (*w.v*), where *w* and *u* are not equal if *u* is a member of *v*.

If we test this definition with the theorem (SUBSET (A B)(D E A B)), it matches the second subset rule with the following bindings:

    (SUBSET (A.(B)) (D E A B)) < (MEMBER A (D E A B)
                                      (SUBSET (B) (D E A B))
    X := A, Y := (B) W := (D E A B)

The first subquestion, MEMBER, is asked and since we can see at a glance that A is a member of the set (D E A B), no trace will be given. The next subquestion, (SUBSET ...), matches the second subset rule with the following bindings.

    (SUBSET (B NIL) (D E A B)) < (MEMBER B (D E A B))
                                   (SUBSET NIL (D E A B))
    X := B, Y := NIL, W := (D E A B)

Again it is apparent that B is a member of (D E A B), so the second subquestion, (SUBSET NIL (D E A B)), is asked. This time it matches the first subset rule:

    (SUBSET NIL (D E A B))

Since this rule has no antecedent conditions, all subquestions have been answered and it is True that the list (A B) is a subset of (D E A B).
    Of course, we assumed that the MEMBER procedure would properly identify elements of a list.

Sec. 3.3   Procedural Logic

```
(MEMBER A (D E A B))
(MEMBER U (W.V)) < (MEMBER U V)

      U := A, W := D, V := (E A B)
      (MEMBER A (E A B))
      (MEMBER U (W.V)) < (MEMBER U V)
        U := A, W := E, V := (A B)
            (MEMBER A (A B))
            (MEMBER U (U.V))
              U := A, U := A, V := (B)
```

The first query asked if A was a member of (D E A B); A was compared to D and failed to match, so the second rule provided a subquestion, "is A a member of (E A B)." Again A failed to match E, so the third subquestion, "is A a member of (A B)" resulted. This time the first rule of MEMBER applied and A was found to be equal to the A of (A B). Since A was equal to an element of the list (D E A B), then A is a member of that list.

As a further example of list computations, the procedure "Union" is defined. The union of two lists is a third list containing a single representation of each element that occurs in either list. The union of (A B C) and (A B D) is (A B C D).

```
(UNION NIL W W)
(UNION (X.Y)  W  Z) < (MEMBER X W) (UNION Y W Z)
(UNION (X.Y)  W  (X.Z)) < (UNION Y W Z)
```

This translates back to English as:

the union of nil with any list w is w;

if the head x, of a list $x.y$ is a member of the list w, the union list, z, is the union of y and w;

otherwise, the union is x added to z, the union of y and w.

This is a recursive procedure that examines the head of the first list with respect to the second; if the head is a member of the second, it is already represented, so the union is the union of the tail of the first with the second. If the head of the first list is not a member of the second, it must be added to the union of the tail of the first list with the second. The terminal case occurs when the first list is empty; then the second list is the union.

What should be noticed in this example is the manner in which the new union list is constructed. If an item in the first list is not present in the second, it is simply added by consing it to the union of the rest of the first list and the second. In this procedure, the union will always contain the entirety of the second list plus the elements unique to the first. If we were to use the union procedure on the two lists (A B) and (A C D), the union list would be formed in the third argument in the following series:

(A B) + (A C D) → (A C D)
(B) + (A C D) → (B.(A C D)) = (B A C D)
() + (B.(A C D)) → (B.(A C D)) = (B A C D)

It should now be possible for the reader to define logic procedures to construct the intersection and complement of two lists.

A most convincing argument for the effectiveness of procedural logic as a programming language is the demonstration of sorting algorithms. One of the simplest of these is an algorithm that recognizes that a list containing one element is sorted; since the last element of a list is sorted, the procedure merges each preceding element with a sorted list to form a new sorted list. In merging, an element may be added to the front of a list if it is less than or equal to the first element; otherwise, the element is merged to the tail of the list, and the head of the list is merged with the result.

(SORT (X.NIL)(X.NIL))
(SORT (X.Y) W) < (SORT Y U) (MERGE X U W)

(MERGE X NIL (X.NIL))
(MERGE X (Y.Z) (X Y.Z)) < (LESSEQ X Y)
(MERGE X (Y.Z) W) < (MERGE X Z U) (MERGE Y U W)

In the list (D C B), B is found to be the last element, C is then merged to give (B C), and D is then merged to result in (B C D).

A more efficient "Quicksort" algorithm is given by Clark and Tarnlund [1977].

(QSORT NIL R R)
(QSORT (X.L) R0 R) < (PARTIT L X L1 L2)
                    (QSORT L2 R0 R1)(QSORT L1 (X.R1) R)
(PARTIT (X.L) Y (X.L1) L2) < (LESSEQ X Y)
                    (PARTIT L Y L1 L2)
(PARTIT (X.L) Y L1 (X.L2)) < (LESSEQ Y X)
                    (PARTIT L Y L1 L2)
(PARTIT NIL Y NIL NIL)

Study of these two sorting procedures—using a procedural logic interpreter to provide traces of the recursive steps—will show them to be effective programs for accomplishing their task. The syntax given is correct for HCPRVR but will require syntactic changes to run in LOGLISP and PROLOG.

3.4 DEFINITE CLAUSE GRAMMARS

Pereira and Warren [1980] use the term *Definite clauses* instead of *Horn clauses* as they describe methods for writing and using procedural grammars to compute with natural language. Generally, a grammar is a system of terminals (e.g., words) and nonterminals (i.e., rules) that form a recursive descrip-

Sec. 3.4 Definite Clause Grammars

tion of the well-formed strings of a language. Context-free phrase structure grammars with each rule augmented by a procedure have found wide usage in compiler applications for translating high-level programming languages into machine assembly code. A similar procedure is applicable to understanding subsets of natural language.

A context-free grammar rule is of the form

NonTerminal := Phrase
Phrase := Sequence of Terminals and/or nonTerminals

Example:

S := N + V
N := birds, snow
V := fly, melts

The example grammar describes the following four derivation trees:

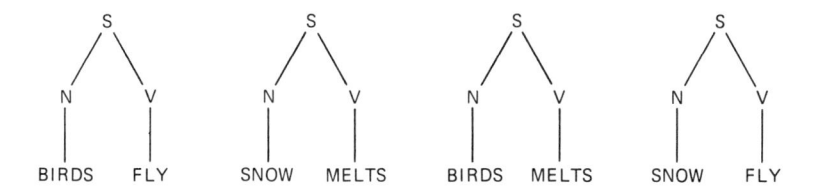

The definition sign, :=, in this grammar is actually an implication in two directions: the comma stands for "or"; and the + is an alternative notation for "and." The rules may be read as the following logical sentences,

$(S \rightarrow N \wedge V)$ $\wedge$ $(N \wedge V \rightarrow S)$
$(N \rightarrow BIRDS \vee SNOW)$ $\wedge$ $(BIRDS \vee SNOW \rightarrow N)$
$(V \rightarrow FLY \vee MELTS)$ $\wedge$ $(FLY \vee MELTS \rightarrow V)$

We should note also that S, N, V, MELTS, and so on, are all propositions (i.e. atomic clauses without variables). If we reverse the arrow and parenthesize the atomic clauses, the grammar can immediately be read as definite or Horn clauses for procedural logic, reading each rule as, "Nonterminal conclusion is True if phrase premises are True."

(S) < (N)(V)
(N) < (BIRDS)   (BIRDS) <
(N) < (SNOW)   (SNOW) <
(V) < (FLY)   (FLY) <
(V) < (MELTS)   (MELTS) <

What will such a program accomplish? If we call it with (N), it will return (N), having established that (N) < (BIRDS), and (BIRDS); if asked for another answer, it will return (N) again, although this time it proved (N) < (SNOW). If called with (S), four answers, all in the form (S), will be returned as each tree in the grammar is explored. If the tree for the top-down proof were recorded, evaluating a conclusion would show all the trees that the grammar provided.

In fact the proof tree can be recorded by adding terms containing variables to some of the clauses in the grammar. But let us also change the predicate names to multiple character constants to distinguish them more easily from variables.

```
(SNT (SNT(X Y))) < (NP X) (VP Y)
(NP (NP X)) < (NOUN X)
(VP (VP X)) < (VB X)
(VB MELTS) <
(VB FLY) <
(NOUN BIRDS) <
```

Notice that each conclusion constructs a list whose head is the name of the rule and whose tail is a list of the lists constructed by its premises. Such an axiom system can now be used to generate all and only the sentences described by the grammar, showing for each its derivation tree. It could also be used to test if a given derivation tree were consistent with the grammar; for example,

```
(SNT (SNT((NP(BIRDS))(VP(MELTS)))) )
```

would be found consistent.

One more term is added containing variables to represent the terminals, and the grammar becomes usable to show the correspondence between a derivation tree and its terminals. (Variables are U, X, Y, Z, and W for this example.)

```
(SNT (U Z) (SNT (X Y))) < (NP U X) (VP Z Y)
(NP U (NP U)) < (NOUN U)
(VP Z (VP Z)) < (VB Z)
(NOUN BIRDS) <
(NOUN SNOW) <
(VB MELTS) <
(VB FLY) <
```

If we now present the theorem, (SNT (BIRDS FLY) W), the trace shows how the grammar computes a parse.

Sec. 3.4 Definite Clause Grammars

(Q-1) (SNT (BIRDS FLY) W)
(A-1) ((SNT (BIRDS FLY) (SNT(X Y))) < (NP BIRDS X) (VP FLY Y))
(Q-2) (NP BIRDS X)
(A-2) ((NP BIRDS (NP BIRDS)) < (NOUN BIRDS))
(Q-3) (NOUN BIRDS)
(A-3) ((NOUN BIRDS))
(R-3) (NOUN BIRDS)
(R-2) (NP BIRDS (NP BIRDS))
(Q-2) (VP FLY Y)
(A-2) ((VP FLY (VP FLY)) < (VB FLY))
(Q-3) (VB FLY)
(A-3) ((VB FLY))
(R-3) (VB FLY)
(R-2) (VP FLY (VP FLY))
(R-1) (SNT (BIRDS FLY) (SNT((NP BIRDS) (VP FLY))))
((SNT (BIRDS FLY) (SNT((NP BIRDS) (VP FLY)))))

[Note: Q-i is a question, A-i shows the match with a rule, and R-i shows a successful answer to the corresponding Q-i.] In the derivation above, the theorem matches the conclusion of the SNT rule, so the variable bindings U = BIRDS and Z = FLY are substituted in the premises. Each premise is then taken as a subquestion, Q-i, which matches a rule, A-i, and the bindings of the variables in the subquestion are propagated through the rule. Finally, the terminal subquestions (NOUN BIRDS) and (VB FLY) correspond to terminal assertions giving the response values R-3, (NOUN BIRDS) and (VB FLY). Substituting the variable bindings for variables in the original theorem, we obtain

(SNT(BIRDS FLY) (SNT((NP BIRDS)(VP FLY))))

providing the parse

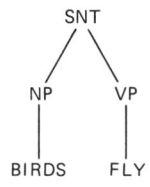

```
        SNT
       /   \
      NP    VP
      |     |
    BIRDS  FLY
```

If we call the theorem with (SNT Y (SNT(NP BIRDS)(VP FLY))), then with no surprise we obtain (BIRDS FLY) for the binding of Y. This symmetry, although trivial in this example, will later be shown to be useful.

We should notice from this demonstration that a context-free phrase structure grammar is a set of propositional sequents that describe the possible derivation trees for terminal strings in its scope. By adding terms with variables to the propositions, the system is changed into a set of predicate logic sequents that relate subtrees and strings. While maintaining the basic phrase structure organization, additional terms can be added to ensure syntactic agreement and semantic sensibility. For example, let us modify the demonstration grammar to ensure syntactic agreement. This can be accomplished by modifying the terminal elements to signify singular or plural and changing the rules to test these features.

(NOUN BIRDS PL)   (NOUN SNOW SING)
(VB FLY PL)   (VB MELTS SING)
(SNT (U Z) (SNT (X Y))) < (NP U X V1) (VP Z Y V1)
(NP U (NP U) V1) < (NOUN U V1)
(VP Z (VP Z) V1) < (VB Z V1)

By adding the variable V1 to both the NP and VP premises of the SNT rule, and marking terminals as SING or PL, the variable V1 imposes an agreement constraint and so rejects BIRDS MELTS and SNOW FLY.

Additional premises can be added to constrain semantic combinations, and arbitrary structures can be constructed in place of the parse tree. These techniques are developed in later chapters as definite clause grammars are described to transform English sentences into various other structures.

3.5 EXERCISES

1. Translate the following sentences into propositional logic and use resolution to prove the theorem. Add the propositions you need.

    (a) A person who has a book can enjoy a rainy Sunday.
    (b) John owns *"The Year of the French."*
        Theorem: John can enjoy a rainy Sunday.

2. Define logic procedures for computing

    (a) the intersection of two lists
    (b) the complement of two lists

    (Documentation for HCPRVR is given in Appendix A. If you have a computing system that uses LISP, bring up HCPRVR and test your procedures on it.)

3. Try the two sorting procedures shown in this chapter in HCPRVR. SETQ TFLAG to True and observe the trace as you call, (SORT (B C D A E) X) for the mergesort, then try (QSORT (B C D A E) X Y). Be sure to declare all the variables used in the two procedures with (VARIABLES M N O ... X Y Z).

    (If you do not have a system that uses LISP, try translating these problems into Prolog and doing the exercise in that language.)

4. Try the grammar given in the last section using HCPRVR. Use TFLAG to trace and QFLAG to obtain additional parsings when the system asks you "Another?"

4

REPRESENTING CONSTITUENTS OF ENGLISH TEXT

4.1 LEVELS OF ENGLISH

Superficially, an English utterance appears as sounds or marks progressing in order one after another. Linguistic analysis, however, shows many levels of structure between the strings of physical events and the eventual conceptualization that is communicated by a discourse. At the physical level are vocalizations and marks on paper. A linguist's trained ear can classify the sounds of any human language into "phonemes" and so translate the vocalizations into "phonemic strings." A written language usually includes an alphabet of particular marks whose combinations represent meaningful units. Certain combinations of phonemes or of characters combine at the next level to form "morphemes," which are the smallest units of meaning in a language. In their turn, sequences of morphemes combine as words or phrases to accumulate more complex meanings.

The *word*, much favored by philosophers and computer scientists, is actually a most difficult term for linguistic definition. For computational purposes, it is often sufficient to define a word as a string of characters bounded by blanks, and recorded in a symbol list. But if a symbol is characterized as having a unitary meaning, such terms as "ice" in "ice cream" fail to qualify, because the combination forms an idiom with its own unique meaning. Frequently used noun–noun phrases in English develop into idioms that eventually cease to reflect the syntactic/semantic combination of their elements. A partial solution is found if a word is defined as that which is a lexical entry regardless of how many blanks may be interposed. But the dictionary contains many elements that are not words; such prefixes as, "un-," "pre-," and "post-," and suffixes such as "-ing," "-ed," "-ion," and "-able" are also legitimate entries. Despite these complications, a few special coding conventions suffice to define a word for practical purposes.

But the morpheme is, in fact, a superior unit of meaning for computational purposes. Languages such as German and Turkish tend to agglutinate meanings by combining morphemes into very large words that have no lexical entries. English sporadically tenses its verbs and marks its nouns and adjectives with special suffixes that make minor modifications to the underlying definitions. Yet, notable computational efficiencies result from basing the lexicon for an English language processor on morphemes rather than words. It is obviously advantageous to have a single entry for each regular verb, such as "regard," rather than one for each of the several forms "regards," "regarded," "regarding." Morphemes such as "-less," "un-," and "dis-" are not as regular as inflectional suffixes in English, with the result that, except for such systems as spelling correctors, there is little advantage in attempting to compute the meaning of their combinations with root forms.

With these caveats about morphemes and words, we may adopt the philosopher's attitude and consider the word as the unit of meaning. Sequences of words combine to form phrases, then phrases form clauses, which in turn combine into sentences or spoken utterances. The sentence is a well-defined unit of written language, but even in formal presentations, speech often includes fragments that are not sentences. Texts, on the other hand, are governed by prescriptive rules for writing, and sentences are usually carefully formed and combined into paragraphs, which in turn combine into sections or chapters and finally into narratives, essays, novels, and books.

Paragraph, chapter, and book are not linguistic units of analysis but rather, of editorial convenience. The combination of clauses into conceptualizations such as schemas and subschemas is a current direction of research in text linguistics, and such work may eventually define new linguistic units that clarify how conceptualizations are communicated. A short sequence of text will illustrate the idea of schemas.

A. The giant rocket was ready.
B. Technicians took shelter.
C. Two red flares rose as a signal.

A schema can provide explicit connectivity among these clauses to show that each of the second and third clauses is a RESULT expansion of the first. Such paraphrases as "A, so B and C," "since A, B, and C" and "B and C when/because A" explicate the causal relations implied by this schema. There may exist appropriate linguistic tests by which any set of clauses may be evaluated as instantiating particular schema forms, but they await further research.

4.2 CONSTITUENTS

Languages are characterized not only by multiple levels, but also by ranks composed of constituents formed of elements from that or the next lower rank. Sentences contain one or more clauses, which in turn contain combinations of phrases that are composed of words or shorter phrases. The syntactic analysis of a sentence is given as a tree of immediate (i.e., adjacent) constituents, each labeled as a given type of phrase.

Consider again the example sentence

Cornwallis sent an army to attack the French troops and Irish rebels at Castlebar.

The following is a form of immediate constituent analysis:

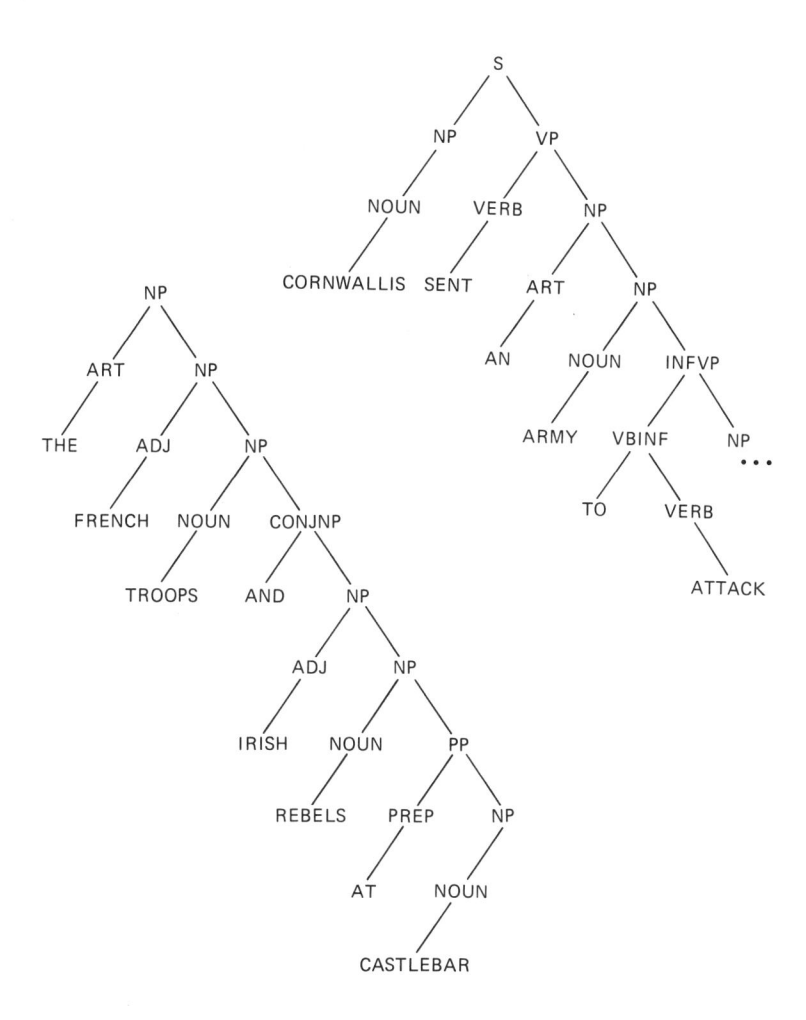

```
                                    S
                                   / \
                                  NP  VP
                                  |   /|\
                                NOUN VERB NP
                                  |   |   /\
                             CORNWALLIS SENT ART NP
                                              |  /\
                                              AN NOUN INFVP
                                                  |    /\
                                                 ARMY VBINF NP
                                                      /\   ...
                                                     TO VERB
                                                         |
                                                       ATTACK

              NP
             /  \
            ART  NP
             |   / \
            THE ADJ  NP
                 |   / \
              FRENCH NOUN CONJNP
                      |    /  \
                   TROOPS AND  NP
                              /  \
                            ADJ   NP
                             |   /  \
                           IRISH NOUN PP
                                  |   / \
                                REBELS PREP NP
                                        |   |
                                        AT NOUN
                                            |
                                        CASTLEBAR
```

The first constituent of this sentence (S) is its subject, the noun phrase (NP), "Cornwallis." The next is a verb phrase (VP), which is composed of the verb "sent" and another NP. This NP decomposes to the two constituents, article (ART) and another NP. This new NP is made up of a noun and an infinitive verb phrase (INFVP) that adds further information. The INFVP is made up of "to," the English infinitive marker, and another verb phrase comprising the verb "attack" and the NP structure composed of a noun and a conjunctive NP (CONJNP), describing the people to be attacked.

The example is shown as a *tree of binary constituents*, that is, each constituent decomposed into exactly one terminal, a terminal and another binary constituent, or two binary constituents. Terminals in the tree are marked as NOUN, ADJ, VERB, and so on, and are then associated with an English word. The regular binary tree offers computational advantages over logically comparable trees containing larger branching factors. It is also the case for English that in all but the very strangest of sentences, the process of analyzing into binary constituents guarantees that any two constituents dominated by a node eventually become adjacent in the analysis process.

Immediate constituent phrase structure is one characteristic that is largely true of English. Where apparently discontinuous constituents (i.e, ones with non-adjacent members) occur as in "She looked the number up," there is a node in the binary constituent tree where the discontinuous elements are brought together. The tree for this example is shown below.

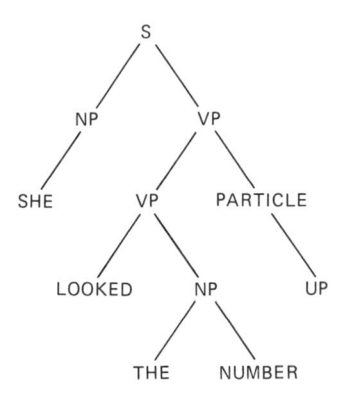

```
                S
              /   \
            NP     VP
           /      /   \
         SHE    VP    PARTICLE
               /  \      \
           LOOKED  NP    UP
                  /  \
                THE  NUMBER
```

In this abbreviated tree, the verb phrase is composed of a verb phrase, "looked" (whose object is "the number") plus a particle, "up." Because the VP and the PARTICLE are eventually adjacent constituents dominated by the top-rank VP, the apparently discontinuous constituents have become available to be treated as continuous at that rank. At that point a transformation can be applied to "look" and "up" to assign the meaning "lookup" to the components.

The binary constituent analyses given above provide a purely syntactic analysis for the sentences. Such analysis shows that the sentence breaks into

Sec. 4.2   Constituents   57

phrases, named as syntactic entities such as: noun phrase, verb phrase, infinitive VP, conjunctive NP, noun, adjective, verb, prepositional phrase (PP), and so on. It also has the desirable property that the terminal English words occur at the bottom of the tree in the same order in which they were presented in the sentence.

One thing it does not show is a certain relation of dominance that always exists between the elements of a binary constituent. For example, in "French army," the noun "army" governs or dominates the adjectival modifier "French"; in "Cornwallis sent an army to attack the Irish," the tree of dominance relations—properly called the *dependency tree*—is as shown:

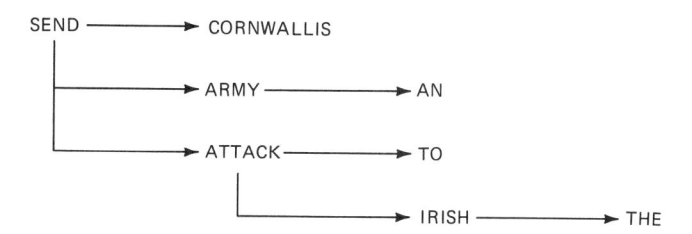

```
SEND ─────────► CORNWALLIS
  │
  ├────────► ARMY ─────────► AN
  │
  └────────► ATTACK ───────► TO
               │
               └─────────► IRISH ─────────► THE
```

In this diagram, dependents to the right of the arrow are dominated by their governors to the left. Rules of dependency are defined on the constituent phrase structure, as follows:

Verbs govern preceding and following NPs, auxiliaries, VPs, adverbials, and PPs that are not more immediately governed.
Nouns dominate articles, adjectives, modifying nouns, and PPs.
Adjectives dominate modifying adverbials.
Prepositions are dominated by preceding nouns and verbs and dominate following nouns.

These rules can be used to transform an immediate constituent phrase structure analysis into a dependency structure. One advantage of such a structure is that the governing terms are lifted to higher levels of the analysis tree and, to the reader, the result is somewhat like a summary of the sentence. This characteristic is referred to as the *summary property*, and later it will prove to be useful for computing summaries of sentences and larger texts.

But more than dominance relates the terms of a dependency structure. For example, in "an army," the article signifies a singular, particular instance of the concept "army." In "the Irish," the article "the" promotes an adjective to a pronominal concept. In "Cornwallis sent an army," the event of "sending" is augmented with specification of a "sender," Cornwallis, and an "object-sent," an army. The "sending" is further specified by the purpose, "attack the Irish," and in the original sentence, also by a location to which the army was sent, "at Castlebar."

This detailed relational structure has attracted linguistic interest since Fillmore [1968] argued that each noun phrase in English was actually in a case relation to some verb in the sentence. Although the relation was often explicitly marked with a preposition, conventions of English syntax allow the preposition to be omitted from many surface forms. The validity of the omission argument can be seen from such paraphrases as the following:

John gave the library books.
Books were given to the library by John.
The event was a giving of books to the library by John.

In the original sentence, the subject, object, and indirect object were each represented as NPs and the reader used his or her understanding of those special positions in the sentence to recognize their relation to the verb. The paraphrases, in contrast, are so arranged as to force the use of a preposition to explicitly mark the relation between each NP and the verb.

A similar phenomenon occurs within the noun phrase. Winograd [1972] offered the following example NP:

the first three old red city fire hydrants without covers you can find

The dependency structure is

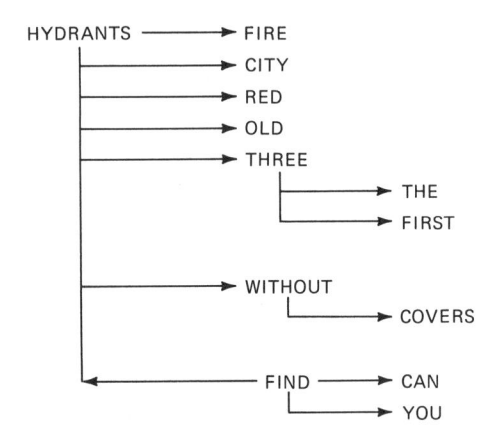

```
HYDRANTS ───────► FIRE
         ├──────► CITY
         ├──────► RED
         ├──────► OLD
         ├──────► THREE
         │            ├──────► THE
         │            └──────► FIRST
         ├──────► WITHOUT
         │            └──────► COVERS
         └──────── FIND ──────► CAN
                       └──────► YOU
```

Winograd used this example to show the syntactic slots available in a noun group (i.e., NP): namely, Determiner, Ordinal, Number, Adjective*, Classifier*, Noun, and Prepositional groups and Clause groups. Adjective* and Classifier* use the *-suffix to indicate multiple possible occurrences. The slots are mainly syntactic names but various more detailed relations are signified by the choice of terms used to fill them. In some sense, the slots for an NP are cousins to the case arguments for verbs, and the concept "hydrant," as representative of a physical object, can be specified as to size, shape, color, number, type, and so on, and additionally qualified, as above, by "without covers" and "you can find."

Like the slot names for nouns, linguists tend to use rather abstract classifications for the verb cases. Such terms as Agent, Patient, Benefactor, Object, Source, Goal, and so on, are typically cited. The term *roles* was suggested by Fillmore as a semantic specialization of cases to particular verbs. Each verb is characterized by the roles in which its arguments participate. For examples,

    Buy—Buyer, Seller, Object-bought, Price
    Steal—Thief, Victim, Booty
    Drive—Driver, Passenger, Vehicle, From, To
    Communicate—Sender, Receiver, Instrument, Message

Often, for such computational purposes as a particular, specialized English language system for making appointments, or reservations, it proves desirable to analyze verbs at the role level. But for any application recognizing a wide range of English texts, the nearly syntactic generality of cases results in simpler analysis and application systems. For nouns, the slots DET, ORD, NUMBER, and CLASS are certainly at an appropriate level of generality, but adjectival modification requires further specification into the finer categories of SIZE, LENGTH, WIDTH, COLOR and so on, in order to achieve a useful level of relations.

Returning to our example of Cornwallis sending an army to attack the Irish, our intuitions about the additional information in the dependency connections is satisfied by using case labels to connect verbs with their arguments and slot labels to specify the relations of nouns and their modifiers. By the two processes of dependency analysis and case or slot labelling, the syntactic structure of a sentence is transformed into its semantic relational form:

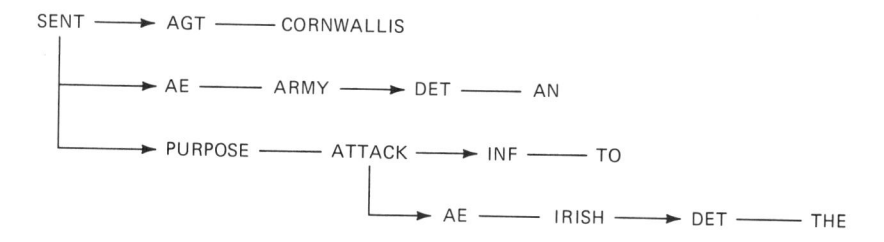

```
SENT ──▶ AGT ──── CORNWALLIS
  │
  ├──▶ AE ──── ARMY ──▶ DET ──── AN
  │
  └──▶ PURPOSE ──── ATTACK ──▶ INF ──── TO
                        │
                        └──▶ AE ──── IRISH ──▶ DET ──── THE
```

The arcs, AGT for agent, AE for affected entity, INF for infinitive, Det for determiner, and so on, label the dependency relations given earlier, and so transform the sentence into a semantic relation composed of words connected by directed, labeled relation arcs. One further step, the substitution of root forms with inflectional relations, such as

```
SEND—TNS—PAST         for SENT
ATTACK—TNS—INF        for ATTACK—INF—TO
ARMY—NBR—SING         for ARMY
```

completes the translation to semantic relational form.

In this form each relation answers an English question. Examples include:

```
SEND AGT CORNWALLIS      WHO SENT?
SEND TNS PAST            SEND WHEN?
SEND AE ARMY             SEND WHAT?
SEND PURPOSE ATTACK      WHY SEND?
ARMY NBR SING            HOW MANY?
ATTACK AE IRISH          ATTACK WHOM?
```

Several possible questions, such as "Who was to attack the Irish?", "What was the army to do?," and "Which Irish?" are not directly answered by the semantic relational structure, but require inference rules of the sort:

If X sends Y for purpose Z
Then Y has purpose Z

Thus since Cornwallis, X, sent an army, Y, for the purpose to attack, Z, the army's purpose is the attack.

Of course such rules must be carefully limited and qualified if they are to be generally true. "Which Irish?" can be answered only in terms of a larger context such as the previous mention of "Irish patriots" or "Irish rebels." Chapter 10, which deals with paraphrase and question answering, examines such rules in detail. Subsequent sections of this chapter describe translations into semantic relational form for a variety of English constituents.

4.3 INFLECTIONAL CONSTITUENTS

In well-formed sentences of English, nouns and verbs agree in number, verbs are marked for tense, and adjectives are marked for the degrees positive, comparative, and superlative. For most nouns and verbs, a suffix is added to a root form to achieve the marking. For adjectives, either the suffixes /null/, /er/, or /est/, or the qualifying adverbs "more" or "most," are used to mark degree. Figure 4.1 summarizes these markings.

The paradigm of Figure 4.1 holds for regular inflections, but many of the most common English nouns and verbs are irregular (e.g., is, am, are, be; have, has, had; sing, sang, sung; goose, geese; etc.) and the English speaker must simply memorize the adjectives that must use "more" and "most" instead of the inflectional suffixes.

A semantic relation is defined as a root form optionally followed by a series of relation-name value pairs. The lexicon for a computational language

Sec. 4.3 Inflectional Constituents

Root Form	Inflection[a]	Relation Name
Send	//	Person1/2-Pres
Sends	/s/	Person3-Pres
Sending	/ing/	Participle
Send	/en/	Past
Girl	//	Singular
Girls	/s/	Plural
Girl's	/'s/	Possessive
Bright	//	Positive
Brighter	/er/	Comparative
Brightest	/est/	Superlative

[a] // is the null inflection.

Figure 4.1 Inflectional constituents.

processer is organized and entered by root forms for those words that follow the regular inflectional rules. Using a suffix-stripping procedure to obtain an entry to the lexicon, the tense, number and degree relations, and the appropriate suffix are all recorded in the semantic relation that is computed for each word. For the examples above, the following semantic relations result:

```
(SEND TNS PAST SFX T/D)
(SEND TNS PARTICIPLE SFX ING)
(SEND TNS PRES PERSON (P1 P2 SING) SFX NIL)
(SEND TNS PRES PERSON (P3 SING) SFX S)
(GIRL NBR SING SFX NIL)
(GIRL NBR PLUR SFX S)
(GIRL NBR SING CASE POSSESSIVE SFX 'S)
(GIRL NBR PLUR CASE POSSESSIVE SFX S')
(BRIGHT DEGREE POS SFX NIL)
(BRIGHT DEGREE COMPAR SFX ER)
(BRIGHT DEGREE SUPERL SFX EST)
```

The example "girls'" is added to the set to show the combination of two inflectional suffixes. The "T/D" value for SFX in the first expression, shows that a "T" is to be added after the "D" is deleted to form the word "sent." An adjective such as "beautiful" which requires "more" or "most" requires syntactic processing of two constituents to form a new one,

```
(BEAUTIFUL DEGREE COMPAR SFX NIL QFY MORE)
(BEAUTIFUL DEGREE SUPERL SFX NIL QFY MOST)
```

The initial lexical entries for these examples are given marked as present, singular, or positive with null suffixes.

```
(SEND TNS PRES SFX NIL)
(GIRL NBR SING SFX NIL)
(BRIGHT DEGREE POS SFX NIL)
```

These values are changed as needed by the lexical lookup that follows suffix stripping. The procedures to accomplish the changes are described in Chapter 5. In that chapter it will also be seen that lexical entries contain more information characterizing each word by semantic features, mapping it into a taxonomy of concepts, and frequently providing other definitional information in the form of process descriptions.

Articles, adverbs, and conjunctions are represented minimally in the lexicon; pronouns are given special features marking case, gender, and number to be used in determining to what concept in the discourse they refer. The general form of a lexical entry follows:

[<ROOT-FORM> <PART-OF-SPEECH> <REL-PAIR*>]

The <REL-PAIR*> signifies a series of relation names and values such as those shown above (i.e., NBR, TNS, DEGREE, SFX, GENDER, CASE, etc.) with appropriate values characterizing the entry. Additional relations include FEATURE, PROCESS, PICTURE, and so on, which can relate the word to any amount of semantic information desired. The information carried in the lexicon is referred to by translation and inference rules used by the language processing systems.

4.4 CLAUSAL CONSTITUENTS

Simple sentences are independent clauses, but in general sentences may contain several clauses explicitly or implicitly related to the independent one. In the Cornwallis example, two clauses are included,

C1. Cornwallis sent an army
C2. to attack the French troops and Irish patriots.

Each clause contains a verb and some of its arguments; the first clause is the independent one in this case, while the second, beginning with "to attack," is an infinitive clause whose subject "an army" is inferrable from the fact that it modifies "army." But it has been noted that this clause is actually the PURPOSE argument for the verb, "sent." It can easily be seen that two simple sentences could paraphrase the example:

Cornwallis sent an army.
The army was to attack the French...

Sec. 4.4   Clausal Constituents

From this it is apparent that the repetition of "army" and of the past-tense marker were deleted when these two conceptualizations were combined into one sentence; what remained was the infinitive verb "to attack," related by one arc to "send" and another to "army." Previously, we showed only the PURPOSE arc relating the infinitive clause to the verb "send" of the independent clause. The semantic relation that better represents this situation is,

(SEND AGT CORNWALLIS
   AE (ARMY AGT* (ATTACK AE FRENCH PURP* ?SEND)))

This is patterned after the mathematical notation,

(ARMY : (ATTACK AGT ARMY AE FRENCH...))

where the colon is read "such that." In this representation, AGT* and PURP* are back-pointing arcs meaning that "army" is the agent of "attack" and that "attack" is the purpose of "send." The notation "?SEND" is meant as a pointer to the first "SEND" in the relation. Alternatively, the sentence could be represented as two interrelated semantic relations.

(SEND AGT CORNWALLIS AE ARMY PURPOSE ?ATTACK)
(ATTACK AGT ?ARMY AE FRENCH)

In either case, the semantic relation (SR) contains the "?-" prefix, referring to the last or next occurrence of the root form prefixed. Such more detailed SRs are computed when sentences and clauses are completed and combined into schemas and discourse trees, but at the first level of analysis the SR structure remains incomplete, as follows:

(SEND AGT CORNWALLIS AE ARMY
   PURPOSE (ATTACK AE FRENCH))

It should be noted that these representations have generally been abbreviated by ignoring modifiers and inflectional relations on rootforms, and so far nothing has been said about whether the sentence is in active or passive voice, imperative, interrogative, or subjunctive mood, or what the detailed form is for such complex verbs as "will have been going to fly." As the discussion progresses some of these deficiencies will be corrected.

The examples dealt with so far have included regular verbs such as "send" and "attack." Many sentences involve the verbs "to be" and "to have," each of which may signify several semantic relations. The following examples show some simple cases of "to be."

Mary is lovely.
Mary is a chinchilla.
Mary is under the couch.

The first attributes the quality of loveliness, which can be approximated as the relation of appearance (AP):

(MARY AP LOVELY)

The second shows a class relation, superset (SUP):

(MARY SUP CHINCHILLA)

The third locates (LOC) her.

(MARY LOC (COUCH PREP UNDER))

Here, the convention is followed that a simple sentence using the verb "to be" is represented as a noun phrase. Sometimes it is desirable to represent these sentences in the following fashion:

(BE AE MARY AP LOVELY TNS PRES VOICE ACTIVE)
(BE AE MARY SUP CHINCHILLA TNS PRES VOICE ACTIVE)
(BE AE MARY LOC (COUCH PREP UNDER) TNS PRES VOICE ACTIVE)

and later transform them into the simpler nominal form. When a form of the verb "to have" is used, the same conventions hold.

Mary has fur.
John has Mary.
Mary has mange.

In these three examples, the relations signified by "has" are, respectively, HASPART, POSSESS, and ASSOCiated with. This latter term is admittedly a catchall used with "have" verbs and possessives for those relations that are not clearly HASPART or POSSESS.

In the case of both "have" and "be" as verbs, there are paraphrase forms, such as:

lovely Mary,
the chinchilla, Mary,
Mary on the couch,
Mary's fur,
John's Mary,
Mary's mange.

One important goal for semantic relations in their representation of text is that they should offer a common notation for syntactic paraphrases, such as those shown in the examples above. This leads to the argument that the verb representations "HAVE" and "BE" should be deleted and the nominal representation chosen. The consequence is generally that questions can be answered with fewer computations. If the verb is tensed or modified by an adverb, the added relation value pairs are simply carried into the noun-headed semantic relation. If the relation is used to generate a noun phrase, the tense and adverbial relations may be ignored or translated as noun modifiers.

4.5 ADJECTIVAL AND ADVERBIAL CONSTITUENTS

For simple adjectives such as those in "large river," "bright light," and "long rocket," the semantic relation name is generally taken as the superclass for the adjective. So the semantic relations for the foregoing examples appear as follows:

>(RIVER SIZE LARGE)
>(LIGHT INTENSITY BRIGHT)
>(ROCKET LENGTH LONG)

The relation names are thought of as labels for scales and the words "large," "bright," and "long" stand for qualitative representations of positions on the scales. For some purposes it will certainly prove desirable to translate these qualitative values into numerical ones, but for many language processing purposes it is unnecessary.

There is a fascinating phenomenon of sense sharing in adjectival contrast pairs, illustrated in the following pairs:

>sharp−dull
>dull−bright
>bright−dark
>dark−light
>light−heavy
>heavy−dull

While this may suggest cognitive relations to the psychologist, linguistically it reminds us that the appropriate sense meaning of the adjective must be selected in order to determine the appropriate scale name.

Comparative and superlative forms of adjectives must also be considered; for examples:

>John is taller than Mary
>John is the heaviest boy in the school
>The more people, the merrier the party

Generally, in discussing these forms, a logical model is used in notations such as the following:

```
GR(HT(JOHN),HT(MARY))
(X) BOY(X) INSCHOOL(X) GR(WEIGHT(JOHN),WEIGHT(X))
(X)(Y) NUMBER-OF-PEOPLE(X),MERRIMENT-OF-PARTY(Y),
    INCREASE(X) → INCREASE(Y)
```

In the notation above, (X) is read as "For all X," and NUMBER-OF-PEOPLE(X) is the relation that is read as, "X is a number-of-people." Such logical representation is most useful for understanding the exact relationships expressed in a sentence, but it projects an illusion of precision that is not actually present. The heights of John and Mary are not known; the sentence only communicated the relation greater-than and so implied that height must be represented by a number. The second expression is clearly inadequate unless we add the fact that the boys in school are other than John. The last expression has been severely foreshortened; it should actually establish that the people are going to the party, that the party includes the people, and that merriment points to some numerical scale. Even with such corrections to the logical representation, it is not clear that the added complexity of notation will improve the precision of language-processing operations.

The same examples can be represented more directly in semantic relations.

```
(JOHN HEIGHT (TALL DEGREE COMPAR SFX -ER *THAN MARY))
(JOHN SUP (BOY WEIGHT (HEAVY DEGREE SUPERL SFX -EST)
    LOC (SCHOOL PREP IN DET THE))
(PERSON NBR PLURAL QFY MORE DET THE
    IMPLY (PARTY MERRIMENT (MERRY DEGREE COMPAR
            SFX -ER DET THE)
    DET THE))
```

The clear advantages to this form are that all the information given in the English is coded into the relations, and the relations themselves are neutral with respect to mathematical or logical interpretation. Since the meaning of the statements may vary depending on the context in which they occur and the task in which they are to be used, the neutrality of the semantic relations proves to be an advantage.

4.6 DETERMINERS, NEGATIONS, AND CONJUNCTIONS

Articles such as "the," "a," and "an" are values for the relation determiner (DET). Other determiners, such as "this," "these," and "those," require an identifying arc such as DXDET (deictic determiner). English quantifiers such

Sec. 4.6 Determiners, Negations, and Conjunctions 67

as "some," "every," "all," "more," "many," and "most" use the relation QFY (quantifier). Thus "all of the seven hydrants" is represented as below.

(HYDRANT NBR PL QUANT SEVEN DET THE QFY ALL)

For representing negation, the special arc NEGative is used associated with the English term it modifies; for examples:

No dog bit a postman.
No postman was bitten.
The dog did not bite a postman.

```
(BITE TNS PAST AGT (DOG NEG NO NBR SING)
             AE (POSTMAN NBR SING DET A))
(BITE TNS PAST AUX(BE TNS PAST) VOICE PASSIVE
             AE (POSTMAN NBR SING NEG NO))
(BITE TNS PRES AUX (DO TNS PAST) NEG NOT
             AGT (DOG NBR SING DET THE)
             AE (POSTMAN NBR SING DET A))
```

Semantic relations can also be used to represent the quantified logic forms of these statements in such a manner as to support the rules for changing quantifiers as negations are brought to the outside of the expression, but for the present purpose, the semantic relations emphasize expression of the English rather than their logical equivalents.

In English any set of syntactically similar constituents can be conjoined by "and" or "or" to result in great conciseness of expression. For computational purposes, conciseness is also a great virtue, so instead of following the customary practice of expanding a conjunctive sentence into several simple ones, the convention was adopted to use the relational symbols *AND and *OR. An example sentence will illustrate.

Scientists and generals withdrew and crouched behind earth mounds.

```
(WITHDRAW TNS PAST AGT (SCIENTIST NBR PLURAL
                    *AND (GENERAL NBR PLURAL))
       *AND (CROUCH TNS PAST
              LOC (MOUND NBR PLUR TYPE EARTH
                    PREP BEHIND)))
```

The conjoined "scientists and generals" were related with *AND, as were "withdraw and crouch." Using the representation to answer questions requires back-pointers from "crouch" and "general" to "withdraw" and "scientist," respectively. With these backlinks, inference rules are written to answer the following types of questions,

Where did the generals crouch?
Did the generals withdraw?
To where did the scientists withdraw?

The desired answers are, respectively, "behind earth mounds," "the generals withdrew," and "behind earth mounds." If we let R stand for a verb such as "withdraw" or "crouch," we can state rules such as the following to obtain the desired answers from the representation.

$$(R\ BKLNK\ R')(R'\ AGT\ X) \rightarrow (R\ AGT\ X)$$
$$(R\ *AND\ R')\ (R'\ U\ V) \rightarrow (R\ U\ V)$$

The first rule translates to English as: "If X is the agent of R', and R' is conjunctively linked to R, then X is also the agent of R." The second rule states: "If R' is related by arc U to V, and R is conjunctively related by *AND to R', then R is also related by arc U to V." The use of these rules is explained in Chapter 9 on questioning text. Here it is sufficient to state that the *AND convention does reduce redundancy at very little cost in computation. It is also consistent with the philosophy that the semantic relations should closely resemble the English they represent. In a later paragraph, *THAN is introduced following the same sort of conventions for using it as an infix relation, and in subsequent chapters such arc names as *TO, *FOR, and other *- prefixes are sometimes used to characterize some general semantic relations by connotative names.

4.7 SENTENTIAL CONSTITUENTS

Two kinds of embedded sentential constituents, clauses joined by conjunctions and those linked by comparatives, have already been considered. Many other forms also exist, for example:

1. She wants lots of chocolate to eat.
2. The rocket was too high to be seen.
3. After the battle was fought, the war was finished.
4. Whenever it rains the streets are wet.
5. The streets were wet because it rained.

Although these examples are few, they will serve to show several conventions for representing embedded sentences in semantic relations. Example 1 can be paraphrased in several ways:

Sec. 4.7 Sentential Constituents

> She wants lots of chocolate that she can eat,
> > for her to eat,
> > to eat,
>
> She wants to eat lots of chocolate.

The two clauses are

> She wants chocolate.
> She may/will eat chocolate.

Although the semantic relations will record the syntactic variations in these sentences (including voice and mood), the essential representation will be as follows:

> (WANT TNS PRES AGT SHE AE (CHOCOLATE AMOUNT LOTS PREP OF)
> PURPOSE (EAT TNS PRESENT MODAL CAN
> AGT SHE RELPRON THAT))

The PURPOSE arc introduces the embedded clause for all these examples, although the clause introduced by "eat" will vary depending on its syntactic form. At a later point when the semantic relations are compiled into a discourse network, pronoun references will be calculated and the missing arguments of the embedded clause will be provided.

> (WANT TNS PRES AGT ELIZA AE (CHOCOLATE...)
> PURPOSE (EAT TNS PRES MODAL CAN AGT ELIZA
> AE (CHOCOLATE...)))

The syntactic information will at that time be carried into the resulting network data structure, but will be ignored for most question-answering operations, and used only when it is desired to translate the relation back to natural language.

Example 2, "The rocket was too high to be seen," is treated much like a comparative of the form, "the rocket was higher than one could see."

> (ROCKET HEIGHT (HIGH DEGREE COMPAR SFX -ER
> *THAN (SEE TNS PRES MODAL COULD
> AGT ONE)))
> (ROCKET HEIGHT (HIGH INTENS TOO
> *THAN (SEE TNS PRES
> MODAL (BE TNS INF))))

The relation *THAN joins the two clauses using the same convention as that of *OR and *AND. The meaning deriving from combining the intensifier or the comparative with the MODAL in both cases is that the rocket could not be seen. Notice that the second form reflects the actual sentence, leaving to some inference rule the question of who might see the rocket. The two clauses, in simplified form, assert:

>The rocket was high.
>It couldn't be seen.

It would prove most desirable at the point of combining clauses into a discourse structure if a simple RESULT arc were used to produce

>(ROCKET DET THE HEIGHT HIGH
>   RESULT (SEE TNS PRES MODAL COULD NEG NOT
>   AGT ONE AE ROCKET))

As usual, inference rules must be written to explicate such a particular meaning for language-processing purposes.

Example 3, "After the battle was fought, the war was finished," illustrates temporal conjunction of two clauses:

>the battle was fought
>the war was finished

>(FIGHT TNS PAST AE (BATTLE DET THE) AUX (BE TNS PAST)
>   VOICE PASSIVE TIME AFTER
>   SEQ> (FINISH TNS PAST AE (WAR DET THE)...)

If we generalize this to account also for "before" and "while," the following SRs result.

>The war was finished before the battle...

>(FINISH...AE (WAR DET THE) TIME BEFORE
>   SEQ> (FIGHT TNS PAST...AE (BATTLE...))

>The war was finished while the battle...

>(FINISH AE (WAR DET THE) TIME WHILE
>   SEQ> (FIGHT...))

The convention is followed that the clauses are ordered by sequence arcs in accordance with text sequence. The actual, physical ordering of the clauses is not necessary; the use of SEQ> and SEQ< arcs can serve the same purpose and so maintain the order in which the clauses were actually presented, while signalling temporal order with the time arcs. Such stylistic devices as flashbacks or scene shifts may be handled with the SEQ< arc.

Sec. 4.7 Sentential Constituents

Example 4 illustrates a pair of clauses joined by implication. "Whenever it rains the streets are wet." The semantic relation follows.

```
(RAIN TNS PRES AE IT TIME WHENEVER
    IMPLY> (STREET NBR PLURAL DET THE STATE WET))
```

An alternative form, "the streets are wet when it rains," receives a similar treatment with the arc IMPLY<, indicating the opposite direction of implication.

```
(STREET NBR PLURAL DET THE STATE WET
    IMPLY< (RAIN ... TIME WHEN AE IT))
```

The conjunctions "because" and "since" receive comparable treatment. Example 5, is illustrated below.

The streets were wet because it rained.

```
(STREET ... STATE WET CAUSAL BECAUSE
    IMPLY< (RAIN ... AE IT))
```

An alternative formulation,

Because it rained, the streets were wet.

```
(RAIN ... AE IT CAUSAL BECAUSE
    IMPLY> (STREET ... STATE WET))
```

The general principles for encoding embedded clauses in semantic relations are

1. encode the actual connective relational word.
2. form an explicit sequential arc using SEQ<, SEQ>, IMPLY>, or IMPLY<.

One other causal relation between clauses, that of bi-implication or EQUIValence, is found primarily in appositions and in some sentences with the verb "to be." For examples,

Cornwallis, the viceroy of Ireland, led the army.
To defeat the French (i.e., to win the war), one should ...
To defeat the French is to win the war.

Representation of these sentences should now be an (un)easy exercise for the reader.

4.8 THEORY OF SEMANTIC RELATIONS

Earlier in this chapter it was shown that syntactic constituents of sentences could be transformed into dependency relations where one element governed or dominated another. By adding labels denoting the nature of the dependency relation, elementary semantic triples of the form <word relation-name word> were formed. When the additional constraint was added that the "word" should be an inflection-free root form, these triples became elementary semantic relations. Combining these triples into larger forms resulted in examples of complex semantic relations, according to the following pattern:

[<ROOT-FORM> (RELATION-PAIR*)]

where the optional, repeated instances of RELATION-PAIR were of the form

[<RELATION-NAME><SEMANTIC-RELATION>]

Rootforms are restricted to entries in the dictionary but, in addition to ordinary words, they include suffixes, and such terminal elements as SINGULAR, PLURAL, COMPARATIVE, SUPERLATIVE, PAST, and FUTURE. The relation names are also selected from a definite, limited list of values, such as AGENT, AFFECTED-ENTITY, INSTRUMENT, TNS, VOICE, MOOD, MODAL, SIZE, SHAPE, DEGREE, QFY, NEG, IMPLY, EQUIV, SUP, QUANT, DET, and so on. Although the list is assumed to be definite, and limited in size, it is still a weakness of the system that the complete list has not yet been defined. The semantic relation associated as the value of a relation-name may be a terminal or a complex SR. A simpler definition of a semantic relation is

> A *Semantic Relation* is a root form, or a root form followed by a list of relation-name value pairs, where each value is itself a semantic relation.

With an appropriate choice of naming conventions, these definitions suffice to account for the structure of conceptual dependencies, partitioned semantic networks, and many other forms of associative networks, as described in Findler [1979]. By adding conventions for encoding linguistic information in these relations, a form called surface semantic relations (SSRs) can be distinguished from other associative network schemes. The SSRs are constrained to represent what was said rather than what might be meant. The test of this property is that the SSR representing a sentence should suffice to generate, among other syntactic paraphrases, exactly that sentence. SSRs are further constrained to maintain the hierarchical summary property that they share with dependency trees. The elements of SSRs are properly words or root forms of words connected by semantic relation names that are meaningful to the (instructed) reader. The "meaning" of an SSR is a variable thing, depending on the context in which it is found and the purpose for which it is used. Such meanings are given explicitly in implication rules for answering questions, constructing paraphrases or translations, communicating commands, and so on; they do not reside in the SSR itself. Additional aspects of the meaning of the root forms are found in the dictionary and, particularly, in the taxonomic relations in which they participate with other root forms.

These principles constrain surface semantic relations to be a formal language that explicitly represents the dependency structure of a natural-language sentence as a root form dominating a set of labeled dependents. Considering the ease with which people identify constituents of their language and can make judgments of dependency relations within constituents of sentences, it is tempting to suggest that the system can be taken as an early-stage process in a psychological theory of text understanding. But to do so is to plunge into a morass of conflicting formulations by psychologists of what might be happening when people read or hear natural language. It is my personal view that there are no satisfactory experimental methods for validating such theories, with the result that the acceptance of psychological theories of language understanding, like those in philosophy and linguistics, depends largely on consensual judgments by the respective professions.

As computational and logical theory for representing natural language understanding, semantic relations need only be shown to be consistent and effective ways to satisfy criteria of text understanding; that is, they must be effective in synthesizing those behaviors that are criterial in the process of understanding language. When taken as a theory of text understanding, they must be considered to be a mathematical theory that accounts well for the behavior, but one far more abstract than the observables of psychological study.

4.9 LOGIC OF CASE RELATIONS

The case-relational representation is a short form used to represent a statement in clausal logic. For the example, "Cornwallis sent an army to attack the French" a quantified logic translation, assuming the conjunction of clauses, is

```
SOME X Y Z U V INST(X, CORNWALLIS)
INST(Y, SEND)
INST(Z, ARMY)
INST(U, ATTACK)
INST(V, FRENCH)
AGT(Y, X)
AE(Y, Z)
PURPOSE(Y, U)
TNS(Y, PAST)
AE(U, V)
TNS(U, INF)
DET(Z, AN)
DET(V, THE)
```

The INST relation designates a particular instance of a concept. If we Skolemize these existential variables by assigning a subscripted constant (i.e., CORNWALLIS1, SEND1, ARMY1, ATTACK1 and FRENCH1) to stand for each particular instance of a concept, we then obtain a conjunction of universally quantified literal clauses as follows:

```
INST(CORNWALLIS1, CORNWALLIS)
INST(SEND1, SEND)
INST(ARMY1, ARMY)
INST(ATTACK1, ATTACK)
INST(FRENCH1, FRENCH)
AGT(SEND1, CORNWALLIS1)
AE(SEND1, ARMY1)
PURPOSE(SEND1, ATTACK1)
TNS(SEND1, PAST)
AE(ATTACK1, FRENCH1)
TNS(ATTACK1, INF)
DET(ARMY1, AN)
DET(FRENCH1, THE)
```

Since each constant includes its concept name we can abbreviate the notation further by allowing the INST predicates to be implied by their subscripted concepts. We can then gather these clauses into semantic relational sets by representing any common first arguments as the initial or head term associated with a set of pairs composed of the predicate name and its second argument. For example, in the expression above, the SEND1 predicates combine as follows:

```
(SEND1 AGT CORNWALLIS1 AE ARMY1 PURPOSE ATTACK1 TNS PAST)
```

Since there are additional predications about ARMY1 and ATTACK1,

```
(ARMY1 DET AN)
(ATTACK1 AE FRENCH TNS INF)
```

and for FRENCH1, (FRENCH1 DET THE) the final composition appears as follows:

```
(SEND1 TNS PAST AGT CORNWALLIS1 AE (ARMY1 DET AN)
PURPOSE (ATTACK1 TNS INF AE (FRENCH1 DET THE))
```

By gathering the clauses into sets, each subscripted constant is uniquely identified by its context and the subscripts can be deleted to result in the final SR form.

```
(SEND TNS PAST AGT CORNWALLIS AE (ARMY DET AN)
PURPOSE (ATTACK TNS INF AE (FRENCH DET THE))
```

In formulas that include universal quantifiers and/or negations QFY and MODAL relations are formed [e.g. (ARMY QFY ALL DET THE), (ARMY MODAL NONE)] and embedded in the set. The SR form is thus shown to be an alternative, abbreviated notation for first-order logic.

The interpretation of the SR is identical to that of the classical logic. There is an instance of a sending event, tense past; there is an instance of Cornwallis (during the time span of this sending), an instance of an army, of an attacking event, and of the French; the agent of the sending is the instance of Cornwallis, the purpose of the sending is an instance of attacking, and the affected entity of the attack is the instance of the French. Each of these instances is an instance of its general concept, which is defined over universally quantified variables. An instance of an event concept can be visualized as a brief movie with particular roles instantiated by particular, temporally marked instances of appropriate concepts such as Cornwallis, the army, the attack, and the French. The "objects" represented by the instantiation are interpreted as classes of experience.

SRs provide a most concise notation—17 symbols vs. 45 in this example—that uses additional code in its interpreter to avoid redundancy in the coding of events. In addition, by gathering the clauses into sets headed by verbs and nouns, a useful indexing form is obtained to minimize the search when proving theorems or answering questions. The cost of these abbreviations can be seen in Chapter 9, where the procedures MATCHPR and MEMPR are described for locating particular relation arc-value pairs in an SR. The SRs that result from analyzing a text are treated simply as assertions by the logic interpreter, but additional rules for matching these complex assertions are provided in procedural logic. For additional discussion of the logic of case structures, see Bruce [1975] and Allen and Frisch [1982], and for treatment of quantifiers in SRs, see Simmons and Chester [1977].

4.10 EXERCISES

1. Represent the following sentences in SSR form:

    (a) A great black and yellow rocket stood in the New Mexico desert.
    (b) It weighed 5 tons.
    (c) Two red flares rose as a signal to fire the rocket.
    (d) Slowly at first the giant rocket rose.
    (e) Soon it was too high to be seen.

    After parsing these sentences, the answers to the exercise may be read in Figure 8.2.

5

TRANSLATING SENTENCES TO SEMANTIC RELATIONS

5.1 PARSING AND TRANSLATION

The surface semantic relations described in Chapter 4 can be computed from English sentences by using an immediate constituent, phrase structure grammar that is augmented with restrictions and transformations. This computational process is generally called "parsing", but even in the simplest cases where only a syntactic tree is to be computed, there is actually a translation from an English string to another string that represents a labeled syntactic tree. Other "parsings" translate natural-language strings into semantic relations or into quantified forms of predicate logic. A simple example of computing a syntactic tree for "Cornwallis met the French commander" will illustrate:

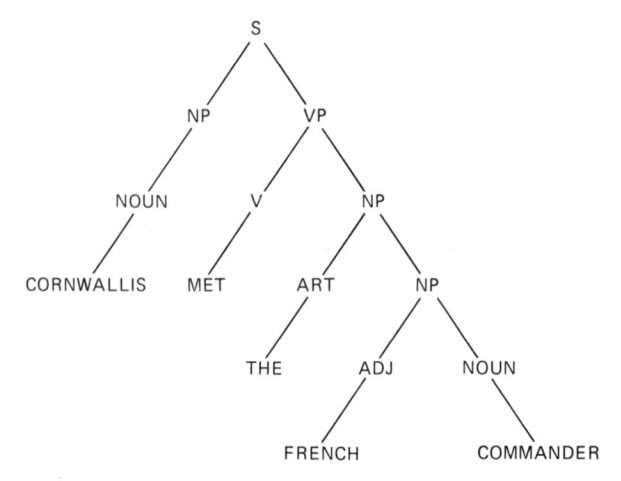

```
                    S
                   / \
                 NP   VP
                 |   / \
               NOUN V   NP
                 |   |  / \
          CORNWALLIS MET ART  NP
                         |   / \
                        THE ADJ NOUN
                             |   |
                          FRENCH COMMANDER
```

This tree can also be expressed as a list, that is, as a string of characters using parentheses to distinguish nodes and their descendents.

(S(NP(NOUN CORNWALLIS))
(VP(V MET)(NP(ART THE)(NP ADJ FRENCH)(NOUN COMMANDER)))))

A phrase structure grammar such as the following suffices to describe the translation.

S → NP + VP
NP → NOUN
NP → ART + NP
NP → ADJ + NP
VP → VERB
NOUN → CORNWALLIS, COMMANDER
ADJ → FRENCH
VERB → MET
ART → THE

The parsing can be accomplished by a procedure that starts with the symbol S, using the associated rule to expand it to (S(NP VP)), then recursively expands the symbols in the expanded list (NP VP), until the terminal elements of the sentence are matched. For example, (S(NP VP)) first expands the NP to give (S(NP(NOUN CORNWALLIS)) (VP)), then expands the VP to give (S (NP...) (VP(VERB MET) NP)), then expands the NP to eventuate in (S...(VP...(NP (ART THE) (NP(ADJ FRENCH)(NOUN COMMANDER))))). When the procedure finds a terminal element such as NOUN and attempts to match it to the string element "the", it fails, and must then back up and select the next available NP rule. The procedure terminates when all elements of the string have been matched successfully, or when all relevant rules of the grammar have been tried and no tree can be found to span the string.

The syntactically labeled tree is called the parse of the sentence and the procedure that applies the grammar is a parser. Using the same grammar, a very similar procedure that is not constrained to match a terminal string is called a generator, and it may use either a random process to select words for each terminal, or various methods to constrain the selection to form meaningful sentences. It will be seen later that one procedure can accomplish both the parsing and generation processes.

The procedure described above is basic to a "top-down" parser, one that starts with S and applies grammar rules until it finds a set that matches the elements of the input string. A comparably concise procedure produces a "bottom-up" parse starting with elements of the input string and finding rules from the grammar that combine its elements into constituents until some rule beginning with "S" accounts for the constituents of the entire string. Parsers are also classified by orientation, as left-to-right or right-to-left, depending on which direction they generate or scan the input string; and by termination criteria, first-path, best-path, or all-paths. The essential mathematics of parsing algorithms is treated in detail by Aho and Ullman [1972]. Expressing the varying flows of control for parsing in procedural logic is examined in Chapter 10.

If an English sentence is represented by a parse tree, the relation holding between each pair of elements is seen to be the path that connects them. In the above example, (NP(NOUN CORNWALLIS)) is dominated by S and coordinate to (VP(VERB MET)(NP . . .)); this configuration defines the relation subject-of-a-sentence. The relation object-of-a-sentence is defined as an NP that is dominated by a VP which in turn is dominated by S, provided that the NP is not coordinate to a following NP. The NP "the French commander" satisfies this definition in the example. If each part of speech (i.e., noun, verb, adjective, and so on) is divided into several subclasses that characterize their similarities and differences in contextual possibilities of occurrence, the parse tree can uniquely represent very fine differences in apparently similar sentences. Thus the parse tree with its labels can be seen as a formal language powerful enough to represent the meanings of sentences. As a formal language, the parse tree contains unambiguous objects in explicit relation; an ambiguous English sentence may give rise to several parse trees, but each tree will be a precise representation of one of its meanings. But parse trees are not a particularly perspicuous language. They are readable only to people very well trained in that form of representation, who also understand the grammar that is used to prepare them.

5.2 DEPENDENCY TREES

Transforming the parse tree into a labeled dependency structure results in a much more readable formal language. The labeled dependency trees lift the most significant words to provide the summary property, have fewer nodes and levels, and use labels that are generally more meaningful to the reader. Consequently, they result in simpler approaches to computation.

Labeled dependency trees can be obtained by augmenting a phrase structure grammar with tests and transformations. The tests establish whether two (or more) constituents can make a semantically well-formed constituent; and if they can, the transformations produce it. Considering the constituents (ADJ FRENCH) and (NOUN COMMANDER), for example, we wish to test whether FRENCH and COMMANDER can form a semantic constituent. It will not do to have rules that simply record all possible combinations of words—there are too many combinations to store directly. It also will not do to accept every adjective-noun pair as well-formed—combinations such as "eager bananas" might occur in environments like "the monkey being eager bananas were brought." The tests must be formulated between these two extremes.

Sec. 5.2   Dependency Trees

Words are organized lexically into taxonomic hierarchies. "French" is a national origin, "commander" is a person, "eager" is a state of motivation, and "banana" is a fruit. A person is a being which is a physical object. Since there are hundreds of terms such as "Irish," "German," "Cuban," and "Mongolian" that are also names of national origin, thousands of descendents of "person," and vast numbers of words that describe instances and classes of physical objects, an effective level at which to write the semantic rules is obtained by ascending the taxonomic structure. The semantic combinations "national-origin physical-object" and "motivation-state animal" are well-formed adjective noun pairs of wide generality. Thus, "French commander," "Cuban banana," and "eager commander" are all well-formed by these rules, but "eager banana" fails to find a well-formed semantic combination of features.

When a constituent passes the test of semantic well-formedness, a transformation is applied to select the governing term and to provide a label for the semantic relation. The information required by the test and transformation can be given in the simple form of an n-tuple such as (NATL POBJ NATL), which, in the context of an adjective–noun combination (e.g., "French commander") provides the information to form the constituent (COMMANDER NATL FRENCH). These n-tuples are called *semantic event forms* (SEFs). The lexical entry characterizing a word must include either (or both) a superset link to the taxonomic structure or a semantic feature such as PERSON, ANIMate, PhysicalOBJECT, and so on. The complete test requires the following steps:

1. For each constituent, find a semantic feature,
2. Listing the features in the order of the constituents, find a matching semantic event form,
3. Rewrite the words of the constituents in the order given by the dependency rules associated with the syntactic constituent, inserting the last term of the SEF as the relation name.

The dependency rules are those given in chapter 4 which state, among other relations, that a noun governs preceding and following adjectives.

Considering again, the example sentence, "Cornwallis met the French commander," the lexicon provides the following features:

```
CORNWALLIS   FEAT PERSON
MEET         FEAT JOIN
FRENCH       FEAT NATL
COMMANDER    FEAT PERSON
```

and the list of semantic event forms includes,

```
PERSON JOIN AGT
JOIN PERSON AE
NATL X NATL      "As before, the X matches anything."
```

As each syntactic constituent is formed in the analysis of the sentence, the semantic test and transformation is applied to construct the corresponding node in the labeled dependency tree. Ignoring for the moment how "met" is changed to its root form "meet," the resulting tree is as follows:

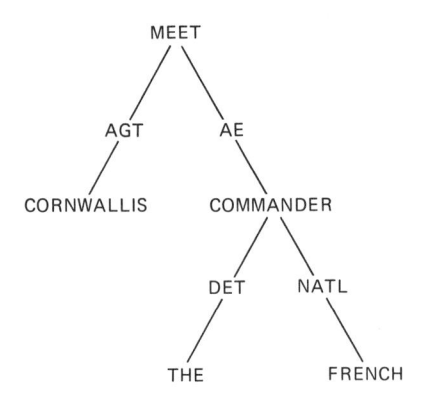

```
              MEET
             /    \
           AGT    AE
           /        \
      CORNWALLIS  COMMANDER
                  /      \
                DET      NATL
                /          \
              THE        FRENCH
```

Each triple in the tree, (i.e. COMMANDER NATL FRENCH, MEET AE COMMANDER, and MEET AGT CORNWALLIS) was derived from the SEFs given above. No semantic test is required to label an arc, DET; the article class provides sufficient information for the purpose.

This tree is more readable than the phrase structure tree shown earlier and it provides an instant summary of the sentence. The reader, in addition to understanding the graphic notion of a tree, need only master the notation of arc names to have a full understanding of the representation. Computationally, a question such as "Who met whom?" is easily answered by matching corresponding elements of the foregoing tree with the following question tree:

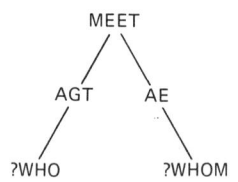

```
          MEET
         /    \
       AGT    AE
       /        \
     ?WHO     ?WHOM
```

The prefixed question marks signal that "WHO" and "WHOM" are restricted variables, to be matched against the candidate answer.

Linear representations are compared below for the semantic relations and the phrase structure analysis.

Semantic Relations:

(MEET AGT CORNWALLIS AE (COMMANDER DET THE NATL FRENCH))
(MEET AGT ?WHO AE ?WHOM)

Sec. 5.3 Computing Semantic Relations

Phrase Structure:

```
(S(NP(NOUN CORNWALLIS))(VP(VERB MET)
                         (NP(ART THE)
                         (NP(ADJ FRENCH)
                            (NOUN COMMANDER)))))
(QS(NP(RPRON WHO))(VP(VERB MET)(NP(RPRON WHOM))))
```

The simplicity and readability of the dependency structure is apparent.

As discussed in Chapter 4, the labeled dependency structure is called a surface semantic relation (SSR). It is a surface structure in that it preserves the syntactic information of the sentence from which it was derived. It is a semantic structure in that it uses explicitly named connections to signify meaningful relations between root forms of words in the text. Deeper semantic relations are derived from additional computations on these surface structures to form narrative and discourse trees, or other complex conceptual representations.

5.3 COMPUTING SEMANTIC RELATIONS

A phrase structure grammar can be applied by some parsing program to a string of natural language to produce a parse tree as output. The parsing program is an interpreter and the grammar is the language it interprets. If the interpreter is named "Parse," then a procedure with three arguments,

[PARSE <SENTENCE>,<PHRASE NAME>,<TRANSLATION>]

can be defined recursively to apply the phrase structure rules, beginning with the node, such as S, given in <PHRASE NAME>, to provide a parse tree as the <TRANSLATION>.

At a slightly lower level of abstraction, the rules themselves can be expressed as procedures.

```
(S <STRING>,<TRANSLATION>)
IF
  (NP <STRING>,<TRANSLATION1><REMDRSTRING>)
  (VP <REMDRSTRING>,<TRANSLATION2>)
(TRANSLATION := (COMBINE TRANSLATION1 TRANSLATION2))
```

For the S procedure, the input is an English string and the output argument is given as a variable. In the NP and VP procedures, the remainder string is what remains after the NP has translated some portion of the input string, and the two translation variables are subtrees of the parse that are combined to give a value for the output argument of the S procedure. It should be remembered from Chapter 3 that these procedures can be called with unbound variables as arguments, and they can even return partial results by assigning values to some but not all of the variables.

Although it is rather difficult to accomplish these procedures directly in any but logic programming languages, direct programming of rules in LISP has been an effective approach to parsing. Winograd introduced procedural parsing of natural English by using LISP functions to define the rules of a phrase structure grammar. He showed a functional equivalence of this approach to the use of an Augmented Transition Network parser. Novak [1977] developed a procedural grammar in LISP functions to account for the English used in 20 physics problems and has argued that it is among the most effective ways to compute analyses of English.

This procedural approach to parsing is particularly well suited to clausal logic programs in PROLOG or HCPRVR. If the grammar is directly expressed in clausal form, each phrase structure rule is interpreted as a procedure that is to be invoked by name and pattern of arguments (i.e., a pattern-invoked procedure). The body of the procedure is the set of antecedents that must be satisfied to prove it. Almost as a side effect, the values of the arguments are manipulated to provide the desired translations. An example of two simple NP rules that combine an article and a noun will clarify the operation.

(NP (X.Y) R ((ART X)(NP1 W)))
  < (ART X)(NP1 Y R W)

(NP1 (U.V) V (NOUN U)) < (NOUN U)

The procedure is called as follows:

(NP (THE ARMY) _REMDR _TRANS)

In the calling pattern the two underscored variables REMDR and TRANS are unbound, but when the procedure has been successfully evaluated they will show, respectively, any remainder string following the NP, and the translation computed by the procedure. The first argument of the procedure, (X.Y), is bound by the interpreter to (THE ARMY) as follows:

X := THE
Y := (ARMY)

Wherever X and Y occur in the procedure, they take on these values, as follows:

(NP (THE.(ARMY)) R ((ART THE)(NP1 W)))
  < (ART THE)(NP1 (ARMY) R W)

Sec. 5.3   Computing Semantic Relations   83

Assuming that there is a lexical entry (ART THE), the first antecedent directly matches it, is thereby proved, and the NP1 antecedent is then called as a procedure with the (U.V) arguments bound throughout as follows:

```
(NP1 (U.V) V (NOUN U)) < (NOUN U)
         U := ARMY
         V := NIL
(NP1 (ARMY.NIL) NIL (NOUN ARMY)) < (NOUN ARMY)
```

The antecedent (NOUN ARMY) matches the corresponding lexical entry and thus proves the NP1 procedure, giving the following values for the variables in the ancestral NP:

```
X := THE
Y := (ARMY)
R := V := NIL
W:= (NOUN U) := (NOUN ARMY)
(NP (THE ARMY) NIL ((ART THE)(NP1(NOUN ARMY)))
```

The semantics of the analysis of these procedures is essentially similar to that for a phrase structure grammar; a procedure call is satisfied if it matches a procedure whose antecedents are all satisfied. If a procedure matches an assertion, it is satisfied. Thus a tree of evaluation is created whose terminal elements are simple assertions. The terminal assertions for the NP example are the lexical assertions (ART THE) and (NOUN ARMY). It should be noticed that the translation is simply a record of the top-down, left-right evaluation of the rules that succeeded in parsing the fragment. Each rule contains in its translation argument a description of its phrase structure antecedents, and those that are successfully evaluated pass their completed descriptions back up the tree to eventuate in a complete syntactic description of the input string.

Figure 5.1 displays a procedural revision of the phrase structure grammar given earlier, and Figure 5.2 shows the analysis history of applying the grammar to the sentence, "Cornwallis met the French commander."

In Figure 5.2, the rule S was called with the sentence as its first argument and an unbound variable for its second. Consulting the grammar, we see that (S...) < (NP...)(VP...). The NP without an article is the one that succeeds, by calling an NP1. The NP1 returns (NOUN CORNWALLIS), the translation of a terminal constituent. The initial NP is now complete and it contains the translation (NP(NOUN CORNWALLIS)). The VP rule is now called with the string "met the...," and it finds the assertion (VERB MET) and calls an NP with the remaining string, "the French commander." First

84　　　　　　　　　　　Translating Sentences to Semantic Relations　　Chap. 5

==
```
            (NOUN CORNWALLIS)
            (NOUN COMMANDER)
            (ADJ FRENCH)
            (ART THE)
            (VERB MET)
            (S X (S V W)) < (NP X R V)(VP R NIL W)
            (NP (X.Y) Z (NP(ART X)(NP1 W)))
                 < (ART X)(NP1 Y Z W)
            (NP X R (NP W)) < (NP1 X R W)
            (NP1(X.Y) R ((ADJ X)(NP1 W)))
                 < (ADJ X)(NP1 Y R W)
            (NP1(X.Y) Y (NOUN X)) < (NOUN X)
            (VP (X.Y) R (VP(VERB X)) W)
                 < (VERB X)(NP Y R W)
```
==

Figure 5.1 Grammar for syntactic tree for Cornwallis sentence.

the article "the," then the adjective "French," and finally, the noun "commander" are found to satisfy the various NP and NP1 rules to result in a completion of the NP translation as

(NP(ART THE)(NP1(ADJ FRENCH)(NOUN COMMANDER)))

==
```
     (S (CORNWALLIS MET THE FRENCH COMMANDER) (S V W))
     (NP(CORNWALLIS . MET THE...) (MET THE...) (NP W)
     (NP1(CORNWALLIS . MET THE...) (MET THE...) (NOUN CORNWALLIS))
     (VP (MET . THE FRENCH...) NIL (VP (VERB MET) W)
     (NP (THE FRENCH COMMANDER) NIL (NP(ART THE) W)
     (NP1 (FRENCH COMMANDER) NIL (NP1 (ADJ FRENCH) W)
     (NP1 (COMMANDER) NIL (NOUN COMMANDER))

     (NP1'(FRENCH COMMANDER) NIL (NP1 (ADJ FRENCH)(NOUN COMMANDER)))
     (NP' (THE FRENCH COMMANDER) NIL (NP(ART THE)(NP1(ADJ FRENCH)
                                          (NOUN COMMANDER))))
     (VP' (MET . THE...) NIL (VP(VERB MET)(NP(ART THE)(NP1(ADJ...]
     (NP1'(CORNWALLIS . MET...)(MET THE...)(NOUN CORNWALLIS) )
     (NP' (CORNWALLIS . MET...)(MET THE...)(NP(NOUN CORNWALLIS)) )
     (S' (CORNWALLIS MET...) (S(NP(NOUN CORNWALLIS))
                  (VP(VERB MET)
                     (NP(ART THE)(NP1(ADJ FRENCH)
                              (NOUN COMMANDER))) ]
```
==

Figure 5.2 Parse history for the Cornwallis sentence.

Sec. 5.4   Semantic Translation   85

The instantiated rules NP1', NP', VP', and S' show how the values of the translated constituents are combined and passed back up to the original call to S. The resulting translation into a parse tree is as follows:

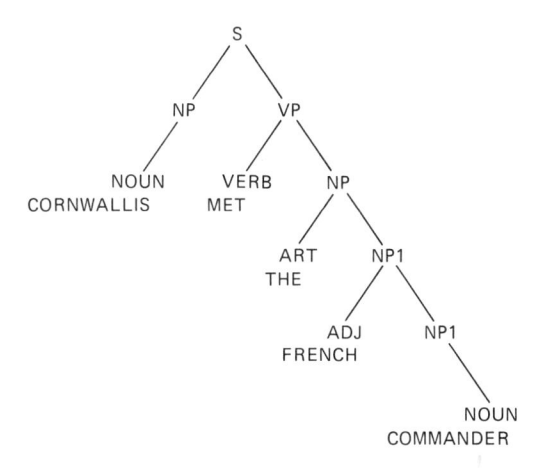

```
                    S
                   / \
                  NP  VP
                  |   / \
                NOUN VERB NP
              CORNWALLIS MET / \
                           ART  NP1
                           THE  / \
                              ADJ  NP1
                            FRENCH  \
                                   NOUN
                                 COMMANDER
```

The same tree is represented in linear parenthetical form as

        (S(NP(NOUN CORNWALLIS))
         (VP(VERB MET)
          (NP(ART THE)(NP1(ADJ FRENCH)
            (NP1(NOUN COMMANDER))))))

This example parsing process shows that a phrase structure grammar can be restated as clausal logic procedures in such a manner that the proof that the input string is a sentence results in a parse tree as its translation. When so restated, the phrase structure names become the names of procedures whose successful evaluation describe a flow of control through the grammar. The record of this flow suitably labeled is the familiar immediate constituent phrase structure analysis of the sentence. At this point we could follow the methods of semantic transformations used by Woods et al. [1972] or by Sager [1981] and translate the resulting syntactic descriptions into some more desirable semantic form, such as surface semantic relations. To do this would require the preparation of another grammar of transformations on phrase structure trees.

5.4 SEMANTIC TRANSLATION

The process of automatic translation requires two grammars, one for each language to describe their constituents, and a set of rules for transforming constituents of the one into those of the other. The constituents of English are phrase structure subtrees such as those just computed. For surface semantic relations (SSRs) the constituents are sets of elementary semantic relations, comprised of words dominating relation name/SR pairs. The rules for translating from one to the other require that the governor of an English constituent be selected and then related by semantic relation name to its dependents according to rules given earlier. A key fact about parsing English is that the immediate constituent phrase structure grammar describes an ordering by which elements of English strings can be combined into a parse tree. If we, in fact, want to translate from string to SSR, we need only to follow the ordering; we do not need to record the parse tree. As each phrase structure rule succeeds, the elements of an English constituent have been established and *these elements can at that time be translated to SSRs.*

It is computationally efficient to accomplish the translation at that point since constraints are imposed on the constituent to decide whether in addition to being syntactically well-formed, it is also semantically so. In a top-down approach with backup, this is a particularly effective strategy for minimizing the length of time that an ill-formed constituent can survive.

To accomplish the translation directly from English strings to SSRs, the phrase structure grammar is augmented with additional information and testing procedures. The lexical entries are enriched with root forms, inflectional information, and semantic class or feature markers. A set of semantic event forms is provided to relate combinations of semantic classes to appropriate semantic relation names. The construction of translations in the constituent rules becomes slightly more complicated.

An NP rule for forming adjective-noun constituents will introduce the approach. The lexical entries, the rule, and the SEFs are as follows:

```
(ADJ EAGER (EAGER ) MOTIV)
(ADJ FRENCH (FRENCH) NATL)
(NOUN BANANA (BANANA NBR SING) VEG)
(NOUN COMMANDER (COMMANDER NBR SING) PERSON)

(NP1 (X.Y) R (V U X1.V1))
   < (ADJ X X1 FA)(NP1 Y R FN (V.V1))
     (SEF FA FN U)
(NP1 (X.Y) Y FN X1) < (NOUN X X1 FN)

(SEF MOTIV PERSON MOTIV)
(SEF NATL X NATL)
```

Variables in these rules are U, V, V1, X, X1, Y, R, FA, and FN. The unbound variable, X, in the last SEF will match any term. It means that all such phrases as "Cuban idea," "French food," or "Irish commander" are well formed semantic units. When the NP1 rule is called, (NP1 (FRENCH COMMANDER) U V), the input string is bound to the variables of the rule as follows:

Sec. 5.4   Semantic Translation

```
X := FRENCH
Y := (COMMANDER)
(NP1 (FRENCH . COMMANDER) R (V U FRENCH . V1))
   < (ADJ FRENCH X1 FA)(NP1 (COMMANDER) R FN (V.V1) )
     (SEF FA FN U)
```

The first antecedent is matched against the lexicon:

```
(ADJ FRENCH X1 FA)
(ADJ FRENCH (FRENCH) NATL)
      X1 := (FRENCH)
      FA := NATL
```

The next antecedent is matched against an NP1 rule to give:

```
(NP1 (COMMANDER . NIL) NIL FN X1)
   <(NOUN COMMANDER X1 FN)
```

Its single antecedent matches the dictionary entry:

```
(NOUN COMMANDER (COMMANDER NBR SING) PERSON)
      X1 := (COMMANDER NBR SING)
      FN := PERSON
```

The result is that the NP1's translation argument is completed and its semantic feature has been provided for use by the rule in which it was called.

```
(NP1 (COMMANDER . NIL) NIL PERSON (COMMANDER NBR SING))
```

The third constituent (SEF FA FN U) now has the values substituted for FA and FN, to give

```
(SEF NATL PERSON U)
```

which matches

```
(SEF NATL X NATL)
      X := PERSON
      U := NATL
```

so the topmost NP1 is now completed with the following values:

```
(NP1 (FRENCH COMMANDER) PERSON (COMMANDER NATL (FRENCH)
                                          NBR SING) )
```

The two constituents "French" and "commander" were translated by their lexical entries into (FRENCH) and (COMMANDER NBR SING), respectively. The features NATL and PERSON were used in (SEF NATL X NATL) to find the appropriate relation name, and the combination, (COMMANDER NATL FRENCH NBR SING), was constructed as a new translation constituent. This is the general, regular process for translating from English constituents to constituents of SSRs.

If we consider some other adjective-noun constituents (e.g., French banana, eager commander, and eager banana), it will be found that the SEFs permit the first two and refuse the third.

>   French banana → NATL FRUIT
>   (SEF NATL X NATL)
>   eager commander → MOTIV PERSON
>   (SEF MOTIV PERSON MOTIV)
>   eager banana → MOTIV FRUIT
>   No SEF matches

5.5 PROCEDURAL GRAMMAR FOR A SENTENCE

These ideas can now be organized into enough procedural grammar to translate our first example sentence into surface semantic relations.

> Cornwallis sent an army to attack the French troops and Irish rebels at Castlebar.

The lexicon and grammar presented in Figures 5.3 and 5.4 were tested with the program HCPRVR to result in the analyses shown below. The variable TEST was bound to the sentence as shown,

```
TEST :=
(S (CORNWALLIS SENT AN ARMY TO ATTACK THE FRENCH TROOPS
AND IRISH REBELS AT CASTLEBAR) X)
```

The grammar was applied to the sentence using the logic procedure TRY, which returned the translation of the sentence into surface semantic relations bound in place of the variable X in the call.

Sec. 5.5 Procedural Grammar for a Sentence   89

==

```
GRAMMAR RULES:
(((S X (V U W . V1))
 < (NP X NF R W) (VP R VF NIL (V . V1)) (NF VF U)))

(((NP (X . Y) NF R (U DET X . V))
 < (ART X) (NP1 Y NF R (U . V)))
 ((NP X NF R V) < (NP1 X NF R V)))

(((NP1 (X . Y) NF R (U S X1 . V))
 <
 (ADJ X X1 FA)
 (NP1 Y NF R (U . V))
 (FA NF S))
 ((NP1 (X . Y) NF R (X1 U X2 *AND V))
 < (NOUN X (X1 U X2) NF) (CONJNP Y NF R V))
 ((NP1 (X Y . Z) NF R (X1 W X2 S (V PREP Y . V1)))
 <
 (NOUN X (X1 W X2) NF)
 (PREP Y)
 (NP1 Z NF1 R (V . V1))
 (NF Y NF1 S))
 ((NP1 (X . Y) NF Y X1) < (NOUN X X1 NF)))

((((CONJNP (AND . Y) NF R V) < (NP Y NF R V)))

(((VP (TO Y . Z) VF R (Y1 INF TO W Y2 . V))
 <
 (VERB Y (Y1 W Y2) VF)
 (VCOMP Z VF R V))
 ((VP (X . Y) VF R (X1 U X2 . V))
  < (VERB X (X1 U X2) VF) (VCOMP Y VF R V)))

(((VCOMP NIL VF NIL NIL))
 ((VCOMP X VF R (S V . W))
  < (NP X NF R1 V) (VF NF S) (VCOMP R1 VF R W))
 ((VCOMP X VF R (S V . W))
  < (VP X VF1 R1 V) (VF1 VF S) (VCOMP R1 VF R W))
 ((VCOMP (X . Y) VF R (S (V PREP X . V1) . W))
 <
 (PREP X)
 (NP Y NF R1 (V . V1))
 (VF X NF S)
 (VCOMP R1 VF R W))
```

==

Figure 5.3 SSR grammar rules for Cornwallis sentence.

90   Translating Sentences to Semantic Relations   Chap. 5

```
============================================================
LEXICON:

((((NOUN CORNWALLIS (CORNWALLIS NBR SING) PERSON))
  ((NOUN ARMY (ARMY NBR SING) PERSON))
  ((NOUN TROOPS (TROOP NBR PLUR) PERSON))
  ((NOUN REBELS (REBEL NBR PLUR) PERSON))
  ((NOUN PATRIOTS (PATRIOT NBR PLUR) PERSON))
  ((NOUN CASTLEBAR (CASTLEBAR NBR SING) PLACE)))

(((VERB SENT (SEND TNS PAST) ACT))
  ((VERB ATTACK (ATTACK TNS PRES) ACT)))

(((ADJ FRENCH (FRENCH) NATL))
  ((ADJ IRISH (IRISH) NATL)))

(((ART AN))  ((ART THE)))

(((PREP TO))  ((PREP AT)))
--------------------------------------------------------
SEMANTIC EVENT FORMS:

(((PERSON ACT AGT)) ((PERSON AT PLACE LOC))
 ((ACT PERSON AE))   ((ACT ACT PURPOSE))
 ((ACT AT PLACE LOC)))
============================================================
```

                     Figure 5.4   Lexical assertions for Cornwallis sentence

```
              *(TRY TEST)
              ((S (CORNWALLIS SENT AN ARMY TO ATTACK THE FRENCH
              TROOPS AND IRISH REBELS AT CASTLEBAR) (SEND AGT
              (CORNWALLIS NBR SING) TNS PAST AE (ARMY DET AN
              NBR SING) PURPOSE (ATTACK INF TO TNS PRES
              AE (TROOP DET THE NATL (FRENCH) NBR PLUR
              *AND (REBEL NATL (IRISH) NBR PLUR
              LOC (CASTLEBAR PREP AT NBR SING))))))))

              *RTIME
              (0.16300000 SECS)
```

      This complex expression is "pretty-printed" by the LISP function SPRINT.

```
              *(SPRINT VAL)
              ((S (CORNWALLIS SENT AN ARMY TO ATTACK THE FRENCH
                   TROOPS AND IRISH REBELS AT CASTLEBAR)
                  (SEND AGT
                        (CORNWALLIS NBR SING)
                        TNS
                        PAST
                        AE
```

Sec. 5.5 Procedural Grammar for a Sentence

```
                (ARMY DET AN NBR SING)
                PURPOSE
                (ATTACK INF
                       TO
                       TNS
                       PRES
                       AE
                       (TROOP DET
                              THE
                              NATL
                              (FRENCH)
                              NBR
                              PLUR
                              *AND
                              (REBEL NATL
                                     (IRISH)
                                     NBR
                                     PLUR
                                     LOC
                                     (CASTLEBAR PREP AT
                                            NBR SING)]
```

One of the first things to notice is the amount of syntactic information contained in the structure. It abounds with such relations as NBR PLUR, TNS PRES, INF TO, PREP AT, and so on. These carry the syntactic cues that will allow the grammar to accept the analysis as input and transform it back to English, as will be shown shortly. Another notable feature that is prominent in the SSR tree is the fact that a rough summary is obtained by reading the first element following each left parenthesis in the pretty-print—SEND CORNWALLIS ARMY ATTACK TROOP REBEL CASTLEBAR. A more careful examination shows that this is due to the summary property of labeled dependency trees, which lift the primary terms into prominent positions. The important consequence is that a procedure to construct sentence summaries is very easy to write (see Chapter 9 for a general summarizing procedure).

The grammar was written to be symmetric so that it could accomplish generation of English from the SSRs as well as to parse English sentences into them. To confirm this property, the variable TEST1 was set to contain X, an unbound variable, in the place of the English string argument, and the SSR in the translation argument.

```
            *(SETQ TEST1 (LIST 'S 'X (CADDAR VAL)))
            (S X (SEND AGT (CORNWALLIS NBR SING) TNS PAST
              AE (ARMY DET AN NBR SING) PURPOSE (ATTACK INF TO
              TNS PRES AE (TROOP DET THE NATL (FRENCH) NBR PLUR
              *AND (REBEL NATL (IRISH) NBR PLUR LOC (CASTLEBAR
              PREP AT NBR SING))))))
            *(TRY TEST1)
            ((S (CORNWALLIS SENT AN ARMY TO ATTACK THE FRENCH
```

```
                    TROOPS AND IRISH REBELS AT CASTLEBAR)
                    (SEND AGT (CORNWALLIS NBR SING) TNS PAST
                    AE (ARMY DET AN NBR SING) PURPOSE (ATTACK
                    INF TO TNS PRES AE (TROOP DET THE NATL (FRENCH)
                    NBR PLUR *AND (REBEL NATL (IRISH) NBR PLUR
                    LOC (CASTLEBAR PREP AT NBR SING))))))

                    *RTIME
                    (0.12400000 SECS)
```

In the TRY of TEST1, the grammar was applied to the SSR and resulted in generating the original sentence.

The RTIMEs shown in the two computer protocols above are, respectively 0.16 and 0.12 seconds which are the amounts of central processor time required by HCPRVR to accomplish the computations on a DEC KI 2060. The computation times increase fairly rapidly with the length of the sentence, and only slowly with the size of the lexicon and grammar. They are mentioned only as reassurance that the logic parsing methods are not hopelessly inefficient compared to those directly programmed in LISP or other languages. It is also worth mentioning that the times vary by as much as seconds depending on the load factor of the operating system.

The grammar was constructed to produce a second parse that related "at Castlebar" to "attack" rather than to the conjunction "French troops and Irish rebels." After the first parse was completed, the system asked if another was desired, to which the answer was, Yes.

```
                    ANOTHER? *Y

                    ((S (CORNWALLIS SENT AN ARMY TO ATTACK THE FRENCH
                    TROOPS AND IRISH REBELS AT CASTLEBAR)
                        (SEND AGT
                            (CORNWALLIS NBR SING)
                            (CORNWALLIS NBR SING)
                            TNS
                            PAST
                            AE
                            (ARMY DET AN NBR SING)
                            PURPOSE
                            (ATTACK INF
                                TO
                                TNS
                                PRES
                                AE
                                (TROOP DET
                                    THE
                                    NATL
                                    (FRENCH)
                                    NBR
```

Sec. 5.5   Procedural Grammar for a Sentence   93

```
                              PLUR
                              *AND
                              (REBEL NATL (IRISH) NBR PLUR))
                        LOC
                        (CASTLEBAR PREP AT NBR SING)))))
```

ANOTHER? *Y

NIL

Notice that (LOC CASTLEBAR...) is now part of ATTACK, and that no other parse existed using the example grammar.

The grammar, shown in Figures 5.3 and 5.4, is a tiny one, devised simply to illustrate the organization of vocabulary, semantic event forms and grammar rules in application to the example sentence. A micro-grammar—still tiny—to account for a 13 sentence text is shown in Appendix B. This one serves to illustrate how to incorporate semantic tests and transformations into a phrase structure organization of logic procedures.

A close examination of the S, VP, and VCOMP rules will clarify the method by which the phrase structure, semantic testing, and transformational components are integrated. The S rule accounts for a simple subject-verb-object sentence, requiring an NP followed by a VP.

```
(((S X (V U W . V1))
 < (NP X NF R W) (VP R VF NIL (V . V1)) (NF VF U)))
```

The NP and VP rules each have five arguments:

[<NAME> <STRING> <FEATURE> <REMAINDER> <TRANSFORM>]

NAME is usually chosen as a linguistic phrase structure term, STRING is the input sentence, FEATURE is the semantic class associated with the governing word of the phrase, REMAINDER is the remaining string after the phrase has accounted for a substring, and TRANSFORM is the translation into surface semantic relations. The third antecedent rule is a semantic event form with the structure

[<NOUN-FEATURE> <VERB-FEATURE> <RELATION-NAME>]

In previous examples this relation has been shown with the predicate name SEF. By deleting this name, the rules are indexed by their first feature, and the computations involving SEFs need only examine short lists whose first element is that feature, to result in significant savings of search time.

The translation is given in the third argument of the calling pattern, (S X (V U W.V1)). This argument specifies a list structure whose first three elements are the values of the variables V, U, and W, and whose remainder is the list V1. When the NP and VP antecedents have been satisfied, they appear as follows:

    (NP (CORNWALLIS SENT AN ARMY...)
     PERSON
     (SENT AN ARMY TO ATTACK...)
     (CORNWALLIS NBR SING))

     X := (CORNWALLIS SENT AN ARMY...)
     NF:= PERSON
     R := (SENT AN ARMY TO ATTACK...)
     W := (CORNWALLIS NBR SING)

    (VP (SENT AN ARMY TO ATTACK...)
     ACT
     NIL
     (SEND AE (ARMY...) PURPOSE (ATTACK...)...)

     R := (SENT AN ARMY TO ATTACK...)
     VF:= ACT
     V := SEND
     V1:= (AE (ARMY...) PURPOSE (ATTACK...)...)

    (PERSON ACT AGT)
     NF:= PERSON
     VF:= ACT
     U := AGT

The transformation (V U W.V1) assembles these values:

    (SEND AGT (CORNWALLIS NBR SING) AE (ARMY...) PURPOSE...)

The variables in the transformation refer to values that have been bound when the antecedents of the rule were satisfied. In LISP, the same list structure could be created in two ways,

    (CONS V(CONS U (CONS W V1)))

or

    (APPEND (LIST V U W) V1)

In clausal logic, the structure is assembled simply by designating its elements as members of a list.

  More difficult transformations are illustrated by the VP and VCOMP rules whose bindings for evaluating the string "to attack at Castlebar," are shown below.

```
(((VP (TO Y . Z) VF R (Y1 INF TO W Y2 . V))
<
(VERB Y (Y1 W Y2) VF)
(VCOMP Z VF R V))
      Y := ATTACK            Z := (AT CASTLEBAR)
      VF := ACT              R := NIL
      (Y1 W Y2) := (ATTACK TNS PRES)
      V := (LOC (CASTLEBAR PREP AT NBR SING))
```

In this rule the transformation is (Y1 INF TO W Y2.V), which forms the structure (ATTACK INF TO TNS PRES LOC (CASTLEBAR NBR SING PREP AT)). The infinitive marker had to be added to the lexical entry, and the resulting list appended to the value of V, returned by the call to VCOMP. The easiest way to accomplish this while maintaining a flat list was to obtain the complete specification for the verb in the call (VERB Y (Y1 W Y2) VF); the verb form had exactly those three parts, Y1, W, and Y2, and then it was possible, explicitly, to insert INF TO following Y1.

The VCOMP rule system is designed to gather a list of all the constituents following the verb until the end of the clause or sentence is reached.

```
((VCOMP (X . Y) VF R (S (V PREP X . V1) . W))
<
(PREP X)
(NP Y NF R1 (V . V1))
(VF X NF S)
(VCOMP R1 VF R W)))
         X := AT                      Y := (CASTLEBAR)
         VF := ACT                    R := NIL
         NF := PLACE                  R1 := NIL
         (V.V1) := (CASTLEBAR NBR SING)
         S := LOC                     W := NIL
```

A VCOMP rule forms, tests, and translates a constituent, calling another VCOMP with any remaining part of the sentence. VCOMP with input NIL returns NIL. The translation part of a VCOMP forms a pair, RELATION-NAME, VALUE, and concatenates this to the value returned by the embedded call to VCOMP. In the example above, the translation to be formed is (S (V PREP X . V1) . W). Substituting for the values of variables, it becomes (LOC (CASTLEBAR PREP AT NBR SING) NIL). Instead of independently forming a prepositional phrase (PP), this rule first strips the preposition, then forms a noun phrase. This strategy allows the transformation to refer directly to the preposition instead of searching the result returned by a PP. The variable V1 is the translation of whatever noun phrase was returned, and V, the noun head, is extracted, then listed with PREP and its value and appended to V1 to form the translation of a PP.

A similar system of rules, NCOMP, is not shown in the example grammar, but is used in a similar fashion to gather all postmodifying noun phrases. In writing grammars to translate subsets of English to SSRs, the constraints of *conciseness, symmetry, and summarizability* are maintained. *Conciseness* is illustrated by the combination of feature markers with the lexical entry and by the use of the SEFs for the double purpose of testing for semantic well-formedness and providing the relation name that describes the relation. Conciseness is an inherent part of the clausal logic approach to translation in its use of designation of lists rather than functional description of them. Therefore, a rule need not contain functions such as CAR, CDR, CONS, and APPEND, nor need it explicitly contain conditional statements; as a very high level language, all these operations are signified by the form of procedural logic statements.

The *symmetric property* is valuable in that it results in the need for only one grammar to describe a translation in two directions. Although symmetry is easier to accomplish in clausal logic grammars than in other forms, the grammar writer must prepare rules that maintain the property. For example, such functions as Append are not symmetric; (APPEND '(A B) '(C D)) and (APPEND '(A B C) '(D)) both result in '(A B C D). But if an attempt is made to "UnAPPEND"(X '(A B C D)), there is no information as to what segment of the list to break out. Later it will be seen that there are symmetric and nonsymmetric ways in which to write such transformations as that required to translate "60 feet of flame" into (FLAME MSR FEET QU 60...).

The *summary property* derives from the definition of labeled dependency structures. If the translation of a sentence is presented as a dependency tree with each higher node governing those that occur below, the tree may be truncated at any level below the root to give the basis for generating a summarizing statement. Again, the grammar writer must avoid rules and transformations that would change these relations. This property is of obvious utility for applications of natural-language processing to text.

5.6 EXERCISES

1. Computing a syntactic structure

   Birds Sing => (SNT(NP(NOUN(BIRD NBR SING)))
                       (VP(VERB(SING TNS PRES MRK PL))))

Sec. 5.6   Exercises

<NAME -STRING -PARSE -REMDR>

((SNT X (SNT V V1) NIL) < (NP X V R)(VP R V1 NIL))
((NP (X.Y)(NP(NOUN X1)) Y) < (NOUN X X1))
((NOUN BIRDS (BIRD NBR PL)))
((VP (X.Y) (VP(VERB X1)) Y) < (VERB X X1))
((VERB SING (SING TNS PRES MRK PL))

(a) Assert the grammar (be sure to declare variables).
(b) (?(SNT(BIRDS SING) V NIL))
(c) (SETQ J (SUBST 'X (CADAR VAL)))
(d) (TRY J)—Notice that the grammar is symmetric.
(e) (SETQ TFLAG T)—Repeat steps b through d.
(f) Expand the grammar to include:
  Birds sing songs
  Birds sing gaily

2. Computing Semantic Case Relations
  Rule Form:

  <NAME -STRING -SEMREL -SEMFEAT -REMDR>

  SEF Form:

  <-SEMFEAT -SF1 ... -SFN -ARCNAME>

  BIRDS SING ⟹ (SING AGT (BIRD NBR PL) TNS PRES MRK PL)

  ((SNT X (V -ARC W.V1) -VF NIL) < (NP X W -NF R)
      (VP R (V.V1) -VF NIL) (-NF -VF -ARC))
  ((NP (X.Y) X1 -NF Y) < (NOUN X X1 -NF))
  ((VP (X.Y) X1 -VF NIL) < (VERB X X1 -VF))
  ((NOUN BIRDS (BIRD NBR PL) ANIM))
  ((VERB SING (SING TNS PRES MRK PL)))
  ((ANIM ACT AGT))

(a) Assert and try the grammar, test it for symmetry, and trace its operation.
(b) Expand it to include "Birds sing songs gaily," to compute (SING AGT (BIRD NBR PL) AE (SONG NBR PL) MANNER (GAILY) TNS PRES MRK PL)
  Hint: Use a VCOMP rule to accumulate arguments that follow the verb.

  ((VCOMP X (-ARC V.W) -VF NIL) < (NP X V -NF R1)(-VF -NF -ARC)
      (VCOMP R1 W -VF NIL))
  ((VCOMP NIL NIL -VF NIL))

((VP (X.Y) (X1 X2 X3.V) -VF NIL) < (VERB X (X1 X2 X3) -VF)
  (VCOMP Y V -VF NIL)

(ADV GAILY (GAILY) MANNER)
SEFs:
(ACT INFO AE) (ACT MANNER MANNER)

3. Type in the grammar of Figures 5.3 and 5.4 and trace the Cornwallis sentence.

6

COMMANDING A ROBOT BLOCK STACKER

6.1 BACKGROUND

A classic study in natural language processing was the thorough procedural semantic system of Winograd [1972] to command and question a simulated robot arm in a world of blocks. The blocks world was a favorite in the first decade of the MIT Artificial Intelligence Laboratory. It was used to develop control systems for actual robot arms; to study principles of visual recognition by computers; to relate understanding of what the television camera saw to commands to the robot arm; and for the design and testing of an English subset for communication.

The beauty of the blocks world was its simplicity. For vision studies, it provided definite objects with clear lines and corners. The blocks could vary in size, shape, and color, and could be few or many in number. They were truly simplistic representatives of the world of physical objects, but for the camera and robot arm they were true objects subject to gravity, reflective of light, casting shadows, even crushable if the robot hand exerted too much pressure. Successions of experimental programs for visual recognition in this world gradually teased out effective methods for recognizing straight lines, edges, corners, and finally, shapes. Similar successions of programs for controlling the robot arm and coordinating it with vision laid the groundwork for the present generation of computer-controlled parts assembly robots. The blocks world was so attractive as a controlled environment that it traveled from Boston to California, Edinburgh, and even to Tokyo.

Even in such an apparently simple environment, fairly intricate problems could be studied. The frame problem was one example; how could the computer keep track of what parts of the blocks world changed or did not, as a result of its actions? The problem of economical sequencing was another: What was the best order in which to accomplish a command that involved unstacking and replacing blocks to achieve a given configuration? There were also problems of deadlock, in which the robot, in order to accomplish one configuration, had to undo another one essential to the solution. More important to Winograd was his realization that this simple world, which could be encompassed by a small English vocabulary, could nevertheless serve as a laboratory for the study of a wide variety of English expressions. Assertions, commands, and questions all had their places. English tensing and mood conventions had computable meanings. The nouns with their modifiers identified physical objects. The verbs "to be" and "to have" had important uses, and the few action verbs that applied to this miniature world found their meaning in terms of operations by the robot arm. The possibilities for communication with a robot arm in the blocks world delimited a subset of useful English. Winograd linguistically defined such a subset and brilliantly demonstrated its computational meaning as a language that his computer could interpret as a set of procedures and their arguments.

Winograd's pioneering program was for the time an excellent demonstration of a modularly organized system that accomplished a succession of most complex operations with a notable degree of computational elegance, despite its length of about 100,000 words of LISP programs. A decade later, his linguistic approach (i.e., procedural semantics) continues to be of considerable interest, but the programs can be replicated in a tiny fraction of the space their ancesters required. The blocks world retains its value for limiting the domain of discourse and for providing a comprehensible demonstration that some meanings of natural language are representable as procedures. Clausal logic procedures for translating English reveal their power and simplicity in this classic world of robot arm and blocks.

6.1.1 Simulating Hand and Blocks

Blocks have color, shape, size, and may support or be supported by other objects. Cubes, rectangular solids, pyramids, and spheres are instances of what might be meant by blocks. A hand can grasp, lift, descend, hold, move to a place, and release a block. Commands to such a system include the following examples:

> Pick the green block up.
> Put it on the red one.
> Put the biggest blue block on the smallest green one.
> Put the blue block on the green and the red on the blue.

Sec. 6.1   Background

Put the blue on the green and pick up the red one.
Put it down.
Put the red block on the blue block on the table.
Put the blue block on the table on the red block.

Additional verbs, such as "place," "get," "remove," "stack," and so on, can be used, and names such as "cube," "pyramid," or "brick" can characterize the various blocks. An appropriate set of questions can query what the hand is holding, what object is where, what was done last, and the why and how of actions, all following Winograd's examples.

But for the purpose of showing the clausal logic approach to the blocks world, only commands need be considered, and the simple world can be simplified even further. The standard blocks world has three dimensions; its table has definite locations characterized by x-y coordinates; the robot arm must be instructed to move in a three-dimensional coordinate system; and each block is characterized by a position in three-dimensional space. If we reduce this world to two dimensions, allow the table indefinitely many locations, and characterize a block's position simply by stating what it is on, the system is drastically simplified, yet with little loss to the purpose of showing how a command language is translated into procedures.

In this reduced blocks world the robot needs only one operation, "Put X on Y." If the hand is to grasp an object, the robot puts the object on the hand; if it is to release it, the robot puts it on the table. Otherwise, the robot must put an object on some other object or on the table. This operation is called "Puton." In order to put X on Y, X must be clear (i.e., it must not support any other object), X must not be a table, Y must either be clear or be the table, and Y must not be a pyramid or a sphere. The following clauses define "Puton" and its supporting procedure, "Clear":

```
(PUTON X Y) < (NEQ X TABLE)(CLEAR X)(NEQ Y PYRAMID)
              (NEQ Y SPHERE)(CLEAR Y)
              (DELETE(ON X W)) (ASSERT (ON X Y))

(CLEAR TABLE) <
(CLEAR X) < (ON Y X) (PUTON Y TABLE)
(CLEAR X) <
```

These relations state that the table is always clear: that is, indefinitely many blocks may be on the table and it may still take more. For any other object, X, if some object Y is on X, then put Y on the table. If nothing is on X, it is clear. The attempt to put something on a sphere or pyramid will fail because these objects are excluded by the definition of PUTON. The relations ASSERT and DELETE, respectively, add and remove assertions with respect to the world model; NEQ is satisfied if its arguments are not equal.

It should be noticed that if we had three blocks stacked on the table as follows:

```
          REDBLOCK
          GREENBLOCK
          BLUEBLOCK
    TABLE------------------------
```

the command "put the blue block on the green block" would result first in the call (PUTON BLUEBLOCK GREENBLOCK). This would test first with, (CLEAR BLUEBLOCK), which would recursively call (PUTON GREENBLOCK TABLE), which would require clearing the green block by putting the red one on the table. An outline of the recursion is instructive.

```
(PUTON BLUEBLOCK GREENBLOCK)
|(CLEAR BLUEBLOCK)
|ON BLUEBLOCK GREENBLOCK) ASSERT
||(ON GREENBLOCK BLUEBLOCK) DELETE
|||(PUTON GREENBLOCK TABLE)
||||(CLEAR GREENBLOCK)
|||||(ON REDBLOCK GREENBLOCK) DELETE
||||||(PUTON REDBLOCK TABLE)
|||||||(CLEAR REDBLOCK) TRUE
|||||||(CLEAR TABLE) TRUE
|||||||(ON REDBLOCK TABLE) ASSERT
|||||(CLEAR TABLE) TRUE
||||(ON GREENBLOCK TABLE) ASSERT
||(CLEAR GREENBLOCK) TRUE
|(ON BLUEBLOCK TABLE) DELETE
(ON BLUEBLOCK GREENBLOCK) ASSERT
```

To conserve space, the DELETE operations are somewhat out of place, but the effect of recursive procedure calls marching inward until satisfied, then marching outward until the initial call is completed, is graphically portrayed.

If the command is given, "Pick up the red block," the result is to assert (ON REDBLOCK HAND). "Put it down" results in the deletion of this assertion and the new assertion, (ON REDBLOCK TABLE). But if instead of "Put it down," the command "Pick up the blue block" were given, it would be discovered that the hand was not clear, and in clearing, the red block would be put on the table. Otherwise, the hand is pure fiction and the robot simulates movement by changing "ON" relations. Since the hand does not actually participate in any commands except "pick up" and "put down," the command "Put the hand on the red block and the green block on the hand" can be legal, with the result:

Sec. 6.1   Background   103

```
                    GREENBLOCK
                    HAND
                    REDBLOCK
             TABLE--------------------------
```

Ordinarily the hand has no "ON" relation, and if the situation shown above ever occurs, there is no robot command that will restore the hand to its original unsupported condition. This situation can be avoided if the DELETE operation fails when its argument is not an assertion—thus (DELETE (ON HAND X)) would fail because there is no (ON HAND ...) in the database. But the anomaly is harmless and is allowed to remain as a reminder that even such a simple robot as this can show unexpected behavior.

6.1.2 Defining the Blocks

The blocks that the robot manipulates are characterized by name, shape, size, and color. Four cubes and a pyramid will suffice for our example. The following assertions describe their characteristics.

```
        (INST REDBLOCK CUBE)           (INST BIGBLUE CUBE)
        (INST BLUEBLOCK CUBE)          (INST GREENBLOCK CUBE)
        (INST GREENPYRAMID PYRAMID)    (INST TABLE TABLE)

        (SUBCLASS PYRAMID BLOCK)       (SUBCLASS CUBE BLOCK)

        (SIZE REDBLOCK 1)              (SIZE BIGBLUE 3)
        (SIZE BLUEBLOCK 1)             (SIZE GREENBLOCK 2)
        (SIZE PYRAMID 2)

        (COLOR REDBLOCK RED)           (COLOR BIGBLUE BLUE)
        (COLOR BLUEBLOCK BLUE)         (COLOR GREENBLOCK GREEN)
        (COLOR PYRAMID GREEN)
```

These assertions form the basis for answering questions that identify the objects referred to in natural-language commands. For example, "the red cube" is analyzed into (CUBE COLOR RED DET THE), which provides data for the questions

```
                    (INST X CUBE)(COLOR X RED)
```

which match
```
            (INST REDBLOCK CUBE)(COLOR REDBLOCK RED),
```

thus identifying the cube named REDBLOCK.

An example such as "the largest cube" requires a procedure that searches among the cubes to discover the largest one.

(LARGESTCUBE X Z) < (LARGERCUBE Y X)(LARGESTCUBE Y Z)
(LARGESTCUBE X X) <

(LARGERCUBE Y X) < (SUP Y CUBE)
(NEQ X Y)(SIZE X X1)(SIZE Y Y1)
(GREATER Y1 X1)

The principle of these procedures is first to find any cube, Y, that is larger than X. If one is found, seek a larger one. If none is found, X is the largest. In case there is a set of largest cubes, any one of them succeeds.

The assertions (SUBCLASS CUBE BLOCK) and (SUBCLASS PYRAMID BLOCK) permit the use of the word "block" to refer to both cubes and the pyramid. "A red block" is analyzed into (BLOCK DET A COLOR RED), which gives rise to the question (INST X BLOCK)(COLOR X RED). Using a rule of transitivity,

(INST X Z) < (SUBCLASS W Z)(INST X W)
(INST X BLOCK) < (SUBCLASS CUBE BLOCK)(INST X CUBE)

any cube is seen to be a block.

6.2 THE ENGLISH COMMAND SUBSET

A grammar for a command subset of English can be derived from analyzing the example sentences shown earlier.

Pick the green block up.
Put it on the red one.
Put the biggest blue block on the smallest green one.
Put the blue block on the green and the red on the blue.
Put the blue on the green and pick up the red one.
Put it down.
Put the red block on the blue block on the table.
Put the blue block on the table on the red block.

All the sentences are in the imperative mood and only two verbs are represented. The verb "put" is used in two forms, one requiring two explicit noun phrase arguments, the other using a particle to imply the location of the "putting." The particle may occur immediately following the verb or at the end of the sentence (e.g., "Pick up the blue block," "Pick the blue block up," "Put it

Sec. 6.2 The English Command Subset

down," "Put down the block"). Noun phrases include straightforward adjective-noun identifiers (e.g., "the green block," "the blue block," "the red block," and "the table"). The pronouns "it" and "one" occur in such commands as "Put it on the red one." The noun is deleted in such commands as "Put the blue on the green." Superlatives involving "biggest" and "smallest" are included, and both noun and verb phrases participate in conjunctive constructions. Prepositional identifiers are included as in "the blue block on the table." No embedded sentences such as "the block which is on the blue block" are included, but the identifying prepositional phrases require the same procedural semantics and may be considered as elliptical forms of embedded sentences.

The commands in this set are invariably a verb followed by noun phrase and possibly particle arguments, and the verbs all occur in simple present tense. Their lexical assertions are as follows:

```
(VERB PUT ON TWO PUTON)
(VERB PUT ON ONE PUTON)
(VERB PUT DOWN ONE PUTON)
(VERB PICK UP ONE PICKUP)
(VERB PICKUP UP ONE PICKUP)
```

The general form is

[VERB _PRINTFORM _PARTICLE _NBROFARGS _OPERATOR]

The underscore prefix is used to mark a term as a variable, as an augmentation of the general use of the letters P through Z. Two verb phrase rules are provided:

```
(VP (X Y.Z) _PARTIC _NBR-ARGS _OPER Z)
    <(VERB X _PARTIC _NBR-ARGS _OPER)
    (PREP Y _PARTIC)

(VP (X.Y) _PARTIC _NBR-ARGS _OPER Y)
    < (VERB X _PARTIC _NBR-ARGS _OPER)
```

In the first rule, X and Y are the first two elements of the English string and Z is the remainder. The body of this rule matches the string element X against the verb entries and thereby finds values for the particle, number of arguments, and operator variables. The rule applies only if the verb is immediately followed by a preposition whose value corresponds to the particle argument of the verb. If no preposition immediately follows, the second rule is used. The remaining string, either Z from the first, or Y from the second rule, is passed as the input argument to a following NP rule.

The lexical entries for nouns and adjectives are as follows:

```
(NOUN BLOCK BLOCK)         (NOUN TABLE TABLE)
(NOUN HAND HAND)           (NOUN PYRAMID PYRAMID)
(NOUN CUBE CUBE)

(ADJ RED RED COLOR)        (ADJ GREEN GREEN COLOR)
(ADJ BLUE BLUE COLOR)
(ADJ BIG 3 SIZE)           (ADJ SMALL 1 SIZE)
(ADJ BIGGEST (BIG DEGREE SUPERL SFX EST VAL MAX) SIZE)
(ADJ SMALLEST (SMALL DEGREE SUPERL SFX EST VAL MIN) SIZE)
```

Every noun phrase rule accesses this information to enable it to form questions about the objects in the model. An adjective-noun combination such as "red block" forms the question (COLOR X RED) which matches a data assertion (COLOR REDBLOCK RED), thus identifying the object referred to as "REDBLOCK." "Big block" forms (SIZE X 3), which matches (SIZE GREENPYRAMID 3) and (SIZE BIGBLUE 3). But noun phrases also include postmodifiers in the form of prepositional phrases, such as "the big block on the green cube," and so reduce the ambiguity.

The noun phrase rules successively strip off articles, pronouns, adjectives, and prepositional phrases to compute the identity of the particular object. The general form of an NP or NP1 is

```
(NP _STRING _OBJECT _REMDR)
    < (WORDCLASS _VALUE1)(PHRASE _REMDR _VALUE2)
      (SEMANTICS _VALUE1 _VALUE2 _OBJECT)
```

The word class rule examines the first element of the input string and returns a value for it. The following phrase rules find a value for the remainder of the string, and semantic testing rules procedurally test these two values as true assertions in the model. If a pronoun is used, or if the adjective does not modify a noun, the OBJECT is assigned the value of the current context carried over from the last command. When a command is successfully evaluated, its first object argument is asserted as a new context.

It will prove instructive to examine the analysis of "a big one on the red" in the context

```
        BIGBLUE
        REDBLOCK BLUEBLOCK GREENPYRAMID
TABLE-----------------------------------------------------------------
```

The topdown evaluation begins with an NP, strips an article, calls an NP1 that strips the adjective "big," calls another NP1 which strips both "one" and "on" from the string, then calls an NP which strips the "the" and calls an NP1

Sec. 6.2　The English Command Subset

for "red." Since no procedural testing is accomplished until the final (NP1 (RED)...) is called, the explanation best starts here, working backward.

```
(NP1 (RED) V NIL) < (ADJ RED X1 X2)(X2 V X1)

    (ADJ RED X1 X2)
    (ADJ RED RED COLOR)
       X1 := RED
       X2 := COLOR

    (X2 V X1) = (COLOR V RED)
               (COLOR REDBLOCK RED)
       V := REDBLOCK
```

If there is no noun, one acceptable form of noun phrase is an isolated adjective. The lexical assertion provides bindings for X1 and X2 in the first antecedent of the rule. The second antecedent uses those bindings to ask a question of the model (COLOR V RED), and this matches the assertion (COLOR REDBLOCK RED), thus binding V to REDBLOCK.

This NP1 was an antecedent (indirect via an NP call), of the higher-level NP1, which is now completed except for the semantic question (ON V REDBLOCK).

```
(NP1 (ONE ON THE RED) V NIL)
    < (NOM ONE V)(PREP ON ON)
      (NP1 RED REDBLOCK NIL) (ON V REDBLOCK)

(ON V REDBLOCK)
(ON BIGBLUE REDBLOCK)

      V := BIGBLUE
```

The (NOM X V) relation succeeds if X is a noun or a pronoun, returning a block name as its value for V. This NP1, too, was an antecedent of a higher-level NP1 containing the adjective "big," which is now also complete except for its semantic question.

```
(NP1 (BIG ONE ON THE RED) BIGBLUE NIL)
    < (ADJ BIG 3 SIZE)(NP1 (ONE ON THE RED) BIGBLUE NIL)
      (SIZE BIGBLUE 3)

(SIZE BIGBLUE 3)
(SIZE BIGBLUE 3) SUCCESSFUL MATCH.
```

In this case the semantic question had no unbound variables, but it had to be asked to determine that the additional qualification "big" was satisfied by the candidate "BIGBLUE," which was "on the red block." If the example had been "little one on the table," several candidates for "one on the table" might have been available. For example, GREENPYRAMID, BLUEBLOCK, and GREENBLOCK might all have been on the table. Then the question (SIZE GREENPYRAMID 1) would have been asked and failed. This would cause the embedded NP1 to find another candidate, say BLUEBLOCK, for which the question (SIZE BLUEBLOCK 1) would be satisfied. The sequence of this finding of a new candidate is important in terms of the efficiency of the system. The last antecedent of an NP1 rule used for analyzing "on the table" is the semantic question (ON V TABLE). If V := GREENPYRAMID failed at the higher level, this question would fail and seek an alternative binding for V, namely one of the two other candidates, BLUEBLOCK and GREENBLOCK.

This kind of backup is generally suitable for finding all possible interpretations of a sentence, but in procedural semantics, for the case of a superlative (e.g., "the biggest blue block on the table") a more efficient approach is given by the NPSET rule. This rule returns a list of all candidates that satisfy its conditions, rather than simply the first. As a result, "biggest" is provided with a set of candidates to examine. Since in procedural semantics, superlatives generally must examine all members of a list, backup alone simply does not answer the need. Whenever a superlative is detected, the NPSET rule is called:

        (NP1 (X.Y) V R) < (ADJ X (X1 DEGREE SUPERL.X2) X3)
            (NPSET Y (W.W1) R) (MEMPR (VAL Z) X2)
            (SUPERL X3 Z (W.W1) V)

The lexical entry for "biggest" is

        (ADJ BIGGEST (BIG DEGREE SUPERL VAL MAX) SIZE)

When the adjective has been found the variables of the rule are

        X3 := SIZE
        X2 := (VAL MAX)
        Z := MAX = (MEMPR (VAL Z) X2)

The NPSET rule is then evaluated to return the list (W.W1), containing names of objects (e.g., BLUEBLOCK, REDBLOCK, GREENBLOCK) that satisfied it. The procedure SUPERL is called with the following bindings:

        (SUPERL SIZE, MAX, (BLUEBLOCK, REDBLOCK, GREENBLOCK) V)

It is defined as follows:

        (SUPERL X Y (W.W1) V) < (Y X (W.W1) V)

Sec. 6.3 Analyzing Commands   109

```
(MAX X NIL V V)
(MAX X (W.W1) V V1) < (X W Z)(MAXR Z V V2)(MAX X W1 V2 V1)

(MAXR X X X)
(MAXR X Y X) < (GR X Y)
(MAXR X Y Y)
```

The SUPERL procedure takes a predicate name such as SIZE as its first argument, MAX or MIN as its second, then forms a call such as (MAX SIZE LIST CURRENTMAXM FINALMAXM). MAX in its turn forms the question (SIZE REDBLOCK X)(MAXR X CURRENTMAX RESULT) to bind RESULT to the maximum of X and CURRENTMAX. MAX then recursively proceeds down the list. When the list is empty, the rule (MAX X NIL V V) assigns the value of CURRENTMAX to FINALMAX. This is simply a clausal logic version of an ordinary program to find the maximum value of an attribute for the members of a list.

The NPSET rule differs from ordinary NP rules in one important way; it returns a set of values rather than a single one. When the phrase "biggest block" calls an NPSET, the rule for a noun returns a list of all blocks [i.e.,(SUP REDBLOCK BLOCK), (SUP BIGBLUE BLOCK), and so on]. The SUPERL procedure then has a list from which to select the biggest. "The biggest blue block on the table" calls an NPSET for "block on the table" and returns a list of blocks on the table [i.e., ((ON BLUEBLOCK TABLE)(ON REDBLOCK TABLE)(ON GREENPYRAMID TABLE))] from which the adjective, "blue" creates a sublist (BLUEBLOCK) from which "biggest" can only select the item BLUEBLOCK. [*Technical Note:* In order to return a set of values, the NPSET rule must actually preempt the flow of control by getting the axioms. To find all objects, Y, on the table, use (SETV W (GET Y "AXIOMS)), and select the subset with (MEMBERS (ON X TABLE) W Z). The bindings of Z then include, for the present example, ((ON BLUEBLOCK TABLE)(ON REDBLOCK TABLE) (ON GREENPYRAMID TABLE)). SETV sets the value of a logic variable to the value returned by a LISP function.]

6.3 ANALYZING COMMANDS

A command in this subset of English is always a verb phrase followed by one or more arguments. The verbs are marked as to how many arguments they will accept; thus "pickup" takes a single argument, and "put" may take one argument and a particle, as in "Put it down," or two arguments, as in "Put the red block on the table." There is a procedure, COMMAND, requiring a verb phrase followed by NXTARGS, which accumulates noun phrases and an optional particle. When these arguments have been analyzed, "command" calls the robot with the result, and so changes the simulated world.

The simplest example is "Pick the red block up." The blocks world will change from the first configuration shown below to the one following it.

```
            REDBLOCK
            BLUEBLOCK    GREENPYRAMID    BIGBLUE
TABLE----------------------------------------------------------------

    REDBLOCK
    HAND

            BLUEBLOCK    GREENPYRAMID    BIGBLUE
TABLE----------------------------------------------------------------
```

The rule COMMAND has the following structure:

```
(COMMAND _STRING) < (VP _STRING _PARTIC _NBRARGS _OPER _REMDR)
        (NXTARGS _NBRARGS _PARTIC _REMDR _VAL _REMSTRING)
        (_OPER._VAL)
        (CONJVP _OPER _PARTIC _NBRARGS _REMSTRING)
```

As before, the underscore prefix marks variables for easier reading. The call (COMMAND (PICK THE RED BLOCK UP)) results in the value

_STRING := (PICK THE RED BLOCK UP)

The VP analyzes this string and returns with the following additional bindings:

_PARTIC := UP
_NBRARGS := ONE
_OPER := PICKUP
_REMDR := (THE RED BLOCK UP)

The procedure NXTARGS is defined with the constants ONE and TWO to seek a particular number of noun and prepositional phrase arguments. The command "Pick up the blue block on the table" requires only one argument, so the NP "the blue block on the table" satisfies it. In contrast, "Put the blue block on the table" requires two arguments, so the first NP must be "the blue block" and the second, "the table." Ordinarily, the command will be given when the blue block is in the hand or stacked on another block, and the procedural test of (ON BLUEBLOCK TABLE) will fail, causing the NP to terminate with "the blue block." But because of the two-argument requirement, no confusion can arise even if the blue block is on the table when the command is (unnecessarily) given. When no second argument is found, the NXTARGS TWO... forces a backup and the prepositional phrase is rejected. This logic is of importance in certain ambiguous situations to be examined later.

Sec. 6.3   Analyzing Commands   **111**

The procedure NXTARGS is defined below for the ONE argument case.

```
(NXTARGS ONE _PARTIC _STRING (_VAL) _REMDR)
   < (NP _STRING _VAL _REMDR1)
     (OPTPARTIC _REMDR1 _PARTIC _REMDR)
```

When called with "the red block up," the bindings are

```
_PARTIC   := UP
_STRING   := (THE RED BLOCK UP)
_VAL      := REDBLOCK
(_VAL)    := (REDBLOCK)
_REMDR1   := (UP)
_REMDR    := NIL
```

The NP identified REDBLOCK, leaving the REMDR1 as (UP). The OPTional-PARTICal rule found that the remainder matched its particle and completed the sentence.

At this point, the COMMAND rule combines its OPER and VAL to form the list (PICKUP REDBLOCK), which calls the procedure (PICKUP X) with an appropriate argument. The result, as shown above, is to remove REDBLOCK from the BLUEBLOCK and place it on HAND.

The two-argument case occurs in an example such as "Put the red block on the blue block on the table." If the blocks world is in the state illustrated below, there is no difficulty.

```
              REDBLOCK    BLUEBLOCK
    TABLE----------------------------------------------
```

The analysis of the string "red block on the blue block on the table" first finds a constituent "blueblock on the table" which corresponds to the model, then attempts to satisfy "redblock on blueblock..." and the model rejects the possibility, so the first NP for the string is terminated with "the red block," and "blueblock on the table" becomes the identifier of BLUEBLOCK. This provides two arguments for (PUTON REDBLOCK BLUEBLOCK) and the operation can be carried out. There are two contrasting situations that can also occur:

```
              REDBLOCK
              BLUEBLOCK
    TABLE----------------------------------

              REDBLOCK
              BLUEBLOCK
              GREENBLOCK
    TABLE----------------------------------
```

The first of these situations satisfies the noun phrase "the red block which is on the blue block which is on the table" and returns the value REDBLOCK. This would be an appropriate interpretation if the command were "Pick up the red block on the blue block on the table," or "Put down the red block...," but it provides only one argument for the verb "Put...on," which requires two. The NXTARGS TWO... rule, finding no further string from which to obtain a second argument, refuses this interpretation and causes the NP to back up and produce the value REDBLOCK from "red block on the blue block," leaving the remainder, "on the table," to provide a second argument. The third model situation, REDBLOCK ON BLUEBLOCK ON GREENBLOCK ON TABLE, allows the noun phrase to obtain the value REDBLOCK from the identifying phrase "the red block on the blue block," leaving a remainder of "on the table" from which to obtain a second argument. The marking of verbs by the number of arguments their operator requires is another aspect of modeling the robot's arm in a manner that causes a sensible interpretation to override the ambiguity of noun phrase identifiers in the blocks world.

6.4 CONJUNCTION OF ARGUMENTS AND COMMANDS

The English subset contains commands such as "Pick the red block up and put it on the green one" and "Put the blue block on the green one and the red one on the blue." Each of these is a conjunction of two commands, and the second illustrates an elided or deleted verb. The final procedure in the command rule given above is a call to CONJVP, the conjunctive verb phrase, defined as follows:

```
<CONJVP _OPER _PARTIC _NBRARGS _REMSTRING>
(CONJVP O P N NIL)
(CONJVP O P N (AND.Y)) < (COMMAND Y)
(CONJVP O P N (AND.Y)) < (NXTARGS N P Y V1 R)
                        (O.V1) (CONJVP O P N R)
```

The first line above shows the general form of the rule. Subsequent lines use abbreviated variables in those positions. The first case, (CONJVP O P N NIL), shows that the rule is satisfied if there is no string remaining; it is the null case. The second and third cases require the next element of the remaining string to be the word "and." The second case is satisfied if there is a complete command, including a verb. The third case provides for a deleted verb by passing the relevant particle and number-of-args to NXTARGS. When NXTARGS succeeds, the command is formed by concatenating O, the operator from the last command, with V1, the value list of arguments NXTARGS returned. There is reasonable efficiency in this system of rules; the first test is for a null remaining string, the second tests if the first word of the string is an "and," using the COMMAND rule, if the next element is a verb; finally, if these two rules have failed, the case of a deleted verb is assumed, the argument string is parsed, and the operator is added from the previous command.

A conjunctive NP is also provided to account for such commands as "put the red block and the blue on the green and the table." This NP also requires its input string to begin with the word, "and," and it, also, is optional. In this particular realization of the blocks world, conjoined noun phrases have very limited usefulness, and the CONJNP rule is correspondingly limited. Conjunctive NPs would become of much more importance if the English subset were enlarged to include commands such as

> Place the red, green, and blue blocks in a stack.
>
> If the red and blue blocks are in a stack, make a new stack of the red and the green and another of the blue block and the green pyramid.

6.5 PROCEDURAL SEMANTICS

The robot's microworld is a set of objects—table, hand, and blocks—and an operation, puton, that can change the "on" relation between pairs of objects. The primitive question in this world is "on(x, y)" whose answer is true if x is a block, y is an object, and x is on y. Otherwise the answer is false. The relation, "puton(x, y)" is true if x is a block, there is no z on x, y is not a pyramid or sphere, and there is no w on y. This relation creates a new world by deleting any relation, on(x, v), and asserting, on(x, y). The semantics of these relations is their mapping into the values, True and False; their pragmatics is their effect on changing the state of the blocks world.

An English command in this world also has syntactic, semantic, and pragmatic structure. The command is syntactically well-formed if all its constituents can be identified by the English grammar. It is semantically well-formed if each of its constituents translates into a constituent of the command language of the model. The command is pragmatically well-formed if each argument corresponds to a true statement in the model and the operation is successfully performed.

If an English statement includes vocabulary not in the dictionary (e.g., brick, tetrahedron, place, and so on), it is badly formed with respect to the given grammar. If it includes syntactic structures not defined by rules in the grammar (e.g., the block *which is* on the green one), it is badly formed for that grammar. The translation of an English constituent into a constituent of the command language is part of the definition of the rule that recognizes the English constituent, so unless there are errors in the grammar, any well-formed constituent of the English subset has a corresponding well-formed command constituent. But well-formed command language constituents may include such pragmatic impossibilities as REDBLOCK ON PYRAMID, TABLE ON HAND, PUTON TABLE PYRAMID, and so on. They may also refer to pragmatically possible states of the block world that do not correspond to its existing state. The role of procedural semantics is to restrict interpretation of English constituents to those that can refer to existing states of the blocks world.

If we refer to GREENBLOCK ON PYRAMID, the questions INST(x, greenblock), INST(y,pyramid), and ON(x, y) fail to discover any pair x, y, to satisfy all of them. If we command PUTON GREENBLOCK PYRAMID, the command fails because although there is a green block and a green pyramid, the pyramid is found by a question in PUTON to be unable to support any object. Apart from this use of procedural semantics, ambiguities are commonly found in the use of prepositional phrases which can modify either a noun or a verb argument. A phrase such as "the red block on the blue block on the table" will certainly refer to the red block, but if it is on a blue block, "on the blue block" means "which is on the blue block." If the blue block is on the table, an ambiguity arises as to whether "on the table" further specifies the blue block or provides another argument for the verb. This ambiguity is resolved at the higher level of establishing a suitable number of arguments for the robot command. At this higher level it is necessary to assume that the intent of a command is to change the world—else the following situation would remain ambiguous.

PUT THE RED BLOCK ON THE GREEN BLOCK ON THE TABLE.

```
            REDBLOCK
            GREENBLOCK
   TABLE--------------------------------
```

It would surely be a strange machine that took REDBLOCK as a first argument for PUTON, and responded "The red block is already on the green block on the table." The assumption that the command wants to change the world leads to the interpretation that the red block on the green block is to be put on the table.

Other ambiguities arise from the fact that there are two blue blocks and two green ones. Unless there is a further specification by size, "the big/small blue block," or by shape, "the green cube/pyramid," or by postmodification, "on the x," either member of the pair satisfies the phrase.

To a large extent, this procedural semantics deals in extensional definitions of objects in the model. A noun phrase designates a set of blocks; a verb phrase selects an operation name; and a command instantiates a relation and its arguments. These objects onto which the English subset maps are actually discovered by examining the correspondence of a constituent description with a constituent—an extensional instance—in the list of statements comprising the model. In contrast, the textual semantics of the last chapter translates an English subset into a language of semantic relations. A semantic relational constituent is judged to be well-formed if its elements are instances of a semantic event form. The semantic event forms are an inventory of how abstract concepts in the subset combine into well-formed SR constituents. In one sense, the SEFs are an extensional description—an enumeration—of well-formed abstract constituents in a language. But each SEF is composed of abstract concepts that may include hundreds of instances, so the set is itself an intensional description of a much larger set of instance constituents. The semantic tests of textual semantics bear at least a superficial similarity to those of the blocks world; in both situations, a proposed constituent of the translation is compared to a model to determine if there is a match. But the blocks world is one instantiation among many possible worlds in the model. It is a particular set of "on" relations that hold at a given time. The SEFs describing a text world are more abstract; many possible instantiations each form a particular text world. The procedural semantics of the blocks world tests each command constituent as consistent with one possible model, the one at hand. A similar procedural semantics for text must eventually be developed, to test further each well-formed semantic relation as consistent with one possible model—the current interpretation of the text. The beginnings of such an approach begin to emerge in the study of text schemas described in Chapters 8 and 9.

6.6 EXERCISES

1. *Blocksworld.* The following is a program that forms a basis for understanding the ideas in the text. Type it into HCPRVR or translate it to PROLOG and run it with the stacking commands. The final procedure, SHOWORLD, will print the state of the world whenever it is called. Ruleforms are:

    ```
    <BLOK -NAME -COLOR -SHAPE -SIZE -SUPPORTIVE -STACKABLE>
    <ON -NAME1 -NAME2>
    ```

    The Objects and Their Relations:

    ```
    (((BLOK PYRAMID1 GREEN PYRAMID LARGE NOSUPRT STACKABLE))
     ((BLOK REDBLOCK RED CUBE SMALL SUPRT STACKABLE))
     ((BLOK BIGBLUE BLUE CUBE BIG SUPRT STACKABLE))
     ((BLOK BLUEBRICK BLUE BRICK BIG SUPRT STACKABLE))
     ((BLOK TABLE NIL NIL NIL SUPRT NIL))
     ((BLOK HAND NIL NIL NIL SUPRT NIL)))

    (((ON REDBLOCK BIGBLUE))
     ((ON BIGBLUE TABLE))
     ((ON PYRAMID1 TABLE)))
    ```

The Relations MEMBER and MEMBERS:

(((MEMB X (X . Y))) ((MEMB X (U . Y)) < (MEMB X Y)))
(((MEMBS (X . Y) Z) < (MEMB X Z) (MEMBS Y Z)) ((MEMBS NIL Z)))

Nominal Forms and Noun Phrase Rules:

(((NOM RED RED))
((NOM BLOCK CUBE))
((NOM BLOCK BRICK))
((NOM BRICK BRICK))
((NOM CUBE CUBE))
((NOM BIG LARGE))
((NOM SMALL SMALL))
((NOM BLUE BLUE)))

((((NP (X . Y) V R) < (ART X) (NP1 Y V NIL R))
((NP X V R) < (NP1 X V NIL R)))

(((NP1 (X Y . Z) W U R)
 <
 (PREP Y Y1)
 (NOM X X1)
 (NP Z V R)
 (Y1 W V)
 (BLOK . W1)
 (MEMBS (X1 . U) W1)
 (SPLIT W1 W W2))
((NP1 (X . Y) V U R) < (NOM X X1) (NP1 Y V (X1 . U) R))
((NP1 (X . Y) W U Y)
 <
 (NOM X X1)
 (BLOK . W1)
 (MEMBS (X1 . U) W1)
 (SPLIT W1 W W2)))

The Verbs:

Command < Vp
VP < VERB PARTICLE NP
   < VERB NP PP
   < VERB NP OPTPARTIC
OPTPARTIC < PARTIC
OPTPARTIC <

Lexical Form:

```
        <VERB -WORD <FEATURE LIST> -OPERATOR>
         (((VERB PICKUP (ONE) PICKUP))
          ((VERB PICK (UP ONE) PICKUP))
          ((VERB PUT (TWO) PUTON))
          ((VERB PUT (DOWN ONE) PUTDOWN))
          ((VERB GO (TO ONE) GOSAM)))

         (((VP (X Y . Z) (_OP _BLOK))
           <
           (VERB X _VF _OP)
           (PARTIC Y)
           (MEMB Y _VF)
           (NP Z _BLOK NIL)
           (_OP _BLOK))
          ((VP (X . Y) (_OP _BLOK))
           <
           (VERB X _VF _OP)
           (MEMB ONE _VF)
           (NP Y _BLOK R)
           (OPTPARTIC R _VF)
           (_OP _BLOK))
          ((VP (X . Y) (_OP U W))
           <
           (VERB X _VF _OP)
           (MEMB TWO _VF)
           (NP Y U R)
           (BLOK U X2 X3 X4 X5 STACKABLE)
           (PP R W R1)
           (BLOK W X2 X3 X4 SUPRT X6)
           (_OP U W)))

         ((((OPTPARTIC NIL X)) ((OPTPARTIC (X . Y) Z) < (PARTIC X)))
          (((PARTIC DOWN)) ((PARTIC UP)) ((PARTIC TO)))
          (((PP (X . Y) V R) < (PREP X X1) (NP Y V R)))
          (((PREP ON ON))((ART THE))((ART A))((ART AN)))
```

A Block-Stacking Robot:

```
        (((PUTDOWN X) < (PUTON X TABLE)))

        (((PUTON X Y) < (CLEAR X) (CLEAR Y) (D* (ON X W)) (A* (ON X Y))))

        ((((CLEAR TABLE)) ((CLEAR X) < (ON W X)(PUTON W TABLE))
        ( (CLEAR X)) )

        (((PICKUP X) < (PUTON X HAND)))
        -------------------------------------------------
        ((SHOWORLD) < (ON X Y) (RPRINT (ON X Y)) FAIL)
```

2. *Extending the Robot's Intelligence.* Given the command "Put the red block on the blue one and the blue one on the red," the robot described above detects no inconsistency and carries out the two commands in sequence. Also if commanded, "Put the red block on the blue one and the blue one on the green," the result is not a three block stack, but the following:

```
                     BLUEBLOCK
          REDBLOCK   GREENBLOCK
TABLE-------------------------------------------------
```

This strange result occurs from interpreting the conjunctive relation as indicating sequential rather than simultaneous conditions.

To obtain the simultaneous interpretation, the procedural semantics system must be modified to postpone operations of a conjunction of commands until they are analyzed further. This analysis examines a sequence to reject contradictions or to reorder the operations to achieve the conjunctive intention. The following rules illustrate the method.

[((PUTON X Y)(PUTON Y X)) < (RPRINT CONTRADICTION)]

e.g., Puton Redblock Blueblock AND Puton Blueblock Redblock;

[((PUTON X Y)(PUTON Y Z)) < (PUTON Y Z)(PUTON X Y)]

e.g., Puton Redblock Blueblock AND Puton Blueblock Greenblock; and

[((PUTON X Y)(PUTON U V)) < (PUTON X Y)(PUTON U V)]

e.g., Any acceptable sequence

These rules can be expressed more generally for lists of commands, and some of the more subtle problems involved in planning can be attacked in a similar fashion. The difficulties of planning sequences of actions are discussed by Sacerdoti [1977] for robot systems and by Bruce and Newman [1978] for cooperative and competetive plans with side effects.

The robot can be further enhanced to introspect its own behavior. By recording each PUTON and CLEAR operation and their arguments, a stack can be maintained that forms the basis for the robot to answer HOW and WHY questions about its behavior. If a method is introduced for saving the actual situation, the robot can answer HOW CAN−COULD−WOULD questions; in this event the robot operates in the possible world to answer the question, then restores the original situation. These question-answering methods derive rather directly from Winograd's SHRDLU.

With the improvements outlined above, the robot becomes a much more intelligent system, one that considers intentions before acting on plans and one that records its actions for future retrospection. The initial robot represented a skill for assembling sequences of stacking operations to achieve a PUTON command; the enhanced versions surround this skill with rudimentary planning behavior and the basis for reasoning about its actions.

7

QUERYING A DOCUMENT DATA BASE

7.1 A SHELVING ROBOT

We might generalize the block-stacking robot described in Chapter 6 to a robot shelf-manager for a library. If we think of our experiences with libraries, it is soon apparent that the collection is a set of books each one sitting on—or absent from—its shelf location, and each characterized in reference files by one or more cards that include its title, author, publisher, and classification number. It is noteworthy that the classification number places a book in relation to its neighbors rather than giving a particular shelf and slot location. Librarians are thus relatively free to reorganize the physical locations of books as long as they maintain their ordering in accordance with the classification numbers. The classification numbers are also organized so that indefinitely many books may be added between any two that the library now has. If, as the librarian does, we characterize each physical shelf as the current home of a series of classification numbers, a shelving robot need merely derive the shelf name from the classification number, then seek along that shelf until either it finds a book or discovers where it can fit, depending on whether its task is to locate or shelve an item.

Such a robot would require access to a document data management system (DDMS) to discover locations for titles, authors, and so on, and to keep track of which books are present or on loan. By analogy with the block-stacking robot, the shelving robot would need only the two primary commands,

[PUTIN <CLASSIF-NBR> <SHELF-LOC>]
[REMOVE <CLASSIF-NBR> <SHELF-LOC>]

The books could be organized within shelves as triples:

[<CLASSIF-NBR> LEFTOF <CLASSIF-NBR>]

and the insertion or removal of an item would involve changing the LEFTOF relation, and marking presence or absence in the file.

Although the shelving robot might be a reasonable system for studying the accomplishment of actions in the physical world of a library, our interest is primarily in translating from natural-language commands and queries into their pragmatic meanings. Since Chapter 6 considered robot commands, this one can largely ignore the manipulative aspects of the robot and concentrate instead on its ability to understand and answer questions (i.e., the capabilities of its document query system).

7.2 BACKGROUND

One classic natural-language problem introduced in the early 1960s was to devise a system to query a formal data base in ordinary English. By 1968 three experimental systems had been introduced that accomplished the task. Thompson and Thompson [1975] had developed a system called REL for a user to define a subset of English to query a relational data base. Kellogg [1968] showed an English query system for a subset of the national census data base, and Woods [1968] published a dissertation applying English queries to portions of the Airlines' Guide. Each of these systems defined a lexicon and grammar for a subset of natural English and a system for mapping questions into formal queries of the data base structure. A decade later, these systems or their descendents still exist as research vehicles, but they have been joined by many more. A few corporations currently offer natural-language interface packages for data bases, although these still must be customized for the particular application.

Although the major research efforts in this area are characterized by carefully wrought, linguistically defensible grammars, some applications use a shortcut method called "semantic parsing." This method defines an English subset by using patterned sequences of semantic class names and function words. A query to a naval data base [Hendrix et al., 1978] is defined as a pattern that matches the left half of a pattern-operation rule. For example, "Print the length of the Kennedy" matches the pattern <PRESENT> THE <ATTRIBUTE> OF <SHIP>. The right half of this rule is a program that constructs an appropriate query to the data base. Such terms as PRESENT, ATTRIBUTE, and SHIP are lexical classes whose contents include both words and additional rules. Key words such as "print," "show," "list," and so on, are instances of the class PRESENT. In addition to key words such as "length" and "beam," the class ATTRIBUTE also includes rules such as ATTRI-

BUTE → <ATTRIBUTE> AND <ATTRIBUTE>, thus allowing the power of an augmented phrase structure grammar (i.e., a phrase structure ordering of pattern-operation procedures).

The apparent advantage of this approach using semantic classes and patterns of classes to translate queries is that a nonlinguistically trained user can fairly easily describe the form of a query in terms of function words and semantic classes. Two weaknesses become apparent. First, a lack of linguistic generalization results in redundant rules; for example, <attribute> of <ship> and <attribute> of <officer> are both included instead of the generalization, <attribute> of <noun>. Second, as the grammar increases in size, lacking a consistent classification system, eventually new forms contradict old ones and changes to the language become unmanageable. The same hazard exists for any ad hoc grammar even if it uses customary linguistic classifications of nouns, NPs, and so on. Unless every effort is devoted to developing word and phrase classes that are consistent across the entire language, a large grammar may eventually collapse in a welter of contradictions.

In contrast to this approach are the query grammars developed by Petrick [1973], Robinson [1982], and Sager [1981]. In these examples the grammar was under development over a period of several years; the Petrick grammar based on linguistic transformational theory, Robinson's a context-free approach augmented with procedures, and the Sager one derived from linguistic string transformations. Although no conclusive evidence is available, it is a strong hypothesis that the syntactic portions of these grammars will successfully generalize beyond the subsets of English to which they have been applied. It is certain that the "semantic grammars" are highly specialized. The Hendrix group at SRI, for example, recognizing the limitations of their semantic grammar approach, adopted the Robinson grammar for advanced interface work.

Clausal logic forms of natural-language query grammars for data bases have been developed by Dahl [1981] and Coelho [1979], among others, in PROLOG. In fact, since PROLOG was originally developed under the impetus of Colmerauer's research in natural language understanding, it is particularly well suited to natural-language analysis. Predictably enough, logic programmers in PROLOG have a preference for translating natural language into fully quantified predicate logic as the query language for a data base.

Their PROLOG grammars translate English queries into logical assertions with explicit quantification, then as a side effect of resolving such assertions with the data base, return any or all answers. Coelho described a natural-language system for managing a library data base for a group of artificial intelligence bibliographic entries. A user could conduct a dialogue with the system to find particular references, to insert new ones, or to classify documents according to the classes of their bibliographic references. The bibliographic entries of the system were categorized into subdomains, and the domain categories were used to minimize search. The Portugese grammar translated user queries and commands into quantified statements that were interpreted by PROLOG with respect to the data base assertions. The grammar covers a useful and flexible subset of Portugese, and the system supports sensible dialogues.

The weakness in translating natural language to quantified logic is that any strict predicate calculus is unsuitable to express the nuances of natural language; standard conventions for representation of comparatives, superlatives, and metaphor are lacking, and the formalism gives a delusionary sense of precision where none may be present in the language it translates. Further, although data base queries translate readily into quantified forms, the user usually wants access to all entries that satisfy the query, although he or she may wish only to examine a few in interactive mode and obtain an off-line printout for the entire set; it is thus not obvious that translation into fully quantified logic is necessary or desirable.

One of the most recent advances in natural-language data base development is offered by Kaplan [1979], who also provides a partial survey of existing systems. The two considerations of *portability* and *cooperative response* are emphasized in Kaplan's work. Portability refers to the need for a grammar to be independent of the actual form and content of the data base so that the natural-language component can be constructed once and transferred to other data bases with minimal changes. Cooperative response augments the query logic by a system that applies when a null answer to a question is encountered. In this event the query system reports a relevant indirect response. For example, if the question is asked,

"What grade did L. R. Smith get in CS378, Spring 1980?" the system encounters a null response, then examines the subquestions, "Course CS378," "Student L. R. Smith," "Date Spring 1980," with respect to the course data and discovers that CS378 was offered in the Spring of 1980, but that L. R. Smith was not registered. As a result it constructs an informative reply:

"No Student L. R. Smith in CS378, Spring 1980." If the course had not been offered, the system would reply,

"CS378 was not given in Spring 1980."

The knowledge to provide this information was contained in the data base and Kaplan presents a program logic for examining the subquestions to return a useful indirect response.

The principle of portability is served by insisting that the lexicon used by the natural-language grammar remain independent of the actual entries in the data base. This can be accomplished by requiring that all field names and values entered in the data base be recognized directly from the data entries rather than by independent entries in a linguistic lexicon. In a later section of this chapter, methods for accomplishing cooperative responses and maintaining portability are discussed at greater length.

7.3 A DOCUMENT DATA MANAGEMENT SYSTEM

A straightforward relational data base containing bibliographic references will serve to demonstrate how procedural logic programs can be used to translate English words, phrases, and sentences into insertion commands and queries to the data base. First, a menu-driven system will be constructed to acquire document data from a user; it will then be expanded to accept queries and present documents to satisfy requests. Then the system will be generalized to accept natural language queries, and the grammar for noun phrases and a range of positive, comparative, and superlative adjectival modifiers will be shown and discussed.

Bibliographic references vary in style from publisher to publisher and journal to journal, but generally must contain the names of authors, title, publishers, publisher location, date, and pages. Advanced text formatting systems such as Scribe [Reid and Walker, 1980] request the essential information from a user and apply particular formatting conventions in the printing process. To obtain this information a menu-driven system—one that requests specific values from the user—is often used. Such a system prints a request (e.g., TITLE?), reads the user response, then asks for another item of data, say PUBLISHER?. When it has accumulated a complete reference, the system adds it to its data base. In a similar fashion a menu-driven system can accumulate the particulars for a request for documents and then ask it of the data base.

The demonstration system defines a document relation as an n-tuple,

[DOC DOCNBR TITLE AUTHOR PUBLISHER CITY DATE TYPE PAGES]

An instantiated relation appears as follows:

(DOC 101 (THE THINKING COMPUTER) (RAPHAEL BERTRAM) FREEMAN
(NEW YORK) 1976 BOOK 324)

A formal query to a list of relations is a nine-tuple starting with the predicate name DOC and including constants or variables in each of the remaining eight positions. For example, in HCPRVR a query for all documents by Bert Raphael is evaluated by TRY.

(?(DOC X Y (RAPHAEL BERTRAM) X1 X2 X3 X4 X5))

The result includes DOC 101 illustrated above.

To compile a set of document references with a menu-driven system, the procedure DOCREAD can be written first to compute the next document number, then to request title, author, and so on. At the time of acquisition, the procedure can also create a data dictionary which can be used to accept approximate titles and author names as well as to serve as a lexicon of nouns for the natural-language processor to be developed in a later section.

The procedure DOCREAD in its simplest version appears in Figure 7.1. The procedure NEXTNBR provides the next number in the data base sequence. RPRINT TITLE? queries the user for a title and RD* TITLE assigns to the variable TITLE what the user has typed. The procedure INDEX, shown below, is called with the classname TITLE; it examines each word in the title and if it is not a function word such as "and," "the," or "of," the word is asserted with a pointer to the entire title. For example, "thinking" creates the following structure:

(THINKING PTR TITLE (THE THINKING COMPUTER))

As a consequence, Raphael's title can be accessed by either, or any combination of, "thinking" and "computer."

```
(DEFPROP DOCREAD
 (((DOCREAD)
   <
   (NEXTNBR X)
   (RPRINT (DOCNBR: X))
   (RPRINT TITLE?)
   (RD* _TITLE)
   (INDEX TITLE _TITLE)
   (RPRINT AUTHOR?)
   (RD* _AUTHOR)
   (INDEX AUTHOR _AUTHOR)
   (RPRINT PUBLISHER?)
   (RD* _PUBLIC)
   (INDEX PUBLISHER _PUBLIC)
   (RPRINT CITY?)
   (RD* _CITY)
   (INDEX CITY _CITY)
   (RPRINT YEAR?)
   (RD* _YEAR)
   (RPRINT TYPE?)
   (RD* _TYPE)
   (RPRINT PAGES?)
   (RD* _PAGES)
   (A* (DOC X _TITLE _AUTHOR _PUBLIC _CITY _YEAR _TYPE _PAGES))))
 AXIOMS)
```

Figure 7.1 Document acquisition procedure.

Sec. 7.3 A Document Data Management System

The result of reading in the data is to create bindings for the variables TITLE, AUTHOR, PUBLISHER, and so on. After the last term, PAGES, has been read, the procedure A* asserts the resulting DOC relation to the data base. Additional entries must be prepared for the data dictionary for each class term of the relation; these are asserted in the form

```
[<Reference word> CLASS <FIELDNAME> <Ordinal Position>]
    (DOCNBR CLASS DOCNBR 1)
    (DOCNBRS CLASS DOCNBR 1)
    (TITLE CLASS TITLE 2)
    (TITLES CLASS TITLE 2)
    (AUTHOR CLASS AUTHOR 3)
    (AUTHORS CLASS AUTHOR 3)
    ...
    (PAGE CLASS PAGE 9)
    (PAGES CLASS PAGE 9)
```

A list of special variables is also declared in the relation DOCVARS:

```
(DOCVARS _DOCNBR _TITLE _AUTHOR _PUBLISHER _CITY _DATE _TYPE
    _DATE _PAGES)
```

These data as well as acceptable variant forms of the words in data entries must be entered by hand for later use in question answering.

Figure 7.2 shows the procedure DOCQUERY, which is a menu-driven approach for accepting simple document specifications from a user.

Like DOCREAD, this procedure queries the user for input on each element of the document relation. The user may respond with an appropriate specification (e.g., a title or an author name) or with NIL. The procedure CONVERT examines the input; if it is NIL, it returns the unbound variable associated with the field. If the field is indexed [e.g., (INDEXED TITLE)], the word is looked up to discover the full term it points to and the associated variable is bound to the full term. If the field is not indexed, the variable is bound to the input. The slash following (CONVERT...) prevents the system from backing up in the event of failure to ask the user to revise each given specification.

An example protocol for designating a document and for finding one is shown in Figure 7.3.

```
============================================================
            (DEFPROP DOCQUERY
             ((DOCQUERY)
               <
               (RPRINT DOCNBR:)
               (RD* X)
               (CONVERT DOCNBR X _DOCNBR)
               (RPRINT TITLE:)
               (RD* X1)
               (CONVERT TITLE X1 _TITLE)
               (RPRINT AUTHOR:)
               (RD* X2)
               (CONVERT AUTHOR X2 _AUTHOR)
               (RPRINT PUBLISHER:)
               (RD* X3)
               (CONVERT PUBLISHER X3 _PUBLISHER)
               (RPRINT CITY:)
               (RD* X4)
               (CONVERT CITY X4 _CITY)
               (RPRINT YEAR:)
               (RD* Y1)
               (CONVERT YEAR Y1 _YEAR)
               (RPRINT TYPE:)
               (RD* Y2)
               (CONVERT TYPE Y2 _TYPE)
               (RPRINT PAGES:)
               (RD* Y3)
               (CONVERT PAGES Y3 _PAGES) /
               (ASK (DOC _DOCNBR _TITLE _AUTHOR _PUBLISHER _CITY _YEAR
                     _TYPE _PAGES))))
             AXIOMS)
============================================================
```

Figure 7.2 A document query procedure.

The indexing and retrieval are accomplished by the following procedures, including those at the top of page 128.

```
            (DEFPROP INDEX
             (((INDEX _C NIL))
              ((INDEX _CLASS (X . Y)) < (FNCTWD X) (INDEX1 _CLASS Y (X . Y)))
              ((INDEX _CLASS X) < (INDEX1 _CLASS X X))
              ((INDEX _CLASS X)))
             AXIOMS)

            (DEFPROP INDEX1
             (((INDEX1 _C NIL X))
              ((INDEX1 _CLASS (X . Y) W)
                <
                (OR [FNCTWD X] [A* (X PTR _CLASS W)])
                (INDEX1 _CLASS Y W))
              ((INDEX1 _CL X Y) < (A* (X PTR _CL Y))))
             AXIOMS)
```

Sec. 7.3   A Document Data Management System   **127**

===

(DOCREAD)

(DOCNBR: 105)
TITLE? *(The Handbook of Artificial Intelligence)

AUTHOR? *(Avron Barr and Edward A Feigenbaum)

PUBLISHER? *(william kaufmann)

CITY? *(Los Altos Calif)

YEAR? *1981

TYPE? *book

PAGES? *409

((DOCREAD))

ANOTHER? *n
NIL
_____

*(docquery)

DOCNBR: *nil

TITLE: *(Artificial Intelligence)

AUTHOR: *barr

PUBLISHER: *nil

CITY: *nil

YEAR: *nil

TYPE: *nil

PAGES: *nil

(DOC 105 (THE HANDBOOK OF ARTIFICIAL INTELLIGENCE)
 (AVRON BARR AND EDWARD A FEIGENBAUM) (WILLIAM KAUFMANN)
 (LOS ALTOS CALIF) 1981 BOOK 409)

((DOCQUERY))

ANOTHER? *n
===

Figure 7.3 Asserting and querying a document.

```
(DEFPROP CONVERT
  (((CONVERT _CLASS NIL X))
   ((CONVERT _CLASS X W) < (INDEXED _CLASS) (FIND X _CLASS W))
   ((CONVERT _CLASS X X)))
AXIOMS)

(DEFPROP FIND
  (((FIND (X . Y) _C Z) < (X PTR _C Z) (FIND Y _C Z))
   ((FIND NIL _C W))
   ((FIND X _C W) < (X PTR _C W)))
AXIOMS)
```

INDEX examines an input string to discard function words such as "and," "of," "a," "the," and so on, which are recorded in the form (FUNCTWD THE), and creates for each content word an assertion of the form (<WORD> PTR <CLASS> <ENTRY>). The result is a set of assertions that index each multiword entry by each content word that it contains.

CONVERT uses the procedure FIND to access these words for any indexed field. It should be noticed that FIND accepts a list of words and when it discovers that the first points to a particular indexed value, it passes that value as an argument to constrain the selection of values for the rest of the words in the request; if subsequent words do not confirm the value nominated by the first one, backup occurs until a value is found that satisfies all the words in the request. If no such value is found, the request will fail and further backup will occur.

We should notice that this elementary menu-driven retrieval system offers only the capability for accepting (approximate) equalities; we cannot request documents with pages greater than 100, or date less than 1978, and so on. The machine can be augmented to accept Boolean conditions and inequalities, but to do so the formal request language must be expanded. In the following section the formal language is appropriately expanded but the menu-driven query approach is abandoned in favor of a full natural-language interface.

7.4 A FORMAL QUERY LANGUAGE

A flexible query language provides for an operation to be carried through on one or more fields of a set of documents. The document subset is specified by restricting the values of the fields using Boolean combinations of equality and inequality relations. Such a query language is defined syntactically below.

```
QUERY := OPERATOR + CLASS + SPECIFICATION*
OPERATOR := PRINT
SPECIFICATION := EQUALITY v INEQUALITY
EQUALITY := CLASS + VALUE
INEQUALITY := RELATION + CLASS + VALUE
INEQUALITY := BOOLEAN + SPECIFICATION
```

Sec. 7.4 A Formal Query Language

```
RELATION := GREATER v LESSER v GREATEST v LEAST
BOOLEAN := AND v OR v NOT
CLASS := DOCNBR v TITLE v AUTHOR v PUBLISHER v CITY v TYPE v DATE
         v PAGE
VALUE := ATOM :(ATOM PTR CLASS VALUE) v (NUMBERP ATOM)
```

The chart above uses the symbol * to signify possible repetitions, + for conjunction, v for disjunction, and := to mean "is defined by." The only operation listed is PRINT, but others such as TOTAL, AVERAGE, or REPORTFORM, could easily be added. The CLASS following the operator specifies the fieldname for the operator to work on, and the SPECIFICATION identifies a set of documents. This element is composed of EQUALITIES and INEQUALITIES; the EQUALITIES specify particular values of a CLASS, while the INEQUALITIES impose the more complex conditions of Boolean and numerical relations on the values sought. In the system to be described, Boolean conditions are not included.

A value is either a number or an atom that points to an indexed field [e.g., "intelligence" is an element of (INTELLIGENCE PTR TITLE (THE HANDBOOK OF ARTIFICIAL INTELLIGENCE))]. The document TYPES—"book," "article," and so on—are indexed by hand to form pointer predicates; other nonindexed types are numbers.

The language is designed for interactive use and since HCPRVR provides QFLAG for presenting all answers one at a time, the quantifiers "all," "some," and numbers are not needed to indicate how many answers are to be printed. In fact, since the demonstration system is designed only to provide an example of a natural-language interface for data management programs and the only operator is PRINT, the operator portion of the language can also be ignored, since the output will always be presented. If no CLASS is specified in a request, TITLE will be assumed as a default value.

Example queries in the abbreviated formal query language include the following:

1. (TITLE (AUTHOR BARR)(DATE 1981)) i.e., titles of Barr's 1981 publications.
2. (PUBLISHER (TITLE INTELLIGENCE)(AUTHOR BARR)) i.e., publisher of Barr with title including intelligence.
3. (PUBLISHER (TYPE BOOK)(AUTHOR BEAUGRANDE)(DATE 1980)) i.e., publisher of books by Beaugrande in 1980.
4. (AUTHOR (GREATEST PAGE NIL)(TYPE BOOK) (GREATER DATE 1980)) i.e., author of longest book since 1980.
5. ((TYPE BOOK)(AUTHOR BEAUGRANDE)(GREATER PAGE (PAGE (GREATEST PAGE NIL)(AUTHOR LEVINE)))) i.e., books by Beaugrande longer than the longest book by LeVine.
6. ((LEAST PAGE NIL)(TYPE ARTICLE)) i.e., shortest article.

The first three examples are simple requests involving (approximate) equalities; the remainder include inequalities. Examples 5 and 6 are incomplete in that they do not include a print field; in these cases the CLASS to be printed defaults to TITLE. It can be noticed that this is a concise, recursive formal language not particularly well engineered for ordinary users, intended instead as the query language most convenient for translation from English questions.

The interpreter for the formal language uses two procedures, REVAL and GETVAL, to evaluate a formal language request. GETVAL first sorts the specifications into EQUALITIES and INEQUALITIES, and uses the equalities to instantiate a document vector. The inequality conditions are applied to each document that is returned until they are satisfied; then the field to be printed is extracted and REVAL prints it. If QFLAG has been set to TRUE, the user is then asked whether or not another answer should be found.

7.4.1 Program Description of the Formal Language Interpreter

The procedures for interpreting the formal query language are shown in Figure 7.4. The top-level call is to DO, which applies the grammar (shown in Figure 7.5) to result in a list of equalities and inequalities, V; REVAL uses GETVAL, passing the ordinal number of the TITLE field for default, and prints the resulting answer.

In GETVAL, the procedure SORTS separates the EQS and the INEQS; obtains the list of special variables, DOCVARS; deletes any previous answers by using D*; uniquely asserts a global variable CURRENTVAL with a value of zero (for use by the GREATEST and LEAST relations); then uses FINDALL to identify the subset of documents satisfying the query. FINDALL asserts its subset to an ANSwer stack as a side effect, so the final procedure of GETVAL, EXTRACT returns the value V, the particular field to be printed.

FINDALL uses VECTOR to form a document relation instantiated by the equalities of the query, then calls APPLY* to evaluate each document returned by VECTOR; if the document satisfies all the inequality conditions, it is asserted to the ANSwer stack and the FAIL forces a backup to find any other document satisfying the query. Naturally, if a candidate document does not satisfy the inequalities, it is rejected and backup causes VECTOR to seek another. When there are no more documents satisfying a query, the second FINDALL definition applies just in case some answer has been recorded as an (ANS V) predicate. All documents satisfying the query can be found by asking (?(ANS.X)) and replying yes to the query "Another?"

VECTOR, for every equality, obtains an ordinal number corresponding to a CLASS [e.g., (AUTHOR CLASS AUTHOR 4)] and replaces that position in the vector with the value the query provided for that class. Thus the equality (AUTHOR (ROBERT BEAUGRANDE)) substitutes (ROBERT BEAU-

Sec. 7.4 A Formal Query Language   **131**

===
(DEFPROP DO
 (((DO _STR _ANS) < (VP _STR R X) (NP R V) (REVAL V _ANS)))
 AXIOMS)

(DMACRO DO (L) (%DO (CDR L)))

(DEFPROP DO PP-DO PRINTMACRO)

(DEFPROP REVAL
 (((REVAL ((X Y) . Z) W) < (GETVAL 3 ((X Y) . Z) W) (RPRINT W))
  ((REVAL ((X Y Z) . V) W) < (GETVAL 3 ((X Y Z) . V) W) (RPRINT W))
  ((REVAL (X Y) Y) < (ATOM* X) (RPRINT Y)))
 AXIOMS)

(DEFPROP GETVAL
 (((GETVAL N _LST V)
   <
   (SORTS _LST _EQS _INEQS)
   (DOCVARS W)
   (OR [D* (ANS X)] [TRUE])
   (UNIQUEA* (CURRENTVAL 0))
   (FINDALL _EQS _INEQS W)
   /
   (EXTRACT N V)))
 AXIOMS)

(DEFPROP SORTS
 (((SORTS NIL NIL NIL))
  ((SORTS ((X Y) . Z) ((X Y) . W) V) < (SORTS Z W V))
  ((SORTS ((X Y Z) . W) V ((X Y Z) . U)) < (SORTS W V U))
  ((SORTS (X Y) ((X Y)) V) < (ATOM* X)))
 AXIOMS)

(DEFPROP DOCVARS
 (((DOCVARS (DOC _DOCNBR _TITLE _AUTHOR _PUBLISHER _CITY _YEAR _TYPE _PAGES))))
 AXIOMS)

(DEFPROP UNIQUEA*
 (((UNIQUEA* (X . Y)) < (OR [D* (X . W)] [TRUE]) (A* (X . Y))))
 AXIOMS)

(DEFPROP FINDALL
 (((FINDALL _EQS _INEQS _DOCVARS)
   <
   (VECTOR _EQS _DOCVARS V)
   (APPLY* _INEQS V)
   (A* (ANS V))
   (FAIL))
  ((FINDALL X Y Z) < (ANS V)))
 AXIOMS)

Figure 7.4 Interpreter for the formal query language.

```
(DEFPROP VECTOR
 (((VECTOR NIL W W) < W)
  ((VECTOR ((X Y) . Z) W W2)
   <
   (X CLASS X1 N)
   (REPLACENTH N Y W W1)
   (VECTOR Z W1 W2)))
 AXIOMS)

(DEFPROP APPLY*
 (((APPLY* NIL W))
  ((APPLY* ((R M1 M2) . W) V)
   <
   (SPLIT M2 U _NBR)
   (M1 CLASS X N)
   (NTH* N V V1)
   (R V1 _NBR)
   (APPLY* W V)))
 AXIOMS)
```
===

Figure 7.4 (*continued*)

===

```
(DEFPROP VP
 (((VP (X . Y) Y _OPER) < (VERB X _OPER)) ((VP X X PRINT)))
 AXIOMS)

(DEFPROP NP
 (((NP (X . Y) V) < (ART X) (NP1 Y V)) ((NP X V) < (NP1 X V)))
 AXIOMS)

(DEFPROP NP1
 (((NP1 (X U . Y) (X1 V))
   <
   (CLASSNOUN X X1 N)
   (NCOMP (U . Y) V1)
   (GETVAL N V1 V))
  ((NP1 (X . Y) V) < (ADJ X _REL _CL) (COMPARATIVE _REL)
   (COMPAR _REL _CL Y V))
  ((NP1 (X Y . Z) ((R2 _C1 NIL) . V))
   <
   (ADJ X _REL _CL)
   (SUPERL _REL)
   (ADJ Y R1 _C1)
   (SEF _REL R1 _C1 R2)
   (NCOMP Z V))
  ((NP1 (X Y . Z) ((_REL _CL NIL) (_CL1 Y1) . V))
   <
```

Figure 7.5 Procedural logic grammar for the English subset: noun phrase and verb phrase rules.

Sec. 7.4 A Formal Query Language

```
          (ADJ X _REL _CL)
          (SUPERL _REL)
          (NOUN Y Y1 _CL1)
          (NCOMP Z V))
          ((NP1 (X Y . Z) ((R1 M1 (M1 M2)) (_CL1 Y1) . V))
          <
          (ADJ X _REL M1)
          (NOUN Y Y1 _CL1)
          (SEF _REL M1 Y1 R1 M2)
          (NCOMP Z V))
          ((NP1 (X Y . Z) ((R _CL N) . V))
          <
          (ADJ X _REL _CL)
          (POSITIVE _REL)
          (NOUN Y Y1 _CL1)
          (SEF _REL _CL Y1 R N)
          (NP Z V))
          ((NP1 (X Y . Z) ((_CL X1) . V))
          <
          (NOUN X X1 _CL)
          (CLASSNOUN Y _CL N)
          (NCOMP Z V))
          ((NP1 (X Y . Z) ((_CL X1) . V))
          <
          (CLASSNOUN X _CL N)
          (NOUN Y X1 _CL)
          (NCOMP Z V))
          ((NP1 (X . Y) ((_CL X1) . V))
          <
          (UNLESS (CLASSNOUN X _Y _Z))
          (NOUN X X1 _CL)
          (NCOMP Y V)))

       (DEFPROP NCOMP
          (((NCOMP NIL NIL))
          ((NCOMP (X . Y) V) < (PREP X X1 X2) (NP Y V))
          ((NCOMP (X Y . Z) V) < (VERB X X1) (PREP Y Y1 Y2) (NP Z V))
          ((NCOMP X V) < (ADVERBIAL X V))
          ((NCOMP X V) < (NP X V)))
          AXIOMS)
==========================================================
```

Figure 7.5 (*continued*)

GRANDE) for the fourth position in the query vector. When VECTOR has instantiated each equality as a vector position and the list of equalities is NIL, the relation (VECTOR NIL W W) < W) applies to find a document that W matches; backing up results in successive bindings for W as long as new documents are found.

APPLY* accepts a list of inequality relations and applies each to the candidate document given to it as the binding for its second argument. Notice that the third argument of a relation is SPLIT into U and NBR. A relation such as (GREATER PAGE (PAGE 200)) is the standard form into which the grammar translates an expression such as "longer than 200 pages," so the SPLIT is used to make the number available as an atom. For the max/min relations there is a NIL in the third argument, so SPLIT returns NIL and NIL as its two output arguments. APPLY* then obtains the ordinal number of the class term [e.g., (PAGE CLASS PAGE 9)] and extracts that nth value (e.g., 324) from the candidate to form a completed inequality relation. Each relation is defined as a procedure, so the actual application of the relation (R V1 NBR) [e.g., (GREATER 324 200)] is accomplished by the call (R V1 NBR), where V1 is the value extracted from the candidate document, and NBR is the reference value from the query.

The relations GREATER and LESSER use the corresponding LISP functions; GREATeST and LEAST seek, respectively, maximum and minimum values. The procedure GREATST is as shown:

```
(DEFPROP GREATST
 (((GREATST V NIL)
   <
   (CURRENTVAL N)
   (GREATER V N)
   (OR [D* (ANS . X)] [TRUE])
   (UNIQUEA* (CURRENTVAL V))))
AXIOMS)
```

To find a maximum value for a field in an unordered list, GREATST compares the value in the document being examined with the value in CURRENTVAL; if the new value is greater, any previous document is deleted from the ANSwer stack, the new value is asserted in CURRENTVAL, and APPLY*, which applies the inequalities, will assert the new document to the answer stack. If the new value is not greater than the old, GREATST fails, and the document is rejected. When all documents in the subset have been checked, the one with the maximum field value is the only one on the ANSwer stack. LEAST works in the same fashion using the predicate LESSER.

7.5 THE ENGLISH QUERY LANGUAGE

The syntax of the English subset is simply an optional verb followed by a noun phrase. The verb is selected from "Print," "Show," or "List," while the noun phrase includes an optional article followed by optional adjectives, a noun, and optional postmodifiers in the form of prepositional, adjectival, adverbial, or participial phrases. Examples of complete English queries follow.

Sec. 7.5   The English Query Language

1. List the titles of books by Chester.
2. Show authors of books longer than Beaugrande's.
3. Print pages of articles by LeVine.
4. Show publisher of the author of Artificial Intelligence.
5. List the title of a book longer than the longest book written by LeVine.
6. Print articles written since 1979.
7. Show books with dates before 1980.

In addition, incomplete queries are also accepted.

8. Books by Chester
9. Pages of book by Feigenbaum
10. A book shorter than the longest book
11. The city of Barr
10. Chester
12. Shortest article since HCPRVR

A recursive transition net graph of this grammar shows the default possibilities:

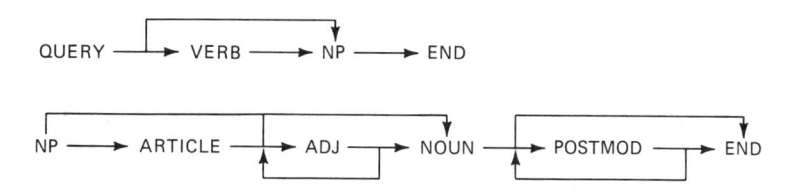

```
QUERY ──┬─► VERB ──┬─► NP ──► END
        └──────────┘
```

```
NP ──► ARTICLE ──┬─► ADJ ──┬─► NOUN ──┬─► POSTMOD ──┬─► END
                 └─────────┘          └─────────────┘
```

A QUERY path through this net shows that the verb, the adjective and postmodifier loops are all optional; only a noun is required. The postmodifier is shown below.

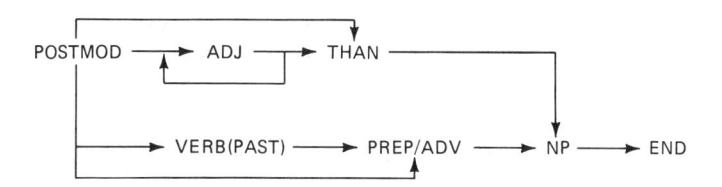

```
POSTMOD ──┬─► ADJ ──┬─► THAN ──────────┐
          │         │                   │
          └─► VERB(PAST) ──► PREP/ADV ──► NP ──► END
```

The postmodifier can be one or more adjectives followed by THAN and an NP, or an optional past participle verb form followed by a prepositional or adverbial phrase. The adjective string in a postmodifier is optional, as in "a longer book than Beaugrande's," where the adjective preceded the noun and the postmodifier is merely THAN NP. A maximal adjectival form is "a long book more recent than the newest book written by Barr."

7.5.1 Program Description of Procedural Logic Grammar

The syntactic description given above serves as a basis for the design of the procedural grammar; as in previous chapters, one or more procedural rules are required for each syntactic constituent. Also as before, each rule accepts an English string as an input argument and provides a semantic translation as its output—in this application the translation is to the formal query language defined earlier. Figure 7.5 shows the constituent rules of the procedural logic grammar; one VP, one NP, and nine NP1 rules encompass the syntactic description of the English subset. The NP1 rules accumulate adjective modifiers and then generally use NCOMP to select postmodifier rules; COMPAR, ADVERBIAL, and THANCLause, shown in a later figure, analyze postmodifying phrases.

The VP rule examines the first element of the input string for a verb; if found it is recorded but ignored by the rest of the grammar and the remaining string is passed to the NP. If no verb is present, the entire string is passed to the NP. The NP strips an article if one is present—treating "all," "any," or "some" as articles—ignores it, and calls an NP1 with the remaining string. The several NP1 rules are organized to accept one or more adjectival modifiers, treating positive, comparative, and superlative forms appropriately. The NCOMP rules accumulate any postmodifier phrases, seeking introductory verbs and prepositions before recursively calling an NP on the remainder of each such phrase. Since a command is a verb followed by an NP, this grammar does not require that the NP return a remainder string; instead, it expects NPs embedded within NPs.

The first NP1 rule seeks a class noun representing a field name, followed by one or more modifying noun phrases to specify and limit field values.

```
(((NP1 (X U . Y) (X1 V))
<
(CLASSNOUN X X1 N)
(NCOMP (U . Y) V1)
(GETVAL N V1 V))
```

If it is satisfied, it then passes control to the formal language interpreter by calling GETVAL with the ordinal number associated with the class noun and V1, the list of equalities and inequalities derived from following noun phrases. This NP1 is thus the driving procedure for the entire analysis and translation; since it is an NP1 it can also be reached when a command such as "Show the publisher of the article by the author of the longest book" includes an embedded query (i.e.,"... author of the longest book"). In the event of an embedded query, the output values (X1 V) are realized, for example, as

Sec. 7.5 The English Query Language   **137**

(AUTHOR (BARR AND FEIGENBAUM)), since GETVAL was called on the subquery. The remaining NP1 rules are devoted to recognizing various forms of adjectival constructions and the noun itself.

Three forms of noun are recognized: numbers, class nouns, and value nouns.

```
(DEFPROP NOUN
  (((NOUN X X1 _CL) < (NUMCLASS X X1 _CL))
   ((NOUN X X1 _CL) < (UNLESS (NUM* X)) (X PTR _CL X1))
   ((NOUN X W X1) < (UNLESS (NUM* X)) (X CLASS X1 N)))
  AXIOMS)
(DEFPROP NUMCLASS
  (((NUMCLASS X X DATE) < (NUM* X) (GREATER X 1800.) / )
   ((NUMCLASS X X PAGE) < (NUM* X)))
  AXIOMS)
```

The NUMCLASS rule uses NUM* to recognize an arabic numeral and tests it to determine if it refers to year or pages. The other two rules examine words indexed when documents were input: for example,

```
(TITLES CLASS TITLE 3)
(BARR PTR AUTHOR (BARR AND FEIGENBAUM))
```

[The apparently redundant number test (UNLESS(NUM* X)) is actually necessary to prevent inappropriate assignments when additional parses are sought during backup.]

When nouns are modified by adjectives, *Semantic Event Forms* are used to determine the resulting meaning. Consider the phrases, "short book," "long book," "short article," "long article." The SEFs given in Figure 7.6 include appropriate entries.

===
```
(DEFPROP SEF
  (((SEF GRAVG PAGE ARTICLE GREATER 30.))
   ((SEF LESSAVG PAGE BOOK LESSER 300.))
   ((SEF LESSAVG PAGE ARTICLE LESSER 30.))
   ((SEF GRAVG PAGE BOOK GREATER 300.))
   ((SEF GREATST GRAVG DATE GREATST))
   ((SEF GREATST LESSAVG DATE LEAST))
   ((SEF LEAST GRAVG DATE LEAST))
   ((SEF LEAST LESSAVG DATE GREATST))
   ((SEF GREATER GRAVG DATE GREATER))
   ((SEF GREATER LESSAVG DATE LESSER))
   ((SEF LESSER GRAVG DATE LESSER))
   ((SEF LESSER LESSAVG DATE GREATER))
   ((SEF LESSAVG DATE X LESSER 1978.))
   ((SEF GRAVG DATE X GREATER 1977.)))
  AXIOMS)
```
===

Figure 7.6 Semantic event forms.

"Short" and "long" are characterized, respectively, as LESSAVG and GRAVG in their lexical definitions, which also show that they refer (in document contexts) to the number of pages.

((ADJ SHORT LESSAVG PAGE))
((ADJ LONG GRAVG PAGE))

The nouns translate to TYPE BOOK and TYPE ARTICLE. Taking the appropriate information from these lexical forms, an SEF is constructed and matched against the SEF set as follows.

(SEF LESSAVG PAGE BOOK U V)
(SEF LESSAVG PAGE BOOK LESSER 300)

(SEF GRAVG PAGE ARTICLE U V)
(SEF GRAVG PAGE ARTICLE GREATER 30)

The SEF match returns the values for the relation and reference values to be used as inequality tests in the resulting formal language query.

An example such as "longer than 100 pages" is translated by an NP1 rule as (GREATER PAGE (PAGE 100)); "longer" signified both the relation GREATER and a reference to PAGE and the repetition "pages" in "100 pages" confirmed the reference and provided the numerical value for the query. Phrases such as "more recent than" or "more ancient than" follow a similar logic, depending on the SEFs to translate the combinations (GREATER GRAVG DATE U V) or (GREATER LESSAVG DATE U V) into relational values (GREATER DATE (DATE 1977)) or (LESSER DATE(DATE 1977)), respectively. Lexical entries for adjectives are shown in Figure 7.7.

```
===========================================================
         ((ADJ GREATEST GREATST X))    ((ADJ NEWEST GREATST DATE))
         ((ADJ OLDEST LEAST DATE))     ((ADJ NEW GRAVG DATE))
         ((ADJ EARLIER LESSER DATE))   ((ADJ LATER GREATER DATE))
         ((ADJ SHORT LESSAVG PAGE))    ((ADJ LONG GRAVG PAGE))
         ((ADJ RECENT GRAVG DATE))     ((ADJ OLD LESSAVG DATE))
         ((ADJ SHORTER LESSER PAGE))   ((ADJ LONGER GREATER PAGE))
         ((ADJ NEWER GREATER DATE))    ((ADJ OLDER LESSER DATE))
         ((ADJ MORE GREATER X))        ((ADJ MOST GREATST X))
         ((ADJ LESS LESSER X))         ((ADJ LEAST LEAST X))
         ((ADJ ANCIENT LESSAVG DATE))  ((ADJ LONGEST GREATST PAGE))
         ((ADJ SHORTEST LEAST PAGE))
===========================================================
```

Figure 7.7 Lexical entries for adjectives.

Apart from the use of "than," only three adverbs are included: "before," "after," and "since." Their lexical form is the same as that for adjectives:

```
                    (((ADV SINCE GREATER DATE))
                     ((ADV BEFORE LESSER DATE))
                     ((ADV AFTER GREATER DATE)))
```

Given such phrases as "since 1976" or "before 1980," the adverbial rules require agreement of the two class fields DATE. In more complex phrases, with subquestions such as "since HCPRVR," the subquestion "HCPRVR" resolves to (DATE(TITLE HCPRVR)), which is answered by (DATE 1980), and the parsing of "since HCPRVR" becomes (GREATER DATE (DATE 1980)).

The rules for comparative, than-clause, and adverbial constructions are shown in Figure 7.8. In this figure it can be seen that the adverbial seeks an

```
===========================================================
             (DEFPROP ADVERBIAL
              (((ADVERBIAL (X Y . Z) ((Y1 Y2 V) . W))
                <
                (VERB X X1)
                (ADV Y Y1 Y2)
                (THANCL Y2 Z V))
               ((ADVERBIAL (X . Y) ((X1 X2 V) . W))
                < (ADV X X1 X2) (THANCL X2 Y V)))
              AXIOMS)

             (DEFPROP THANCL
              (((THANCL Y1 (X Y . Z) (_CL X1))
                <
                (NOUN X X1 _CL)
                (CLASSNOUN Y _CL N)
                (NCOMP Z V)
                / )
               ((THANCL _CL (X . Y) (_CL X1)) < (NOUN X X1 _CL) (NCOMP Y V) / )
               ((THANCL _CL X V) < (NP1 (_CL OF . X) V)))
              AXIOMS)
             (DEFPROP COMPAR
              (((COMPAR R _C (X Y THAN . W) ((_RN X1 V) (_CL1 Y1)))
                <
                (ADJ X X1 _CL)
                (NOUN Y Y1 _CL1)
                (SEF R _CL X1 _RN)
                (THANCL _CL W V))
               ((COMPAR R _C (X THAN . W) ((R _C V) (_CL X1)))
                <
                (NOUN X X1 _CL)
                (THANCL _C W V))
               ((COMPAR R _C (THAN . Y) ((R _C Z))) < (THANCL _C Y Z)))
              AXIOMS)
===========================================================
```

Figure 7.8 Rules for adverbials and comparatives.

adverb followed by a than-clause, passing to the than-clause the field name to constrain any following noun phrase. The third THANCL rule, failing to find a simple noun phrase, forms a subquestion (NP1 (CLASS OF.X)) by adding the class name and "of" to the remaining text. This form matches the first NP1 rule forcing the call to GETVAL to resolve the subquestion.

7.6 PROTOCOL OF SYSTEM BEHAVIOR

The recording of a run with the system on a small collection of documents is shown below. The procedure (ANSWERS) is occasionally used to print all answers; it is defined:

((ANSWERS) < (ANS X)(RPRINT X) FAIL)

@run lisp

NIL
*
*(do (show the publisher of beaugrande) x)

(ABLEX NEW JERSEY BOOK)
((DO (SHOW THE PUBLISHER OF BEAUGRANDE) (ABLEX NEW JERSEY BOOK)))

ANOTHER? *y

NIL

(do (the publishers of the author of hcprvr) x)

(UNIV OF TEXAS DEPT OF COMP SCI)
((DO (THE PUBLISHERS OF THE AUTHOR OF HCPRVR)
     (UNIV OF TEXAS DEPT OF COMP SCI)))

ANOTHER? *y

(PROC AAAI)
((DO (THE PUBLISHERS OF THE AUTHOR OF HCPRVR) (PROC AAAI)))

ANOTHER? *n

NIL
*(do (the publishers of the authors of the handbook) x)

(WILLIAM KAUFMANN)
((DO (THE PUBLISHERS OF THE AUTHORS OF THE HANDBOOK)
     (WILLIAM KAUFMANN)))

ANOTHER? *y

*(do (show books about text) x)

Sec. 7.6   Protocol of System Behavior   **141**

(TEXT DISCOURSE AND PROCESS)
((DO (SHOW BOOKS ABOUT TEXT) (TEXT DISCOURSE AND PROCESS)))

ANOTHER? *y

(HEURISTIC LOGIC FOR QUESTIONING ENGLISH TEXT)
((DO (SHOW BOOKS ABOUT TEXT)
    (HEURISTIC LOGIC FOR QUESTIONING ENGLISH TEXT)))

ANOTHER? *y

NIL
*(do (a short book) x)

(HEURISTIC LOGIC FOR QUESTIONING ENGLISH TEXT)
((DO (A SHORT BOOK) (HEURISTIC LOGIC FOR QUESTIONING ENGLISH TEXT)))

ANOTHER? *y

NIL
*(do (a long book by feigenbaum) x)

(THE HANDBOOK OF ARTIFICIAL INTELLIGENCE)
((DO (A LONG BOOK BY FEIGENBAUM)
    (THE HANDBOOK OF ARTIFICIAL INTELLIGENCE)))

ANOTHER? *n

NIL
*(do (all papers by chester) x)

HCPRVR
((DO (ALL PAPERS BY CHESTER) HCPRVR))

ANOTHER? *y

HCPRVR
((DO (ALL PAPERS BY CHESTER) HCPRVR))

ANOTHER? *y

NIL
*(answers)

((DOC 100 HCPRVR (CHESTER D) (UNIV OF TEXAS DEPT OF COMP SCI)
AUSTIN 1979 ARTICLE 15))
((DOC 103 HCPRVR (CHESTER D)(PROC AAAI)(SAN DIEGO) 1980 ARTICLE 5))
NIL
*(do (print the author of a book longer levine) x)

NIL
*(do (print the author of a book longer than levine) x)

(BEAUGRANDE DE ROBERT)
((DO (PRINT THE AUTHOR OF A BOOK LONGER THAN LEVINE)
    (BEAUGRANDE DE ROBERT)))

ANOTHER? *y

(RAPHAEL BERTRAM)
((DO (PRINT THE AUTHOR OF A BOOK LONGER THAN LEVINE)
    (RAPHAEL BERTRAM)))

ANOTHER? *y

(AVRON BARR AND EDWARD A FEIGENBAUM)
((DO (PRINT THE AUTHOR OF A BOOK LONGER THAN LEVINE)
    (AVRON BARR AND EDWARD A FEIGENBAUM)))

ANOTHER? *y

NIL
*(answers)

((DOC 102 (TEXT DISCOURSE AND PROCESS) (BEAUGRANDE DE ROBERT)
(ABLEX NEW JERSEY BOOK) NORWOOD 1980 BOOK 351))
((DOC 104 (THE THINKING COMPUTER) (RAPHAEL BERTRAM) FREEMAN
(NEW YORK) 1976 BOOK 324))
((DOC 105 (THE HANDBOOK OF ARTIFICIAL INTELLIGENCE)
(AVRON BARR AND EDWARD A FEIGENBAUM) (WILLIAM KAUFMANN)
(LOS ALTOS CALIF) 1981 BOOK 409))
NIL
*(do (list the pages of the longest book) x)
409
((DO (LIST THE PAGES OF THE LONGEST BOOK) 409))

ANOTHER? *y

NIL
*(do (pages of shortest book) x)

113
((DO (PAGES OF SHORTEST BOOK) 113))

ANOTHER? *n

NIL
*(do (show the publisher of a book longer than 300 pages) x)

(ABLEX NEW JERSEY BOOK)
((DO (SHOW THE PUBLISHER OF A BOOK LONGER THAN 300 PAGES)
    (ABLEX NEW JERSEY BOOK)))

ANOTHER? *y

Sec. 7.6   Protocol of System Behavior   143

FREEMAN
((DO (SHOW THE PUBLISHER OF A BOOK LONGER THAN 300 PAGES) FREEMAN))

ANOTHER? *y

(WILLIAM KAUFMANN)
((DO (SHOW THE PUBLISHER OF A BOOK LONGER THAN 300 PAGES)
     (WILLIAM KAUFMANN)))

ANOTHER? *y

NIL
*(do (show the author of a long paper) x)

NIL
*(do (show the author of a short paper) x)

(CHESTER D)
((DO (SHOW THE AUTHOR OF A SHORT PAPER) (CHESTER D)))

ANOTHER? *y

(CHESTER D)
((DO (SHOW THE AUTHOR OF A SHORT PAPER) (CHESTER D)))

ANOTHER? *y

(MACHE GREEGER)
((DO (SHOW THE AUTHOR OF A SHORT PAPER) (MACHE GREEGER)))

ANOTHER? *y

(BOLOUR ANDERSON DEKEYSER WONG)
((DO (SHOW THE AUTHOR OF A SHORT PAPER)
     (BOLOUR ANDERSON DEKEYSER WONG)))

ANOTHER? *y

NIL
*(answers)

((DOC 100 HCPRVR (CHESTER D) (UNIV OF TEXAS DEPT OF COMP SCI)
AUSTIN 1979 ARTICLE 15))
((DOC 103 HCPRVR (CHESTER D)(PROC AAAI)(SAN DIEGO) 1980 ARTICLE 5))
((DOC 106 (OVERVIEW OF LAMBDA MACHINE) (MACHE GREEGER)
(SIGART NEWSLETTER #80) (NEW YORK) 1982 ARTICLE 2))
((DOC 107 (THE ROLE OF TIME IN INFORMATION PROCESSING: A SURVEY)
(BOLOUR ANDERSON DEKEYSER WONG) (SIGART NEWSLETTER) (NEW YORK)
1982 ARTICLE 21))
NIL
*(do (show the author of a book by Ablex) x)

(BEAUGRANDE DE ROBERT)
((DO (SHOW THE AUTHOR OF A BOOK BY ABLEX) (BEAUGRANDE DE ROBERT)))

ANOTHER? *n

NIL
*(do (show dates of chester) x)

1979
((DO (SHOW DATES OF CHESTER) 1979))

ANOTHER? *y

1980
((DO (SHOW DATES OF CHESTER) 1980))

ANOTHER? *y

NIL
*rtime

(0.87000000 SECS)
*(do (publisher of levine) x)

(UNIV OF TEXAS DEPT OF COMP SCI)
((DO (PUBLISHER OF LEVINE) (UNIV OF TEXAS DEPT OF COMP SCI)))

ANOTHER? *n

NIL
*(do (show a 1981 paper) x)

NIL
*(do (show a 1982 paper) x)

(OVERVIEW OF LAMBDA MACHINE)
((DO (SHOW A 1982 PAPER) (OVERVIEW OF LAMBDA MACHINE)))

ANOTHER? *y

(THE ROLE OF TIME IN INFORMATION PROCESSING: A SURVEY)
((DO (SHOW A 1982 PAPER)
     (THE ROLE OF TIME IN INFORMATION PROCESSING: A SURVEY)))

ANOTHER? *y

NIL
*(do (book with the oldest date) x)

(THE THINKING COMPUTER)
((DO (BOOK WITH THE OLDEST DATE) (THE THINKING COMPUTER)))

ANOTHER? *n

Sec. 7.6 Protocol of System Behavior

NIL
*(do (the newest book) x)

(THE HANDBOOK OF ARTIFICIAL INTELLIGENCE)
((DO (THE NEWEST BOOK) (THE HANDBOOK OF ARTIFICIAL INTELLIGENCE)))

ANOTHER? *n

NIL
*(do (the most ancient book) x)

(THE THINKING COMPUTER)
((DO (THE MOST ANCIENT BOOK) (THE THINKING COMPUTER)))

ANOTHER? *
*(do (all long books) x)

NIL
*(do (titles of all long books) x)

(TEXT DISCOURSE AND PROCESS)
((DO (TITLES OF ALL LONG BOOKS) (TEXT DISCOURSE AND PROCESS)))

ANOTHER? *y

(THE THINKING COMPUTER)
((DO (TITLES OF ALL LONG BOOKS) (THE THINKING COMPUTER)))

ANOTHER? *y

(THE HANDBOOK OF ARTIFICIAL INTELLIGENCE)
((DO (TITLES OF ALL LONG BOOKS)
     (THE HANDBOOK OF ARTIFICIAL INTELLIGENCE)))

ANOTHER? *y

NIL
*(do (books before 1980) x)

(THE THINKING COMPUTER)
((DO (BOOKS BEFORE 1980) (THE THINKING COMPUTER)))

ANOTHER? *y

NIL

*(do (books since raphael) x)

(HEURISTIC LOGIC FOR QUESTIONING ENGLISH TEXT)
((DO (BOOKS SINCE RAPHAEL)
     (HEURISTIC LOGIC FOR QUESTIONING ENGLISH TEXT)))

ANOTHER? *y

(TEXT DISCOURSE AND PROCESS)
((DO (BOOKS SINCE RAPHAEL) (TEXT DISCOURSE AND PROCESS)))

ANOTHER? *y

(THE HANDBOOK OF ARTIFICIAL INTELLIGENCE)
((DO(BOOKS SINCE RAPHAEL)(THE HANDBOOK OF ARTIFICIAL INTELLIGENCE)))

ANOTHER? *y

NIL
*(answers)

((DOC 101 (HEURISTIC LOGIC FOR QUESTIONING ENGLISH TEXT)
(LEVINE SHARON)(UNIV TEXAS DEPT OF COMP SCI) AUSTIN 1980 BOOK 113))
((DOC 102 (TEXT DISCOURSE AND PROCESS) (BEAUGRANDE DE ROBERT)
(ABLEX NEW JERSEY BOOK) NORWOOD 1980 BOOK 351))
((DOC 105 (THE HANDBOOK OF ARTIFICIAL INTELLIGENCE)
(AVRON BARR AND EDWARD A FEIGENBAUM) (WILLIAM KAUFMANN)
(LOS ALTOS CALIF) 1981 BOOK 409))
NIL
*(do (dates of all papers written since 1976) x)

1979
((DO (DATES OF ALL PAPERS WRITTEN SINCE 1976) 1979))

ANOTHER? *y

1980
((DO (DATES OF ALL PAPERS WRITTEN SINCE 1976) 1980))

ANOTHER? *y

1982
((DO (DATES OF ALL PAPERS WRITTEN SINCE 1976) 1982))

ANOTHER? *y

1982
((DO (DATES OF ALL PAPERS WRITTEN SINCE 1976) 1982))

ANOTHER? *y

NIL
*(answers)

((DOC 100 HCPRVR (CHESTER D) (UNIV OF TEXAS DEPT OF COMP SCI)
AUSTIN 1979 ARTICLE 15))
((DOC 103 HCPRVR (CHESTER D)(PROC AAAI)(SAN DIEGO) 1980 ARTICLE 5))
((DOC 106 (OVERVIEW OF LAMBDA MACHINE) (MACHE GREEGER)
(SIGART NEWSLETTER #80) (NEW YORK) 1982 ARTICLE 2))
((DOC 107 (THE ROLE OF TIME IN INFORMATION PROCESSING: A SURVEY)

Sec. 7.7   Extending the System   **147**

```
(BOLOUR ANDERSON DEKEYSER WONG) (SIGART NEWSLETTER) (NEW YORK) 1982
ARTICLE 21))
NIL
*(np (dates of all short papers written since 1978) x)
((NP (DATES OF ALL SHORT PAPERS WRITTEN SINCE 1978) (DATE 1979)))

ANOTHER? *y

((NP (DATES OF ALL SHORT PAPERS WRITTEN SINCE 1978) (DATE 1980)))

ANOTHER? *y

((NP (DATES OF ALL SHORT PAPERS WRITTEN SINCE 1978) (DATE 1982)))

ANOTHER? *y

((NP (DATES OF ALL SHORT PAPERS WRITTEN SINCE 1978) (DATE 1982)))

ANOTHER? *y

NIL
*(np (publishers of authors of artificial intelligence) x)
((NP (PUBLISHERS OF AUTHORS OF ARTIFICIAL INTELLIGENCE)
     (PUBLISHER (WILLIAM KAUFMANN))))

ANOTHER? *y

NIL
*
@pop
```

[PHOTO: Recording terminated Tue 25-May-82 5:03PM]

7.7 EXTENDING THE SYSTEM

English questioning of the system showed that the formal language, providing value matching and numerical relational constraints, is flexible enough to answer a wide range of questions that might be presented. Actually, though, it lacks several desirable capabilities, such as the following:

1. Consultation of the previous answer as a document subcontext for a question,
2. The use of a taxonomy of concepts to provide understanding of synonyms for data base terms and values,
3. A full Boolean logic of AND, OR, and NOT,
4. A range of operators for computing sums, averages, and statistical reports,
5. A cooperative response logic for explaining why no answer is forthcoming.

Such extensions to the system could bring it to the level of the very best natural-language data base systems currently available.

A context containing the previous answer is already provided in the (ANS X) predicates that contain all answers to the last question. Consultation of that list might be signaled in the language by pronominal references such as "those documents," "them," and so on. A question context may also be provided by saving the translated question in memory. Hendrix and his SRI group included these capabilities in their LADDER system, attending particularly to the use of elision in questions. For example, a user might first request "Show all the books about logic," then follow with, "List those less than 250 pages" or "about math." In the first case, "those" refers to the answer context; in the second, the elision can be presumed to refer to the context provided by the preceding question. But consider the difficulty in distinguishing the two elisions, "less than 250 pages" and "about math"; the first refers to the preceding answer context, whereas the second probably does not. These capabilities require considerable augmentation of the system's default logic and introduction of knowledge about pronoun usage into its grammar.

The ability to use a taxonomic system of concepts is already present in primitive form in the present system; it can recognize that "paper" is a synonym for "article" and "volume" for book. The lexicon accomplishes this recognition on a word-for-word basis, but what is needed is a systematically derived taxonomy that relates the wide variety of words a user might choose to those that actually refer to the data base. To obtain such a taxonomy, the questions posed by a large set of users must be recorded and analyzed. The new vocabulary items they introduce should then be organized into a shallow taxonomy relating their terms to those of the data base. Although expanding the vocabulary is primarily an empirical transaction with a community of users, it could be partially accomplished by a systematic expansion of the data base vocabulary to include all reasonable synonyms shown by English dictionaries and thesauri.

The present system accepts only a conjunction of constraints on a request; Boolean logic would provide the capability for disjunctions and negations as well. In the formal query language no great difficulties are apparent; the logical terms AND, OR, and NOT can be recognized by the same procedure that recognizes numerical relations. A query such as

(SHOW BOOK (OR (AUTHOR JONES)(AUTHOR SMITH)))

requires that the document set be searched twice, once for AUTHOR JONES, and once for AUTHOR SMITH, to provide two sets on which the OR executes a union. Naturally, these operations can be combined for greater search efficiency. Introduction of NOT requires a complementing operation—to return the document sublist, excluding any containing the negated constraint.

The extended system should prove advanced enough to warrant carefully designing its interfaces with the user. In command mode it should accept statements and questions in ordinary English without parentheses and return the answers in similar form. It should probably present the user with the number of documents that satisfy his or her request, accept a number to be printed, and then present the answers. Special operators should be available to allow for computing statistics and presenting reports. Improvements can also be made to the process of adding and deleting bibliographic data base items.

Kaplan's cooperative response logic should also be included. A first step is to provide the capability of saving answers to subquestions. In the event that some particular constraint reduces the saved document list to zero, that constraint can be removed to a failed-list, the question can be completed, the reason for failure reported, and any answer excluding that constraint can be provided. For example, if the question were "papers about logic longer than 50 pages by Chester," the failed-list would accumulate the expression (GREATER PAGE (PAGE 50)). The response would be, "No such documents longer than 50 pages, but excepting this constraint, two hits. How many do you wish to see?" For the sake of computational economy it may be desirable, as Kaplan suggested, to use this mode only as a second try in the event that the question returns a null answer.

This chapter has described a natural-language bibliographic retrieval system in successively more complex stages. From the most elementary beginnings in a menu-driven acquisition and query system, it progressed to a formal language interpreter that accepts a query composed of an operation, an identifier, and a set of constraints. The interpreter uses this information to search a set of bibliographic data relations to select those consistent with the constraints and to present the values of the identifier field that was requested. For a large collection of documents this interpreter must be modified to ensure optimal efficiency in searching, using where possible—as in ELISP—system paging functions to access the files. A classification approach, such as that described by Coelho, can be introduced to reduce further the size of document lists that must be searched.

A natural-language subset grammar translates English queries into the data base formal language in a single process that uses the phrase structure of a command to apply a sequence of semantic transformations of its constituents to form constituents of the formal query language. This chapter's example offers an effective natural-language retrieval system, but one that can be significantly improved by the suggested extensions. In addition to those improvements, the construction of a bibliographic data compiler that can apply a grammar to transform the semiformal language of bibliographic entries into indexed data relations offers scope for challenging research studies.

7.8 EXERCISES

1. Use DOCREAD to create a small data base and query it with DOCQUERY. (Remember to ASSERT function words as FNCTWD predicates.)

2. Augment DOCQUERY to accept inequalities and Boolean combinations of elements.

3. Consulting Chapter 6, augment the natural-language grammar to accept conjunctive, disjunctive, and negative constituents, translating them into the Boolean formal-language constituents you defined in Exercise 2.

4. Modify the system to record its questions; use this information and the previous answers stored in (ANS X) to accept pronouns and ellipsis. (Consult Chapter 6 for program ideas.)

5. Instead of responding NIL to a failed question, return a more cooperative response.

8

CASE STUDIES OF A NARRATIVE SCHEMA

8.1 STUDIES OF DISCOURSE

Previous chapters have been concerned with translating isolated sentences into various formal representations for illustrating semantic relations, commanding a robot, or querying a data base. Translating sequences of sentences into a connected structure of discourse is a much more difficult process that requires definition of the structure to be computed and maintenance of a contextual representation for the sentences that have already been translated. The discourse representation chosen for study in this chapter is a tree patterned after the structure that a human reader might present as an outline of the text.

The prototypical form of discourse is conversation: evanescent speech, loose in syntactic form, dependent on tone, emphasis, gesture, and surround for its coherence, interpretable at many pragmatic, social, and psychological levels for its meaning. Texts are derivative forms of discourse: more permanent, with more regular syntax, dependent on largely self-contained contexts, requiring only knowledge of the topic area and general linguistic understanding. The discourse structure of natural conversation is forbiddingly hard; but although texts may contain recorded conversations among other elements, their discourse structure appears to be just exceedingly difficult, and research has been rewarded with some degree of success in the study of fairly simple narrative forms.

Although texts may be classified in many ways, the dichotomy of narrative and expository discourse makes a clear distinction. Narratives include folk tales, legends, news reports, stories, and novels. Expository texts include encyclopedia articles, scientific papers, editorials, textbooks, instruction manuals, and even dictionaries. Narrative texts depend heavily on a temporal sequence of events, whereas exposition is usually concerned with logical and taxonomic sequences. Part of the problem of discourse analysis is to define structures that organize the clauses of a text into a meaningful whole. Some forms of these structures are taught in writing courses; paragraphing is taught in terms of introductory topic sentences, supporting facts and examples, and strong concluding sentences, and outlining the ideas of an essay or story by showing successive topics and subtopics is taught as a method of organizing composition.

The definition and computation of discourse structures has received much attention in the last 10 years. Books such as Grimes' *Thread of Discourse* [1975] and Halliday and Hasan's *Cohesion in English* [1976] have helped to clarify some of the issues concerning the connectivity of sentences in coherent texts. Papers by Hobbs [1979], Grosz [1977], Sidner [1979], Lockman and Klappholz [1980], and others have been concerned to discover computational algorithms for resolving pronominal reference and developing connected structures to represent texts. As of this writing, no well-defined algorithm has been found to accomplish this task with any degree of generality.

Networks of semantic relations for representing narratives have been studied by Phillips [1975], Young [1977], and Smith, [1981] among others. The network studies are characterized by the development of a context that relates the words of the text to larger concepts implied but not necessarily mentioned. The process of relating each clause in the text to a context is taken as a model of the human process of understanding, and the context that interconnects the words and clauses of the text is the structure of the discourse. Again, in this approach, the methods so far published are largely specialized to the particular texts studied.

Related to the network studies of text is the decade of exploration of scripts, plans, and so on, by Schank and Abelson and their students at Yale. In this case the approach is to translate sentences of text into conceptual dependency structures (i.e., networks of concepts connected by labeled dependency arcs) and then to relate the resulting sentences to organized sequences of action such as scripts, or to account for each dependency structure as part of a plan that some character is developing to satisfy a set of goals. The analysis of a narrative is realized as an instantiated script or structure of plans. The result of this work is a significant set of example scripts applied to such ordinary events as "using a subway," "going to a restaurant or museum," and to newspaper stories of accidents and of terrorist activities. The goal of a general procedure for relating sentences to a discourse structure is more closely approximated in this line of research than in most others. Procedures that relate sentences to conceptual dependencies and these to scripts or plans use general methods to determine if a noun phrase or pronoun is related to a previous topic in the text. The resulting discourse structure—of conceptual dependencies—has been demonstrated to support paraphrase, question-answering, and translation operations.

Two theories of how stories are created are predominant in the computational study of text. The first of these, the theory of story grammars, was introduced by Propp in 1927 [1968] and explored computationally by Klein and Simmons [1963], Rumelhart [1975], Simmons and Correira [1979], and Correira [1980]. In this theory, the sentences of a story are terminal elements of a tree that can be formalized as a grammar. Although Propp's original work used a context-free phrase-structure grammar to describe stories, the computational explorations use complex grammar rules that not only specify syntactically well-formed sequences of story elements but test them for semantic connectivity as well. In addition to the computational studies of story grammars, a group of psychological and text linguistic studies of story trees is collected in a special issue of *Poetics* [January 1980].

A more recent theory introduced by Meehan [1976], proposes that a story is developed as a report of a problem-solving process in which various characters seek to satisfy their goals amid the confusions and conflicts of a social world. Carbonell [1981] further explores this theory in terms of motivated characters solving problems to achieve their goals in competition with others, who may lie, bargain, or cheat to further their own motivations.

These two theories account for stories at two different levels; the story grammar provides a formalism for arranging the *sentences* of a text into a meaningful tree, while the problem-solving theory arranges the *events* underlying the sentences of the story into a tree of causal relations. The latter theory is clearly more satisfactory as a psychological account of story production and understanding, but the former is not without merit as a linguistic theory that can be used to structure text for various computational purposes.

In this chapter we provide two case studies for a narrative schema about the flight of a V-2 rocket, using a story grammar approach in procedural logic, and representing the text as a treelike* structure of relations among surface semantic relations (SSRs). The resulting representations will be shown in the following chapter to have excellent properties for summarizing and answering questions from the text.

8.2 THE V-2 ROCKET STORY

In a series of studies concerned with how people understood and remembered stories, Beaugrande [1980] used a brief narrative about the flight of a V-2 rocket. Simmons and Chester [1982] prepared a clausal logic grammar of the

---

[*Strictly speaking, both story "trees" and event "trees" are in fact rooted hierarchical graphs that allow interconnections among tree nodes and may include loops.]

type described in Chapter 5 and applied it to the following slightly edited version of the text.

> A great black and yellow V-2 rocket forty-six feet long stood in a New Mexico desert. Empty it weighed five tons. For fuel it carried eight tons of alcohol and liquid oxygen.
> Everything was ready. Scientists and generals withdrew to some distance and crouched behind earth mounds. Two red flares rose as a signal to fire the rocket.
> With a great roar and burst of flame the giant rocket rose slowly and then faster and faster. Behind it trailed sixty feet of yellow flame. Soon the flame looked like a yellow star.
> In a few seconds it was too high to be seen; radar tracked it as it sped upward to three-thousand mph. A few minutes after it was fired the pilot of a watching plane saw it return. It plunged into earth forty miles from the starting point.

To understand this story we might first consider a model that simulates the rocket flight as it occurred in time and space. Such a model would require a number of parameters, many of which are not specified by the text. For a simulation model of the rocket, we need to know its length—46 feet, its weight—five tons, its fuel—alcohol and liquid oxygen, eight tons, the thrust of its engine—unknown, its rate of burning fuel—unknown, its location—a New Mexico desert, but its exact location and altitude are unknown. We need to know its heading in terms of a three dimensional vector, its exact time of ignition, and the direction and magnitude of wind velocities at successive altitudes. With all this information, we could develop a set of equations that describe successive locations of the rocket as a function of time, characterize the remaining amounts of fuel, and predict the point of burnout and the approximate point of impact. Such models are commonly used in the aerospace industry to simulate the flight of missiles or to calculate orbits for space exploration. We might wish to use a rough approximation of such a model to translate the sentences into a series of line drawings and equations of the type Novak [1977] uses for analyzing physics problems.

Of course there is more to be simulated in the text than the rocket. There are scientists and generals observing the takeoff; someone fired flares as a signal; there is a radar that tracked the rocket to altitude; and there is the pilot of an observation aircraft stationed somewhere to watch the missile descend. Each of these events can be simulated mathematically and graphically as can the "the sixty feet of yellow flame" that looked like a yellow star. With such detailed simulation models it would be fairly easy to construct a series of time frames modeling successive events described by the text; indeed, if drawings are desired, we must use such detailed simulation models supported by various default mechanisms to infer quantities and locations not given by the text.

Beaugrande's studies of what people recollected after reading the rocket text suggest rather strongly that most people developed images of successive events in the flight. Their errors were amusing and instructive; some people recollected the rocket as silver colored, the fuel as hydrogen and oxygen, the altitude as 30 miles and so on. Weight, size, color and locations of the rocket were often distorted in recollection, suggesting that although people had some sort of image of the event described, it often differed remarkably from the actual description. We can interpret the results of Beaugrande's experiments to mean that although people probably use models of the type described by Meehan, these models are much more schematic than the detailed simulation described above. From his subjects' reports, Beaugrande abstracted a flight schema that was composed of a takeoff, an ascent, a peak, a descent, and an impact. He concluded that his subjects had a preconceived schema or outline for a rocket flight by which this particular instance was organized. Their errors revealed that the preconception often distorted the facts that they had read. As their recollections faded with time, this tendency to distortion toward the schema structure became more pronounced. This experiment is one of a long series that confirm observations of human memory developed in the 1930s by Bartlett [1932].

It was also observed in this and similar experiments that subjects did not recall exact words of the text; but instead, they remembered and described in their own words the events that were given. Generally, this experiment favors Meehan's story theory, but if we are not concerned to construct visual images for our computer simulation, a story tree approach can also be used to apply a schema to the text and so simulate important features of human understanding. Actually, the "story tree" approach is a schema application in which the schema procedure organizes descriptions of the event into a causally related outline form. This organization functions to simplify the task of constructing summaries and answering factual questions from the text. It is not articulated enough, though, to easily answer questions about successive locations of the rocket, fuel states, or other matters that could be inferred from a more detailed model. In this schema tree approach, the sentences are first translated into semantic representations using a grammar of the type given in Chapter 5; then a procedural grammar representing the schema is applied to organize the sentences into an instantiated schema. Detailed information of the type needed for constructing an image series is not required at this level of computation.

8.3 A FLIGHT SCHEMA

As a basis for scoring what people recollected on reading the rocket story, Beaugrande drew a network of semantic relations. The Simmons-Chester clausal logic grammar translated the sentences of the text into an approximation of this structure. That approximation adopted many of Beaugrande's arc names but generally used a simpler notation for labeling the arcs. The sentence translations that were computed are shown in Figure 8.1.

```
===========================================================
            1.((STAND AE (ROCKET DET A SIZE (GREAT)
                           COLOR (BLACK *AND (YELLOW))
                           TYPE V-2
                           LGTH (LONG LGTH (FOOT QU (FORTY-SIX) NBR PL))
                           NBR SING)
                    TNS PAST
                    LOC (DESERT PREP IN DET A LOC (NEWMEXICO) NBR SING))

            2. (WEIGH AE (IT ST (EMPTY) NBR SING)
                    TNS PAST
                    MSR (TON QU (FIVE) NBR PL))

            3. (CARRY PU (FUEL PREP FOR NBR SING)
                    AE (IT NBR SING)
                    TNS PAST

                    AE (ALCOHOL QU (EIGHT) WT (TON NBR PL)
                            PREP OF
                            NBR SING
                            *AND (OXYGEN STATE (LIQUID) NBR SING)))

            4. (BE AE (EVERYTHING NBR PL) TNS PAST ST (READY))

            5. (WITHDRAW AGT (SCIENTIST NBR PL *AND (GENERAL NBR PL))
                    TNS PAST
                    LOC (DISTANCE PREP TO DET SOME NBR SING)
               *AND
               (CROUCH TNS PAST
                       LOC (MOUND PREP BEHIND TYPE (EARTH NBR SING) NBR PL)))
            6. (RISE AE (FLARE QU (TWO) COLOR (RED) NBR PL)
                    TNS PAST
                    PU (SIGNAL PREP AS DET A
                            PU (FIRE INF TO TNS PRES
                                    AE (ROCKET DET THE NBR SING))
                        NBR SING))

            7. (RISE AC (ROAR PREP WITH DET A SIZE (GREAT) NBR SING
                           *AND (BURST SUBST (FLAME PREP OF NBR SING)
                                   NBR SING))
                    AE (ROCKET DET THE SIZE (GIANT) NBR SING)
                    TNS PAST
                    RATE (SLOWLY *THEN (FASTER *AND FASTER)))

            8. (TRAIL LOC BEHIND
                    INSTR (IT NBR SING)
                    TNS PAST
                    SUBST (FLAME QU (SIXTY)
                                  MSR (FOOT NBR PL) PREP OF
                                  COLOR (YELLOW) NBR SING))
```

Figure 8.1 Sentence analysis of rocket story.

Sec. 8.3   A Flight Schema   **157**

```
       9. (LOOK TIME SOON
              AE (FLAME DET THE NBR SING)
              TNS PAST
              AP (STAR PREP LIKE DET A COLOR (YELLOW) NBR SING))

      10. (BE TI (SECOND PREP IN DET A QU (FEW) NBR PL)
              AE (IT NBR SING)
              TNS PAST
              HT (HIGH INTENS TOO
                     RESULT (SEE INF TO AUX (BE TNS PRES) TNS PAST)))

      12. (TRACK INSTR (RADAR NBR SING)
              TNS PAST
              AE (IT NBR SING)
              DUR (SPEED AE (IT NBR SING)
                     TNS PAST
                     DIR UPWARD
                     RTE (MPH PREP TO)
                     QU (THREE-THOUSAND) NBR PL)))

      13. (SEE TI (AFTER TI (MINUTE DET A QU (FEW) NBR PL)
              EVT (FIRE AE (IT NBR SING)
                     AUX (BE TNS PAST) TNS PAST))
              AGT (PILOT DET THE OF (PLANE PREP OF DET A
                                     INSTR* (WATCH TNS PRPRT)
                                     NBR SING)
                          NBR SING)
              TNS PAST
              AE (RETURN AE (IT NBR SING) TNS PRES))

      14. (PLUNGE INSTR (IT NBR SING)
              TNS PAST
              *TO (EARTH PREP INTO NBR SING)
              LOC (MILE QU (FORTY)
                     LOC (POINT PREP FROM DET THE
                                 LOC (START TNS PRPRT) NBR SING)
                     NBR PL)))
```
==

Figure 8.1 (*continued*)

The logic grammar and lexicon for computing these translations are given in Appendix B.1. A connected graph somewhat similar to Figure 8.1 can be constructed for these structures by creating a node for the head element of each SSR joined to case value nodes by arcs labeled with the case names. If a word from an SSR is already present in the graph, new arcs and nodes should be attached to the earlier node. The resulting graph will show considerable connectivity among the SSRs, particularly if the pronouns and other anaphors are resolved.

A story grammar of the types customarily studied would characterize the V-2 rocket story with a tree such as the following:

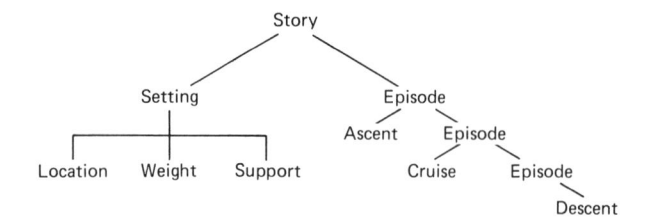

```
                           Story
                          /     \
                   Setting       Episode
                  /  |  \        /     \
                                Ascent   Episode
          Location Weight Support      /     \
                                   Cruise    Episode
                                              \
                                              Descent
```

Below the terminal nodes would be the structure of the sentences that they characterize. Our approach to constructing a Flight schema differs mainly by labeling the nodes differently and by including a specification of the focus for each description or action.

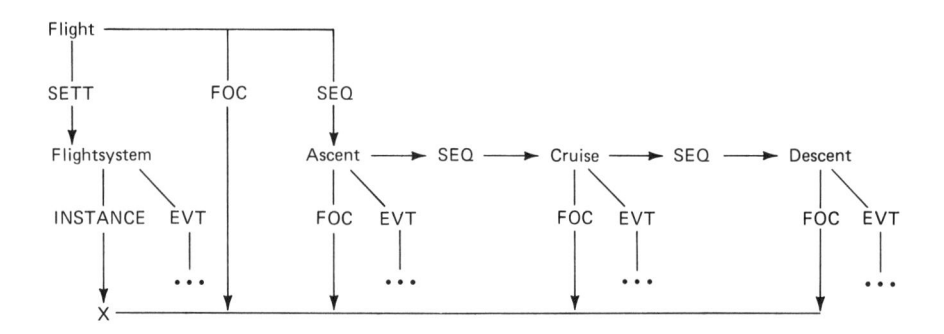

```
Flight
  |
 SETT         FOC         SEQ
  ↓                        
Flightsystem        Ascent → SEQ → Cruise → SEQ → Descent
  |    \              |              |              |
INSTANCE EVT       FOC  EVT      FOC  EVT      FOC  EVT
  ↓      |          |             |             |
  X     ...        ...           ...           ...
```

In this diagram, the flight is about X, some instance of a Flightsystem, the Ascent, Cruise, and Descent of X. Each EVenT arc will relate the sentences of the text to the schema headings. We can see that this schema, like the story tree, imposes an explanatory superstructure of concepts and arc labels to organize the sentences of the story. Unlike the schemas people use, this one is designed to record all the sentences of the narrative under the event arcs. As a result of translating each sentence into SSRs, and organizing these into a tree for the entire story, summaries can easily be computed by deleting nodes to abbreviate the tree.

For example, the briefest summary is "the flight of a rocket." Longer summaries reach deeper into the tree to produce,

> The flight of a rocket which ascended, cruised, and descended.
>
> The flight of a rocket. A V-2 rocket stood in the desert. It rose with a roar and a burst of flame. Radar tracked it. It plunged to earth forty miles from its starting point.

Methods for actually computing such summaries of sentences and stories are given in Chapter 9.

Sec. 8.3   A Flight Schema   **159**

8.3.1 Computing the Schema Instantiation

The schema diagrammed above may also be stated in the sequence notation of clausal logic.

>   (FLIGHT FOC X) < (FLIGHTSYSTEM INST X EVT Y)
>   (ASCENT FOC X EVT Y1)
>   (CRUISE FOC X EVT Y2)
>   (DESCENT FOC X EVT Y3)

This procedure recognizes a flight of X if it can establish the premises that X is a Flightsystem in some event Y, that X is the focus of an Ascent, a Cruise, and a Descent in events Y1, Y2, and Y3. So, if we have already asserted,

>   (FLIGHTSYSTEM INST ROCKET
>   EVT ((STAND AE ROCKET ...)
>   (WEIGHT AE IT...)
>   (CARRY INSTR IT...)))

then we can prove the first antecedent with X bound to Rocket, and Y to the list of sentences following the EVT arc. Similarly, the Ascent, Cruise, and Descent antecedents can be established if these subschema elements have been asserted. But of course the problem lies in the fact that while parsing the sentences of the text, we have not attempted to instantiate these subschemas (i.e., Flightsystem, Ascent, etc.). We need rules to apply the subschemas to the SSRs of the text.

Given a list of SSRs, S, we can define a Flightsystem rule as follows:

>   (FLIGHTSYSTEM X U (FLTSYSTEM EVT (T1 T2 T3)) S R)
>   <
>   (LOCAT X U T1 S R1)
>   (WT X T2 R1 R2)
>   (SUPPORT X T3 R2 R)

This rule uses the three premises LOCAT, WT, and SUPPORT to test the SSRs given in the argument S. LOCAT takes the list of sentence relations, S, and computes the values for X, the instance of a Flightsystem; for U, its location; for R1 a list of sentences remaining; and for T1, the first sentence that satisfied the LOCAT relation. Then the WT relation uses the remainder list, R1, to find the sentence, T2, and SUPPORT then uses WT's remainder, R2, to find T3 and return the remainder list R to FLIGHTSYSTEM.

The actual work of examining sentence relations is accomplished by LOCAT, WT, and SUPPORT. At this point we must descend into quite detailed description to understand the procedures that examine sentences and question them to determine that they have certain necessary properties to qualify as elements of a schema.

```
(LOCAT X U (X POSIT Y LOC U . Q) ((Y . W) . R) R)
<
(RELATE Y POSITION)
(MATCHPR (AE (X1 . Q) LOC U) W W)
(RELATE X X1)
```

The sentence list, S, is now represented as ((Y . W) . R), where (Y . W) is the first SSR and R the remainder. This SSR was (STAND AE ROCKET LOC DESERT...), so Y was bound to STAND and W to the remainder of the sentence relation. The procedure (RELATE Y POSITION) is bound to (RELATE STAND POSITION). This procedure is true if its two arguments are in a SUPerset, INSTance, PART, or EQUIValence relation. STAND is an instance of the concept POSITION, so this premise is proved. MATCHPR extracts the AE argument of which X1 is the first element, and the LOC argument from W, the remainder of the first sentence relation. Then RELATE is called again to ensure that if X is bound, say to rocket, that X1 is a related reference. If X is not bound, as is the case, it takes the value of X1.

The first sentence relation is as follows:

```
(STAND AE (ROCKET DET A SIZE (GREAT)
                  COLOR (BLACK *AND (YELLOW))
                  TYPE V-2
                  LGTH (LONG LGTH (FOOT QU (FORTY-SIX) NBR PL))
                  NBR SING)
       TNS PAST
       LOC (DESERT PREP IN DET A LOC (NEWMEXICO) NBR SING))
```

If we apply the LOCAT rule as described above, we first relate STAND to POSITION. Given the assertion (STAND SUP POSITION), this relation is proved. MATCHPR is then used to extract the AE and LOC arguments: ROCKET... and DESERT..., respectively. The variable X, unbound in the call from FLIGHTSYSTEM, is then compared with ROCKET and by the definition of RELATE, takes on that value. The third argument of LOCAT is thus bound as follows:

```
(ROCKET POSIT STAND LOC (DESERT LOC (NEWMEXICO...)...)
        SIZE GREAT COLOR (BLACK...)...)
```

The variable Q is bound to the remainder of the SSR that started with ROCKET. The result is that the sentence relation has been rewritten as a linguistically nominal structure from its original form headed by the verb STAND.

Sec. 8.3   A Flight Schema   **161**

```
(WT X (X WT Y . Q) ((U . W) . R) R)
<
(RELATE U WEIGH)
(MATCHPR (AE (X1 . Q) MSR Y) W W)
(RELATE X1 X)

(SUPPORT X (X CO (Z PU Y)) ((U . W) . R) R)
<
(RELATE U SUPPORT)
(MATCHPR (AE X1 CO Z PU Y) W W)
(RELATE X1 X)
```

In a similar fashion, WT and SUPPORT evaluate the next two sentences and return their values to FLIGHTSYSTEM, whose event bindings then appear as follows:

```
(FLTSYSTEM EVT ((ROCKET POSIT STAND
                   LOC (DESERT PREP IN
                           DET A LOC (NEWMEXICO)
                           NBR SING)
                   DET A SIZE (GREAT)
                   COLOR (BLACK *AND (YELLOW))
                   TYPE (V-2)
                   LGTH (LONG LGTH (FOOT QU
                           (FORTY-SIX) NBR PL))
                   NBR SING)
         (ROCKET WT (TON QU (FIVE) NBR PL)
                   ST (EMPTY) NBR SING)
         (ROCKET CO (ALCOHOL WT (TON QU (EIGHT)
                           NBR PL)
                   PREP OF
                   *AND
                      (OXYGEN STATE (LIQUID)
                           NBR SING)
                   NBR SING
                   PU (FUEL PREP FOR NBR SING)))))
```

The FLIGHTSYSTEM procedure has gathered the first three sentences as its characterizing event, and in the process it resolved two uses of the pronoun "it" and revised the sentence relations into nominal forms describing the rocket. The verbs "weigh" and "carry" vanished in favor of the relational arcs "WT" for weight and "CO" for contain. The entire Flight schema is given in Appendix B, Section B.2, and its instantiation in the rocket text is shown Section B.3. This instantiation will be used again in Chapter 9.

What has been shown above is a top-down definition and application of the Flight schema. The schema was defined as a procedural logic program that examined a sequence of sentence relations, checking to determine to which subschema each belonged. In the definition presented the schema is a tree of procedures that exactly fits the sequence of sentences given in the rocket story. Although such an exercise is computationally interesting in showing the type of operations required to instantiate a schema from a text, it suffers severely from lack of generality. If the same text were presented with its sentences in a different ordering this schema would fail. The schema could be modified so that each subschema searched the entire list of sentence relations until it was satisfied, or even changed so that some subschemas were optional. Top-down evaluation of schemas is not intrinsically limited to the form illustrated; it can be generalized to whatever extent is desired.

Nevertheless, it is intuitively more appealing to attempt a bottom-up approach in which the sentence relations select subschemas, and subschemas finally select the top-level schema.

8.4 BOTTOM-UP CONTROL OF SCHEMA INSTANTIATION

The natural form of top-down recursive evaluation of procedures is illustrated in the following abstraction:

$$(PRED\ (HD.TAIL)\ (FHD.W)) < (P1\ HD\ FHD)(PRED\ TAIL\ W)$$

The variables are HD, TAIL, FHD, and W. The procedure P1 applied to the head of a list results in a value, FHD, and PRED is then applied to the remainder of the list to result in W. If we had a list of three elements, (A B C), and P1 had the effect of doubling its argument, the tree of recursive evaluation would appear as follows.

$$(PRED\ (A.(B\ C))\ (FHD.W)) < (P1\ A\ FHD)\ (PRED\ (B\ C)\ W)$$

If (P1 A FHD) matches an assertion,

$$(P1\ A\ AA),$$

then the bindings for variables are as follows:

$$HD := A \quad TAIL := (B\ C) \quad FHD := AA$$

The sequence of three recursive calls followed by the final value of PRED is shown below.

Sec. 8.4 Bottom-Up Control of Schema Instantiation

```
              (PRED (A.(B C)) (AA.W)) < (P1 A AA) (PRED (B C) W)
              (PRED (B.(C)) (BB.W) ) < (P1 B BB)(PRED (C) W)
                (PRED (C.NIL) (CC.W) ) < (P1 C CC)(PRED NIL W)
                  (PRED NIL W)
                  (PRED NIL NIL)
                (PRED (C.NIL) (CC) )...
              (PRED (B.(C)) (BB CC) )...
            (PRED (A B C) (AA BB CC))
```

The natural top-down flow of control consists of direct calls to the the conclusion and premises of each procedure, but a level of indirection can be introduced by including premises that index procedures. For the example above, we might have indexed the procedure P1 by its possible arguments, A, B, C, ..., using relations such as (A INDX P1), (B INDX P1), (C INDX P1), and so on. Then, defining a procedure, BOTUP, we provide a flow of control dictated by the arguments given when the procedure is called.

```
                  (BOTUP (X.Y) (W.Z))
                   < (X INDX U)(U X W)(BOTUP Y Z)
```

If the procedure is called with

```
                  (BOTUP (A B C) U),
```

the control trace then appears as follows:

```
              (BOTUP (A B C) (AA.Z))
                < (A INDX P1)(P1 A AA)(BOTUP (B C) Z)
                (BOTUP (B C) (BB.Z))
                  < (B INDX P1)(P1 B BB)(BOTUP (C) Z)
                  (BOTUP (C NIL) (CC.Z))
                    < (C INDX P1)(P1 C CC)(BOTUP NIL Z)
                    (BOTUP NIL NIL)
                  (BOTUP... (CC.NIL)) <...
                (BOTUP... (BB CC.NIL)) <...
              (BOTUP... (AA BB CC)) <...
```

In this recursion, the first premise used an argument to select a procedure, then evaluated the procedure that was selected. The output is the same, but the top-level procedure was defined less directly than in the previous example. It used a system of index assertions to allow the input arguments to select a flow of control. Such an approach applied to natural language allows the words of a sentence or the sentences of a discourse to select the rules in orders corresponding to bottom-up analysis.

With little change in the analysis of the flight story, it is possible to let each sentence select a subschema, to combine identical or syntactically related subschemas, and then to order the subschemas according to a schema. We can define the Flight schema to be composed of subschemas.

(FLIGHT SUBSCHEMA (FLIGHTSYSTEM ASCENT CRUISE DESCENT))

If each sentence of the story can select a subschema such as Flightsystem, Ascent, and so on, the Flight schema can reorder the events from whatever sequence they occurred in the story into the temporal sequence provided by the schema. First, let us abbreviate the story to four sentences:

A V-2 rocket stood in the desert.
It rose with a roar and a burst of flame.
Radar tracked it.
It plunged to earth forty miles away.

The first sentence describes the location of a rocket, so a rule such as

(LOCAT (X.Y) (LOCAT FOC W LOC V EVT (X.Y)))
<   (RELATE X POSITION) (FOCUS Y W)
      (MEMPR (LOC V) Y)

states that if the head of the sentence is a position [e.g., (STAND SUP POSITION)] and its focus—the main argument of the verb—is W, and it has a LOC arc to some location, V, the sentence can be classified as a LOCAT or Location predicate. The second argument of the LOCAT rule summarizes the sentence (LOCAT FOC ROCKET LOC DESERT EVT(STAND AE ROCKET...)). A LOCAT predicate can participate in many schemas, but if for each schema, S_i, there is an indexing predicate, (LOCAT SCH S_i), it is possible to find an S_i that encompasses all the subschemas aroused by subsequent sentences. In the present story, we have (LOCAT SCH FLIGHTSYSTEM) to arouse a rule

(FLIGHTSYSTEM (X.Y) (FLIGHTSYSTEM FOC W1 EVT U))
< (MEMPR (FOC W) Y)(PRONREF W W1)
   (RELATE W1 FLIGHTSYSTEM)
   (MEMPR (EVT U) Y)

This rule takes the LOCAT predicate computed above as its first argument. If the FOCus W of the LOCAT predicate is a pronoun, PRONREF finds its reference; if not, it returns the input argument as the binding for W1. The next requirement is that the focus argument be related to a Flightsystem [i.e., (RELATE ROCKET FLIGHTSYSTEM)]. The event argument of the LOCAT relation is then extracted and the result is to form the Flightsystem element of a Flight, that is, (FLIGHTSYSTEM FOC ROCKET EVT (STAND AE ROCKET...)).

In a similar fashion the next sentence, actually the SSR,

(RISE AE IT AC (ROAR...)...)

uses the assertion

(RISE SCH ASCEND)

to arouse the rule

(ASCEND (X.Y) (ASCEND FOC Y1 EVT (X.Y)))
< (RELATE X RISE)(FOCUS Y (X1.R))
(PRONREF X1 Y1)

Any SSR whose verb is related to ASCEND will have a relation: (RISE SCH ASCEND), (CLIMB SCH ASCEND), and so on. The ASCEND rule tests that the verb is related to "rise," then extracts the main argument and finds its reference if it is a pronoun. It forms an ASCEND predicate, for example:

(ASCEND FOC ROCKET EVT (RISE AE ROCKET...))

Using the index (ASCEND SCH ASCENT), the ASCENT rule is selected.

(ASCENT (ASCEND.Y)(ASCENT.Y))
< (MEMPR (FOC Y1) Y)
(OLDFOC Z)(RELATE Y1 Z)

This rule extracts the focal argument and relates it to the context, OLD-FOCus, to ensure that the ascent predicate is connected to the previous context. The result of this rule is to change from the ASCEND predicate, which may participate in many schemas, to the ASCENT relation, which is part of the Flight. In a larger system with several schemas, there might also be additional subschemas, ASCENT1, ASCENT2, and so on. These might be elements of such schemas as Mountain-Climb, Orbit-Launch, and so on.

In a similar fashion the remaining two sentences select and instantiate CRUISE and DESCENT relations. When all the sentences have instantiated subschemas, the subschemas arouse a candidate schema that attempts to organize all of them into a schema. For example, the ASCENT subschema has the following index relation:

(ASCENT SCH FLIGHT)

and Flight has

> (FLIGHT SUBSCHEM (FLIGHTSYSTEM ASCENT CRUISE DESCENT))

A procedure, SCHEMPARS, extracts in order any of the SUBSCHEM arguments that have been found and constructs

> (FLIGHT SETT (FLIGHTSYSTEM FOC... EVT...)
> SEQ (ASCENT FOC... EVT...)
> SEQ (CRUISE FOC... EVT...)
> SEQ (DESCENT FOC...EVT...))

The SSRs from the sentences selected subschema rules which tested the sentence arguments, resolved pronouns, and tested for connectivity with the context. When all the sentences in the story were accounted for by subschemas, the process was repeated at the next level to arouse a schema which extracted any of its elements that had been found and formed a story tree as shown above.

8.4.1 Bottom-Up Program Description

The bottom-up analysis is accomplished by a series of procedures, CLAUSGRP, UNARY, BINARY, EVTPR, and SCHEMPARS. Definitions for these are shown in Figure 8.2.

```
================================================================
        (DEFPROP CLAUSGRP
        (((CLAUSGRP NIL T W) < (SCHEMPARS T W))
         ((CLAUSGRP ((PARAGRAPH) . Y) T T1) < (UNIQA* (SCHCNTX NIL))
                                              (CLAUSGRP Y T T1))
         ((CLAUSGRP (X . Y) T T3)
          <
          (SENTENCE X V)
          (UNARY V V1)
          (BINARY V1 T T1)
          (CLAUSGRP Y T1 T3)))
        AXIOMS)

        (DEFPROP UNARY
        (((UNARY (BE . Y) (PREPAR FOC X1 EVT ((BE . Y))))
          <
          (MEMPR (ST W) Y)
          (RELATE W READY)
          (UNIQA* (SCHCNTX PREPAR))
          (FOCUS Y (X . R))
```

Figure 8.2 Bottom-up control procedures.

Sec. 8.4 Bottom-Up Control of Schema Instantiation

```
      (PRONREF X X1))
    ((UNARY (BE . Y) (ASCENT FOC X1 EVT ((BE . Y))))
     <
     (MEMPR (ST W) Y)
     (RELATE W HEIGHT)
     (FOCUS Y (X . R))
     (PRONREF X X1))
    ((UNARY (X . Y) (PREPAR FOC W EVT ((X . Y))))
     <
     (SCHCNTX PREPAR)
     (FOCUS Y (W . W1))
     (OLDFOC Z)
     (UNLESS (RELATE W Z)))
    ((UNARY (X . Y) V)
     <
     (UNIQA* (SCHCNTX NIL))
     (X SCH S1)
     (S1 (X . Y) (W . W1))
     (W SCH S2)
     (S2 (W . W1) V)))
   AXIOMS)

 (DEFPROP BINARY
   (((BINARY V (T . W) (V1 . W)) < (EVTPR T V V1))
    ((BINARY (X . Y) T ((X . Y) . T)) < (MEMPR (FOC W) Y)
                                        (ONEA* (OLDFOC W))))
   AXIOMS)

 (DEFPROP EVTPR
   (((EVTPR (X . X1) (X . X2) (X EVT W . Y))
     <
     (DEPAIR (EVT U) X1 Y)
     (MEMPR (EVT V) X2)
     (APPEND U V W))
    ((EVTPR (PREPAR . X1) (X . X2) (X SETT (PREPAR . X1) . X2)))
    ((EVTPR (X . X1) (DESCRIP . X2) (X EVT W . Y))
     <
     (DEPAIR (EVT U) X1 Y)
     (MEMPR (EVT V) X2)
     (APPEND U V W)))
   AXIOMS)

 (DEFPROP SCHEMPARS
   (((SCHEMPARS ((X . X1) . Y) (W SETT X2 . W1))
     <
     (X SCHEMA W)
     (W SUBSCHEM (V . V1))
     (SCHEMEM V ((X . X1) . Y) X2)
     (SCHEMELS V1 ((X . X1) . Y) W1)))
   AXIOMS)
```

Figure 8.2 (*continued*)

```
(DEFPROP SCHEMEM
  ((((SCHEMEM X ((X . X1) . Y) (X . X1)))
   ((SCHEMEM X (U . Y) W) < (SCHEMEM X Y W)))
  AXIOMS)

(DEFPROP SCHEMELS
  ((((SCHEMELS NIL Z NIL))
   ((SCHEMELS (X . Y) Z (SEQ X1 . W)) < (SCHEMEM X Z X1)
                                        (SCHEMELS Y Z W))
   ((SCHEMELS (X . Y) Z W) < (SCHEMELS Y Z W)))
  AXIOMS)

(DEFPROP UNIQA*
  ((((UNIQA* (X . Y)) < (REMREL X) (ASSERT (X . Y))))
  AXIOMS)

(DEFPROP FOCUS
  ((((FOCUS W X1) < (MEMPR (AGT X1) W))
   ((FOCUS W X1) < (MEMPR (INSTR X1) W))
   ((FOCUS W X1) < (MEMPR (AE X1) W)))
  AXIOMS)
```
===

Figure 8.2 (*continued*)

The procedure CLAUSGRP is called with a list of unparsed sentences as its first argument. It uses two stacks as its next two arguments. It first calls the procedure SENTENCE to translate an English sentence into surface semantic relations in the manner described in Chapter 5. The procedure UNARY is then called to instantiate a subschema with that sentence. UNARY, in this formulation, has three special rules to deal with copulas: BE AE EVERYTHING ST READY, BE AE IT ST HIGH, and to recognize the special setting state called PREPARATIONS. The SSR corresponding to "everything was ready" is recognized by a UNARY rule as establishing a PREPARATION, and at this point a global register, SCHCNTX, is assigned the value PREPARATION. Each succeeding sentence will be recognized as a PREPARATION until that register is reset to NIL, which occurs when the focus of a sentence shifts back to the main topic of the discourse. This is the purpose of the (UNLESS(RELATE W Z)) in the third UNARY rule. The fourth UNARY rule is the general one that uses the verb of an SSR to select a schema (X SCH S1), and applies the rule (S1 (X.Y)(W.W1)) to obtain a subschema heading as the list (W.W1). In turn, W selects the next higher level of schema, (W SCH S2), and S2 is applied, (S2 (W.W1) V). The variable, V, as a result, is bound to the resulting subschema instantiation. Two stages of subschema evaluation are provided so that such common schemas as ASCEND, DESCEND, and so on, can participate in various higher-level schemas. In the present example, ASCEND participates in ASCENT, which is part of FLIGHT; it may also be a part of such other high-level schemas as mountain climbing, submarine cruising, and so on.

Sec. 8.4 Bottom-Up Control of Schema Instantiation

BINARY combines the resulting subschema with whatever is on the first stack, its second argument, to produce a new stack, its third argument. To accomplish this, it uses EVTPR to form a new subschema for two identical subschemas, or for the combination of Preparations with a subschema, or for adding a Description to a subschema. Having processed the first sentence on a list of sentences, CLAUSGRP calls itself recursively with the rest of the list. When the entire list of sentences has been used to form a stack of instantiated subschemas—the second argument of CLAUSGRP—and the list of sentences is NIL, SCHEMPARS is called to instantiate a schema from the subschemas and so construct a tree structure that orders the subschemas according to the schema regardless of what their textual order was. SCHEMPARS is easily satisfied; it requires only that the first subschema of the schema be present, and accepts any other elements without failing if none exist. A more thorough definition of SCHEMPARS should compute a score as a percentage of schema elements found. Then when several schemas apply to a text, the one with the highest score could be selected. In this study, only the one schema is available, so this feature is unnecessary.

Individual subschema rules are invoked by the verb head of an SSR. The SSR is then tested for various properties required by the subschema. For example, the subschemas LOCAT and FLIGHTSYSTEM are examined below.

```
(((LOCAT SCH FLIGHTSYSTEM))
((LOCAT (X . Y) (LOCAT FOC X2 EVT ((X . Y))))
<
(RELATE X POSITION)
(MEMPR (LOC W) Y)
(FOCUS Y (X1 . R))
(PRONREF X1 X2) ))
```

In the initial SSR of the text, (STAND AE ROCKET... LOC DESERT...), the index relation (STAND SCH LOCAT) was used to invoke the LOCAT procedure. This procedure first tested that X, bound to STAND, is related to POSITION. The lexical assertion (STAND SUP POSITION) confirmed this relation. The procedure MEMPR was then used to extract from the SSR a LOC arc and its value. MEMPR is very like a member procedure, except that it seeks arc-value pairs instead of single elements. The procedure FOCUS was then applied to the SSR to extract the main argument, Agent, Instrument, or Affected Entity in that order of preference. The procedure PRONREF, explained later, then converts any pronoun to its reference. If these tests are all passed, LOCAT forms the structure (LOCAT FOC ROCKET LOC DESERT EVT ((STAND AE ROCKET... LOC DESERT...))). LOCAT then points to the FLIGHTSYSTEM subschema by the relation, (LOCAT SCH FLIGHTSYSTEM), and FLIGHTSYSTEM imposes further constraints.

```
(((FLIGHTSYSTEM SCHEMA FLIGHT))
 ((FLIGHTSYSTEM (X . Y) (FLIGHTSYSTEM FOC W1 EVT U))
 <
 (MEMPR (FOC W) Y)
 (RELATE W1 FLIGHTSYSTEM)
 (MEMPR (EVT U) Y)))
```

The main constraint imposed is to relate the focal argument of the LOCAT subschema to a Flightsystem. Thus, of the many sentences that invoke the LOCAT subschema, only those concerned with birds, bees, airplanes, rockets, and so on, will be recognized as Flightsystems. The two MEMPR calls in this procedure are for the purpose of extracting the focus and event arguments from the LOCAT schema to rewrite it as a FLIGHTSYSTEM. All the other subschema rules that UNARY calls follow a pattern similar to that of LOCAT and FLIGHTSYSTEM.

The procedure PRONREF is of limited adequacy but serves for the present text.

```
(((PRONREF X Z)
 <
 (PRON X1 (X NBR Y))
 (FEAT X X2)
 (OLDFOC Z)
 (FEAT Z X2)
 (NOUN Z1 (Z NBR Y)))
 ((PRONREF X X)))
```

This procedure of the two arguments, X and Z, first tests to determine if X is a pronoun, by looking it up in the list of PRONoun axioms. It then obtains a feature, X2, such as ANIM, MALE, FEMALE, or POBJ. OLDFOCus returns a value for Z, the last sentence focus. The feature characterizing Z must match that of the pronoun and Z must be a noun with the same NBR—singular or plural—as the pronoun. If all these tests are satisfied, the reference for the pronoun X is the noun Z. If X is not a pronoun, the value of PRONREF is X. Although the procedure OLDFOC backs up to find previous topics, no pretense can be made that this is an adequate general logic for finding pronoun references; it is sufficient only for such simple uses of pronouns as those that occur in the rocket story.

8.5 SCHEMA ANALYSIS

The case studies shown in this chapter have concentrated on the top-down and bottom-up computation of outline organizations of a narrative text. The schemas were clausal logic procedures that examined semantic surface relations to determine how they could be fitted into a tree describing a flight. The top-down schema is the most direct approach; a narrative is a Flight if it is a sequence, Flightsystem, Ascent, Cruise, and Descent. A sequence of sentences is a Flightsystem if the topic is an instance of a Flightsystem and the following sequence of sentences describe Locative, Weight, and Support predicates. The sentence sequence that follows is an ASCENT if first there is a set of PREPARations, then a RISE, followed by a DESCRIPtion. Similar detailed statements describe the Cruise and Descent portions of the schema. The obvious limitation to that direct approach was that it included no capability to generalize to other sequences of sentences describing flights.

The top-down approach can be generalized; a Flight is established if *among* a series of sentences there is one or more that describe a flying object and its states, and there are sentences that describe some of an Ascent, a Cruise, and/or a Descent. This generalization can be accomplished by rules that recurse through the entire set of sentences for each element of the flight schema, and also for each element of each subschema. Such repetitive examination of the list of sentences is a notably inefficient processing strategy, so the alternative approach of bottom-up analysis was described.

The bottom-up flow of control is less direct in that the controlling procedures (i.e., CLAUSGRP, UNARY, and BINARY) must select the subschema and schema rules to be used depending on the sentence that is examined. The mechanism to accomplish this includes indexing predicates [i.e., (RISE SCH ASCEND), (ASCEND SCH ASCENT), (FLIGHT SUBSCHEM (FLIGHTSYSTEM, ASCENT...))] that indicate which procedure should be selected for the task at hand. The resulting procedure needed to scan a list of sentences only once to apply a set of relevant schemas, and it was satisfied if some schema encompassed all the sentences of the text, whether all the elements of the schema were used or not. Since there are highly neutral schemas for arbitrary state or descriptive predicates, every sentence can usually be accounted for.

In the case analysis presented, only a single schema and a single narrative were studied; but for the general use of schemas the problem arises of determining which schema *best* fits the text. A general text analysis system would have hundreds or thousands of schemas, and each sentence might arouse several. A narrative such as the Flight might be encompassed under such schemas as a Missile Attack, Satellite Launch, and so on. Subschemas describing locations, states, descriptions, risings, returnings, and so on, will also prove common to many schemas. It is apparent that each subschema and schema must include a scoring variable that reports the extent to which it was satisfied by a given text. Then the best fitting schema can be selected.

But if best-fitting schemas are desired, parallel evaluation of several schemas must be required rather than the first-path approach described above. Fortunately, the parallel approach is well understood in terms of parsing sentences; the Cocke-Kasami-Younger algorithm described by Pratt [1975] provides a method of applying a grammar to obtain an all-paths analysis of sentences. Evaluation of this approach in comparison to first- or best-path analyses has shown that the cost of computing all paths compares quite favorably with that for a single path (see Slocum [1981]). The all-paths approach generally uses a chart (i.e., a special context) that contains instantiations of all rules that apply to each successive sequence of elements in a sentence. Chapter 10 describes an all-paths chart parser in procedural logic.

The schema procedures in this case study were designed to compute an outline of a narrative in the form of a schema instantiation tree. It should be particularly noticed that the general form of a node in that tree was

[<SCHEMA-NAME> <ARC> <VALUE>,..., <ARC> <VALUE>,
EVT (<SSR>...<SSR>)]

Generally, the arcs were limited to FOCus and LOCation and every schema or subschema recorded its sentences as values of the EVenT arc. But the nodes in the tree can just as well record summaries of the sentences they encompass, in any form that is desired, and the literal recording of the sentence can be omitted. Thus a complex sentence such as "Two red flares rose as a signal to fire the rocket" might instantiate a SIGNAL schema as follows.

(SIGNAL FOC (FLARE QU TWO COLOR RED)
PURPOSE (FIRE AE ROCKET))

In the top-down schema that was first described, the schema instantiations revised the state descriptions of a rocket standing in the desert, weighing five tons, carrying eight tons of fuel, into predications on the rocket by changing the English verbs into the form of such arcs as POSITION, WEIGHT, and CONTAIN. It is to be emphasized that the instantiation of schema descriptions provides the opportunity for completely arbitrary transformations of the text into whatever form of knowledge structure is desired.

Finally, although the schemas of this chapter depend on translating sentences into SSRs, no such complete parsing of sentences is actually required to extract information from a text. Such classic key word scanning systems as Eliza by Weizenbaum [1966] and Parry by Colby [1973] as well as the more recent Yale work for scanning newspaper articles to extract script bindings by deJong [1979] can also be accomplished using the control flows illustrated.

8.6 EXERCISES

1. The grammar for translating the rocket story into SSRs, the top-down schema definition, and its instantiation in the story are shown in Appendix B. Load the grammar and the schema and test it on some of the examples given in the text. When you trace the grammar operation, notice the frequency with which the pro-

cedural relation FEAT is called. It is a fairly difficult task to rewrite the grammar and the lexicon using the techniques described in Chapter 5 to incorporate features into the lexical entries and to examine them in the grammar rules. You might wish to attempt this exercise for a subset of the lexicon and grammar.

2. If you have understood the ideas in the top-down schema, you might wish to experiment with schemas that provide differing forms of outline structure to encompass the story. For example, you could include explicit time markings on each element of the Flight schema, or you could compute a summary statement about the events in each element.

9

QUESTIONING AND SUMMARIZING THE TEXT

9.1 BACKGROUND OF RESEARCH

Despite considerable research activity in the translation of natural-language questions to data base query languages, the last decade saw little published work on questioning natural-language texts. The Yale conceptual dependency structure was used by Cullingford [1979] and others to develop representations for newspaper stories, and Lehnert [1978] presented a detailed exploration of methods for questioning instantiated scripts. Wilensky [1978] studied the use of plans for understanding text, and deJong [1979] reported on a system for scanning newspaper stories to instantiate brief scripts. Apart from the Yale work, Grishman and Hirshman [1978] at New York University reported an approach to English questioning of medical records. This approach involved analysis of the medical records with the NYU linguistic string analyzer that applied a grammar with string transformations to translate the natural text medical records into a data base form. English questions were then analyzed in a similar fashion, translated to predicate logic statements, and proved (or disproved) from the data base.

More relevant to this chapter is the recent exploration of PROLOG text grammars by Silva et al. [1979]. In this study, sentences are translated into one or more event records, depending on how many events the sentence describes. An event record is described as a template that has several attributes whose values may be present in the event description provided by a sentence. The authors describe the use of templates as a "slot and filler" approach, which we can understand as similar in structure to those used in conceptual dependency and surface case relations, but much less restricted in choice of arc or slot labels. Higher-level templates are planned to integrate multiple sentences into discourse structures to reflect the meaning of the text as a whole. The authors concluded that PROLOG offers a "solid framework" for the continued development of language understanding modules. Although this PROLOG approach has not yet studied question-answering, it is apparent that the method will depend on translating questions into the same data base form of instantiated templates and matching with the data base. Other lines of research concerning questioning PROLOG data bases including those mentioned in Chapter 7, and recent work by Robinson and Sibert [1980] and Warren and Pereira [1982], describe methods for translating sentences into predicate logic queries and questioning structured data collections.

In 1980 a procedural logic question-answering system was developed at the University of Texas at Austin to test the effectiveness and value of narrative schema instantiation. This system integrates the sentence translation, schema instantiation, and English generation techniques described in earlier chapters, and introduces a question answering and summarizing logic. It has been developed and explored with respect to the rocket text and, although aiming toward a general approach, it still requires development and testing for a much larger body of text. Sharon LeVine, who contributed important logical procedures to the system, described it in considerable detail (see LeVine [1980]). In this chapter the procedural logic text questioning and summarizing system is described as a continuation of the case studies of the narrative schema given previously.

9.2 ASSERTING AN INSTANTIATED SCHEMA AS A TEXT DATA BASE

An instantiated Flight schema resulting from the schema parsing methods of Chapter 8 is shown in Appendix B, Section B.3. That structure can be seen as a labeled outline tree that organized the SSRs of the text as events that instantiated each subschema of the Flight. The structure of the instantiated schema tree is shown as a fairly large list of lists. To avoid extensive searching of this structure it is desirable that each English term in the instantiated schema be immediately accessible on demand. This is accomplished by forming an assertion for each term that begins a list.

```
(FLIGHT FOC ROCKET LOC DESERT
    SETT (FLIGHTSYSTEM FOC ROCKET
                EVT ((ROCKET POSIT STAND
                      TYPE V-2
                      LOC (DESERT...))
                    (ROCKET WEIGHT (TON...))
                        ...))
```

```
    SEQ (ASCENT SETT (PREPARATIONS EVT ((READY...)...))
        EVT ((RISE AE ROCKET...)...)
        SEQ (CRUISE EVT ((TRACK INSTR RADAR...)...)
            SEQ (DESCENT EVT ((PLUNGE...)...)]
```

For the example above, (computed by the top-down schema of Chapter 8), (ASSERT (Flight...)) asserts the entire list; (ASSERT (Flightsystem...)) asserts its sublist; each Rocket event is asserted as a list of the translated SSR; and each nonsyntactic term following an arc (i.e. ROCKET, DESERT, STAND, V-2, TON, etc.) forms an assertion. At first glance this appears to multiply vastly the storage requirements for representing the tree, but LISP comes to our aid by representing the entire list only once; each assertion is simply a pointer to some part of that list. For further convenience, a backlink, BK*, to the next higher list is added to each assertion. Instances of the form are (FLIGHTSYSTEM BK* FLIGHT) and (FLIGHT BK* *TOP*), where *TOP* is a distinguished atom terminating the series. Additional SQ arcs are added to each SSR assertion to preserve explicitly the sequence relations of SSRs in the instantiated schema. Although the assertional structure could be formed by a logic procedure, the mapping functions of LISP accomplish it more quickly and were therefore used in a function called INPREDS.

The result of forming the assertional structure is that each element of the instantiated schema was asserted as a factual proposition (i.e., a conclusion without premises) and each may be directly accessed. For example, the query (FLIGHT.X) results in X being bound to the rest of the instantiated schema structure; (ROCKET.X) returns one of the many assertions starting with ROCKET, and backs up to give each succeeding one as needed. (RISE.W) followed by (MATCHPR (AE W1 AC W2) W W) returns the values for the AE and AC arguments if present in W. The backlinks approximate inverse arcs, allowing access to the structure in both downward and upward directions.

The simplest approach to retrieval from this structure is thus merely the assertion of a word dotted to a variable. For example,

$$\text{(RISE.X)}$$

returns

$$\text{(RISE AE (FLARE NBR PL QU TWO COLOR RED)...)}$$

and, if asked for the next answer, gives

$$\text{(RISE AE (ROCKET...) AC (ROAR...) RATE (SLOWLY...))}$$

Finer constraints are achieved by the use of MATCHPR and MEMPR procedures, and fuzzy matches through synonyms, hyponyms, and so on, are achieved by various procedures that consult a taxonomy for the words of the text. Details of retrieving answers are developed in a later section of the chapter.

9.3 ANALYSIS OF ENGLISH QUESTIONS

Natural-language questions can be analyzed into a *query* and an *identifier*. In "Where was the flight?" the query is "where" and the identifier is "the flight." The verb "was" contains only tense information and adds nothing more to the identifier. If the question were "Was the flight in a desert?," the fronting of the verb "was" signals that the statement is a Yes/No question. The query of this question is the unspoken "Is it true that . . ." and the identifier is "the flight was in a desert." An equivalent question "From where did the flight originate?" offers the query "from where" and the identifier "the flight did originate."

The English question analysis system is restricted to Yes/No forms and to questions that begin with one of the question words "Who," "What," "Where," "When," "How," and "Why." These constraints hardly inconvenience a user, but remarkably simplify the grammar that is required for analysis; without them, almost every English statement would have to be considered as a possible question: for example, In New Mexico there was a desert from which what kind of vehicle rose? In contrast, "What kind of vehicle rose from a New Mexico desert?" is relatively easy to analyze. Thus in the questioning mode, if the input query does not begin with a question word, it must be a YES/NO question.

Computational analysis occurs in several stages. First the question is translated to an SSR with the grammar of Appendix B., Section B.1. The special arc, QOBJ, is used to distinguish the query portion, and the grammar is augmented with a QTERM rule to identify queries. Transformations that remove BE verbs, resolve pronouns, and solve ellipses are then applied to produce an explicit identifier and query. The focus of the question is then recorded in a global context to serve as a partial basis for resolving anaphora in future questions, and the retrieval of an answer is attempted. For our simplest question, "Where was the flight?," the following SSR was produced.

(BE QOBJ LOC TNS PAST AE (FLIGHT NBR SING DET THE))

The procedure QS accomplished the analysis above by first extracting a question term with QTERM, and then the identifier with a rule, Q1, that accepts a verb phrase, or an auxiliary verb followed by a verb phrase or a sentence. Thus the sublanguage of questions for this system is

QUESTION := QTERM + (AUX) + VP v S

Parentheses show optionality, and "v" is the symbol for "or." This definition, except for its insistence on an introductory question word, includes all of English, in that a VP can include sentences as modifiers, and a sentence can be almost anything. But the grammar actually available to the system is limited to statements and questions about the V-2 rocket flight.

After the question has been translated into an SSR, the question-transforming procedure QTF is called.

(QTF (BE QOBJ LOC ... AE (FLIGHT ...)) V W)

The procedure returns

(QTF (BE QOBJ LOC ... AE (FLIGHT ...))) (FLIGHT) LOC)
V := (FLIGHT)   W := LOC

QTF extracted the identifier (FLIGHT) and the query LOC. Notice that (BE TNS PAST) and NBR SING DET THE were deleted from the original SSR computed by QS. The retrieval procedure ASK can now be called:

(ASK (FLIGHT) LOC W)

This follows the pattern outlined earlier, of retrieving (FLIGHT.X) and testing X with (MEMPR (LOC W) X) to return

(ASK (FLIGHT) LOC (IN A NEWMEXICO DESERT))

Actually, ASK does not return English; instead, the W argument appears as

(DESERT BK* G00312 NBR SING DET A LOC NEWMEXICO PREP IN)

This is translated back to the English by a procedure called GEN that uses the same grammar as was used for parsing. This procedure will be discussed later.

The top-level questioning function is QUERY, which accepts the English question and returns an answer.

(QUERY (WHERE WAS THE FLIGHT)
(IN A NEWMEXICO DESERT))

As a result of this query, the global context variables CTXID and CTXLOC are bound, respectively, to FLIGHT and DESERT. Then if the next question

Sec. 9.3 Analysis of English Questions

were "When?" or "When did it happen?" the context variable would resolve the anaphora. We have seen such context variables in use before in commanding the robot hand and in answering data base queries.

Generally, rules for extracting the query map simple question words into semantic relational arcs as follows:

Who   → Agent
What → AE or INSTR
Where → LOC
When → TIME
Why   → PUrpose, CAuse
How   → INSTR or MANNER

When an attribute is questioned in such forms as "how many," "how long," "what color," "what color of flame," and so on, the query expression becomes more complicated. These examples are parsed into the following queries.

How many tons did... → (QU (TON NBR PL))
How long was it → LNGTH
What color was it → COLOR
What color of flame → (COLOR (FLAME))

For such complex queries as "what color of flame," and "how much fuel," the mapping is generally to an (ARC.QUALIFIER), as in (COLOR(FLAME)) or (QU(FUEL)). This notation forms a signal to the retrieval system to seek the qualifier in the candidate answer and then discover if it is modified by the arc. If that qualifier is present and so modified, the value following the arc is the answer. In the example "What color of flame did the rocket trail?" the identifier is (TRAIL INSTR ROCKET) and the query is (COLOR (FLAME)). An (abbreviated) answer candidate is

(TRAIL INSTR ROCKET AE (FLAME COLOR YELLOW))

First, the identifier is successfully matched, then a search is made for the qualifier of the query, to discover (FLAME COLOR YELLOW...), and finally this is examined to discover if it has a value for the arc COLOR. That value YELLOW is the answer.

LeVine [1980, p.14] presented a summary statement of question analysis which is revised as Figure 9.1.

```
===========================================================
         QUERY-FORM ARCNAMES AND ANSWER PROCESS
         ─────────────────────────────────────────────

         WHY     PURPOSE: Return value of PU or CAUSE arc or previous
                          act of schema.

         HOW     INSTRument or MANNer: Return value of one of these.

         WHEN    TIME: Return preceding or following event introduced
                       by appropriate adverb, before or after.

         WHERE   LOCation: Return value of LOC arc.

         WHO     AGenT: Return value of AGT arc.

         WHAT    AE or INSTR: Return value of Affected Entity or
                 INSTR arc.

         ATTRIBUTE       ARCNAME or (ARCNAME.QUALIFIER): Return value
                         associated with ARCNAME. If QUALIFIER is
                         present treat it as a further identification
                         constraint and return the value of its ARCNAME.
                         ARCNAMES are usually such terms as LNGTH, SIZE,
                         COLOR, etc.

         HOW MANY        (QUantity.QUALIFIER) value of QU arc on QUAL.

         HOW MUCH        (MSR.QUALIFIER) value of MeaSuRe arc on QUAL.

         YES/NO          TRUTH: Return "Yes" with matching assertion
                         from text if answer if found; else return "No"
                         with the assertion that matched the identifier
                         and failed the query. A possible third category
                         is "unknown."
===========================================================
```

Figure 9.1 Analysis of query terms.

Lehnert, studying stories primarily involving motivated human actions, was very much concerned with understanding why, for example, John did not eat a burned hamburger, or with inferring that an unmentioned waitress may have served it. She is also concerned to ask what might have happened *if* such and such. This form of question goes beyond the goals of the more literally oriented text questioning with which this system is concerned. We might want to include knowledge beyond the text to answer "What would have happened if the rocket engine exploded?" But this tests common sense rather than immediate understanding of the text. More relevant is a question that the system still cannot answer: "Why were scientists present?" Our world knowledge suggests that scientists who study rockets are much concerned to observe them in action, but the introduction of many such assertions may lead to the dilemma of producing rational but wrong explanations as often as correct ones.

More important to understanding questions about text is the logic suggested by Kaplan [1979] and discussed in Chapter 7. Essentially, this logic provides that when a question fails to find an answer, a second attempt should be made to derive the most meaningful information that answers one of the questions implied by the identifier. LeVine took the first step in her treatment of Yes/No questions summarized in Figure 9.1, but more is needed. If we were to ask of this text, "Why did the admiral fire the scientist?", it would be most desirable to reply to the effect, "No admiral is known and no scientist is known to have been fired." Kaplan shows that procedures for this level of understanding are not excessively difficult or costly, and as text questioning machines develop, such procedures should be included.

9.4 RETRIEVING ANSWERS WITH FUZZY MATCHING

When a set of sentences is translated into surface semantic relations, the nouns and verbs are reduced to root forms and such variations as active and passive voice and declarative or interrogative mood result in SSR structures identical except for syntactic signals. Yet many sentences that answer the same question may use different words and phrasing to do so. A hierarchical taxonomy of vocabulary items can reduce this variation, as can the translation of words into a system of primitive actions and nominal categories such as that developed by Schank. A hierarchical taxonomy is commonly available in machine-readable English dictionaries, but unfortunately, such dictionaries require considerable processing to make the taxonomy accessible to a language computing system (see Amsler [1981]). Brachman [1979] and Fahlman [1979] have explored representation and retrieval properties of verbal concept taxonomies. In the quite small experiments in text question-answering, of which this is one, ad hoc taxonomies are developed as needed to relate questions and answers. For example, such assertions as the following are used in this system:

>   (ROCKET SUP FLIGHTSYSTEM)
>   (FLIGHTSYSTEM SUP VEHICLE)
>   (SCIENTIST SUP HUMAN)
>   (RISE SUP GO)
>   (GO SUP MOVE)
>   (WITHDRAW SUP GO)
>   (YELLOW SUP COLOR)
>   (AFTER SUP TIME)

These are further supported by the rules for inverse and transitivity relations;

(SUP X Y) < (X SUP Y)
(SUP X Y) < (Y INST X)
(SUP X Z) < (SUP X Y)(SUP Y Z)

where SUPerset and INSTance are inverse concept inclusion relations.

This taxonomy, however incomplete, is of great utility in answering such questions as "Where did the people go?" from such sentences as "Scientists withdrew behind earth mounds." If an appropriate assertion were included for every verb in the text in the form [<VERB-NAME> SUP <PRIMITIVE>], for example,

(GO SUP PTRANS)
(WITHDRAW SUP PTRANS)
(RISE SUP PTRANS)
(SEE SUP MTRANS) ... etc.

then the effect of translating the verbs into Schankian primitives would be achieved. The use of a complete lexical taxonomy may prove superior to such an approach.

As in the robot and the document-questioning systems, there is a formal language retrieval system underlying the natural-language translator. The procedures ASK, ASKPR, and ANSWER are the basis of this system. ASK has the form

[ASK <IDENTIFIER> <ARC> <RESULT>]

The question "What color was the rocket?" appears as

(ASK (ROCKET) COLOR X)

and its answer as

(ASK (ROCKET) COLOR (BLACK *AND (YELLOW)))

The essential definition of ASK is as follows:

((ASK (S . V) R T)
<
(CAND (S . V) (U1 . U2))
(ASKPR V U2)
(ANS (U1 . U2) R T))

The first argument of ASK is an identifier in the form of a list: for example, (RISE AE (ROCKET COLOR BLACK)) or (ROCKET). The second argument is the arcname to be queried, although as was discussed above, this may be a list of an arcname and a qualifier such as (QU (FUEL MSR TON)). To answer the question, we might simply take the identifier, say (ROCKET.V), and use it as a query. But this would limit the answer candidates to only those beginning with the word "rocket." The procedure CAND is designed to provide a greater degree of generality.

$$(CAND\ (X.Y)\ (X.W)) < (X.W)$$
$$(CAND\ (X.Y)\ (U.W)) < (SUP\ X\ U)\ (U.W)$$

In the first case of CAND, the head of the identifier is used to retrieve all assertions starting with that word. In the second case, the hierarchical taxonomy is accessed by using the SUP rule defined earlier. In both cases the relational pairs associated with the head of the identifier SSR are temporarily ignored. It is the task of ASKPR to determine that the pairs of the identifier are satisfied by the candidate.

ASKPR is a two argument procedure of the form

[ASKPR <LIST-OF-PAIRS> <CANDIDATE>]

and originally it was defined simply as a recursion of MEMPR through the list. To obtain generality, a new procedure, GMEMPR, was defined that is less strict than MEMPR. ASKPR is defined as

$$(ASKPR\ (U\ V.W)\ T) < (GMEMPR\ (U\ X)\ T)$$
$$(RELATE\ V\ X)\ (ASKPR\ W\ T)$$

Notice that GMEMPR queries the arc, U, given by the identifier and accepts any value, X, that it may have in the candidate, T. GMEMPR is not limited only to the candidate given; it may follow a backlink to a higher-level verb of which the candidate is an argument and seek a deleted subject, and it is specially designed to understand the *AND arc, which is used to encode conjunctions (see Chapter 5). The procedure RELATE uses the taxonomy to compare X from the candidate with V from the identifier. RELATE is defined as

$$(RELATE\ X\ Y) < (SUP\ X\ Y)$$

Actually it spreads a wider net than even this loose definition; it accounts also for equality, for comparison of an atom and a list, a pronoun and its reference, and for parts and their wholes.

In using the three functions CAND, GMEMPR, and RELATE, ASK is designed to obtain controlled fuzzy matches between the identifier of a question and its possible candidate answers. A year of experience with the system has not yet shown that the fuzziness introduces error, but it is to be expected that as the size of the data base increases, such errors will occur.

When a candidate has been found to satisfy the identifier of a question, the procedure ANSWER uses it as a basis for extracting an answer from a specified arc, or for seeking an ancestor, predecessor, or successor in the schema tree as an answer.

[ANSWER <CANDIDATE> <CONSTRAINT> <RESULT>]

ANSWER is defined very much like a case selector; depending on the constraint, specialized procedures such as PURPOSE for a PU arc, LOCUS for a LOC arc, TIME for a TIME arc, and so on, are used first to determine if the arc is directly satisfied by the candidate; or if not, to discover if one of the indirect ways of establishing its value can succeed. The nature of these special—and fuzzy—procedures will become apparent in the examples given below.

The description of the formal language query system shows that questions are expected to range from the simple, unusual case of being answered by a direct match with an identical SSR in the instantiated schema, to a more usual indirect match that accounts for related vocabulary use and disparate structure of expression. The essential feature of text questioning is fuzzy matching, even after the text and question have been reduced to canonical structures. This fuzzy aspect of language is also apparent in work by Yale researchers, where despite the use of primitives, many rules and procedures must be devoted to alternative structures and vocabulary in question and answer.

9.5 QUESTIONS AND ANSWERS

The question-answering logic for the system was developed in two phases; first, 15 questions were written to query the story, then LeVine augmented the logic provided for those questions with additional grammar and procedures to answer YES/NO questions, to explore WHY and WHEN questions, and generally to expand the system capabilities. In this section some example questions and answers will be shown with comments explaining noteworthy characteristics of the answering logic. Later sections explain the generation of English answers and the logic of constructing summaries.

The simplest questions merely query attributes of sentences given by the text.

Sec. 9.5 Questions and Answers

```
(QUERY(WHERE WAS THE FLIGHT) (IN A NEWMEXICO DESERT))
(QUERY(WHAT COLOR WAS THE ROCKET) (BLACK AND YELLOW))
(QUERY(HOW LONG WAS IT) (FORTY-SIX FEET LONG))
(QUERY (HOW MUCH DID IT WEIGH) (FIVE TONS))
(QUERY (HOW MUCH FUEL DID IT CARRY)
        (EIGHT TONS OF ALCOHOL AND LIQUID OXYGEN))
(QUERY (WHAT WAS THE PURPOSE OF THE FLARES)
        (AS A SIGNAL TO FIRE THE ROCKET))
(QUERY (HOW DID THE ROCKET RISE)
        (SLOWLY THEN FASTER AND FASTER) )
(QUERY (WHAT KIND OF VEHICLE WAS FLOWN) (V-2))
(QUERY (WHERE WAS THE PILOT)
        (FORTY MILES FROM THE STARTING POINT))
(QUERY (WHAT COLOR FLAME TRAILED THE ROCKET)
        (YELLOW) )
(QUERY (WHO SAW IT) (THE PILOT OF A WATCHING PLANE))
```

The only indirection in the questions above are the use of "it" and the phrase "kind of vehicle", which required an answer qualifier, (TYPE(VEHICLE)).

The following group of examples explore questions that require examining contextual groups of sentences to obtain answers.

```
(QUERY (WHY DID RADAR TRACK THE ROCKET)
        (BECAUSE IT WAS TOO HIGH TO BE SEEN) )
(QUERY (WHY WERE SCIENTISTS PRESENT)
        (BECAUSE THE ASCENT WAS BEGINNING) )
```

The first query was answered by the pair of sentences "Soon it was too high to be seen. Radar tracked it to an altitude of...." The first sentence ended the ASCENT phase of the schema and the second started the CRUISE. Since the two subschemas are taken as causally related, the ending of the first is a reason for the second. The second question obtained its answer by taking a step upward in the schema. The sentence about scientists and generals was schematized as a SETTING event of the ASCENT portion of the FLIGHT; since no purpose arc was given in the sentence, the fact that it was an ASCENT was used as an answer. Since the Rocket story is a simple narrative, lacking description of motivated human actions, the purposive answer logic described by Lehnert [1977,1978] has little scope in this exploration.

An answer to a WHEN question is obtained by finding a preceding or following arc.

```
(QUERY (WHEN DID THE GENERALS HIDE)
        (BEFORE THE GIANT ROCKET ROSE WITH A GREAT
        ROAR AND BURST OF FLAME) )
(QUERY (WHEN DID RADAR TRACK THE ROCKET)
        (AFTER ROCKET WAS TOO HIGH TO BE SEEN) )
```

The choice of a following act in the first query was dictated by the fact that the preceding sentences described states in a setting part of the schema. The second query followed the default of seeking the last event. WHEN questions are also answered by sentences introduced by temporal phrases.

Two YES/NO questions are shown below.

```
(QUERY (WERE THE FLARES YELLOW)
       (NO TWO RED FLARES ROSE AS A SIGNAL TO FIRE
        THE ROCKET) )
(QUERY (DID THE ROCKET RISE SLOWLY)
       (YES WITH A GREAT ROAR AND BURST OF FLAME
        THE GIANT ROCKET ROSE SLOWLY THEN FASTER
        AND FASTER) )
```

For this type of question each candidate answer is saved in a context register. If no answer succeeds, a "NO" is prefixed to the the last candidate as an answer; otherwise, a "YES" is prefixed to the complete sentence that satisfied the query.

The question-answering logic involves a considerable degree of complexity, and few generalizations are warranted from the exploration of a single story with a few dozen questions. We have noted that many questions that appear superficially similar to ones that obtain answers actually entail significant differences in structure when carefully studied. The process of answering questions requires many steps of parsing, transformation, context checking and saving, candidate examination, answer validation, and the generation of English responses. Although when debugged, these processes run off in 10 to 20 seconds of (DEC 20) processing time, the debugging process is quite tedious with many paths to be checked for possible errors. The generalizations inherent in the procedures CANDS, GMEMPR, and RELATE seem to be wellfounded, and the approach described in organizing the analysis and answering processes has no obvious weaknesses, but the degree of specialization of the procedures used in the ANSWER logic is at least suspicious. It is clear that a great deal of research on answering questions from text is still required before the understanding of the process settles into simple structure.

9.6 GENERATING ENGLISH ANSWERS

In Chapter 5 it was noted that the rules that translated sentences into SSRs were symmetric and that a sentence rule given a string would return a translation, or given an SSR translation would return a corresponding English string. The short sentence "Empty it weighed five tons" will be used as an example of this.

```
*(SS (EMPTY IT WEIGHED FIVE TONS) X)
((SS (EMPTY IT WEIGHED FIVE TONS)
     (WEIGH AE (IT ST (EMPTY) NBR SING) TNS PAST
      MSR (TON QU (FIVE) NBR PL))))
```

Sec. 9.6   Generating English Answers

```
ANOTHER? *N

(SS X (WEIGH AE (IT ST (EMPTY) NBR SING) TNS PAST
      MSR (TON QU (FIVE) NBR PL)))
((SS (EMPTY IT WEIGHED FIVE TONS)
      (WEIGH AE (IT ST (EMPTY) NBR SING) TNS PAST
          MSR (TON QU (FIVE) NBR PL))))

ANOTHER? *N
```

In the first example the sentence rule SS was called with the sentence as a first argument and an unbound variable, X, as a second. It returned the translation and asked if another interpretation was desired. Then SS was called again, this time with the variable X in place of the sentence, and the SSR that it had just obtained given as the second argument. From the SSR it computed the sentence from which the SSR had been derived.

The symmetry of the grammar can be maintained provided that the SSR contains signals representing the tense, number, voice, and mood of the sentence, and provided that the grammar rules use only procedures that have inverses. This symmetry is put to excellent use in generating answers to questions, in that the same grammar that was used to translate sentences and questions into SSR forms produces the English expression of the answer. The symmetry inheres not only in the sentence level rules but in each phrase rule as well, so the short answers produced for the example questions shown above were computed from the one grammar that the system uses for both purposes.

It was noted both that the schematized text changed some of the structures that the grammar translated, and that when the text was asserted, additional backlink and sequence arcs were added to the SSRs. Further, the question-answering process often substituted a referent for a pronoun in the text and sometimes introduced additional phrases such as "Before," "After," and so on. After all this, a procedure called BREV was frequently used to construct a briefer version of a phrase or sentence as an answer. All these changes must be accommodated before the grammar can recognize a structure as one corresponding to what its rules produce.

The procedure GEN uses deletion processes to recognize and accommodate the changes.

```
((GEN (X . Y) (X . V)) < (PHRASE X) (GEN Y V))
((GEN (P . X) Y)
    <
    (DELPAIR (SQ U) X X1)
    (DELPAIR (TPC U1) X1 X2)
    (DELALPR BK* X2 X3)
    (SGEN (P . X3) Y))
((GEN X Y) < (ATOM* X) (SGEN X Y)))
```

The first GEN rule examines the structure for an introductory string of English words using PHRASE. This string is appended as a list to the answer, so PHRASE merely tests that list as containing a string of English. The main GEN rule calls the logic procedures DELPAIR and DELALPR to delete sequence, topic, and backlink (i.e., BK* arcs), then calls SGEN to apply the grammar to the resulting cleaned-up SSR. The two deletion procedures delete values from a list given as an argument and return a new list without those values. The third GEN rule is the special case of generating a single word, which is used frequently in short answers.

SGEN is a case selector procedure that tests its first argument to determine what grammar rule to apply.

```
((SGEN (X . Y) S) < (VV X1 (X . X2)) (SS S (X . Y)))
((SGEN (X . Y) S) < (VBE X1 (X . X2)) (SS S (X . Y)))
((SGEN X (THE X)) < (NOUN X X1))
((SGEN (X SUP Y) (THE X IS A Y)))
((SGEN (X . Y) S) < (NOUN X X1) (NP S (X . Y) NIL))
((SGEN (X . Y) S) < (MEMPR (PREP U) Y) (PP S (X . Y) NIL))
((SGEN (X . Y) S) < (ADJ X) (ADJP S (X . Y) NIL))
((SGEN (X . Y) S) < (ADJ X) (POSTMOD S (X . Y) NIL))
((SGEN (X . Y) S) < (ADV X) (ADVPH S (X . Y) NIL))
```

The premises of these rules examine the SSR given as the first argument and then apply an appropriate grammar rule specifying as its first argument the string S to be computed as the value of the second argument in the conclusion. If a verb or a copulative verb, VBE, is present, a sentence is generated. If a single noun is to be generated, "The" is prefixed. If the SSR starts with a noun, an NP is constructed; with an adjective an adjectival phrase or a postmodifying adjectival phrase; or if it contains a preposition, a prepositional phrase is built.

The two main procedures, GEN and SGEN, are all that are required to compute well-formed English strings from the much distorted SSRs given as initial inputs. If paragraphs or stories were to be generated, a similar process could be used provided that the logic and style of the paragraph and sentence structures were computed in terms of SSRs. Naturally, the decisions of what to say, when to paragraph, when to use anaphora, and hundreds of stylistic considerations make the generation of content vastly more difficult than its translation into English.

9.7 COMPUTING SUMMARIES

Schema instantiation of the type illustrated in Chapter 8 results in an organization of the SSRs into a tree that corresponds to a labeled outline of the structure of a story. For efficiency in question-answering, the elements of the schema instantiation were asserted to construct an indexed data base. Our

Sec. 9.7 Computing Summaries

first experiences with computing summaries used the data base, and the question-answering system contains procedures BREV, GIST, SUMMARY, and so on, to summarize all or any part of the Flight. Further experience with schematization led to the development of the bottom-up approach for applying schemas to text, to the use of the flattened schema structure shown below, and the realization that summary computation was not only an aspect of question-answering, but a useful goal in itself. As a result, in this section a procedure is presented for computing summaries directly from the instantiated schema. The two minor modifications required to compute summaries from the data base are also noted.

Since the instantiation of a schema results in a tree that organizes text into a labeled outline form, computation of summaries is essentially a process of selecting subtrees and abbreviating them to any extent desired.

The schema instantiated by the bottom-up analysis resulted in the following structure:

```
(FLIGHT SETT (FLIGHTSYSTEM FOC ROCKET LOC DESERT
                           EVT (1,2,3))
        SEQ (ASCENT FOC ROCKET
                    SETT (FOC ROCKET
                          EVT (4 5 6))
                    EVT (7 8 9 10)
             SEQ (CRUISE FOC ROCKET
                         EVT (11 12)
                  SEQ (DESCENT FOC ROCKET
                               EVT (13 14) ]
```

The value of each EVT arc is abbreviated to the sequence numbers (from Figure 8.1) of the sentence SSRs they include. In this instantiation, each of the SSRs is headed by a verb directly as translated from the English (in contrast to the top-down schema which modified the SSRs to form noun-headed structures for state descriptions). The entire structure is a list representing a tree in the form of a head word and a list of pairs. The first element of each pair is an arc name, SETT, SEQ, FOC, or EVT. The second element of a pair (i.e., the value of the arc) is a word or a tree, except in the case of the EVT arc, where convenience dictates a simple list of SSRs. It can be noticed in the diagram above that SSRs involving state descriptions have been classified as Setting events associated with the Flight and with the Ascent. Other descriptive SSRs were ordered in the event structures so as to follow the acts they describe.

An elementary summarizing function can be defined to provide short, medium, or long summaries from an instantiated schema. Its form is

[SUMMARIZE <SCHEMA> <NODE> <LENGTH> <SUMMARY>]

SCHEMA is the name of the instantiated schema to be summarized, NODE is the part to be summarized, LENGTH of LONG, SHORT, or MEDIUM can be specified, and SUMMARY is the summarization resulting from the computation. A more sophisticated procedure would use NODE to find the instantiated schema, as was actually done in the version that used the data base. We can define SUMMARIZE as follows:

```
(SUMMARIZE (X.Y)  W N  V)
  < (TREEMEMB W (X.Y) W1) (SUMUP W1 N V)
```

TREEMEMB seeks for a node, W, in the instantiated schema (X.Y) and returns the matching substructure, W1. SUMUP will do all the work of selecting, abbreviating, and translating into English, to compute the summary, V. (If the instantiated schema has been asserted as a data base, SUMMARIZE requires only three arguments, [SUMMARIZE <NODE> <LNGTH> <SUMMARY>], and instead of TREEMEMB, the procedure (CAND W W1) will return the subtree desired to be summarized.)

```
(TREEMEMB X (X.Y) (X.Y))
(TREEMEMB X (U.Y) W)
  < (MEMPR (R W) Y) (TREEMEMB X W)
(TREEMEMB X (EVT.Y) W)
  < (MEMBER (X.U) Y W)
```

TREEMEMB takes a single word, such as ASCENT or RISE as its first argument; if this word starts the tree given as its second argument, that tree is the value. Otherwise, the procedure recurses down the the tree until either it finds a subtree so labeled, or an event SSR starting with that word. SUMUP examines that result to discover SETTing, SEQuence, and EVT arcs. When an EVT arc has been selected by SUMUP, SUMRIZE is called to apply BREV once, twice or thrice to abbreviate the SSRs and so form a SHORT, MEDIUM, or LONG summary structure. The procedure SUMRIZE and its defining procedures BREV and SGEN are included in Figure 9.2. The procedure SGEN, discussed previously, transforms the results to English sentences. The essential principle of these procedures is to extract one or more nodes from an instantiated schema, find their event arcs, abbreviate the SSRs recorded there, and translate the result to English.

The system can be improved in several ways; a title corresponding to the head of the subschema and its focus value can be extracted, and the focus can be used to substitute as necessary for pronouns in the SSRs. Better approaches to abbreviation can be developed, and the superstructure labels of the instantiated schema can be used more effectively to produce such high-level summaries as "The flight of a rocket that ascended cruised and descended."

The tested procedures for summarizing an instantiated schema are shown in Figure 9.2, except for BREV and SGEN explained earlier. These procedures are somewhat more complicated than the simple example explained above. It can be noticed that the actual schema tree has lists of lists where the example used lists, and SUMUP deletes first a SEQ arc, then any number of

Sec. 9.7 Computing Summaries

SEQuence arcs as it traverses the flattened schema structures. The actual generation is accomplished by SUMRIZE, which uses BREV to abbreviate an SSR, and SGEN to transform it to English. If the summarize procedure is adapted to work from the asserted data base, GEN should be called to clean up the modified SSRs before calling SGEN to translate them to English. A hack for making a title using (THE <NODE>) is apologetically included in the value that SUMMARIZE returns. Some examples of application to the schema of Appendix B, Section B.3, are shown in Figure 9.3. The results shown in the latter figure are the actual structures returned by the procedures of Figure 9.2. The examples are labeled as LONG, SHORT <NODE>, followed by the sentences that were computed. Each example is a truncation of the actual return from calls to SUMMARIZE, showing the key word used and the length parameter.

```
=========================================================
              (((SUMMARIZE (X . Y) X _LNGTH ((THE . X) . V))
                 < (SUMUP (X . Y) _LNGTH V))
              ((SUMMARIZE (X . Y) Z _LNGTH ((THE Z) . V))
                 < (TREEMEMB Z (X . Y) W) (SUMUP W _LNGTH V)))

              (((TREEMEMB X ((X . Y)) (X . Y)))
              ((TREEMEMB X (X . Y) (X . Y)))
              ((TREEMEMB X ((U . Y)) V) < (MEMPR (EVT V) Y)
                                          (MEMBER (X . X1) V))
              ((TREEMEMB X (U . Y) W) < (MEMPR (R . V) Y)
                                         (TREEMEMB X V W)))

              (((SUMUP (X . Y) N W) < (DEPAIR (SETT U) Y Y1)
                                       (SUMUP U SHORT W1)
                                       (SUMUP (X . Y1) N W2)
                                       (APPEND W1 W2 W))
              ((SUMUP (X . Y) N W) < (DEPAIR (SEQ U) Y Y1)
                                      (SUMUP U N W1)
                                      (SUMUP (X . Y1) N W2)
                                      (APPEND W1 W2 W))
              ((SUMUP (X . Y) N W) < (MEMPR (EVT U) Y)
                                      (SUMRIZE U N W))
              ((SUMUP X N W) < (SUMRIZE X N W))
              ((SUMUP X N NIL)))

              ((SUMRIZE NIL N NIL))
              ((SUMRIZE (X . Y) MEDIUM (X1 . W)) < (BREV X V)
                                                    (SGEN V X1)
                                                    (SUMRIZE Y SHORT W))
              ((SUMRIZE (X . Y) LONG (X1 . W)) < (BREV X V)
                                                  (SGEN V X1) (SUMRIZE Y MEDIUM W))
              ((SUMRIZE (X . Y) SHORT (X1)) < (BREV X V)
                                               (SGEN V X1)))
=========================================================
```

Figure 9.2 Procedures for summarizing instantiated schemas.

==
        (FLIGHT LONG
            (THE FLIGHT)
                (A GREAT BLACK AND YELLOW V-2 ROCKET FORTY-SIX FEET
                    LONG STOOD IN A NEWMEXICO DESERT)
                (THE GIANT ROCKET ROSE WITH A GREAT ROAR AND BURST
                    OF FLAME)
                (IT TRAILED SIXTY FEET OF YELLOW FLAME)
                (SOON THE FLAME LOOKED LIKE A YELLOW STAR)
                (RADAR TRACKED IT)
                (THE PILOT OF A WATCHING PLANE SAW IT RETURN)
                (IT PLUNGED INTO EARTH FORTY MILES FROM THE
                    STARTING POINT)

        (FLIGHT SHORT
            (THE FLIGHT)
                (A GREAT BLACK AND YELLOW V-2 ROCKET FORTY-SIX FEET
                    LONG STOOD IN A NEWMEXICO DESERT)
                (THE GIANT ROCKET ROSE WITH A GREAT ROAR AND BURST
                    OF FLAME)
                (RADAR TRACKED IT)
                (IT PLUNGED INTO EARTH FORTY MILES FROM THE STARTING POINT)

    (ASCENT LONG
     (THE ASCENT)
       (THE GIANT ROCKET ROSE WITH A GREAT ROAR AND BURST OF FLAME)
       (IT TRAILED SIXTY FEET OF YELLOW FLAME)
       (SOON THE FLAME LOOKED LIKE A YELLOW STAR))

    (ASCENT SHORT
          (THE ASCENT)
            (THE GIANT ROCKET ROSE WITH A GREAT ROAR AND BURST
                OF FLAME)))

    (CRUISE SHORT (THE CRUISE) (RADAR TRACKED IT))

    (CRUISE LONG
          (THE CRUISE)
            (RADAR TRACKED IT)
            (THE PILOT OF A WATCHING PLANE SAW IT RETURN))

    (DESCENT LONG
          (THE DESCENT)
            (IT PLUNGED INTO EARTH FORTY MILES FROM THE STARTING POINT))

    (RISE LONG
          ((THE RISE)
            (THE GIANT ROCKET ROSE WITH A GREAT ROAR AND BURST OF FLAME)
            (IT TRAILED SIXTY FEET OF YELLOW FLAME)
            (SOON THE FLAME LOOKED LIKE A YELLOW STAR)))
==

Figure 9.3 Examples of computed summaries.

9.8 EXERCISES

1. Using the instantiated schema of Appendix B, Section B.3, write a LISP function to assert each list and sublist as an HCPRVR axiom whose predicate name is the atom head of the list. The function should add BK* links for backlink references to the list that each sublist is embedded in.

2. Write relational procedures for CANDS, ASK, ASKPR, and ANS and experiment with formal-language questioning of the resulting axiom system.

3. Experiment with BREV, GEN, and SGEN to form English answers to your questions.

4. Experiment with the grammar of Section B.1 to translate questions into SR form.

5. The hardest task of all is to develop a more suitable QTF (question transforming procedure) to translate the SSR representing a question into the appropriate identifier + query form. (I am not satisfied with the one we used).

6. Experiment with the instantiated schema given in Section B.3 and the programs for computing summaries, with a view to improving the summarizing procedure.

10

PARSING AND PARAPHRASE

Earlier chapters showed forms of Horn clause grammars for translating single sentences into semantic relations and for assembling sentences into hierarchical discourse structures. Chapter 8 introduced a method for separating control flow of the interpreter from the rules it used to compute a discourse structure; the result was a bottom-up computation that used the SRs of the discourse to select schema rules effectively for organizing a discourse structure. This chapter develops control-flow ideas further in the context of syntactic parsing, and in paraphrase and translation procedures that transform SRs into other SRs which use different words and phrases to express equivalent meanings.

10.1 PARSING PROCEDURES

One of the earliest natural-language parsing systems was the Harvard Predictive Analyzer [Kuno and Oettinger, 1962]. It applied a context-free phrase structure grammar using a top-down flow of control, interpreting each rule such as

$$S \rightarrow NP + VP$$

to predict that if an NP were found, a VP would follow. Example sentences, such as

Time flies like an arrow

Sec. 10.1 Parsing Procedures

were demonstrated to have several purely syntactic interpretations. To compute all interpretations for this sentence from a context-free grammar is still an interesting task that demonstrates effectively the operations for which a parser is designed. By varying properties of the grammar and the parser and measuring the length of time to accomplish the parsings, it is possible to evaluate various strategies for accomplishing the computation.

10.1.1 Top-Down and Bottom-Up Parsing

A top-down analysis can use a context free grammar to transform a language string into a syntactic tree structure, beginning by selecting a rule that describes the root S or SNT for Sentence. Examples of such rules are:

$$\begin{array}{l}
SNT \to NP + VP \\
NP \to NOUN \\
NOUN \to BIRDS \\
NOUN \to FLY \\
SNT \to VP \\
VP \to VERB + ADVERB \\
VP \to VERB + VP \\
VP \to VERB \\
VERB \to FLY \\
SNT \to ADVERB + SNT \\
ADVERB \to AWAY
\end{array}$$

The first element of the right-hand side of the rule selected (e.g., SNT → NP + VP) is used either to find another rule or to match the first element of the string. When a rule contains terminal elements (i.e., elements that are not left-hand sides of rules), either the terminal element matches the current element in the string, or that branch of the parsing tree is abandoned and the algorithm selects another rule that might apply. If the sentence "Fly away" were to be attempted by rule 1 above, SNT → NP + VP would be selected; the NP would be satisfied by the noun sense of FLY, but the VP would fail on AWAY. As a result the first SNT rule would fail and the second would then be selected, SNT → VP, and the VP rule that allowed for a VERB followed by an ADVERB would then succeed. The process of failing and selecting a new alternative is called "backup"—an essential aspect of a top-down parser.

The successful syntactic parse of "Fly away" shows the instantiation of a subtree from the grammar

(SNT(VP(VERB FLY)(ADV AWAY)))

or in tree structure,

```
        SNT
         |
         VP
        /  \
    VERB   ADVERB
      |      |
     FLY    AWAY
```

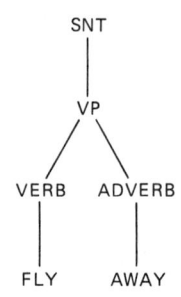

Naturally, such a simple grammar showed nothing about tense, mood, or voice of the sentence; to decide that tense is "present," mood is "imperative," and voice is "active" more complex rules are required.

A bottom-up flow of control can also be used with the same simple grammar. The bottom-up parser selects the first element of the string and seeks to match it to the right-hand side of a rule (e.g., FLY matches NOUN → FLY). It then seeks any rule in which NOUN is the right-hand side (e.g., NP → NOUN). Since there is no rule for which NP is the sole element on the right side, it then selects the next element from the string; AWAY matches ADVERB → AWAY. Since there is no rule with ADVERB as the sole element on the right, the algorithm seeks to find a rule whose right-hand side is → NOUN + ADVERB; none exists. At this point the bottom-up procedure could backup and reassign values to provide VERB → FLY, ADVERB → AWAY, and then discover the match, VP → VERB + ADVERB, and the final rule, SNT → VP, to complete the parse. Generally, though, a bottom-up procedure computes all possible matches for each element and stores them for future reference in a complex list called a chart. In this all-paths, bottom-up procedure, when all constituent matches have been computed and stored on the chart, those constituents labeled SNT that account for all the words in the string are selected as legitimate parses.

A top-down procedure can also use a chart, so that instead of discarding all its computations when it backs up, it will have saved the successfully computed constituents; then, going forward again it may be able to use some of the constituents without recomputing them. In the ambiguous string

Fly, fly away,

the two analyses

(SNT(VP(VERB FLY)(VP(VERB FLY)(ADVERB AWAY))))

and

(SNT(NP(NOUN FLY))(VP(VERB FLY)(ADVERB AWAY)))

10.2 A STRICTLY TOP-DOWN PARSER

Today's procedural logic interpreters provide a strict top-down analysis; given a goal SNT with premises NP and VP, the NP is first evaluated, then the VP. Taking advantage of this flow of control in the interpreter, grammars may be written directly in the form of Horn clauses. A context-free grammar for the two word sentence "birds fly" shows how the rules can be augmented with structure-building operations to produce a parse with no other parser than the procedural logic interpreter itself.

```
(SNT X (SNT V V1)) < (NP X V R)(VP R V1 NIL)
(NP (X.Y) (NP (NOUN X) Y) < (NOUN X)
(VP (X.Y) (VP (VERB X) Y) < (VERB X)
(NOUN BIRDS)
(VERB FLY)
```

Proving the goal (SNT (BIRDS FLY) W) results in the following trace:

```
(SNT (BIRDS FLY) W)
 (SNT (BIRDS FLY)(SNT(NP V)(VP V1)))
  (NP (BIRDS FLY) (NP(NOUN BIRDS)) FLY)
   (NOUN BIRDS)
   *(NOUN BIRDS)
  *(NP (BIRDS FLY) (NP(NOUN BIRDS) FLY)
  (VP (FLY) (VP(VERB FLY)) NIL)
   (VERB FLY)
   *(VERB FLY)
  *(VP (FLY)(VP(VERB FLY)) NIL)
 *(SNT (BIRDS FLY)(SNT(NP(NOUN BIRDS))(VP(VERB FLY))) )
```

(* marks the subquestions as they are successfully answered) The analysis completed in the second argument is a parse tree,

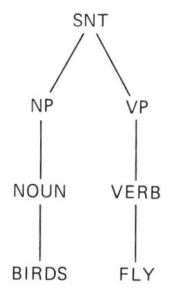

Earlier chapters have shown very complex grammars to find syntactic constituents, test them for semantic and pragmatic well-formedness, and transform them into constituents of such target languages as SRs and robot and data management command systems. All these grammars were procedural in that they were composed of Horn clause procedures to be directly interpreted by HCPRVR.

An alternative mode using declarative statements as a grammar requires that a parser be written to interpret those statements as grammar rules. The advantage of such an approach is that we can choose our own flow of control in the parser: top-down or bottom-up, first-path or all-paths, as desired. The disadvantage is that another level of interpretation may reduce the efficiency of the computation. The loss of efficiency in applying the rules, however, may well be compensated for by a reduction in the number of rules to be found or applied, or by compiling the rules and interpreter.

One of the simplest top-down, first-path parsers is shown in the following procedure:

```
((TDPARSE X (X U1 V1) Y Z)
<
(RULE U V X)
(TDPARSE U U1 Y R1)
(TDPARSE V V1 R1 Z))
((TDPARSE X (X U1) Y Z) < (RULE U X) (TDPARSE U U1 Y Z)))
```

The declarative rules for this (and subsequent parsers) are the following:

```
(((RULE NP ART NP1))         ((RULE SNT NP VP))
 ((RULE NP1 NOUN PP))        ((RULE VP1 VERB NP))
 ((RULE NP1 NOUN NP1))       ((RULE NP1 NOUN))
 ((RULE NP NP1))             ((RULE VP1 VERB))
 ((RULE VP VP1 PP))          ((RULE PP PREP NP))
 ((RULE VP VP1))             ((RULE SNT VP))

 ((RULE NOUN TIME))          ((RULE VERB TIME))
 ((RULE NOUN FLIES))         ((RULE VERB FLIES))
 ((RULE VERB LIKE))          ((RULE PREP LIKE))
 ((RULE ART AN))             ((RULE NOUN ARROW)))
```

This parser is called with the sentence

```
(TDPARSE SNT _PARSE (TIME FLIES LIKE AN ARROW) NIL)
```

The symbol SNT is a constant that states the name of the constituent to be constructed in the variable PARSE from the string given as the third argument; the fourth argument, the remainder, is required to be NIL. In the definition of TDPARSE,

Sec. 10.2 A Strictly Top-Down Parser

```
(TDPARSE X...) < (RULE U V X)(TDPARSE U...)(TDPARSE V...)
(TDPARSE X...) < (RULE U X) (TDPARSE U...)
```

a two-constituent rule is first sought, and if discovered, TDPARSE is called to compute the first constituent and then the second. If no binary rule is discovered, a unary rule is sought and applied by a recursive call to TDPARSE. For example, (TDPARSE SNT...) asks first for some (RULE U V SNT) and finds a match with (RULE NP VP SNT), so (TDPARSE NP...) and then (TDPARSE VP...). A trace for the Noun Phrase, "Time flies" is shown below.

```
(TDPARSE NP _VAL (TIME FLIES) NIL)
 (RULE U V NP)
 *(RULE NOUN NP1 NP)
  (TDPARSE NOUN (TIME FLIES) R)
   (RULE U V NOUN)
   (RULE U NOUN)
   *(RULE TIME NOUN)
  *(TDPARSE NOUN (NOUN TIME) (TIME FLIES) (FLIES))
  (TDPARSE NP1 V (FLIES) R1)
   (RULE U V NP1)
   ...
   (RULE U NP1)
   *(RULE NOUN NP1)
  *(TDPARSE NOUN (NOUN FLIES) (FLIES) NIL)
    (RULE U V NOUN)
    (RULE U NOUN)
    *(RULE FLIES NOUN)
   *(TDPARSE NOUN (NOUN FLIES) (FLIES) NIL)
  *(TDPARSE NP (NP(NOUN TIME)(NP1(NOUN FLIES)))(TIME FLIES) NIL)
```

The starred clauses represent solutions to subquestions encountered while proving the NP. (An actual computer trace would show many more subquestions that have been deleted to enhance readability.) It should be noticed that the procedure TDPARSE includes structure-building operations that generally produce a list, (<SYMBOL> <STRUCTURE>) [e.g., (NOUN FLIES), (NP1(NOUN FLIES)), (NP (NOUN TIME)(NP1...))]. The grammar rules contain no operations, just a representation of context-free phrase structure rules. TDPARSE controls the order in which the rules are selected and the construction of the parse tree; if we reversed the order of the two definitions of TDPARSE, the order in which rules would be examined would change, but the parse tree would be the same.

Although this two-line parser may be notable for its brevity, it is equally remarkable for its inefficiency; it asks several hundred subquestions in the process of parsing a two-word sentence from the example grammar, and it takes about 25 seconds to obtain all parses for "Time flies like an arrow." This contrasts with about 3 seconds for all parses with our best procedural logic parsers, 1/2 second when the grammar is written as interpretable Horn clauses, and 30 milliseconds for our best LISP parser! The first source of inefficiency lies in the fact that it is a pure top-down parser; no distinction is made between phrase rules and those used for identifying word classes. Examination of the unary rule form, (<variable> <symbol>), shows that in attempting to identify a word as a noun, for example, every word will be examined until one is found to match the input string. The cost will climb as an exponential function of the number of vocabulary items. So the first improvement is to segregate word classes as special rules, (WC <word> <symbol>), and to add another TDPARSE definition:

(TDPARSE S (S W) (W.Y) Y) < (WC W S)

S is the symbol, say NOUN
W is the first element in the string
Y is the tail of the string and the remainder to be parsed

Just this change reduces the cost on the test sentence from 25 to 6 seconds. The list of assertions, RULE, is considerably shortened, so that when searching for a unary or binary rule, far fewer candidates need be considered. The effect is to have introduced a bottom-up component into the top-down parse at the point where the most alternatives exist as word-class rules, to allow the first element of the string to index its rule. More efficiency could be gained by shifting the WC rules to infix notation, (W WC S), where W is the word from the string, WC a constant, and S the word-class name. The result of this change would reduce vastly the number of elements to be examined when seeking a word's word class since the rules would now be indexed by the typographic form of the word, rather than by the common predicate name.

The result is the three rule parser shown in Figure 10.1, with its parses of the test sentence and its cost for all parses given by RTIME. Although TDPARSE is designed as a first-path parser, by setting HCPRVR's variable, QFLAG, to True, the system requests whether the user wishes to seek another derivation, so providing all paths before it announces NIL to signify no more.

10.3 BOTTOM-UP PARSING

The principle of a bottom-up parse is to allow for the words in the sentence string to select first-level, word-class constituents, then for first-level constituents to select higher-level ones, until finally the highest level, SNT, is achieved, accounting for all elements in the string. Figure 10.2 shows the two procedures, PARSE and STKPARS, to accomplish this process with the aid of a

Sec. 10.3 Bottom-Up Parsing

```
(((TDPARSE X (X W) (W . Y) Y) < (WC W X))
 ((TDPARSE X (X U1 V1) Y Z)
  <
  (RULE U V X)
  (TDPARSE U U1 Y R1)
  (TDPARSE V V1 R1 Z))
 ((TDPARSE X (X U1) Y Z) < (RULE U X) (TDPARSE U U1 Y Z)))
```

```
*(TDPARSE SNT X (TIME FLIES LIKE AN ARROW) NIL)

((TDPARSE SNT
          (SNT (NP (NP1 (NOUN TIME) (NP1 (NOUN FLIES))))
               (VP (VP1 (VERB LIKE) (NP (ART AN) (NP1 (NOUN ARROW))))))
          (TIME FLIES LIKE AN ARROW)
          NIL))

ANOTHER? *y
((TDPARSE SNT
          (SNT (NP (NP1 (NOUN TIME)))
               (VP (VP1 (VERB FLIES))
                   (PP (PREP LIKE) (NP (ART AN) (NP1 (NOUN ARROW))))))
          (TIME FLIES LIKE AN ARROW)
          NIL))

ANOTHER? *y

((TDPARSE SNT
          (SNT (VP (VP1 (VERB TIME) (NP (NP1 (NOUN FLIES))))
                   (PP (PREP LIKE) (NP (ART AN) (NP1 (NOUN ARROW))))))
          (TIME FLIES LIKE AN ARROW)
          NIL))

ANOTHER? *y

((TDPARSE SNT
          (SNT (VP (VP1 (VERB TIME)
                        (NP (NP1 (NOUN FLIES)
                                 (PP (PREP LIKE)
                                     (NP (ART AN)
                                         (NP1 (NOUN ARROW)))))))))
          (TIME FLIES LIKE AN ARROW)
          NIL))

ANOTHER? *y
NIL

*rtime (5.7680000 SECS)
```

Figure 10.1 First-path top-down parser.

stack. The first PARSE clause is used to terminate the parse just in case the sentence string is NIL and the stack contains a list with one sentence analysis, ((SNT.X)). Otherwise, PARSE calls a unary rule for the first word of the sentence and passes control to STKPARS with the stack containing the instantiation of that unary rule, for example,

(STKPARS ((NOUN TIME).T1) T2)

STKPARS attempts to satisfy a unary or binary rule with elements from the stack; if it succeeds, it calls itself to attempt further high-level constituents, otherwise returning the stack, whereupon PARSE recurses with the stack and the next word in the string, until the string is empty. If at that point no encompassing SNT has been obtained, backup occurs to find an alternative parsing path.

As with our first top-down parser, the primary virtue of this first-path, bottom-up parser is its brevity; its inefficiency derives from frequent backup and from not segregating word class rules. The RTIME value of 31.2 seconds is notably bad.

10.4 CHART PARSING

The parsers so far shown compute a first path and use backup when a path fails or when additional parses are desired. Both can be easily modified to obtain all paths in a parallel fashion, recording each successful constituent as an assertion in a distinguished context called a chart. The idea of a chart is due to Martin Kay [1971], who showed a method for drawing a graph showing all constituents in an all-paths, bottom-up parser. The sentence "Time flies" can be parsed by the example grammar, giving the two interpretations

(SNT(NP(NP1(NOUN TIME)))(VP(VP1(VERB FLIES))))
(SNT(VP(VP1(VERB TIME))(NP(NP1(NOUN FLIES))))))

To show this on a chart, the words of the sentence are taken as arcs connecting numbers:

0--TIME--1--FLIES--2

Each word class for a word adds another arc, then the unary classes NP1, NP, VP1, VP are added.

Sec. 10.4 Chart Parsing

```
(((PARSE NIL ((SNT . X)) (SNT . X)))
 ((PARSE (X . Y) T1 T3) < (WC X X1) (STKPARS ((X1 X) . T1) T2)
                         (PARSE Y T2 T3))
(((STKPARS ((X1 . X) . Z) W) < (RULE X1 X2)
                              (STKPARS ((X2 (X1 . X)) . Z) W))
 ((STKPARS ((X1 . X) (Y1 . Y) . Z) W)
  <
  (RULE Y1 X1 X2)
  (STKPARS ((X2 (Y1 . Y) (X1 . X)) . Z) W))
 ((STKPARS X X)))

((PARSE (TIME FLIES LIKE AN ARROW)
        NIL
        (SNT (NP (NP1 (NOUN TIME)))
             (VP (VP1 (VERB FLIES))
                 (PP (PREP LIKE) (NP (ART AN) (NP1 (NOUN ARROW))))))))

ANOTHER? *y
((PARSE (TIME FLIES LIKE AN ARROW)
        NIL
        (SNT (NP (NP1 (NOUN TIME) (NP1 (NOUN FLIES))))
             (VP (VP1 (VERB LIKE))
                 (NP (ART AN) (NP1 (NOUN ARROW))))))

ANOTHER? *y
((PARSE (TIME FLIES LIKE AN ARROW)
        NIL
        (SNT (VP (VP1 (VERB TIME) (NP (NP1 (NOUN FLIES))))
             (PP (PREP LIKE)
                 (NP (ART AN) (NP1 (NOUN ARROW))))))

ANOTHER? *y
((PARSE (TIME FLIES LIKE AN ARROW)
        NIL
        (SNT (VP (VP1 (VERB TIME))
                 (NP (NP1 (NOUN FLIES)
                          (PP (PREP LIKE)
                              (NP (ART AN)
                                  (NP1 (NOUN ARROW))))
                 ))))))

ANOTHER? *y
NIL
*rtime
(31.199000 SECS)
```

Figure 10.2. Bottom-up parser with backup.

```
            |--VERB--|--NOUN---|
            |        |         |
            |--NOUN--|--VERB---|
            |        |         |
            0--TIME--1--FLIES--2
            |        |         |
            |--NP1---|--NP1----|
            |--NP----|---NP----|
            |--VP1---|---VP1---|
            |--VP----|---VP----|
```

Then the combinations of unary phrases are drawn to show connections between NOUN-0,1 and NP1-1,2 to form an NP-0,2:

$$NP\text{-}0,1 + NP1\text{-}1,2 \text{--} NP\text{-}0,2$$
$$VERB\text{-}0,1 + VP\text{-}1,2 \text{--} VP\text{-}0,2$$
$$NP\text{-}0,1 + VP\text{-}1,2 \text{--} SNT\text{-}0,2$$
$$VP\text{-}0,1 + NP\text{-}1,2 \text{--} SNT\text{-}0,2$$
$$NP\text{-}0,1 + NP1\text{-}1,2 \text{--} NP\text{-}0,2$$

As the notation above suggests, the chart we draw can be easily represented as a data structure that identifies each constituent uniquely by the constituents and nodes it spans. The complete parse of a sentence constructs a chart as a list of all its constituents uniquely identified by context.

In procedural logic we can adopt this data structure idea by asserting each unique constituent to a special context. If we identify a constituent as a 4-tuple of the form

<SYMBOL, CONSTITUENT, INPUT-STRING, REMAINDER>

which occurs in calls to a parsing rule,

(CHPARS _SYM _CON _STR _REM)
< ... (ASSERT (_SYM _CON _STR _REM) *)

where the function ASSERT with two arguments creates a new axiom marked for the * context. If we now wish to discover if a constituent already exists on the chart, we merely ask

(CHPARS S C ST R) < (S C ST R)

The special context marker is used only by a procedure for clearing out axioms, and all axioms are accessible to the prover. The procedure call (CLEAR *) removes all axioms marked with the symbol that is its argument, and is called at the beginning of each parse to eliminate any assertions left by a previous parsing.

Sec. 10.4   Chart Parsing   205

==

(((CHPARSE: X) < (NOT (CLEAR *)) (CHPARS X) (SHOWPARSE X)))

(((CHPARS NIL)) ((CHPARS X) < (EQ X (W . Y))
                              (BUILDUP W W X Y) (CHPARS Y)))

(((SHOWPARSE X) < (SNT Z X NIL) (RPRINT Z ---------) (FAIL)))

(((BUILDUP Z U X Y) < (Z U X Y) /)
 ((BUILDUP Z U X Y) < (ASSERT (Z U X Y) *) (BUILDUP1 Z U X Y)))

(((BUILDUP1 Z U X Y) < (BRULE V Z) (BUILDUP V (V U) X Y) (FAIL))
 ((BUILDUP1 Z U X Y)
  <
  (BRULE V W Z)
  (W U1 X1 X)
  (BUILDUP V (V U1 U) X1 Y)
  (FAIL))
 ((BUILDUP1 Z U X Y)))
_____

(CHPARSE: (TIME FLIES LIKE AN ARROW))

(SNT (VP (VP1 (VERB TIME) (NP (NP1 (NOUN FLIES))))
     (PP (PREP LIKE) (NP (ART AN) (NP1 (NOUN ARROW))))))
_____

(SNT (NP (NP1 (NOUN TIME))) (VP (VP1 (VERB FLIES))
                             (PP (PREP LIKE) (NP (ART AN)
                                  (NP1 (NOUN ARROW))))))
_____

(SNT (VP (VP1 (VERB TIME) (NP (NP1 (NOUN FLIES)
                    (PP (PREP LIKE) (NP (ART AN)
                                  (NP1 (NOUN ARROW)))
))))))
_____

(SNT (NP (NP1 (NOUN TIME) (NP1 (NOUN FLIES))))
     (VP (VP1 (VERB LIKE) (NP (ART AN)
                             (NP1 (NOUN ARROW))))))
_____

NIL
*rtime (3.1770000 SECS)
==

Figure 10.3 An all-paths, bottom-up chart parser (programmed by Dan Chester).

An all-paths, bottom-up chart parser of this type, written by Dan Chester, is shown in Figure 10.3. This parser follows the bottom-up chart principle by applying all rules possible at each stage in scanning the input string, and recording them as starred assertions. When this process has been completed, SHOWPARSE prints every SNT constituent that has a NIL remainder, accomplishing this by printing the first one, then failing with the FAIL axiom, and printing another until no more are found. The FAIL axiom is undefined, so it always fails.

CHPARS of a string X splits the string into a CAR, W and a CDR, Y, calls BUILDUP to apply all rules, then recurses on the CDR of the string. BUILDUP first seeks to determine if the constituent it is attempting to form has already been computed in that context.

(BUILDUP _SYMBOL _WORD _STRING _REMAINDER)

asks the subquestion

(_SYMBOL _WORD _STRING _REMAINDER).

If that exact constituent has previously been computed, it will have been asserted and the query will be successful; otherwise, it will fail. If it is successful, the cut symbol, / , is used to avoid trying any other BUILDUP rules; that constituent is proved and in the event of backup, when the cut is encountered, no further attempts at any other BUILDUP rules will be attempted. If the constituent has not previously been computed, BUILDUP asserts it and calls BUILDUP1 to apply unary and binary rules. When a rule is successfully applied, the procedure is deliberately failed to force backup to find another rule. When no other rules exist, BUILDUP1 succeeds with the last, unconditional axiom.

The control flow in this procedure is more complex than any previously shown, using FAIL to force backup to apply all rules, applying / to prevent redundant construction of constituents, and A* to assert them as new axioms during the process of parsing a sentence. The procedure is efficient—within the limits of interpreted code—requiring about 3 seconds to obtain all parsings. This RTIME should be contrasted with that for the bottom-up, backup parser shown in Figure 10.2. (These times are for a DEC 2060 with a KI processor, using compiled HCPRVR code interpreting the parser definitions. They are useful primarily for comparisons of these parsers, but they incidentally show the still high cost of computation that is entailed by uncompiled procedural logic programs. In general contrast, our best compiled LISP parser accomplishes the all-paths parsing in 33 milliseconds, and writing the grammar in Horn clauses results in a cost of 1/2 second.)

The reader is encouraged to understand these programs by running them in HCPRVR or translating them to PROLOG and testing them. It is generally quite hard to comprehend the depth of recursion in parsing except by watching the descending calls and their returns in a trace of the procedure. Several other variations in parsers can be programmed easily when these are understood; a top-down, all-paths, chart parser, a left-corner parser, a system to look ahead when applying rules, a first-path bottom-up chart parser, and numerous other variations discussed in the parsing literature are all attractive exercises for deepening the comprehension of control flow in sentence analysis (see Aho and Ullman [1972]).

10.5 TRANSLATION AND PARAPHRASE

The problem of automated translation was the first proposed application of computation to natural language; unfortunately, it is one of the hardest. After a few prominent and dedicated researchers concluded quite correctly that they could not solve the problem, they managed—quite inappropriately—to convince the scientific community of the United States that the problem was too difficult to study directly. Today large-scale efforts appear to be underway to achieve useful automated translation of technical materials among European common-market member languages, and Japan supports more than one large project. In the United States, only a tiny trickle of public funding is devoted to this purpose, and no American corporations as of this writing have found the problem tractable or attractive enough to support the large effort that will be required to prepare grammars for this purpose.

The computational problem has been fairly well understood since Satterthwaite [1965] and Tosh [1965] described the basic approach in terms of the following paradigm.

Parse input language string to deep syntactic structure:

$$IL \rightarrow DS1$$

Map from IL terms in DS1 to target language terms to form an equivalent deep structure, DS2:

$$IL\text{-}DS1 \rightarrow TL\text{-}DS2$$

Generate target language strings from DS2:

$$TL\text{-}DS2 \rightarrow TL$$

A similar paradigm was stated by Andreyev in terms of dependency structures [Booth, 1967]. The paradigm was followed successfully by Vauquois [1979] in Europe and by Lehmann et al. [1980] in the United States. Artificial intelligence researchers, including Wilks [1973] and Schank and Riesbeck [1980], added further support to this paradigm while introducing a semantically oriented deep structure to improve the representation of meaning preserving constraints on the translation.

Although the computational paradigm is reasonably well established, the linguistic effort required to describe large subsets of natural-language grammar is so considerable that there is still no assurance that the problem is tractable from an engineering viewpoint. To take a local example from the Texas Linguistics Research Center, the first 15 years' effort toward accumulating German–English translation grammars had to be scrapped when a modern (i.e. 1975) approach to grammar description and parsing was adopted. From about 1977 to the present a low level of effort on German–English grammars has resulted in a vocabulary of 20,000 to 30,000 entries, and less than 1000 complex grammar rules. This accumulation has proved sufficient for translation of about 200 pages of technical German into good-quality English, and efforts continue to increase both vocabulary and grammar.

But almost certainly the considerable progress in the development of natural-language understanding systems will sooner or later obsolete this collection, too, and force restatement of the language descriptions in more powerful rules that will extend the present sentence-by-sentence procedures to translations that depend on larger contexts.

For small subsets of natural language (i.e., from a few paragraphs to perhaps a short book) the translation task is manageable. Bilingual students in a computational linguistics or artificial intelligence seminar frequently take considerable pleasure in demonstrating systems sufficient to translate a few sentences, with a fairly general linguistic approach. After examining the basic paraphrase logic for translation, some student efforts will be shown for English–French, Spanish–English, and English–Japanese, using both context-free and context-sensitive transfer rules to accomplish the task.

10.6 PARAPHRASING SENTENCES

Parsing a sentence string translates it into one or another formal language. In the example parsings so far shown in this chapter, the formal language is merely a list representation of a linguistic phrase structure tree. But previous chapters have shown the usefulness of parsing into semantic relations and their incorporation into larger discourse structures which can be used for answering questions of various types. Paraphrase is a rather general term which is defined by Merriam-Webster as follows:

> Paraphrase: a restatement of a text, passage, or work giving the meaning in another form.

Thus to "restate" a sentence as a parsing, or to translate a sentence to SRs, or to logic, or from English to Japanese are all examples of paraphrase. Perhaps to restate a question as its answer goes beyond this definition, yet we have seen that answering a question depends strongly on the fact that the question's form identifies statements that might be answers, so in some sense

Sec. 10.6 Paraphrasing Sentences

the answer is truly an amplified restatement of the question. Generally, all computations on a natural language are designed to restate meanings as formal-language assertions—implied by the language string in the context of a particular knowledge system. But "good-quality translation" is a special kind of restatement; let us call it "fair paraphrase" to signify the subset of paraphrases that preserve—without significant addition or deletion—the meaning of the original string.

An example of fair paraphrase is seen in the following two sentences.

The old man from Spain ate perch.
The elderly Spaniard dined on fish.

I detect no significant difference in "the old man from Spain" and "the elderly Spaniard" except that "Spaniard" is not uniquely male. But the meanings of "ate perch" and "dined on fish" are subtly different in that the physical particularities of eating perch are submerged in the more social notion of dining on fish. The generalization from "perch" to "fish" has also discarded unique qualities associated with "perch." Nevertheless, I judge these to be fair paraphrases and thereby suggest the idea that fair paraphrase and translation are relative notions that can be quantified by psychological measurements derived from human judgments of similarity between paraphrase pairs.

We can translate the first sentence into surface semantic relations (SSRs) to produce the following structure.

```
(EAT TNS PAST AGT (MAN AGE (OLD) DET THE NBR SING
         *FROM (SPAIN PREP FROM NBR SING))
 AE (PERCH NBR SING/PL) )
```

Then the following set of context-sensitive transfer rules will transform this structure into another SSR.

```
(EAT PAPH DINE ((CONSTRAIN AGT PERSON)(ADDIF AE PREP ON)))
(MAN PAPH SPANIARD ((DEPAIR *FROM SPAIN)))
(OLD PAPH ELDERLY NIL)
(PERCH PAPH FISH NIL)

(DINE AGT (SPANIARD AGE ELDERLY NBR SING DET THE)
 AE (FISH PREP ON NBR SING/PL))
```

The first rule says that EAT may be paraphrased by DINE provided that the agent of EAT is a subclass of the concept PERSON, and if there is an AE argument, the PREPosition ON should be added to its value. Notice that in "Pedro ate at a restaurant" there is no affected entity argument, so the ADDIF AE would not add the preposition. The second rule limits the substitution of SPANIARD for MAN to just the case where there is a *FROM (i.e., Source) argument whose value is related to SPAIN; this rule might also apply to "a man from Barcelona." The two remaining rules offer free substitution without constraints.

To apply these rules requires an interpreter that will accept a string to be paraphrased and return its translation. A first-path, bottom-up procedure is indicated to accomplish the paraphrase by allowing each element of the input SR to select and apply any rule associated with it. If several rules are applicable, the first one that succeeds is chosen; if none succeeds, the null paraphrase, translation of an element into itself, is the default. An interpreter for these rules and the example of their application are given in Figures 10.4 and 10.5. The procedure TRANSLATE first attempts to REPLACE the head of its SR, then calls TRANSPAIR to translate the SR's argument pairs. REPLACE seeks a paraphrase rule, (X PAPH U V); if it finds one, it uses APPLY* to apply the constraints, V, to the arguments of the SR, and if they are satisfied replaces the original head, X, with the paraphrase, U, and the original arguments, R, with the revised arguments, Y1. When TRANSLATE is given an atom, the second TRANSLATE rule applies to return an atom as a translation. If no PAPH rule is found, REPLACE returns the atom or list it was given.

Since an SR is invariably either an atom or a head followed by case-name SR pairs, the recursion is perfectly regular, requiring of TRANSPAIR only that it call TRANSLATE for each pair and account for the NIL case that ends a list of pairs.

APPLY* takes a list of constraints and an SR and calls APPLY1 to apply each constraint. The constraints CONSTRAIN, ADDIF, and DEPAIR are each associated with arguments; APPLY1 is a mini-interpreter that recognizes each constraint name and calls appropriate procedures MEMPR, RELATE, DEPAIR, and REPAIR to apply the constraint arguments to the SR and so revise it to a new one. MEMPR is used to establish an argument that is tested by RELATE to conform to a constraint. MEMPR and RELATE were described in Chapter 8. In the ADDIF case, if the case name is present, REPAIR modifies the SR by adding a new argument pair to it. DEPAIR is defined to remove a particular pair from an SR. This set of procedures offers a first approximation to those that are required for changing an SR to a paraphrase or translation.

In Figure 10.5, the call to TRANSLATE with the perch-eating SR is shown, followed by the result in which the SR for "The elderly Spaniard ate fish" is computed.

The paraphrased SSR contains all the necessary detail for the English grammar to translate it into the string "The elderly Spaniard dined on fish." Although the grammar is not shown, the entire paraphrase procedure follows the translation paradigm described earlier;

> A sentence is parsed into a deep structure (i.e., SSR1).
> Context sensitive transfer rules transform SSR1 to SSR2.
> The grammar generates a translation sentence from SSR2.

Sec. 10.6 Paraphrasing Sentences

```
========================================================
        (DEFPROP TRANSLATE
         (((TRANSLATE (S . R) (S1 . R2))
            <
           (REPLACE S R (S1 . R1))
           (TRANSPAIR R1 (S1 . R1) R2))
          ((TRANSLATE X Y) < (ATOM* X) (REPLACE X NIL Y)))
         AXIOMS)

        (DEFPROP TRANSPAIR
         (((TRANSPAIR (A V . R) (S . R1) (A V1 . R2))
            <
           (TRANSLATE V V1)
           (TRANSPAIR R (S . R1) R2))
          ((TRANSPAIR NIL X NIL)))
         AXIOMS)
        (DEFPROP REPLACE
         (((REPLACE X Y (U . Y1)) < (X PAPH U V) (APPLY* V Y Y1))
          ((REPLACE X NIL X))
          ((REPLACE X W (X . W))))
         AXIOMS)
        (DEFPROP APPLY*
         (((APPLY* (X . Y) V W) < (APPLY1 X V V1) (APPLY* Y V1 W))
          ((APPLY* NIL Y Y)))
         AXIOMS)

        (DEFPROP APPLY1
         (((APPLY1 (CONSTRAIN R W) V V) < (MEMPR (R X) V) (RELATE X W))
          ((APPLY1 (DEPAIR R W) V V1) < (DEPAIR (R W1) V V1) (RELATE W W1))
          ((APPLY1 (ADDIF R (W W1)) V V1)
             < (REPAIR (R (X . Y)) V (R (X W W1 . Y)) V1)))
         AXIOMS)
        (DEFPROP DEPAIR
         (((DEPAIR X NIL NIL))
          ((DEPAIR (X Y) (X Y . W) W))
          ((DEPAIR (X Y) (U V . W) (U V . Z)) < (DEPAIR (X Y) W Z)))
         AXIOMS)
        (DEFPROP REPAIR
         (((REPAIR (R X) (R X . Y) (R1 Z . Y)))
          ((REPAIR (R X) (U V . Y) (R1 Z) (U V . W))
                         < (REPAIR (R X) Y (R1 Z) W))
          ((REPAIR X NIL Y NIL)))
         AXIOMS)
========================================================
```

Figure 10.4 Interpreter for paraphrase rules.

```
===========================================================
              (TRANSLATE (EAT TNS
                              PAST
                         AGT
                         (MAN DET
                              THE
                              AGE
                              (OLD)
                              *FROM
                              (SPAIN PREP FROM NBR SING)
                              NBR
                              SING)
                         AE
                         (PERCH NBR SING))
                    W)
              ((TRANSLATE (EAT TNS
                               PAST
                          AGT
                          (MAN DET
                               THE
                               AGE
                               (OLD)
                               *FROM
                               (SPAIN PREP FROM NBR SING)
                               NBR
                               SING)
                          AE
                          (PERCH NBR SING))
                    (DINE  TNS
                           PAST
                           AGT
                           (SPANIARD DET THE AGE (ELDERLY) NBR SING)
                           AE
                           (FISH PREP ON NBR SING))))
===========================================================
```

Figure 10.5 Paraphrasing an SSR.

In this case of paraphrase only the English grammar and the transfer rules are needed; generally for translation between languages a grammar for each and a set of transfer rules from terms of one language to those of the other are required.

10.7 TRANSLATION EXAMPLES

In his term paper for a computational linguistics course, a student developed two grammars, one French and one English, to account for the following sentences:

Sec. 10.7 Translation Examples

The first settlement of the French in Texas was a tiny colony. Harboring a hundred souls it perched on the coast of Texas. Its founders lodged within its frail ramparts the grandest visions of empire.

The parsing into SSRs are given below for the third sentence, first in English, then in French.

```
(LODGE AGT (FOUNDER ASSOC (ITS) NBR PLUR) TNS PAST
    LOC (RAMPART PREP WITHIN ASSOC (ITS)
            SIZE (FRAIL) NBR PLUR)
    AE (VISION DET THE SIZE (GRANDEST)
            ASSOC (EMPIRE PREP OF NBR SING) NBR PLUR))
```

Ses fondateurs plaçaient dans ses fragiles ramparts les immenses visions d'empire.

```
(PLACER AGT (FONDATEUR ASSOC (SES) NBR PLUR) TNS PAST
    LOC (RAMPART PREP DANS ASSOC (SES)
            TYPE (FRAGILES) NBR PLUR)
    AE (VISION DET LES SIZE (IMMENSES)
            ASSOC (EMPIRE PREP D NBR SING) NBR PLUR))
```

Some English and French vocabulary entries are compared below.

```
(NOUN FOUNDERS (FOUNDER NBR PLUR) HUMAN)
(NOUN VISIONS (VISION NBR PLUR) TOBJ)
(VERB LODGED (LODGE TNS PAST) ACT)
(ADJ GRANDEST)

(NOUNF FONDATEURS (FONDATEUR NBR PLUR) HUMAN)
(NOUNF VISIONS (VISION NBR PLUR) TOBJ)
(VERBF PLACAIENT (PLACER TNS PAST) ACT)
(ADJF IMMENSES)
```

The grammar rules for these sentences in the two languages differ only slightly, and the semantic event forms (see Chapter 5) that show allowable combinations of semantic features of elements in constituents are practically identical unless they contain prepositions. In that case they differ by using French or English forms.

Revealing the inadequacy of studying translation in small samples, the student prepared a dictionary:

```
(SETQ LAROUSSE '(
    (ITS . SES)
    (THE . LES)(OF.D)(WITHIN.DANS)(FRAIL.FRAGILES)
    (GRANDEST.IMMENSES)(LODGE.PLACER)
    (FOUNDER.FONDATEUR)(VISION.VISION)
    (RAMPART.RAMPART) ))
```

Apart from the inappropriate GRANDEST-IMMENSES entry, the dictionary, although sufficient for the sentence at hand, is simply context free and thus inadequate for general-purpose application. Articles and prepositions make this particularly apparent; sometimes "the" will be translated as "le," "les," "l'...," and "of" as "d'," "du," or "des." Despite an inadequate lexical approach this exercise shows the power of symmetric grammars in translation. The translation from English to French used the English grammar to transform into a case structure which was then input to the French grammar to produce a French sentence; from French to English used the French grammar to parse and the English one to generate. Only one grammar for each language was required.

In a similar fashion for the same seminar, Takao Usui showed translations between English and Japanese.

>The congress of the United States meets at the capitol building. There the members of Congress make the laws of our country.
>
>Amerika no gikai wa kyapitoru biru ni atsumuru. Sokode gikai no memba wa warewareno kuni no horitsu o tsukuru.

Again in his first effort, only context-free mapping rules were used, and the lexical structure has no generality.

For Spanish–English translation, Francisco Bravo-Ahuja developed lexical structures that directly translated Spanish into English semantic relations under the control of the Spanish grammar.

```
(S-NOUN COHETE (ROCKET SING3 MASC) POBJ)
(S-ADJ AMARILLO (SING3 MASC) YELLOW COLOR)
(S-RVERB (ENCONTRABA (STAND PAST SING3) POSITION)
(S-VERB LLEVABA (CARRY PAST SING3) CONTAIN)
(S-ART LOS THE (PLUR3 MASC))
(S-ART EL THE (SING3 MASC))
```

The features SING3, PLUR3, MASC, POBJ, COLOR, and so on, are used for minimal context testing, so as transfer rules these are not strictly context free. In this system also the use of symmetric grammars was demonstrated for translation in both directions with one grammar for each language.

10.8 CONTEXT-SENSITIVE TRANSLATION FROM ENGLISH TO JAPANESE

Following his initial exercise in translation Usui [1982] attempted the more general context-sensitive approach using the rocket story of Chapter 8. In this

Sec. 10.8 Context-Sensitive Translation from English to Japanese

effort he first translated the rocket story into Japanese, then constructed a grammar to produce Japanese SSRs from the text, and designed context-sensitive lexical and transfer rules for translating the English SSRs into Japanese SSRs of exactly the form produced by the Japanese grammar. For automatic translation this system used the English grammar of the rocket story published by Simmons and Chester [1982] to transform English sentences into SSRs, then applied the transfer rules to translate these into Japanese SSRs, finally using the Japanese grammar to generate Japanese sentences.

The English analyses were given in Figure 8.1; a comparison of English and Japanese SSRs for the first two sentences are shown below.

```
(STAND AE (ROCKET DET A SIZE (GREAT)
             COLOR (BLACK *AND (YELLOW))
             TYPE V-2)
             LGTH (LONG LGTH (FOOT QU (FORTY-SIX) NBR PL))
             NBR SING)
       TNS PAST)
       LOC (DESERT PREP IN DET A LOC (NEWMEXICO) NBR SING))

(TATSU AE (ROCKET POSTP GA
           LGTH (NAGASA POSTP NO
                 MSR (FEET POSTP NO QU (*46 FORM ORG)))
                 QU (*46 FORM ORG)))
           SIZE (OHKII FORM ORG)
           COLOR (KUROI FORM CONT *AND(KIIROI FORM ORG))
           TYPE (V-2))
       LOC (NAKA POSTP NI
            LOC (SABAKU POSTP NO LOC (NEWMEXICO)))
       AUX (IRU TNS PAST) TNS PAST)
```

```
(WEIGH AE (IT ST (EMPTY) NBR SING)
       TNS PAST
       MSR (TON QU (FIVE) NBR PL))

(ARU AE (SORE POSTP WA) ST (KARA POSTP DE)
     WGT (OMOSA POSTP GA
           MSR (TON POSTP NO QU (*5 FORM ORG)))
     TNS PAST)
```

The symmetry of the Japanese grammar is demonstrated by parsing the first sentence and regenerating the sentence from its SSR. The following console recording is quoted from Usui [1982, pp. 10–12]. His comments are set off by double angle brackets, <<...>>.

```
*(sprint st1)
  << ST1 contains a sentence to be parsed.>>
(S12 (*46 FEET NO NAGASA NO OHKII KUROKU KIIROI V-2 ROCKET
      GA NEWMEXICO SABAKU NO NAKA NI TATTEITA)
     X
     X1)
```

216   Parsing and Paraphrase   Chap. 10

NIL
*(try st1)
   << We call TRY to parse ST1. The CONTINUE question tell us
      that 100 subquestions have been asked; if we repond no,
      the proof will be abandoned.>>

CONTINUE? *y

((S12 (*46 FEET NO NAGASA NO OHKII KUROKU KIIROI V-2 ROCKET
GA NEWMEXICO SABAKU NO NAKA NI TATTEITA) (TATSU AE (ROCKET P
OSTP GA LGTH (NAGASA POSTP NO MSR (FEET POSTP NO QU (*46 FOR
M ORG))) SIZE (OHKII FORM ORG) COLOR (KUROI FORM CONT *AND (
KIIROI FORM ORG)) TYPE (V-2)) LOC (NAKA POSTP NI LOC (SABAKU
POSTP NO LOC (NEWMEXICO))) AUX (IRU TNS PAST) TNS PAST) NIL
))

*rtime
(0.77300000 SECS)
   << It took real CPU time 0.773 secs in UCI LISP, HCPRVR
      DEC 2060 KI10.>>

*(sprint (car val))
   << Now we can look at the answer pretty-printed. VAL con-
      tains the answer.>>
(S12 (*46 FEET NO NAGASA NO OHKII KUROKU KIIROI V-2 ROCKET
         GA NEWMEXICO SABAKU NO NAKA NI TATTEITA)
     (TATSU AE
            (ROCKET POSTP
                    GA
                    LGTH
                    (NAGASA POSTP
                            NO
                            MSR
                            (FEET POSTP
                                   NO
                                   QU
                                   (*46 FORM ORG)))
                    SIZE
                    (OHKII FORM ORG)
                    COLOR
                    (KUROI FORM CONT *AND (KIIROI FORM ORG))
                    TYPE
                    (V-2))
            LOC
            (NAKA POSTP
                  NI
                  LOC
                  (SABAKU POSTP NO LOC (NEWMEXICO)))
            AUX
            (IRU TNS PAST)
            TNS
            PAST)

Sec. 10.8   Context-Sensitive Translation from English to Japanese   **217**

```
            NIL)
NIL
   << Now we set J to (s12 x semantic-relation nil) by using
      VAL.>>
*(setq j (car (subst x (cadar val) val)))
(S12 _X (TATSU AE (ROCKET POSTP GA LGTH (NAGASA POSTP NO MSR
 (FEET POSTP NO QU (*46 FORM ORG))) SIZE (OHKII FORM ORG) CO
 LOR (KUROI FORM CONT *AND (KIIROI FORM ORG)) TYPE (V-2)) LOC
 (NAKA POSTP NI LOC (SABAKU POSTP NO LOC (NEWMEXICO))) AUX (
 IRU TNS PAST) TNS PAST) NIL)

*(try j)
   << We will TRY to generate the original sentence.>>
((S12 (*46 FEET NO NAGASA NO OHKII KUROKU KIIROI V-2 ROCKET
GA NEWMEXICO SABAKU NO NAKA NI TATTEITA) (TATSU AE (ROCKET P
OSTP GA LGTH (NAGASA POSTP NO MSR (FEET POSTP NO QU (*46 FOR
M ORG))) SIZE (OHKII FORM ORG) COLOR (KUROI FORM CONT *AND (
KIIROI FORM ORG)) TYPE (V-2)) LOC (NAKA POSTP NI LOC (SABAKU
POSTP NO LOC (NEWMEXICO))) AUX (IRU TNS PAST) TNS PAST) NIL
))
   << It generated the original sentence, showing the
      symmetry of the grammar.>>
*rtime
(0.60000000 SECS)
```

The general form and flavor of the English-Japanese deep structure transfer rules can be seen from the examples in Figure 10.6. It is notable that Usui developed a set of general case transformation rules in which particular case arguments such as LOC, PUrpose, AGT, MSR, and so on, in the English SSRs are sufficient to signify that a preposition, if any, should be deleted, and an appropriate Japanese post-position signal such as "no" or "ni" should be added. The English grammar was also modified to provide explicit arcs for sentence relations, SNTRL SUBject and SNTRL OBJect, so that the Japanese translation could develop its surface markings of "wa," "no," and "ni."

===
            Case Transformation Rules

            (((LOC JP LOC (W . Y) (W . Y)) < (MEMPR (PREP TO) Y))
             ((LOC JP LOC (W . Y) (X POSTP NI LOC (W . Y1)))
              <
              (MEMPR (PREP X) Y)
              (DEPAIR (PREP X) Y Y2)
              (ADDPR (POSTP NO) Y2 Y1)))

            (((PU JP PU (W . Y) (W . Y1))
              <
              (MEMPR (PREP X) Y)
              (DEPAIR (PREP X) Y Y2)
              (ADDPR (POSTP NI) Y2 Y1))

```
((PU JP PU (W . Y) (W . Y1))
 <
 (MEMPR (INF TO) Y)
 (DEPAIR (INF TO) Y Y2)
 (ADDPR (POSTP NO) Y2 Y3)
 (ADDPR (POSTP TAME) Y3 Y1)))

(((MSR JP MSR (W . Y) (W . Y1))
  <
  (DEPAIR (PREP OF) Y Y2)
  (ADDPR (POSTP NO) Y2 Y1)))
```

Vocabulary Transformation Rules

```
((((IT JP SORE Y Y1) < (DEPAIR (NBR X) Y Y1)))

(((BLACK JP KUROI Y Y1)
  <
  (MEMPR (*AND X) Y)
  (ADDPR (FORM CONT) Y Y1))
 ((BLACK JP KUROI Y Y1) < (ADDPR (FORM ORG) Y Y1)))

(((GREAT JP OHKII Y Y1)
  <
  (MEMPR (*AND X) Y)
  (ADDPR (FORM CONT) Y Y1))
 ((GREAT JP OHKII Y Y1) < (ADDPR (FORM ORG) Y Y1)))

(((YELLOW JP KIIROI Y Y1)
  <
  (MEMPR (*AND X) Y)
  (ADDPR (FORM CONT) Y Y1))
 ((YELLOW JP KIIROI Y Y1) < (ADDPR (FORM ORG) Y Y1)))

((((FORTY-SIX JP *46 Y Y1) < (ADDPR (FORM ORG) Y Y1)))

(((DESERT JP SABAKU Y Y1)
  <
  (DEPAIR (DET X) Y Y2)
  (DEPAIR (NBR X1) Y2 Y1)))

(((ALCOHOL JP ALCOHOL Y Y1)
  <
  (DEPAIR (NBR X) Y Y2)
  (DEPAIR (DET X1) Y2 Y1)))

(((OXYGEN JP SANSO Y Y1)
  <
  (DEPAIR (NBR X) Y Y2)
  (DEPAIR (DET X1) Y2 Y1)))

((((LIQUID JP EKITAI Y Y1) < (DEPAIR (DET X) Y Y1)))
```

Sec. 10.8 Context-Sensitive Translation from English to Japanese

```
(((TON JP TON Y Y1)
  <
  (DEPAIR (NBR X) Y Y2)
  (MEMPR (QU X1) Y2)
  (ADDPR (POSTP NO) Y2 Y1)))

(((SCIENTIST JP KAGAKUSHA Y Y1)
  <
  (DEPAIR (NBR X) Y Y2)
  (DEPAIR (DET X1) Y2 Y1)))

(((FOOT JP FEET Y Y1)
  <
  (DEPAIR (NBR X) Y Y2)
  (MEMPR (QU X1) Y2)
  (ADDPR (POSTP NO) Y2 Y1)))

(((LONG JP NAGASA Y Y1)
  <
  (MEMPR (MSR X) Y)
  (ADDPR (POSTP NO) Y Y1)))

(((ROCKET JP ROCKET Y Y1)
  <
  (DEPAIR (DET X) Y Y2)
  (DEPAIR (NBR X1) Y2 Y1)))

(((BEHIND JP USHIRO Y Y1) < (ADDPR (POSTP NI) Y Y1)))

(((IN JP NAKA Y Y1) < (ADDPR (POSTP NI) Y Y1)))

(((ON JP UE Y Y1) < (ADDPR (POSTP NI) Y Y1)))

(((STAND JP TATSU Y Y1)
  <
  (MEMPR (TNS X) Y)
  (ADPAIR (AUX (IRU TNS X)) Y Y2)
  (DEPAIR (TNS X) Y2 Y3)
  (ADPAIR (TNS X) Y3 Y1)))

(((CARRY JP TSUMU Y Y1)
  <
  (MEMPR (TNS X) Y)
  (ADPAIR (AUX (IRU TNS X)) Y Y2)
  (DEPAIR (TNS X) Y2 Y3)
  (ADPAIR (TNS X) Y3 Y1)))
```

==

Figure 10.6 Example English–Japanese transfer rules.

Generally, the vocabulary transfer rules delete English markings for DETerminer and singular/plural NBR for nouns, add appropriate postposition markers for adverbs and prepositions, and select suitable Japanese auxiliaries to signal the tense of verbs. Some very difficult problems arise in terms of quantity and measure, since Japanese uses a variety of special markers depending on whether one, two, three, or several objects are signified. The interpreter of these rules follows the logic of the translator given earlier in Figure 10.4. A recorded example of their application to the SSRs of the first sentence is shown below.

```
*st1
   << ST1 contains SR of English of the sentence 1 in rocket
      story. The variable U will be bound to the translated
      SRs.>>
(TRANSLATE (STAND AE (ROCKET DET A SIZE (GREAT) COLOR (BLACK
   *AND (YELLOW)) TYPE (V-2) LGTH (LONG MSR (FOOT QU (FORTY-SI
   X) NBR PL)) NBR SING SNTRL SUB) TNS PAST LOC (DESERT PREP IN
   DET A LOC (NEWMEXICO) NBR SING)) U)

*(try st1)

   << We called TRY to translate ST1. Each CONTINUE questions
      100 subquestions.>>
CONTINUE? *y

CONTINUE? *y

((TRANSLATE (STAND AE (ROCKET DET A SIZE (GREAT) COLOR (BLAC
K *AND (YELLOW)) TYPE (V-2) LGTH (LONG MSR (FOOT QU (FORTY-S
IX) NBR PL)) NBR SING SNTRL SUB) TNS PAST LOC (DESERT PREP I
N DET A LOC (NEWMEXICO) NBR SING)) (TATSU AE (ROCKET POSTP W
A SIZE (OHKII FORM ORG) COLOR (KUROI FORM CONT *AND (KIIROI
FORM ORG)) TYPE (V-2) LGTH (NAGASA POSTP NO MSR (FEET POSTP
NO QU (*46 FORM ORG)))) LOC (NAKA POSTP NI LOC (SABAKU POSTP
NO LOC (NEWMEXICO))) AUX (IRU TNS PAST) TNS PAST)))

   << We pretty-print the output. See the following.
      Verb (AUX) transformation, ordinary noun,
      adjectives (both cases), preposition handling (LOC)
      including English word IN changes into NAKA.
      Also SNTRL SUB changes to POSTP WA.>>
*(sprint (car val))
(TRANSLATE (STAND AE
                    (ROCKET DET
                            A
                            SIZE
                            (GREAT)
                            COLOR
                            (BLACK *AND (YELLOW))
                            TYPE
                            (V-2)
```

Sec. 10.8 Context-Sensitive Translation from English to Japanese   221

```
                              LGTH
                              (LONG MSR
                                     (FOOT QU (FORTY-SIX) NBR PL))
                              NBR
                              SING
                              SNTRL
                              SUB)
                       TNS
                       PAST
                       LOC
                       (DESERT PREP
                              IN
                              DET
                              A
                              LOC
                              (NEWMEXICO)
                              NBR
                              SING))
              (TATSU AE
                     (ROCKET POSTP
                            WA
                            SIZE
                            (OHKII FORM ORG)
                            COLOR
                            (KUROI FORM
                                   CONT
                                   *AND
                                   (KIIROI FORM ORG))
                     TYPE
                     (V-2)
                     LGTH
                     (NAGASA    POSTP
                                NO
                                MSR
                                (FEET POSTP
                                       NO
                                       QU
                                       (*46 FORM ORG))))
                     LOC
                     (NAKA POSTP
                            NI
                            LOC
                            (SABAKU POSTP NO LOC (NEWMEXICO)))
                     AUX
                     (IRU TNS PAST)
                     TNS
                     PAST))
NIL
*rtime
(0.85500000 SECS)
```

For readers who can understand Japanese, the first two paragraphs of the translation are presented below for comparison with the English given in Chapter 8.

> 46 feet no ohkii kuroku kiiroi V-2 rocket wa NewMexico sabaku no naka ni tatteita. Kara de sore wa 5 ton no omosa ga atta. Nenryo ni sore wa 8 ton no alcohol to ekitai sanso o tsundeita.

> Subete wa dekita. Kagakusha to shogun wa tohkuni hanarete, dote no ushiro ni suwatta. 2 hon no akai honoh ga rocket o uchiageru tame no aizu ni agatta.

Usui encountered many difficulties in accomplishing the fine grain of the translation. For example, the sentence "It was too high to be seen" requires a paraphrase to the form "It was so high that one could not see it;" such paraphrases are possible using the context-sensitive transfer rules, but not easy. Usui was not satisfied with the generality of his Japanese grammar and concluded that considerable linguistic work was required for a successful translation project. He raised the interesting question for further research on symmetry of grammars: "Can one translation grammar map SRs in both directions between a pair of languages?" In other terms, is it possible to construct symmetric systems of transfer rules for translating between pairs of languages?

10.9 SUMMARY

Earlier in this chapter several methods for using rules and specialized interpreters were shown for controlling the flow of computation despite the HCPRVR top-down evaluation of Horn clauses. Rule forms and an interpreter for paraphrasing sentences were then shown as a realization of the translation paradigm. Examples of context-free translation and finally of English–Japanese translation using rules sensitive to sentence context were presented. A main purpose of the chapter was to demonstrate that rule-based computations in HCPRVR are not intrinsically limited by top-down evaluation. The secondary purpose was to examine the translation paradigm developed by early workers in the field of automatic translation in terms of its expression in procedural logic. This paradigm is expressed easily in Horn clause rules, but the task of defining optimal forms for lexicon and transfer rules is a significant research area that has so far been neglected. The few studies of translation mentioned here emphasize that the linguistic task of accumulating bilingual lexical and transfer rules will require a major effort before it is safe to conclude that automatic translation of technical literature is feasible. It is at least moderately encouraging, though, that the computations using symmetric grammars are neither excessively complex nor costly.

10.10 EXERCISES

1. Load and run the parsers given in Figures 10.1 to 10.3, following the traces of their operation.

2. Modify the grammars to allow for additional sentences such as "The raft floated down the river later burned."

3. Construct a left-corner parser (see Aho and Ullman [1972]).

4. Program a version of Parsifal following Marcus [1980].

5. Load and run the paraphrase system of Figure 10.4. Write a grammar and paraphrase rules to paraphrase a five-sentence paragraph of text.

11

KNOWLEDGE SYSTEMS

11.1 INTRODUCTION

In preceding chapters small grammars and schema systems have been shown to translate subsets of natural English into command languages or into a discourse structure that supports questioning and summarizing procedures. These are systems with specialized knowledge concerning the structure of a small subset of English and the content of a particular task; they follow an AI paradigm of demonstrating specialized intelligence in convenient microworld environments. During the past several years, the microworld paradigm has tended to yield to another, the expert knowledge system.

In this newer paradigm specialized knowledge of an expert—medical diagnostician, geologist, engineer, mechanic, and so on—is encoded as a system of inference rules that represent an organized portion of knowledge about a particular subdiscipline of the expert's field of knowledge. So DENDRAL [Feigenbaum, 1977] encodes specialized knowledge used by chemists to understand spectral analyses of chemical compounds, MYCIN [Shortliffe, 1976] encodes the relations of symptoms and medical tests to disease entities, and PROSPECTOR [Duda et al., 1978] relates geological phenomena to the possible presence of desired minerals. Surveys of these applications have been given by Feigenbaum [1977] and Duda and Gashnig [1981], showing a range of applications to medicine, engineering, geology, chemistry, and computer architecture. In each such application, the expert knowledge system has shown capabilities comparable to those of the experts from whom the knowlege was derived.

The basic rule form for such systems is an IF-THEN statement frequently augmented with a probabilistic weight:

IF secondary K-feldspar replacing plagiocase
in fresh-looking rocks
THEN 4, potassic zone alteration.

The 4 in the consequent shows the degree to which the premise is sufficient to establish the conclusion. Networks of 500 to 2000 such rules encompass significant bodies of specialized knowledge that may be used for diagnosis and for teaching.

European uses of PROLOG include inferential databases of specialized knowledge for determining drug interactions, the application of pesticides, and for air pollution control, reported by Futo et al. [1978], and for design of apartment houses by Markusz [1977]. The logic of these programs is essentially similar to that found in expert knowledge systems, with PROLOG serving as the interpreter for rules expressed as Horn clauses. These systems, like McDermott's [1981] expert for configuring VAX computer systems, are more oriented to task accomplishment or general questioning than the bulk of current American expert systems, which follow the diagnosis paradigm. Most recently, Clark and McCabe [1982] have shown a canonical design in PROLOG for a diagnostic system concerned with finding carburetor faults. Clark is particularly concerned to demonstrate methods for dealing with weighting schemes and the canonical "how" and "why" questions for which these systems provide answers. An example system for analyzing automobile starter problems developed below is based on his logic.

Expert knowledge systems often accept their data in a stylized subset of English if-then statements, and usually report their conclusions in natural-language phrases. Yet they are generally weak as language processors and tend to elicit information primarily by asking yes/no and multiple-choice questions. In this respect they resemble the first generation of computer-aided teaching programs; they present a menu of choices from which the user selects, then step by step interrogate the user until they reach a conclusion. Prospector and other advanced systems allow communication with specialized data languages and limited subsets of English, but generally the inclusion of free natural-language communication is beyond the state of the art.

11.2 AN EXAMPLE EXPERT MECHANIC

In our highly technological culture, specialized handbooks abound for service and repair of houses, appliances, and vehicles. In one such book, Jorgenson [1974] presents a chapter on troubleshooting Volkswagen problems. This chapter includes sections on the starter, charging system, engine, ignition, fuel system, and so on. It is a compilation of expert mechanics' knowledge about the relation of symptoms of mechanical failure to their underlying causes. Six paragraphs from this text are cited in Figure 11.1.

Starter

Starter system troubles are relatively easy to isolate. The following are common symptoms and cures.

1. Engine cranks very slowly or not at all—Turn on the headlights; if the lights are very dim, most likely the battery or connecting wires are at fault. Check the battery using the procedures described in Chapter 7. Check the wiring for breaks, shorts, and dirty connections.

    If the battery and connecting wires check good, turn the headlights on and try to crank the engine. If the lights dim drastically, the starter is probably shorted to ground. Remove the starter and test it using the procedures described in Chapter 7.

    If the lights remain bright or dim slightly when trying to crank the engine, the trouble may be in the starter, solenoid, or wiring. To isolate the trouble, short the two large solenoid terminals together (NOT to ground); if the starter cranks normally, check the solenoid wiring up to the ignition switch and the seat belt interlock relay (1974). If the starter still fails to crank properly, remove the starter and test it.

2. Starter turns, but does not engage with engine—This trouble is usually a defective pinion or solenoid shifting fork. It may also be that the teeth on the pinion, flywheel ring gear, or both, are worn down too far to engage properly.

3. Starter engages but will not disengage when ignition switch is released—This trouble is usually caused by a sticking solenoid, but occasionally the pinion can jam on the flywheel. With manual transaxles, the pinion can be temporarily freed by rocking the car in high gear. Naturally, this is not possible in automatics; the starter must be removed.

4. Loud grinding noises when starter runs—This trouble may mean the teeth on the pinion and/or flywheel are not meshing properly or it may mean the overrunning clutch is broken. In the first case remove the starter and examine the gear teeth. In the latter case, remove the starter and replace the pinion drive assembly.

Figure 11.1 (From Eric Jorgenson, *Volkswagen Service-Repair Handbook*, Clymer Publications, Los Angeles, 1974.)

We can translate this English description of expert knowledge about starters into a tree of possible faults and tests by creating an outline of the text, as follows.

Starter
    Starter turns engine slowly or not at all
        Turn on the headlights
            If dim
                Test battery

Sec. 11.2　An Example Expert Mechanic

        or connecting wires
      Turn on the headlights and crank the engine
        If the lights dim drastically
           Starter probably shorted
           Remove starter and test it
        If the lights remain bright
           Solenoid test
              Short the two large
              solenoid terminals together.
              If starter cranks normally,
              check solenoid wiring to
              ignition switch and seatbelt
              interlock relay.
              If starter still fails, remove
              and check it.
    Starter turns but does not engage with engine
      Remove starter
      Test solenoid shifting fork
      Test pinion
      Test teeth on flywheel ring gear and pinion
    Starter engages but will not disengage when ignition switch
    is released
      Pinion jam on flywheel
         Automatic transaxle—Remove starter and test
         Manual transaxle—Rock the car in high gear
    Loud grinding noises when starter runs
      Remove starter
        Overrunning clutch broken
           Replace pinion drive assembly
        Gear teeth not meshing properly
           Test teeth on flywheel and pinion

  From this hierarchic outline we can perceive a tree of four possible starter faults. For the first of these, two tests are offered: the "headlight dim" test and the "headlight dims with cranking" test. If the headlights are dim, we test for battery troubles or bad connections; for the other symptom we test the solenoid or the starter itself. We can translate the first starter fault into a series of IF-THEN rules, as follows:

IF starter turns engine slowly or not at all
THEN headlight test OR headlight and crank test.

IF headlight test results in dim headlights
THEN battery OR battery connections

IF headlight and crank test results in lights
dimming drastically

THEN starter test

IF headlight and crank test results in lights remaining bright or dimming slightly
THEN solenoid test OR starter test

In a similar fashion, the battery, battery connections, solenoid, and starter tests can be expressed in rules. To apply these rules computationally, we must obtain information by asking questions of the human user. A simple form for accomplishing this is to present a symptom, followed by a yes/no query, followed by instruction-query messages until a terminal fault is reached. For example (computer messages in capitals, user in lowercase):

```
STARTER TURNS ENGINE SLOWLY OR NOT AT ALL? YES/NO?
yes
TURN ON HEADLIGHTS; ARE THEY VERY DIM?
yes
EXAMINE THE ELECTROLYTE IN YOUR BATTERY; IS IT LOW?
no
TEST YOUR BATTERY WITH A HYDROMETER; ANY WEAK CELLS?
no
EXAMINE THE CONNECTIONS TO YOUR BATTERY; ARE THE TERMINALS
DIRTY?
yes
CLEAN THE TERMINALS WITH BAKING SODA; TIGHTEN THE CONNECTIONS;
DOES THAT SOLVE THE PROBLEM?
yes
```

The programming task is to design a rule form that will present messages and read responses under control of the network of implication rules. This can be accomplished by stating each node in the implication system as a procedural logic rule that prints a message, reads a response, and transfers control to another rule.

```
(STARTER) < (PR* (STARTER TURNS ENGINE SLOWLY OR NOT AT ALL?
    YES/NO?)) (RD* X)(EQ X YES) (OR ((HEADLIGHTS)(HEADLIGHTS
    WITH CRANKING)))
(HEADLIGHTS) < (PR* (TURN ON THE HEADLIGHTS; ARE THEY DIM?))
    (RD* X) (EQ X YES) (OR ((BATTERY)(BATTERY CONNECTIONS)))
(BATTERY) < (PR* ...) and so on,
```

Some efficiencies can be obtained, however, both for writing and interpreting the rules if we define a 4-tuple rule form as follows:

[POSFAULT <NAME> <MESSAGE> <TESTS>]

Figure 11.2 shows a series of such POSFAULT rules to represent some starter faults.

Sec. 11.2 An Example Expert Mechanic

```
============================================================
    (((POSFAULT (STARTER)
            (STARTER TURNS BUT ENGINE DOESN'T?)
            ((PINION AND FLYWHEEL) (SOLENOID SHIFTING FORK))))
    ((POSFAULT (STARTER)
            (STARTER CRANKS ENGINE SLOWLY OR NOT AT ALL?)
            ((HEADLIGHTS DIM) (HEADLIGHTS DIM WHILE CRANKING))))
    ((POSFAULT (STARTER)
            (STARTER DOESN'T DISENGAGE WHEN IGNITION SWITCH
             IS RELEASED?)
            ((STICKING SOLENOID) (JAMMED PINION))))
    ((POSFAULT (HEADLIGHTS DIM)
            (TURN ON THE HEADLIGHTS; ARE THEY DIM?)
            ((BATTERY) (BATTERY CONNECTIONS))))
    ((POSFAULT (STARTER)
            (LOUD GRINDING NOISES WHEN STARTER TURNS?)
            ((PINION AND FLYWHEEL) (OVER-RUNNING CLUTCH))))
    ((POSFAULT (HEADLIGHTS DIM WHILE CRANKING)
            (TURN ON THE HEADLIGHTS; CRANK ENGINE WITH STARTER;
             DO THE LIGHTS DIM SHARPLY?)
            ((STARTER TEST))))
    ((POSFAULT (HEADLIGHTS DIM WHILE CRANKING)
            (THE LIGHTS REMAINED BRIGHT?)
            ((SOLENOID TEST) (STARTER TEST))))
    ((POSFAULT (BATTERY) (IS ELECTROLYTE LOW IN BATTERY?)
            ((ELECTROLYTE LOW))))
    ((POSFAULT (BATTERY)
            (TEST YOUR BATTERY WITH A HYDROMETER;
             ARE ONE OR MORE CELLS BELOW NORMAL?)
            ((CHARGE BATTERY))))
    ((POSFAULT (ELECTROLYTE LOW)
            (ADD DISTILLED WATER; GET STARTED WITH JUMPER CABLES;
             RECHARGE BATTERY; DOES THAT SOLVE THE PROBLEM?)
            ((SOLVED))))
    ((POSFAULT (CHARGE BATTERY)
            (RECHARGE THE BATTERY; DID THAT SOLVE THE PROBLEM?)
            ((SOLVED))))
    ((POSFAULT (BATTERY CONNECTIONS)
            (DIRTY BATTERY TERMINALS OR WIRES?)
            ((CLEAN TERMINALS))))
    ((POSFAULT (BATTERY CONNECTIONS)
            (LOOSE OR FRAYED WIRE CONNECTIONS FROM BATTERY?)
            ((FIX CONNECTIONS))))
    ((POSFAULT (CLEAN TERMINALS)
            (WASH TERMINALS WITH BAKING SODA AND TIGHTEN THEM;
             DID THAT SOLVE THE PROBLEM?)
            ((SOLVED))))
    ((POSFAULT (FIX CONNECTIONS)
            (REPLACE FRAYED WIRE AND TIGHTEN ALL CONNECTIONS; OK NOW?)
            ((SOLVED)))))
============================================================
```

Figure 11.2 Possible fault rules.

A simple interpreter for such rules is the procedure MECH:

```
(MECH) < (POSFAULT STARTER X Y)(PR* X) (RD* W) (EQ W YES)
           (POSFAULTS Y)
(POSFAULTS ((SOLVED)) ) <
(POSFAULTS (X.Y)) < (POSFAULT X X1 X2)
(POSFAULTS (X.Y)) < (POSFAULTS Y)
```

The procedure terminates when the test field contains (SOLVED). If the answer to a message is other than yes, this system backs up to apply an alternative POSFAULT rule; for the yes, it goes forward applying the tests contained in the test field.

More is required of a knowledge system, however, than simply leading its user through a decision network. Generally, "how" and "why" questions can be asked at any time. The "why" question is interpreted to mean "Why do you ask?"; its answer is given by a standard response such as "I'm trying to determine if the — is at fault." The "how" question is taken to mean "How did you arrive at that conclusion?" and is answered typically by a list of sentences describing each step in the inference chain. To answer these questions, the interpreter given above is augmented to save its history in a special context register, and to accept and respond to the question "why." For the sake of simplicity, the answer is always given as a list of the steps the system has so far followed (ignoring the standard interpretation given above). When the system asks the user if the solution worked and receives a "yes" in response, it then automatically prints out its inference steps and returns control to the top.

Figure 11.3 shows the interpreter for the POSFAULT rules given in Figure 11.2. The procedure TALKCHOICE is called with the user's response as one of its arguments. If the response is "why," the procedure uses PRLST* to print the steps of its reasoning from last to first; for the response "yes" it creates a new reasoning step and adds it to the context register. In the case of any other response, the procedure POSFAULTS fails, stores the failed test on its context, and tries any remaining test associated with the previous step of its reasoning.

The procedures, RD* and PR* simply read and print. PRLST* prints a list, one element per line, and UNIQA* first deletes the value of a register such as CONTEXT, then asserts it with a new value. The call (CONTEXT X) assigns to X the current value in the context register.

The behavior of this simple mechanic-expert is shown in Figure 11.4. It should be noticed that limited to the few rules shown in Figure 11.2, Mech is far closer to an idiot with a few facts about batteries than to an expert mechanic; the addition of 200 or 300 more rules, however, would bring the system to a level of expertise well beyond that of the typical reader. If the

Sec. 11.2 An Example Expert Mechanic

```
===========================================================
           (((MECH)
             <
             (CONTEXT X)
             (A* (LASTCTX X))
             (UNIQA* (CONTEXT NIL))
             (PR* (WHAT PART OF YOUR CAR IS GIVING TROUBLE?))
             (RD* W)
             (DEVICE W W1)
             (UNIQA* (CONTEXT ((TROUBLE WITH W1))))
             (POSFAULTS (W1))))

           (((POSFAULTS ((SOLVED))) < (CONTEXT X) (PRLST* X) (MECH))
            ((POSFAULTS (X . Y))
             <
             (POSFAULT X X1 X2)
             (PR* X1)
             (RD* W)
             (TALKCHOICE X X1 X2 W))
            ((POSFAULTS (X . Y))
             <
             (CONTEXT W)
             (UNIQA* (CONTEXT ((X IS NOT THE PROBLEM) . W)))
             (POSFAULTS Y)))

           (((TALKCHOICE X X1 X2 WHY)
             <
             (CONTEXT W)
             (PRLST* W)
             (PR* X1)
             (RD* Y)
             (TALKCHOICE X X1 X2 Y))
            ((TALKCHOICE X X1 X2 YES)
             <
             (CONTEXT Y)
             (UNIQA* (CONTEXT ((PROBLEM X2 BECAUSE TEST X POSITIVE) . Y)))
             (POSFAULTS X2)))
===========================================================
```

Figure 11.3 An expert knowledge interpreter.

rules are augmented to include weightings reflecting the probability that a given set of symptoms truly reflects a mechanical fault, the amount of code in the Mech interpreter will grow notably. Additional procedures can also be added to improve the system's ability to communicate with the user. Even lacking these refinements, it is believed that Mech captures essential features of diagnostic experts in a form that can be easily understood by the reader interested in experimenting with such systems.

```
============================================================
              *(mech)

              (WHAT PART OF YOUR CAR IS GIVING TROUBLE?) *starter

              (STARTER TURNS BUT ENGINE DOESN'T?) *no

              (STARTER CRANKS ENGINE SLOWLY OR NOT AT ALL?) *yes

              (TURN ON THE HEADLIGHTS; ARE THEY DIM?) *yes

              (IS ELECTROLYTE LOW IN BATTERY?) *no

              (TEST YOUR BATTERY WITH A HYDROMETER;
                  ARE ONE OR MORE CELLS BELOW NORMAL?) *no

              (DIRTY BATTERY TERMINALS OR WIRES?) *yes

              (WASH TERMINALS WITH BAKING SODA AND TIGHTEN THEM;
               DID THAT SOLVE THE PROBLEM?) *yes

              (PROBLEM ((SOLVED)) BECAUSE TEST (CLEAN TERMINALS) POSITIVE)
              (PROBLEM ((CLEAN TERMINALS))
                      BECAUSE TEST (BATTERY CONNECTIONS) POSITIVE)
              ((BATTERY) IS NOT THE PROBLEM)
              (PROBLEM ((BATTERY) (BATTERY CONNECTIONS))
                      BECAUSE TEST (HEADLIGHTS DIM) POSITIVE)
              (PROBLEM ((HEADLIGHTS DIM) (HEADLIGHTS DIM WHILE CRANKING))
                      BECAUSE TEST (STARTER) POSITIVE)
              (TROUBLE WITH (STARTER))
              _____

              (WHAT PART OF YOUR CAR IS GIVING TROUBLE?) *battery

              (IS ELECTROLYTE LOW IN BATTERY?) *no

              (TEST YOUR BATTERY WITH A HYDROMETER;
                  ARE ONE OR MORE CELLS BELOW NORMAL?) *yes

              (RECHARGE THE BATTERY; DID THAT SOLVE THE PROBLEM?) *yes

              (PROBLEM ((SOLVED)) BECAUSE TEST (CHARGE BATTERY) POSITIVE)
              (PROBLEM ((CHARGE BATTERY)) BECAUSE TEST (BATTERY) POSITIVE)
              (TROUBLE WITH (BATTERY))
============================================================
```

Figure 11.4 Dialogue with expert Mech system.

11.3 APPLICATIONS TO TEACHING

Before the term "expert knowledge systems" was coined, many teaching systems used a similar approach. Specialized languages such as Course-Writer, PLANET, and so on, allowed a teacher to express his course content as a display, followed by one or more queries, with transfer to another topic as a function of the student's answers. In a modern sense, these systems were "experts" both in course content and the ordering of presentation for effective learning. Some advanced tutorial systems such as Sophie [Brown and Burton, 1975] included simulation models of the tasks they taught. The diagnostic capabilities of teaching systems lay primarily in the answer evaluation logic; their presentation strategies were similar to those of diagnostic experts particularly in their display of English explanations and their reliance on short answer forms; and the interpreters for teaching programs, like those for expert knowledge, resolved to a simple sequence of present a display, read a response, evaluate it, and present the next display as a function of the user's answer.

The point of these similarities is to emphasize that it is the representation and accumulation of expert knowledge that is of importance, not the cleverness of an interpretive program. The human expert understands and encodes what certain facts mean, how they combine to permit inferences to be made, and how these inferences lead to useful conclusions; the interpreter simply finds a path through the chunks of knowledge as a function of the user's input. As a consequence, modern expert knowledge systems are easily transformed into teaching systems, as Clancy et al. [1979] demonstrated in the GUIDON system for teaching students analysis of pulmonary functions using rules originally developed in MYCIN for diagnosis.

If we wish to transform our expert mechanic to a teacher, we need only prepare a different though similar interpreter, and modify the form of the rules so that they can apply in both modes. As a teacher, Mech should present a problem, for example:

> THE STARTER CRANKS THE ENGINE TOO SLOWLY
> SELECT A DIAGNOSTIC TEST FROM THE FOLLOWING:
> (PINION AND FLYWHEEL) (HEADLIGHTS DIM WHILE CRANKING)
> (HEADLIGHTS DIM) (STICKING SOLENOID)(STARTER TEST)

The user selects HEADLIGHTS DIM and the system responds:

> TURNED ON THE HEADLIGHTS. HEADLIGHTS DIM.
> SELECT A DIAGNOSTIC TEST:
> (FUSES) (GROUNDS) (SHORTS) (BATTERY) (BATTERY CONNECTIONS)

User selects BATTERY

> LOOKING AT THE BATTERY

SELECT A DIAGNOSTIC TEST:
(TERMINALS)(ELECTROLYTE)(CONNECTIONS)(HYDROMETER)

and so on.

When the user selects an inappropriate test, the system can make the customary negative reinforcement and provide such information as is desired to get back on a reasonable path. Scoring can be a function of the number of appropriate choices and the length of the diagnostic path.

Numerous other teaching designs are possible. One attractive approach is suggested by the immensely fascinating adventure games that currently proliferate on microcomputers. In the canonical form of these games, the user is placed in a cave, a strange land, a haunted house, and so on, and given the task of finding a path to a treasure, despite numerous obstacles to be encountered. The user is allowed a simple sentence form—usually noun-verb—to command various actions such as "climb wall," "draw sword," "attack dragon," and so on. Adventure games are yet another form of expert knowledge system in which an expert—author—develops a consistent model of some special microworld and provides a network of possible paths from its entrance to its exit; the traversal of a path requires a series of actions from the user, whose final score is some function of his or her understanding of the adventure world. An issue of *Creative Computing* [Aug. 1981, Vol 7, #8] was devoted to descriptions of the technology of these games. Like teaching machines, adventure games benefit remarkably from sophisticated graphic displays, and the general expert system, in as much as it is interactive, can be expected to find similar benefits by displaying graphic information. Considering the mechanic's handbook, for example, without its profusion of assembly photographs and exploded diagrams, a user would be hard put to understand the verbal descriptions of complex machinery.

11.4 KNOWLEDGE SYSTEMS FOR UNDERSTANDING LANGUAGE

Perhaps we have overemphasized the user-interactive aspects of knowledge systems; medical diagnosis systems often work with input data in the form of case histories that record the symptoms and test results accumulated for a patient; R1, the computer assembly expert, is dependent on a data base describing the various components and upon a formal language input of the customer's requirements; and the various inferential knowledge bases in PROLOG usually accept formal-language queries. Only teaching systems and games are inherently interactive.

A more important dimension of knowledge systems concerns the nature of their inferential logic. Medical diagnosis, because of the great complexity and variety of human individual differences, is inherently probabilistic; all of a standard set of symptoms may be present in some individual, but the disease may not be the one expected. Prospectors, too, may find all the signs of oil and yet drill a dry hole. Thus an important aspect of many knowledge systems is the technique used to indicate the degree of confidence to be given to a line of inference. These form a subclass which we can call "probabilistic knowledge systems."

In application to understanding natural language, knowledge systems range from relatively deterministic sentence grammars that require strict sequences of phrases, to plausible narrative schemas that are satisfied if some of their elements are present. For understanding discourse and conversation, the knowledge systems provide much weaker lines of inference that we can call "plausible logic."

Notable studies of the knowledge systems useful for understanding English descriptions of human actions are found in Schank and Abelson [1977], Carbonell [1981], and Allen [1979]. These knowledge systems include organized schemas of knowledge such as planboxes, scripts, plans, and goal trees—each a form of complex inference rule. They are used to understand English descriptions by augmenting the language statements with inferred knowledge of human situations, plans, and goals. For example, Carbonell, using situational scripts, belief models for conservative and liberal viewpoints, and goal trees to model the aims of United States and Soviet Union policies, enriches the meaning of "The U.S. Congress is expected to approve the Panama Canal treaty" with a structure equivalent to the following:

```
CANAL-ZONE FROM (CONTROL BY UNITED STATES)
           TO (CONTROL BY PANAMA)
UNITED STATES GOAL VIOLATED
UNITED STATES MILITARY STRENGTH DECREASED:
KNOW ACTOR (COUNTRY TYPE COMMUNIST)
     OBJ (DECREASE ACTOR UNITED STATES
               OBJ (MILITARY STRENGTH)
               VAL (INCREMENT -2))
```

In conjunction with the conservative belief models and the United States and Soviet goal trees, Carbonell's Politics system is able to provide the following answers to questions:

Q1. Should the United States approve the treaty?
A1. No, the treaty is bad for the United States.
Q2. Why is the treaty bad for the United States?
A2. The United States would lose the canal to Panama and the United States would be weaker.
Q3. What might happen if the United States loses the canal?
A3. Russia will try to control the canal.

Using the liberal belief model, a contrasting set of answers is obtained.

Q1. Should the United States approve the treaty?
A1. Yes, the Panama Canal Treaty is good for the United States.
Q2. Why is the treaty good?
A2. The Panama Canal Treaty improves relations with Latin American countries.
Q3. What happens if the United States keeps the canal?
A3. This will cause discontent and conflict in Panama and Latin America.

What is most striking about Politics is its humanlike ability to extrapolate from a simple statement a large system of interpreted meanings. This illustrates at once both the strength and weakness of plausible knowledge systems; to understand a text means to incorporate it somehow into a belief system and so add to it implications—meanings that it implies rather than states. But "rationalization"—the process of finding plausible reasons, becomes maladaptive when too generously applied, and the ideologue who interprets every fact by way of dogmatic beliefs may be revealed as a rationalizing fanatic.

Understanding a speaker's intention from a query is shown by Allen [1979] to involve the use of knowledge in the form of plans and structures that represent actions. For example, the query "Can you reach the salt?" can be understood as a request to pass the salt by use of the following elements of knowledge: [Note, BEN for Beneficiary, PROP for Proposition, AGT for Agent, and OBJ for Object.]

```
PASS (AGT BEN OBJ)
    PRECONDITION (HAVE AGT OBJ)
    EFFECT (HAVE BEN OBJ)

REACH (AGT OBJ)
  PRECOND (NEAR AGT OBJ)
  EFFECT (HAVE AGT OBJ)

REQUEST (SPEAKER HEARER ACTION)
    EFFECT (WANT HEARER ACTION)
    BODY (BELIEVE HEARER (WANT SPEAKER ACTION))

INFORM (SPEAKER HEARER PROP)
    PRECOND (KNOW SPEAKER PROP)
    EFFECT (KNOW HEARER PROP)
    BODY (BELIEVE HEARER
            (WANT SPEAKER (KNOW HEARER PROP)))
```

The analysis of "Can you reach the salt?" appears as follows:

1. Speaker wants Hearer to inform S whether H can reach the salt.
2. H infers S wants H to be able to reach the salt.
3. If H can reach the salt, the effect is that H has the salt.
4. Having the salt enables H to pass the salt.
5. H infers therefore that S wants him to pass the salt.

This line of plausible inference is appropriate at the dinner table, but rather chancy otherwise and although Allen does not show the restriction to mealtime situations, it can presumably be added to the knowledge structure. The same structure of rules is sufficient to understand such alternative forms as:

"Pass the salt."
"I want you to pass the salt."
"Do you have the salt?"
"Is the salt near you?"

More practical applications to understanding a dialogue at a train station are also demonstrated to be comprehended with the aid of a knowledge-based analysis of speech acts.

What we can see in all these examples of knowledge systems is the importance of reasoning from incomplete knowledge to draw plausible conclusions. Another example adapted from Schank and Riesbeck convincingly demonstrates the necessity of such systems for understanding even simple cases of narrative description.

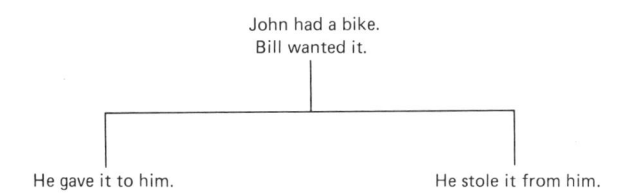

```
                    John had a bike.
                    Bill wanted it.
                           |
              ┌────────────┴────────────┐
              |                         |
        He gave it to him.        He stole it from him.
```

In the first continuation, "he" refers to John, "him" to Bill; in the second, "he" refers to Bill and "him" to John. To assign these pronoun bindings correctly requires specialized knowledge about the verbs "give" and "steal." Wilensky [1978] used the system PAM to develop detailed explanations of every step in an expanded version of this story; our analysis will be in the form of procedural logic rules and schemas. Both analyses succeed in computing forms of discourse structure, and both almost incidently solve the pronoun references.

We might suppose that specialized knowledge about the verbs "give" and "steal" could be represented in Horn clause rules such as the following:

```
(GIVE AGT X OBJ Y *TO Z) < (HAVE AGT X OBJ Y)
                          (WANT AGT Z OBJ Y)
                          (ASSERT (HAVE AGT Z OBJ Y))
(STEAL AGT X OBJ Y *FROM Z) < (HAVE AGT Z OBJ Y)
                              (WANT AGT X OBJ Y)
                              (ASSERT (HAVE AGT X OBJ Y))
```

These rules state that the agent of the giving must have had the object given, the *TO or recipient must have wanted it, and the result is that Z then has the object. With "steal" in contrast, the *FROM or patient of the stealing must have had the object, the agent must have wanted it, and the result is then asserted that the agent has it. (Notice the essential aspect of ownership is ignored for these examples since it is not required to resolve the pronouns. Miller and Johnson-Laird [1976] give a more complete semantic definition for these verbs.)

It is apparent that these rules are too stringent on several counts; the recipient of a giving might not want the gift, the agent of a theft might not want the object but instead wish to discomfort the owner, and if the object of either transaction is something large such as a house or a bank, the recipient may have something other than the physical object—a deed or a note, for example. Stating the rules in the form of semantic relations also calls our attention to the fact that when these rules are applied to analyzed sentences from a text, the variables X, Y, and Z may not match the same things because of the use of pronouns, ellipses, and anaphoric references. It is also the case that an SSR will include much syntactic information from its sentence that the rule does not, and therefore the rules will not exactly match the SSRs.

If, for example, the rule is applied with the "give" and "steal" SRs (ignoring the extra syntactic information contained in the SSRs),

```
(GIVE AGT HE OBJ IT *TO HIM) < (HAVE AGT HE OBJ IT)
                               (ASSERT (HAVE AGT HIM OBJ IT))
```

the first antecedent must be proved. The previous text asserted

```
(HAVE AGT JOHN OBJ BIKE)
(WANT AGT BILL OBJ IT)
```

Clearly, there is no perfect match, yet our knowledge of pronouns tells us that "he" matches "John," "it" matches "bike," and "him" matches "Bill." The situation is similar with "steal":

```
(STEAL AGT HE OBJ IT *FROM HIM) < (HAVE AGT HIM AE IT)
                                  (ASSERT (HAVE AGT HE OBJ IT))
```

In this case the pairings are HIM−JOHN, IT−BIKE, and HE−BILL. Instantiating these rules directly from the sentence will not allow HCPRVR to prove

Sec. 11.5 Knowledge Schemas

the rules for the obvious reason that "he," "him," and "it" will not match "John," "Bill," and "bike."

On the other hand, if we state the rules somewhat differently, the procedure RELATED can resolve pronoun correspondences and return a common definite concept. This procedure compares two terms to discover if they are related by subset, or part-of arcs, or if one is an acceptable pronoun for the other; it returns the original concept word as its third argument.

```
[ ((GIVE.X) → (GIVE.Y)) < (MATCHPR (AGT X1 AE X2 *TO X3) X X)
    (HAVE.W) (MATCHPR (AGT W1 AE W2) W W)
    (RELATED (X1 W1 Y1)(X2 W2 Y2))
    (WANT.Z) (MATCHPR (AGT Z1 AE Z2) Z Z)
    (RELATED (X3 Z1 Y3)(X2 X2 Y2))
    (ASSERT (HAVE AGT Y1 AE Y2))
    (SET Y (AGT Y1 AE Y2 *TO Y3)) ]
```

The input argument (GIVE.X) matches any SSR whose verb is "give." MATCHPR extracts the value of the relevant case arguments for RELATED to compare, the consequent that the recipient had the object is asserted with canonical form concepts, and Y is set to the list of these. The result is that the output argument (GIVE.Y) is an SR that ignores syntactic arguments of the original SSR and has no indirect references.

But there is still no assurance that we can prove that the recipient wanted the gift or perhaps even that the giver had it before the giving. So a further step must be taken to translate this still strict logical form into something fuzzier—a schema that can be satisfied with less stringent antecedent conditions.

11.5 KNOWLEDGE SCHEMAS

As we saw in Chapters 8 and 9, a schema is a complex rule for combining sentences or instantiated schemas into labeled treelike structures. A Transact* schema can be designed for this example, expanded to include possible bargaining steps.

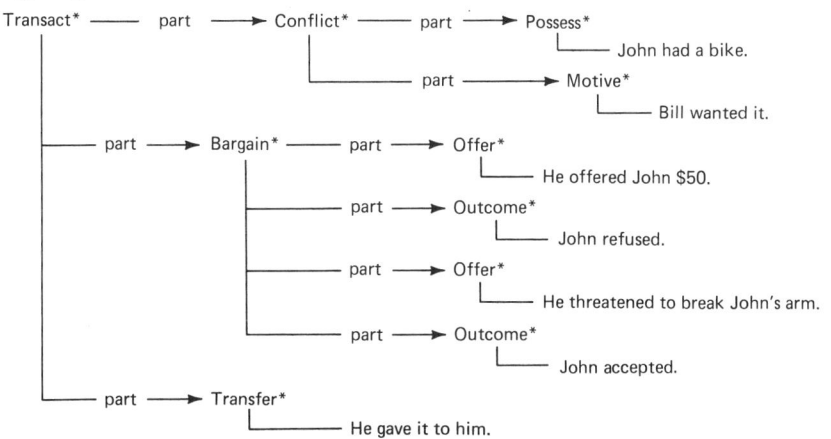

```
Transact* ─── part ───► Conflict* ─── part ───► Possess*
                                                    └── John had a bike.
                                ─── part ───► Motive*
                                                    └── Bill wanted it.
          ─── part ───► Bargain* ─── part ───► Offer*
                                                    └── He offered John $50.
                                ─── part ───► Outcome*
                                                    └── John refused.
                                ─── part ───► Offer*
                                                    └── He threatened to break John's arm.
                                ─── part ───► Outcome*
                                                    └── John accepted.
          ─── part ───► Transfer*
                                    └── He gave it to him.
```

The idea of this schema is that a Transact* may include one or more parts: a Conflict*, a Bargain*, a Transfer*. The transfer component is required. The Conflict* includes one or more of Possess* and Motive*, and the Bargain* one or more of Offer* and Outcome*.

Alterman [1982] has developed a convenient rule form for representing event concepts. Each verbal concept is characterized by up to seven arcs as follows: ANTECEDENT, ENABLE, SUBCLASS, PART, COORDINATE, CONSEQUENT, and SEQUEL. Rules using this information have the following format:

[ARCNAME CONCEPT1 CONCEPT2 <ARC CONSTRAINTS>]

An example using GET and GIVE as concepts is

(ENABLE GET GIVE ((MATCHP AGT AGT)(MATCHP AE AE)))

The rule states that GET and GIVE can be combined if their respective agents and affected entities match. The rule interpreter embeds one SR into another according to the requirements of the arc name. In this case,

(GIVE AGT JOHN AE BIKE...
    ENABLE* (GET AGT JOHN AE BIKE...))

[i.e., John's giving of a bike was enabled by his getting it.] The arc ENABLE* is the inverse of ENABLE; it is used here because the dominating concept of the pair in this context is GIVE. In the process of matching arc values, the controlling procedure finds references and substitutes them for pronouns.

Using just the relations PART and SC (subclass), schema rules for a variation on the transaction narrative were rewritten for Alterman's conceptual analyzer. Their form can be understood from the following sample:

(PART TRANSACT* CONFLICT* ((MATCHP *TO AGT)(MATCHP AE AE)))
(PART CONFLICT* MOTIVE* ((MATCHP AGT AGT)(MATCHP AE AE)))
(SC MOTIVE* WANT ((MATCHP AGT AGT)(MATCHP AE AE)))
(SC CONFLICT* HAVE ((MATCHP *WITH AGT)(MATCHP AE AE)))
(PART TRANSACT* BARGAIN* ((MATCHP *TO AGT)(MATCHP AE *FOR AE)))
(PART BARGAIN* OFFER* ((MATCHP AGT AGT)(MATCHP AE AE)
    (MATCHP *FOR *FOR)))
(PART BARGAIN* OUTCOME* ((MATCHP AGT *TO)(MATCHP AE AE)
    (MATCHP *FOR *FOR)))
(SC OFFER* THREATEN ((MATCHP AGT AGT)(MATCHP AE AE)))
(SC OUTCOME* REFUSE ((MATCHP AGT AGT)(MATCHP AE AE)))
(PART TRANSACT* TRANSFER* ((MATCHP *FROM *FROM)
    (MATCHP AE AE)
    (MATCHP *FOR *FOR)
    (MATCHP *TO *TO)))
(SC TRANSFER* GIVE ((MATCHP *FROM AGT)(MATCHP AE AE)
    (MATCHP *TO *TO)))

Sec. 11.5 Knowledge Schemas 241

The interpreter for these rules takes an SR (or an SSR), extracts the head verb, and seeks it as an element of an SC rule. When it is found, the MATCHP constraints are applied; if there are no arguments for one of the elements, the arguments of the other are transferred to it; if both elements have arguments the rule of matching is essentially that of RELATE—two arguments match if one is a subclass or part of the other, or if one is a pronoun for the other. Referring terms are discarded in favor of the words they refer to. The process recurses on schema terms using PART rules. As a result of applying such rules, ellipsis is often corrected as well by transferring values to arguments not present in the sentence but part of the schema rule.

The result for analyzing two variations on the transaction story are shown in Figures 11.5 and 11.6. UNDERSTANDER was called with the list of SRs shown as the first argument and returned them and the schema organization it computed as a second argument.

```
==========================================================
((UNDERSTANDER
  ((GET (AGT JOHN) (AE BIKE))
   (WANT (AGT BILL) (AE IT))
   (OFFER (AGT HE) (AE MONEY) (*FOR IT))
   (REFUSE (AGT JOHN))
   (STEAL (AGT HE) (AE IT) (*FROM HIM)))

  ((TRANSACT* (*FROM JOHN)
              (*TO BILL)
              (AE BIKE)
              (PART (CONFLICT* (AGT BILL)
                               (*WITH JOHN)
                               (AE BIKE)
                               (PART (MOTIVE* (AGT BILL)
                                              (AE BIKE)
                                              (SC (WANT (AGT BILL)
                                                        (AE BIKE)))
                               ))
                               (PART (POSSESS* (AGT JOHN)
                                               (AE BIKE)
                                               (SC (GET (AGT JOHN)
                                                        (AE BIKE)))
              ))))
              (PART (BARGAIN* (AGT BILL)
                              (*TO JOHN)
                              (PART (OFFER* (AGT BILL)
                                            (AE MONEY)
                                            (*TO JOHN)
                                            (SC (OFFER (*FOR IT)
                                                       (AGT BILL)
```

Figure 11.5 Discourse structure using Alterman's conceptual analyzer: *steal* example.

```
                                              (AE MONEY)
                                              (*TO JOHN)
                                   ))))
                            (PART (REFUSE* (AGT JOHN)
                                           (SC (REFUSE (AGT JOHN))))))
                  (PART (TRANSFER* (*FROM JOHN)
                                   (*TO BILL)
                                   (AE BIKE)
                                   (SC (STEAL (*FROM JOHN) (AGT BILL)
                                              (AE BIKE))))
          )))))))
========================================================
                       Figure 11.5 (continued)
========================================================
       ((UNDERSTANDER
         (((GET (AGT JOHN) (AE BIKE))
          (WANT (AGT BILL) (AE IT))
          (OFFER (AGT HE) (AE MONEY) (*FOR IT))
          (REFUSE (AGT JOHN))
          (GIVE (AGT HE) (AE IT) (*TO HIM)))
         (((HE MONEY BILL IT JOHN BIKE)
           ((TRANSACT* (*FROM JOHN)
                       (*TO BILL)
                       (AE BIKE)
                       (PART (CONFLICT* (AGT BILL)
                                        (*WITH JOHN)
                                        (AE BIKE)
                                        (PART (MOTIVE* (AGT BILL)
                                                       (AE BIKE)
                                                       (SC (WANT (AGT BILL)
                                                                 (AE BIKE)))
                              ))
                              (PART (POSSESS* (AGT JOHN)
                                              (AE BIKE)
                                              (SC (GET (AGT JOHN)
                                                       (AE BIKE)))
                       ))))
                       (PART (BARGAIN* (AGT BILL)
                                       (*TO JOHN)
                                       (PART (OFFER* (AGT BILL)
                                                     (AE MONEY)
                                                     (*TO JOHN)
                                                     (SC (OFFER (*FOR IT)
                                                                (AGT BILL)
                                                                (AE MONEY)
                                                                (*TO JOHN)))))
                                       (PART(REFUSE* (AGT JOHN)
                                                     (SC (REFUSE (AGT JOHN)
                                                     ))))))
```

Figure 11.6 Analysis with Alterman's conceptual understander: *give* example

Sec. 11.6 Constructing Knowledge Schemas

```
                 (PART (TRANSFER* (*FROM JOHN)
                                  (*TO BILL)
                                  (AE BIKE)
                        (SC (GIVE (AGT JOHN) (*TO BILL)
                                  (AE BIKE)))))))
))))
```
===

Figure 11.6 (*continued*)

The knowledge used in these examples is that encoded in the schemas; but Alterman's system is even more general than a schema applier. He has developed a dictionary of some 200 verbs and their interrelations in terms of his seven coherence relations. His conceptual understander uses this dictionary knowledge to organize sentences of text in a manner comparable to that shown above but using concept definitions rather than schemas to construct and label the subtrees. He has shown that the resulting structures are suitable for answering questions and forming summaries.

11.6 CONSTRUCTING KNOWLEDGE SCHEMAS

It is easily possible to make an outline for any ordinary text and from that outline to construct schemas. Unfortunately, several alternative outlines can be constructed by different people, so standard methods for outlining text must be defined rather carefully and systematically to obtain comparable results from different persons. Once an outline has been obtained, it represents a form of discourse analysis—generally, a tree organization of text with headings and subheadings, and sentences or clauses as terminal elements. The question of how to name the headings and subheadings is one of how to classify schemas and concepts. When such an outline has been prepared, it can serve as a guide for writing schemas, one for each node in the outline.

The Transact* schema diagram shown earlier for the bike story was derived from the following outline.

> Transaction
> Conflict
> > Possession "John got a bike"
> > Motive "Bill wanted it"
>
> Bargain
> > Offer "He offered fifty dollars..."
> > Outcome "John refused"
> > ...
> > Offer "He threatened to break Bill's arm"

Outcome <implied>
Transfer
He gave it to him

In this approach to outlining, each event described by a sentence is labeled, and sets of related labels are labeled at higher levels in a recursive process that terminates with the label that encompasses the entire narrative. For schema design, the labels are then suffixed with an asterisk to distinguish them from ordinary concepts.

The alternative method used by Alterman depends on intrinsic conceptual relations among verbal concepts, combining concepts in labeled dependency structures subordinating one concept to another in terms of the relational arc that connects the two. The dependency stuctures that result still maintain the summary property and are enriched by explicit information which the text may have left implicit.

The approach to explicating dependency relations between pairs of sentences is illustrated below.

```
Give by John of bike to Bill
^
|
Result of
|
Threaten by Bill . . .
^
|
Result of
|
Refusal by John of offer
^
|
Result of
|
Offer by Bill of money
^
|
Result of
|
Want by Bill of bike
^
|
Enabled by
|
Get by John of bike
```

This form of analysis requires definition of a set of arc names and careful judgments of how successive sentences are related. Alterman's study of 10 folk tales resulted in a compilation of about 200 verbs whose successive orderings in text led him to define seven relations that appear to encompass the dependencies he encountered. The "enable-result" system illustrated above is much cruder, but can be used as a first approximation to a dependency structure for text sentences.

The contrast between outline and dependency approaches to organizing texts is analogous to the sentence-level contrast of syntactic structure and labeled dependency structure. Both syntactic and dependency analysis results in hierarchical structures for sentences. At both sentence and discourse levels, the contrasting structures are comparably effective in revealing constituent properties of the text; in both cases, the syntactic and the outline structures add labels to constituents, while the dependency structures relate words or text sentences by labeled arcs. At the discourse level, we neither know a "grammar" nor do we know the dependency relations that hold between pairs of clauses. Alterman's work, from this view, is aimed at discovering a set of general dependency relations that hold between clauses—his seven coherence relations. The text grammarians, in contrast, are exploring possible grammar forms for labelling the constituents of discourse—with story grammars and schema structures.

Both the outlining technique and the dependency method sketched above seem to be "natural" forms for analyzing text into hierarchical structures of sentences. The term "natural" is used to suggest that they are easily teachable to people who have little or no understanding of formal linguistics. The problem common to both methods is one of defining in a precise manner the terms and criteria that a person should use to make some "standard" form of analysis. At present, although the methods are easily teachable and depend mainly on a person's nonlinguistic understanding, the lack of formal defining criteria for "standard analyses" must result in widely differing structures assigned by different analysts using either technique.

Throughout this book we have seen that grammars, semantic translators, scripts, frames, and schemas are each examples of compilations of knowledge in variant forms of IF–THEN rules; each such example represents limited knowledge of all possible cases; and each reveals the weakness of limited knowledge by its possibility of erroneous application to some new and unexpected segment of text. It is not the case that every program composed of implication rules is a knowledge system because some such programs (e.g., factorial, subset, Fibonacci function, etc.) are completely algorithmic and completely deterministic. Knowledge systems are heuristic by nature— procedures that are defined for only a partial set of all cases to which they might be applied. For natural language, we are assured that no grammar will ever be complete because the language changes, adding new words and new constructions as people continue to use and modify it. For conceptual definitions, it is apparent that ever finer and finer levels of detail can be articulated. At the discourse level, it appears that schemas sufficiently detailed to account for successive events in a narrative or argument are incomplete knowledge representations, limited both in their capability for generalization and in their ability to reject inappropriate instances. A lifetime's experience of reading in one field, say geology, hardly equips a person with the schemas required for reading physics, and even the geologist's schemas may encounter new and unexpected narratives that lead their user mistakenly down a garden path which terminates in confusion.

11.7 THE KNOWLEDGE PARADIGM

All of the knowledge systems discussed in this chapter depend on the use of explicit implicational rules. Of course, there are other systems very similar in principle that are more procedural in nature: for example, the KRL, KLONE series (see Bobrow and Winograd [1977] and Brachman [1979]). The expert knowledge systems are frequently probabalistic in nature using numerical values both to indicate the probable truth of a conclusion and to indicate the probability that a given rule applies to a particular sequence of symptoms. Knowledge systems for text are even less certain; they offer plausible conclusions if some of their antecedents are satisfied. In the forms of schemas, plans, scripts, and goal trees, they provide possible explanations that organize the sentences of a text or dialogue into plausible structures of meaning. None of these systems offers positive assurance as to the truth of their conclusions.

Newell [1981] analyzes the knowledge level to arrive at the instructive conclusions that:

1. Knowledge is forever an abstraction—the extension of a finite set of rules that lead to an infinite set of conclusions.
2. Knowledge results from a process applied to a symbol system—it is an action rather than a structure.
3. Knowledge is inseparable from the agent that applies the process—people and programs reify knowledge.
4. Knowledge and rationality are intimately related in a principle of rationality:

> If an agent has knowledge that one of its actions will lead to one of its goals, then the agent will select that action. [p. 8]

Throughout his discussion, Newell emphasizes the heuristic nature of knowledge.

> Knowledge: Whatever can be ascribed to an agent, such that its behavior can be computed according to the principle of rationality. [p. 10]
>
> To ascribe to an agent the knowledge associated with structure S is to ascribe whatever the observer can know from structure S. [p. 13]
>
> The knowledge level is only an *approximation*, and a relatively poor one on many occasions—we called it radically incomplete. [p. 12]

Most knowledge systems of any consequence are, like human knowledge, necessarily incomplete. They include rules for dealing with a particular set of cases and may be surprised at any moment by the appearance of a rare and unpredicted situation. McDermott [1981], in a discussion of his experiences with R1, the computer expert, states the point succinctly.

It is not clear that all (or even most) of R1's supporters realize that R1 will always make mistakes. The problem is that at least some of R1's supporters think of it as a program rather than as an expert. There is of course a big difference between programs and experts. Finished programs, by definition, have no bugs. When experts are finished, on the other hand, they're dead. [p. 28]

Of course, large applied programs suffer from the same limitation and errors continue to be found decades after delivery of such relatively straightforward systems as those used for producing paychecks, let alone their operating systems.

Considering these views of knowledge from authors of knowledge systems, what is so attractive about the knowledge paradigm? First, not all uses of knowledge are so hazardous; algorithms for well-understood problems such as computing factorials, Fibonacci series, parsing formal languages, and so on, can be expressed in implication rules to result in perfectly reliable programs. The rule forms in which knowledge systems are represented are not the reason for their heuristic nature. Second, large complex programs generally suffer from the same incompleteness of definition that is so apparent in knowledge systems; they, too, are subject to human limitations of understanding. Knowledge systems are typically characterized by relatively independent modular units, so erroneous units can easily be replaced and new units can be added without interfering with existing ones. They are particularly adaptable to the guessing games of medical diagnosis, analysis of conversation, and discourse structuring of text. In their very fallibility they lend themselves to the simulation of commonly fallible human thought processes as no precise mathematical model can. Yet a knowledge system that represents a perfectly understood mathematical, scientific, or engineering process need be no less reliable than the process itself.

11.8 CLOSURE

Throughout this book we have seen that grammars, semantic translators, schemas, parsing procedures, and expert systems can all be realized as computations using IF−THEN rules of various forms. We have seen that procedural logic is a concise and effective technique for expressing and interpreting these rules as programs. Without intending to claim that natural-language discourse is itself a formal-logical system, we have seen that formal-logical systems can be used to analyize and process those fragments of discourse that we understand procedurally. It is true that the meaning of a discourse is usually subtle, multi-dimensional, and implicit. It is also true, however, that computers must deal first and foremost with their actual input, that is, with the "surface text" as a sequence of signs and symbols. Until computers can compute effectively with that surface input—parse it, analyze it, generate it, paraphrase it, summarize it, query it, and so on—we cannot have a reliable link to the knowledge that underlies language communication. In this sense, "grammar" is a set of rules and procedures for accomplishing these tasks on linguistic sequences. We can render not only classical phrase-structure grammars, but also scripts, frames, schemas, and expert knowlege, as logical systems that state conditions and actions applicable to text or dialogue. Of course, the resulting plausible interpretations will not provide certainty about the text meaning; but, after all, human communication is not, and cannot be, an enterprise of certainty. One can never know absolutely what another person means, because consciousness is not identical in different minds; but one can follow plausible rules and decide what the other probably means, and what one should probably do about it.

It is not contended that procedural logic is the only technique for encoding procedural rules that represent knowledge, or even necessarily the best technique. As Newell reminds us, "knowledge" is "the extension of a finite set of rules that lead to an infinite set of conclusions." The complexity of human communication is beyond the power of any single computational approach, we owe a great debt to many approaches: the conceptual dependency and dynamic memory systems from Yale, the truth-maintenance systems and frame languages from MIT, the problem-solving and production systems from Carnegie-Mellon, the procedural semantics and speech-act systems from Toronto, the expert knowledge systems from Stanford, and many more. Nonetheless, it is argued that the procedural logic approach presented here is well adapted to contemporary computing environments, particularly to the LISP machine families, and to the task of developing formal systems for natural-language computations. Hence, procedural logic offers a currently accessible vehicle for making immediate headway on the linguistic and cognitive problems we must solve.

Each perspective on computation helps us to understand what it is to know something or mean something. Indeed, artificial intelligence and cognitive science can be defined as explorations toward understanding knowledge and meaning. Insomuch as procedural logic provides us with a capability for representing what we do understand in a language natural to our thought, yet interpretable as computer programs, it promises notable contributions to these sciences.

11.9 EXERCISES

1. Explore and augment the V-W Trouble Shooting system.
2. Make it into a teaching system.
3. As a fairly serious project can you make a general system like Novak's [1977], for translating descriptions into pictures?
4. What are *your* answers to the questions given in the Preface?

A

USING HCPRVR

Daniel Chester
University of Delaware
September 1982

Instructions for using a simple theorem prover called HCPRVR are given, followed by a brief explanation of its operation. HCPRVR has been used to parse and generate English sentences and to interpret program specifications.

A.1 INTRODUCTION

HCPRVR, a simple Horn clause theorem prover written in Lisp, is a straightforward application of the problem reduction technique to a very simple logical formalism. The three major classes of expressions in this formalism are *terms, atomic formulas,* and *axioms*. The syntax for these classes are given by the following BNF rules:

        <term> ::= <constant> | <variable> | (<list of terms>)
        <constant> ::= <literal atom>
        <variable> ::= <literal atom> | _<literal atom>
        <list of terms> ::= | <term> | <term> <list of terms> |
                    <term> . <term>
        <atomic formula> ::= (<predicate name> <list of terms>)

249

```
<predicate name> ::= <constant>
<axiom> ::= ( <fact> ) |
            ( <conclusion> < <list of premisses> )
<fact> ::= <atomic formula>
<conclusion> ::= <atomic formula>
<list of premisses> ::= <premiss> |
                        <premiss> <list of premisses>
<premiss> ::= <variable> | <atomic formula> | /
```

A.2 INITIAL DATA

Literal atoms are declared to be variables by typing

(VARIABLES atom1 atom2 ... atomN)

Literal atoms beginning with underscore (_) are always variables and do not have to be declared. Axioms are declared by typing

(AXIOMS '<list of axioms>)

To see the axioms associated with a predicate name (i.e., axioms that have that predicate name in the conclusion), type

(GET '<predicate name> 'AXIOMS)

A.3 THEOREMS

In this system, all theorems are in the form of atomic formulas. This is not really restrictive because we can prove the disjunction of formulas P1 and P2 by adding the axioms (Q < P1) and (Q < P2) and then proving Q. We can prove the conjunction of P1 and P2 by means of the function ?, i.e., by evaluating (? P1 P2).

Negation is not a primitive concept in this formalism. To deal with the negation of an atomic formula, we have to introduce a dual predicate name for the complementary concept and add appropriate axioms. For example, if (ON X Y) is an atomic formula and we want to deal with the negation of ON, we have to add axioms about the formula (NOT_ON X Y). (As far as the prover is concerned, NOT_ON is just another predicate name; it is the extra axioms that identify it as the negation of ON.) If you want to work in a formalism that has negation as a primitive logical concept, I suggest that you look at Chapter 6 of *Automated Theorem Proving: A Logical Basis* by David Loveland, (North Holland Publishing Company, New York, 1978. xiii + 395 pages). He describes a theorem prover that extends this prover in both its formalism and its algorithm.

A.3.1 Proving Theorems

To prove a theorem stated as an atomic formula, type

$$(TRY\ '<atomic\ formula>)$$

or

$$(?\ <atomic\ formula>)$$

If the theorem has been assigned as the value of a <Lisp variable>, type

$$(TRY\ <Lisp\ variable>)$$

A conjunction of formulas can be proved by typing

$$(?\ <formula1>\ <formula2>\ \ldots\ <formulaN>\ )$$

Note that ? is a Lisp FEXPR. If there are assignments to the variables in the formulas that make them true, TRY or ? will evaluate to the list of formulas with the variables replaced by their assignments. If no such assignments are possible, TRY or ? evaluates to NIL. Only one set of assignments will normally be found, although several sets of assignments may be possible. (Actually, "answer a question" would be better terminology than "prove a theorem" for what HCPRVR does. For instance, (TRY '(ON X TABLE)) answers the question "Is there something on the table?" The answer might be ((ON FORK TABLE)), meaning "The fork is among the things on the table.")

A.4 PREDICATE NAMES AS FUNCTIONS

Occasionally, it is useful to let a predicate name be a Lisp function that gets called instead of letting HCPRVR prove the formula in the usual way. The predicate name ASSERT, for example, is a LISP function that adds new axioms dynamically. Predicate names that are also functions are FEXPRs and expect that their arguments have been expanded into lists in which all bound variables have been replaced by their values. These predicate names must be marked as functions by having the Lisp property FN set to T [e.g., by executing (PUT '<predicate name> 'FN T), so that HCPRVR will interpret them as functions]. See Section A.9 for a list of built-in predicate names.

A.5 GLOBAL VARIABLES

There are several global variables that the user should know about in order to make the most effective use of HCPRVR. These variables and their significance are:

> AFLAG   When AFLAG is T, the trace of HCPRVR includes the axioms

that are being tried for each relation being traced. The default value is NIL.

DEPTH   This determines the depth to which expressions in traces are printed. The default value is 4.

LENGTH   This determines the length to which expressions in traces are printed. The default value is 6.

LIMIT   This is an integer that controls how many steps of the proof will be tried before HCPRVR asks whether it should continue. When it prints CONTINUE?, typing Y or YES will allow it to resume proving, typing N or NO will cause HCPRVR to stop; anything else will be evaluated and the value printed, followed by the CONTINUE? query again. The default value of LIMIT is 100.

QFLAG   This flag determines how HCPRVR terminates. If QFLAG is NIL, the default value, a call to TRY or ? returns the first solution it finds or NIL. If QFLAG is T, a call to TRY or ? prints the first solution it finds, followed by the query ANOTHER?. If you type Y or YES the system will look for another solution; any other input will terminate the program with the current solution.

SHORTFORM   This flag is set to T or NIL in order to control whether the full unification algorithm is executed. When SHORTFORM is T, the test that prevents a variable X from being bound to a term like (F A X B) is omitted. Strictly speaking, this is not logically correct, but it has proved adequate for most applications, and runs a little faster.

RTIME   At the end of each call to TRY or ? this variable is set to a message stating how many seconds the computation took.

TFLAG   This flag is set to T or NIL in order to control a trace of the proof. When TFLAG = NIL, no trace is shown. When TFLAG = T, each atomic formula about to be proved is printed with the prefix (Q-n) attached, where n is the length of the remaining goal stack. When the formula is proved, it is printed again with the prefix (R-n) attached. Do not use the Lisp TRACE function to trace PROVE or MATCH because HCPRVR works with circular lists. Use the RTRACE function if you only want to trace a few relations.

VAL   This variable is set to the value returned by TRY so that it can be reexamined without running the prover again.

A.6 PARSING SENTENCES

As an illustration of how HCPRVR can be used to parse sentences, a trivial example will be given. Parsing is done by axioms that combine syntax with semantic tests. Each syntactic category is a predicate name that requires three terms after it. The first term is a list of words. The second term is a

Sec. A.6 Parsing Sentences

representation for an initial segment of the word list which makes a phrase belonging to the syntactic category. The last term is the remainder of the word list after the phrase is removed. Thus, in the atomic formula (NP (THE CAT IS ON THE MAT) (CAT DET THE) (IS ON THE MAT)) the second term, (CAT DET THE) represents the NP phrase THE CAT.

By letting syntactic categories be predicates with three arguments, we can make axioms that pull phrases off of a list of words until we get a sentence that consumes the whole list. In addition, arbitrary tests can be performed on the phrase representations to check whether they can be semantically combined. Usually, the phrase representation in the conclusion part of an axiom tells how the component representations are combined, while the premises tell how the phrase should be factored into the component phrases, what their representations should be, and what restrictions they have. Thus, the axiom

```
((S X (U ACTOR V . W) Z) < (NP X V Y) (VP Y (U . W) Z)
                          (NUMBER V N1) (NUMBER U N2)
                          (EQ N1 N2))
```

says that an initial segment of word list X is a sentence if first there is a noun phrase ending where word list Y begins, followed by a verb phrase ending where word list Z begins, and both phrases agree in number (singular or plural). Furthermore, the noun phrase representation V is made the actor of the verb U in the verb phrase, and the rest of the verb phrase representation, W, is carried along in the representation for the sentence.

A.6.1 Example

Here is a sample grammar that will parse the sentence THE CAT IS ON THE MAT.

```
(VARIABLES X Y Z U V W N1 N2)

(SETQ GRAMMAR '(
((S X (U ACTOR V . W) Z) < (NP X V Y) (VP Y (U . W) Z)
                          (NUMBER V N1) (NUMBER U N2)
                          (EQ N1 N2))
((NP (THE . X) (U DET THE) Y) < (N X U Y))
((N (X . Y) X Y) < (CAT X N))
((VP X (U LOC V) Z) < (V X U Y) (PP Y V Z) (FEAT V LOC))
((V (X . Y) X Y) < (CAT X V))
((PP (ON . X) (ON LOC U) Y) < (NP X U Y) (FEAT U POBJ))
((FEAT (X . Y) Z) < (FEAT X Z))
((CAT CAT N))
((CAT IS V))
((CAT MAT N))
((FEAT CAT POBJ))
((FEAT MAT POBJ))
((FEAT ON LOC))
```

```
((NUMBER (X . Y) Z) < (NUMBER X Z))
((NUMBER CAT SING))
((NUMBER MAT SING))
((NUMBER IS SING))
))

(AXIOMS GRAMMAR)

(SETQ THEOREM '(S (THE CAT IS ON THE MAT) X NIL))
```

The sentence can now be parsed by typing either

```
(? (S (THE CAT IS ON THE MAT) X NIL))
```

or (TRY THEOREM). The pretty-printed form of VAL after this computation is

```
(S (THE CAT IS ON THE MAT)
   (IS ACTOR (CAT DET THE) LOC (ON LOC (MAT DET THE)))
   NIL)
```

A.7 THEORY OF OPERATION

A.7.1 General Organization

HCPRVR works essentially by the problem reduction principle. Each atomic formula can be thought of as a problem. Those that appear as facts in the list of axioms represent problems that have been solved, while those that appear as conclusions can be reduced to the list of problems represented by the premises. Starting from the formula to be proved, HCPRVR reduces each problem to lists of subproblems and then reduces each of the subproblems in turn until they have all been reduced to the previously solved problems, the "facts" on the axiom list. The key functions in HCPRVR that do all this are PROVE and MATCH.

A.7.2 The PROVE Function

PROVE is the function that controls the problem reduction process. It has one argument, a stack of *subproblem structures*. Each subproblem structure has the following format:

(<list of subproblems>.<binding list>)

where the list of subproblems is a sublist of the premises in some axiom and the CAR of the binding list is a list of variables occurring in the subproblems, paired with their assigned values. When PROVE is initially called by TRY, it begins with the stack

Sec. A.7 Theory of Operation

$$(\,(\,(\,<\text{formula}>\,)\,\text{NIL}\,)\,)$$

The algorithm of PROVE works in depth-first fashion, solving subproblems in the same left-to-right order as they occur in the axioms and applying the axioms as problem reduction rules in the same order as they are listed. PROVE begins by examining the first subproblem structure on its stack. If the list of subproblems in that structure is empty, PROVE either returns the binding list, if there are no other structures on the stack (i.e., if the original problem has been solved), or removes the first structure from the stack and examines the stack again. If the list of subproblems of the first subproblem structure is *not* empty, PROVE examines the first subproblem on the list. If the predicate name in it is a function, the function is applied to the arguments. If the function returns NIL, PROVE fails; otherwise, the subproblem is removed from the list and PROVE begins all over again with the modified structure.

When the predicate name of the first subproblem in the list in the first subproblem stucture is *not* a function, PROVE gets all the axioms that are stored under that predicate name and assigns them to the local variable Y. At this point PROVE goes into a loop in which it tries to apply each axiom in turn until one is found that leads to a solution to the original problem. It does this by calling the MATCH function to compare the conclusion of an axiom with the first subproblem. If the match fails, it tries the next axiom. If the match succeeds, a *new* subproblem structure is put on the front of the stack. This new subproblem structure consists of the list of premises from the axiom and the binding list that was created at the time MATCH was called. Then PROVE calls itself with this newly formed stack. If this call returns a binding list, it is returned as the value of PROVE. If the call returns NIL, everything is restored to what it was before the axiom was applied and PROVE tries to apply the next axiom.

The way that PROVE applies an axiom might be better understood by considering the following illustration. Suppose that the stack looks like this:

$$(\,(\,(\text{C1 C2}).<\text{blist}>\,)\,\ldots\,)$$

The first subproblem in the first subproblem structure is C1. Let the axiom to be applied be

$$(\text{C} < \text{P1 P2 P3})$$

PROVE applies it by creating a new binding list blist', initially empty, and then matching C with C1 with the call (MATCH C <blist'> C1 <blist>). If this call is successful, the following stack is formed:

$$(\,(\,(\text{P1 P2 P3}).<\text{blist'}>\,)\,(\,(\text{C1 C2}).<\text{blist}>\,)\,\ldots\,)$$

Thus problem C1 has been reduced to problems P1, P2 and P3 as modified by the binding list blist'. PROVE now applies PROVE to this stack in the hope that all the subproblems in it can be solved.

In the event that the axiom to be applied is (C), that is, the axiom is just a fact, the new stack that is formed is

((().<blist'>) ((C1 C2).<blist>) ...)

When PROVE is called with this stack, it removes the first subproblem structure and C1, and then begins working on problem C2.

A.7.3 The MATCH Function

The MATCH function is a version of the unification algorithm that has been modified so that renaming of variables and substitutions of variable values back into formulas are avoided. The key idea is that the identity of a variable is determined by *both* the variable name and the binding list on which its value will be stored. The value of a variable is also a pair: the term that will replace the variable and the binding list associated with the term. The binding list associated with the term is used to find the values of variables occurring in the term when needed. Notice that variables do not have to be renamed because MATCH is always called (initially) with two distinct binding lists, giving distinct identities to the variables in the two expressions to be matched, even if the same variable name occurs in both of them.

MATCH assigns a value to a variable by CONSing the variable name-value pair to the CAR of the variable's binding list using the RPLACA function; it also puts that binding list on the list bound to the Lisp variable SAVE in PROVE. This is done so that the effects of MATCH can be undone when PROVE backtracks to recover from a failed application of an axiom.

A.8 SPECIAL FEATURES

The following Lisp functions are provided in HCPRVR:

(RTRACE name1 name2 ... nameN)

RTRACE is an FEXPR that marks predicate names name1 through nameN to be traced. This function allows traces to be selective. (RTRACE) evaluates to a list of the predicate names currently being traced.

(UNRTRACE name1 name2 ... nameN)

UNRTRACE is an FEXPR that stops the selective tracing of predicate names name1 through nameN. (UNRTRACE) stops the tracing of all predicate names. *Note:* RTRACE and UNRTRACE do not affect the nonselective traces caused by the TFLAG variable.

Sec. A.9   Predicates   **257**

(CLEAR context)

CLEAR is an FEXPR that clears memory of all axioms with an expression matching context in the second position in the axioms [i.e., where the arrow (<) usually appears]. (CLEAR <) removes only axioms of the form (<formula> <). (CLEAR) removes all axioms except those of the form (<formula>) or (<conclusion> < <premise1> ... <premiseN>).

(RELATIONS)

RELATIONS evaluates to a list of all the predicate names for which axioms are stored.

A.9 PREDICATES

The following predicate names are already included in HCPRVR:

(EQ x y)

Succeeds if x equals y.

(NEQ* x y)

Succeeds if x does not equal y.

(ATOM* x)

Succeeds if x is an atom.

(VAR* x)

Succeeds if x is an unbound variable.

(ASSERT x1 ... xN)

ASSERT stores the axiom (x1 ... xN). When N > 1, x2 may be any symbol or Lisp expression, which is used to distinguish a subset of axioms. x2 is the "context" of the axiom. (See CLEAR.)

(UNLESS x)

Calls (? x). UNLESS succeeds if and only if (? x) fails.

(SETV* x expr)

Sets the variable x to the Lisp evaluation of expr. Any logic variables that appear in expr are replaced by their values before evaluation.

(RAND*)

Sometimes succeeds; the pattern of successes is random. *Note:* RAND* is also a Lisp random selection function that can be called in a SETV* formula. If Y is bound to the list (z1 ... zN), the formula (SETV* X (RAND* . Y)) binds X to some zI that has been chosen randomly from the list Y.

(RPRINT x1 ... xN)

The arguments x1 through xN are printed on successive lines.

(RTERPRI)

Prints a carriage-return line-feed.

(RREAD x)

Binds x to one Lisp S-expression taken from the terminal.

This is the cut symbol. It has no effect until PROVE attempts to back up past it, at which time PROVE immediately fails the subproblem that it is attempting to solve. For example, suppose that the axioms that expand a subproblem C are (C < A / B) and (C < D E), and that they are stored in that order. The first axiom is tried first. If subproblem A fails, the second axiom is tried. If A succeeds, the cut symbol also succeeds and subproblem B is tried. If B fails or some later failure causes PROVE to backtrack past it, subproblem C fails immediately; PROVE does not backtrack into A or go on to the second axiom. *Note:* / should always be followed by a blank space.

A.10 SELECTED READINGS

For implementation details of other Horn clause theorem provers, consult the following:

Black, F. S., A Deductive-Question Answering System, in *Semantic Information Processing,* M. Minsky (ed.), MIT Press, Cambridge, Mass., 1968, pp. 354–402.

Warren, D. H. D., Pereira, L. M., and Pereira, F. C. N., PROLOG—The Language and its Implementation Compared with LISP. *Proc. ACM Symp. Artif. Intel. Programming Languages, SIGPLAN Notices,* Vol. 12, p. 8/*SIGART Newsl.,* Vol. 64, pp. 109–115, Aug. 1977.

For an axiomatization of the STRIPS problem solver, see:

Warren, D. H. D., WARPLAN: A System for Generating Plans, DCL Memo 76, Dept. Comp. Logic, School Artif. Intell. University of Edinburgh, June 1974.

For discussion of processing natural language with Horn clause theorem provers, see:

Dahl, V., Quantification in a Three-Valued Logic for Natural Language Question-Answering Systems, *IJCAI '79,* Tokyo, 1979, pp. 182–187.

Simmons, R., and Chester, D., Relating Sentences and Semantic Networks with Clausal Logic, Dept. Comp. Sci., University of Texas, Austin, 1980; *Commun. ACM,* 1982, in press.

For added inspiration, read:

Brown, F., and Schwind, C., Outline of an Integrated Theory of Natural Language Understanding, DAI Res. Rep. 50, Dept. Artif. Intell., University of Edinburgh, Mar. 1978.

```
COMMENTED HCPRVR PROGRAM
[;; ***************HCPRVR PROGRAM********************]

[;; HCPRVR IS A HORN CLAUSE THEOREM PROVER]

(SPECIAL FORMULAS QFLAG AFLAG TFLAG RANDOM* SHORTFORM LIMIT
 DEPTH LENGTH COUNT VAL TEMP SAVE X COMMAND)
(SPECIAL RTIME GLOBALCOMMAND GLOBALSLASHFLAG)
(NOCALL FORMULAS COUNT TEMP SAVE X COMMAND GLOBALCOMMAND
 GLOBALSLASHFLAG)
(NOCALL PROVE EXPAND1 STRIP ISFCN INDEX MATCH ABSENT TFLAG*
 TPRINT SKIM)
(NOUUO NIL)

[;; *****************DEPTH AND LENGTH VARIABLES**********]

[;;DEPTH AND LENGTH CONTROL THE AMOUNT OF PRINTING DURING RTRACES]

(SETQ DEPTH 4)
(SETQ LENGTH 6)

[;; ****************LIMIT VARIABLE****************]

[;; LIMIT DETERMINES THE NUMBER OF CALLS TO PROVE BEFORE USER
 IS ASKED IF HE WANTS TO CONTINUE]

(SETQ LIMIT 100)

[;; *****************? FUNCTION****************]
```

[;; ? IS THE TOP LEVEL FUNCTION THAT DOES NOT EVALUATE ITS
ARGUMENTS]
[;; THE CALLING FORMAT IS:
(? <FORMULA1> <FORMULA2> --- <FORMULAN>)]
[;; IT TRIES TO FIND A SET OF ASSIGNMENTS TO THE VARIABLES IN THE
FORMULAS THAT MAKES THEM ALL BE TRUE SIMULTANEOUSLY]
[;; IF SO, IT SETS VAL TO THE LIST OF FORMULAS WITH THE VALUES
SUBSTITUTED IN; IF NOT, IT RETURNS NIL]

(DF ? (FORMULAS)
(TRYN FORMULAS]

[;; ****************TRY FUNCTION*****************]

[;; TRY IS THE TOP LEVEL FUNCTION THAT EVALUATES ITS ARGUMENT]
[;; THAT ARGUMENT MUST BE A SINGLE FORMULA]
[;; OTHERWISE IT BEHAVES LIKE ?]

(DE TRY (FORMULA) (TRYN (LIST FORMULA]

(DE TRYN (FORMULAS)
(MAKEVARIABLES FORMULAS)
(PROG (COUNT TM GLOBALSLASHFLAG GLOBALCOMMAND)
(SETQ COUNT (ADD1 LIMIT))
(SETQ TM (TIME))
(SETQ VAL NIL)
(COND ((NULL (PROVE (LIST (LIST FORMULAS NIL)))) (SETQ VAL NIL)))
(SETQ RTIME (LIST (*QUO (DIFFERENCE (TIME) TM) 1000.0) 'SECS))
 (RETURN (COND (QFLAG NIL)
                    (VAL]

[;; *******************PROVE FUNCTION****************]

[;; PROVE IS THE THEOREM PROVING ALGORITHM]
[;; ITS ARGUMENT IS A LIST OF SUBPROBLEM STRUCTURES]
[;; EACH SUBPROBLEM STRUCTURE HAS THE FORM
    (<LIST OF SUBPROBLEMS> <BINDING LIST>)]
[;; IT EXPANDS EACH SUBPROBLEM ACCORDING TO SOME AXIOM UNTIL THEY
ALL FULLY EXPAND SUCCESSFULLY OR SOME SUBPROBLEM CANNOT BE EXPANDED]
[;; PROVE SEARCHES THE SPACE OF EXPANSIONS IN A DEPTH-FIRST FASHION,
APPLYING AXIOMS IN THE ORDER THAT THEY WERE READ IN AND EXPANDING
LISTS OF SUBPROBLEMS (FORMULAS) IN LEFT-TO-RIGHT ORDER]

(DE PROVE (X)
(PROG (Y SAVE Z W)
(SETQ COUNT (SUB1 COUNT))

[;; THE C LOOP ASKS THE USER IF HE WANTS TO CONTINUE THE SEARCH
AFTER EVERY N CALLS TO PROVE, WHERE N = LIMIT]
[;; Y OR YES CAUSES CONTINUATION; N OR NO CAUSES TERMINATION; ANY
OTHER EXPRESSION WILL BE EVALED AND ITS VALUE PRINTED]

Sec. A.10   Selected Readings   **261**

```
C(COND ((ZEROP COUNT)
        (PRINT 'CONTINUE?)
        (COND ((MEMBER (SETQ COMMAND (READ)) '(Y YES))
               (SETQ COUNT (ADD1 LIMIT)))
              ((MEMBER COMMAND '(N NO)) (RETURN))
              (T (PRINT (EVAL COMMAND)) (GO C)))))
B(COND ((NULL (CAAR X))
        (COND ((NULL (CDR X))
               (SETQ VAL (EXPAND1 (CDAR X) FORMULAS))
               (RETURN (COND (QFLAG (SPRINT VAL) (TERPRI)
                                    (PRINT 'ANOTHER?)
[;; IF QFLAG IS NOT NULL AND PROVE FINDS A SOLUTION, IT PRINTS THE
SOLUTION AND ASKS WHETHER USER WANTS ANOTHER SOLUTION]
[;; IF THE INPUT FROM THE TTY IS Y OR YES, PROVE
SIMULATES A FAILURE AND FINDS ANOTHER SOLUTION]
[;; ANY OTHER INPUT TERMINATES PROVE]
                                    (COND ((MEMBER (READ) '(Y YES))
                                           NIL)
                                          (T (CDAR X))))
              ((CDAR X)))))
        ((SETQ X (CDR X))
         (OR (AND (TFLAG*) (PRINT (LIST 'R- (LENGTH X)))
                           (TPRINT (EXPAND1 (CDAR X) (CAAAR X))))
             T)
         (SETQ X (CONS (CONS (CDAAR X) (CDAR X)) (CDR X)))
         (GO B))))
 ((ISFCN (CAAAR X) (CDAR X))
  (COND (EVAL (EXPAND1 (CDAR X) (CAAAR X)))
        (SETQ X (CONS (CONS (CDAAR X)
                            (CDAR X))
                      (CDR X)))
        (GO B)))))
 (AND (TFLAG*)
      (PRINT (LIST 'Q- (LENGTH X)))
      (TPRINT (EXPAND1 (CDAR X) (CAAAR X))))
 (SETQ Y (GET (INDEX (CAAAR X) (CDAR X)) 'AXIOMS))
A(COND ((ZEROP COUNT) (RETURN))
       ((NULL Y)
        (COND ((EQ (CAAAR X) '/ )
               (OR GLOBALSLASHFLAG (SETQ GLOBALSLASHFLAG (CDAR X)))))
        (RETURN))
       ((AND (MATCH (CAAR Y)
                    (SETQ Z (LIST NIL))
                    (CAAAR X)
                    (CDAR X))
             (OR (AND AFLAG
                      (TFLAG*)
                      (PRINT (LIST 'A- (LENGTH X)))
                      (TPRINT (EXPAND1 Z (CAR Y))))
                 T)
             (SETQ W (PROVE (CONS (CONS (STRIP (CDAR Y)) Z) X))))
        (RETURN W))
```

```
              (T (MAPC (FUNCTION (LAMBDA (X) (RPLACA X (CDAR X)))) SAVE)
                 (SETQ SAVE NIL)
                 (SETQ Y (COND ((NULL GLOBALSLASHFLAG) (CDR Y))
                               ((EQ GLOBALSLASHFLAG Z)
                                (SETQ GLOBALSLASHFLAG NIL))))
                 (GO A))) ))

(DE EXPAND1 (LST X)
(COND   ((NOT (ATOM X)) (CONS (EXPAND1 LST (CAR X))
                              (EXPAND1 LST (CDR X))))
        ((NUMBERP X) X)
        ((GET X 'VARIABLE)
         (COND ((SETQ TEMP (ASSOC X (CAR LST) NIL))
                (EXPAND1 (CDDR TEMP) (CADR TEMP)))
               (X)))
        (X))))

(DE STRIP (X)
(COND   ((NULL X) NIL)
        (T (CDR X)))))

(DE ISFCN (Z ZLST)
(COND ((ATOM (SETQ Z (INDEX Z ZLST))) (GET Z 'FN)))))

(DE INDEX (Z ZLST)
(PROG   () A
(COND   ((NOT (ATOM Z)) (SETQ Z (CAR Z)) (GO A))
        ((SETQ TEMP (ASSOC Z (CAR ZLST) NIL))
         (SETQ Z (CADR TEMP))
         (SETQ ZLST (CDDR TEMP))
         (GO A))
        (Z (RETURN Z)))))

[;; ****************MATCH FUNCTION******************]

[;; MATCH IS THE UNIFICATION ALGORITHM IMPLEMENTED SO THAT RENAMING
OF VARIABLES AND SUBSTITUTION FOR VARIABLES ARE UNNECESSARY]
[;; A VARIABLE IS REALLY A VARIABLE NAME PLUS A BINDING LIST]

[;; THE FOLLOWING IS THE ORIGINAL DEFINITION OF MATCH;
IT IS INCLUDED HERE BECAUSE IT IS EASIER TO READ]

[;;
(DE MATCH (X XLST Y YLST)
(PROG ()
A (COND ((AND (ATOM X)
              (NOT (NUMBERP X))
              (GET X 'VARIABLE)
              (SETQ TEMP (ASSOC X (CAR XLST) NIL)))
         (SETQ X (CADR TEMP))
         (SETQ XLST (CDDR TEMP))
```

```
                    (GO A)))
B (COND ((AND (ATOM Y)
              (NOT (NUMBERP Y))
              (GET Y 'VARIABLE)
              (SETQ TEMP (ASSOC Y (CAR YLST) NIL)))
         (SETQ Y (CADR TEMP))
         (SETQ YLST (CDDR TEMP))
         (GO B)))
  (COND ((AND (EQ X Y) (EQ XLST YLST)) (RETURN T))
        ((AND (ATOM X)
              (NOT (NUMBERP X))
              (GET X 'VARIABLE)
              (OR SHORTFORM (ABSENT X XLST Y YLST)))
         (SETQ SAVE (CONS XLST SAVE))
         (RPLACA XLST (CONS (CONS X (CONS Y YLST)) (CAR XLST)))
         (RETURN T))
        ((AND (ATOM Y)
              (NOT (NUMBERP Y))
              (GET Y 'VARIABLE)
              (OR SHORTFORM (ABSENT Y YLST X XLST)))
         (SETQ SAVE (CONS YLST SAVE))
         (RPLACA YLST (CONS (CONS Y (CONS X XLST)) (CAR YLST)))
         (RETURN T))
        ((AND (NOT (ATOM X)) (NOT (ATOM Y)))
         (COND ((MATCH (CAR X) XLST (CAR Y) YLST)
                (SETQ X (CDR X))
                (SETQ Y (CDR Y))
                (GO A))))
        ((EQ X Y) (RETURN T))))))
]

[;; THE FOLLOWING DEFINITION OF MATCH EXECUTES FASTER]

(DE MATCH (X XLST Y YLST)
(PROG ()
A(COND  ((ATOM X)
         (COND ((NOT (NUMBERP X))
                (COND((GET X 'VARIABLE)
                      (COND ((SETQ TEMP (ASSOC X (CAR XLST) NIL))
                             (SETQ X (CADR TEMP))
                             (SETQ XLST (CDDR TEMP))
                             (GO A))
                            (T (PROG ()
                               B(COND ((AND (ATOM Y)
                                            (NOT (NUMBERP Y))
                                            (GET Y 'VARIABLE)
                                            (SETQ TEMP (ASSOC Y
                                                 (CAR YLST) NIL)))
                                       (SETQ Y (CADR TEMP))
                                       (SETQ YLST (CDDR TEMP))
                                       (GO B))))
                                (COND   ((AND (EQ X Y) (EQ XLST YLST))
                                         (RETURN T))
```

                                              ((OR SHORTFORM
                                                    (ABSENT X XLST Y YLST))
                                                (SETQ SAVE (CONS XLST SAVE))
                                                (RPLACA XLST
                                                    (CONS (CONS X (CONS Y YLST))
                                                          (CAR XLST)))
                                                (RETURN T))
                                              ((RETURN NIL))))))
                              ((GO C))))
                          ((GO C)))))
  B(COND ((ATOM Y)
          (COND ((NOT (NUMBERP Y))
                  (COND ((GET Y 'VARIABLE)
                          (COND ((SETQ TEMP (ASSOC Y (CAR YLST) NIL))
                                  (SETQ Y (CADR TEMP))
                                  (SETQ YLST (CDDR TEMP))
                                  (GO B))
                                (T (COND ((OR SHORTFORM
                                              (ABSENT Y YLST X XLST))
                                          (SETQ SAVE (CONS YLST SAVE))
                                          (RPLACA YLST
                                                (CONS (CONS Y
                                                            (CONS X XLST))
                                                      (CAR YLST)))
                                          (RETURN T))
                                         ((RETURN NIL))))))
                        ((RETURN (EQ X Y)))))
                ((RETURN (EQ X Y))))))
    (COND ((MATCH (CAR X) XLST (CAR Y) YLST)
           (SETQ X (CDR X))
           (SETQ Y (CDR Y))
           (GO A))
          ((RETURN NIL)))
  C(COND ((ATOM Y)
          (COND ((NOT (NUMBERP Y))
                  (COND ((GET Y 'VARIABLE)
                          (COND ((SETQ TEMP (ASSOC Y (CAR YLST) NIL))
                                  (SETQ Y (CADR TEMP))
                                  (SETQ YLST (CDDR TEMP))
                                  (GO C))
                                (T (COND ((OR SHORTFORM
                                              (ABSENT Y YLST X XLST))
                                          (SETQ SAVE (CONS YLST SAVE))
                                          (RPLACA YLST
                                                (CONS (CONS Y
                                                            (CONS X XLST))
                                                      (CAR YLST)))
                                          (RETURN T))
                                         ((RETURN NIL))))))
                        ((RETURN (EQ X Y)))))
                ((RETURN (EQ X Y))))))]

[;; ****************ABSENT FUNCTION***************]

Sec. A.10 Selected Readings

```
[;; ABSENT IS THE TEST FOR NONOCCURRENCE OF A VARIABLE IN ITS
INTENDED VALUE; THIS TEST IS SKIPPED WHEN SHORTFORM = T]

(DE ABSENT (X XLST Y YLST)
(PROG () A
(COND ((ATOM Y)
        (COND ((OR (NUMBERP Y)(NOT (GET Y 'VARIABLE))) (RETURN T))
              ((SETQ TEMP (ASSOC Y (CAR YLST) NIL))
               (SETQ Y (CADR TEMP))
               (SETQ YLST (CDDR TEMP))
               (GO A))
              ((RETURN (NOT (AND (EQ X Y) (EQ XLST YLST)))))))
      ((ABSENT X XLST (CAR Y) YLST)
          (SETQ Y (CDR Y))
          (GO A)) )))))

(DE NEWAXIOM (X)
(PROGN (MAKEVARIABLES X)
(PUT (INDEX X '(NIL)) 'AXIOMS (APPEND (GET (INDEX X '(NIL)) 'AXIOMS)
   (LIST X)) 'AXIOMS)))))

(DE MAKEVARIABLES (X)
(COND ((NULL X) NIL)
      ((NOT (ATOM X))(MAKEVARIABLES (CAR X))(MAKEVARIABLES (CDR X)))
      ((EQ (CAR (EXPLODE X)) '_)(PUTPROP X T 'VARIABLE)]

[;; ***************AXIOMS FUNCTION************]

[;; AXIOMS STORES A LIST OF AXIOMS ]
[;; THE AXIOMS HAVE THE FORM ( <FORMULA> ) OR
    ( <FORMULA> < <FORMULA1> <FORMULA2> --- <FORMULAN> ) ]

(DE AXIOMS (X) (MAPC 'NEWAXIOM X)))

(SETQ SHORTFORM T)

(DE VARIABLE (X) (PUT X 'VARIABLE T)))

[;; ************VARIABLES FUNCTION************]

[;; THE VARIABLES FUNCTION IS USED TO DECLARE A LIST OF ATOMS TO
BE VARIABLES]

(DF VARIABLES (X) (MAPC 'VARIABLE X)))

(VARIABLES X Y Z U W)

(DE TPRINT (X) (PRINLEV (SKIM X LENGTH) DEPTH))

(DE TFLAG* () (OR (GET (INDEX (CAAAR X) (CDAR X)) 'RTRACE) TFLAG))

[;; ****************TFLAG VARIABLE*****************]
```

[;; SETTING TFLAG TO T CAUSES ALL STEPS OF THE PROOF TO BE TRACED]

(SETQ TFLAG NIL)

[;; ******************RTRACE FUNCTION****************]

[;; RTRACE TRACES THE PROOF SELECTIVELY]
[;; IT EXPECTS A LIST OF RELATION NAMES; ONLY STEPS INVOLVING THESE
RELATIONS ARE TRACED]
[;; IF RTRACE IS CALLED WITHOUT A LIST, IT PRINTS A LIST OF ALL THE
RELATIONS CURRENTLY SET TO BE TRACED]

(DF RTRACE (X) (COND (X (MAPC '(LAMBDA (X) (PUT X 'RTRACE T)) X))
              ((MAPCAN (FUNCTION (LAMBDA (X)
                           (MAPCAN (FUNCTION (LAMBDA (Y)
                                   (COND ((GET Y 'RTRACE)
                                          (LIST Y)))))
                                  X)))
                      OBLIST]

[;; ****************UNRTRACE FUNCTION*************]

[;; UNRTRACE UNDOES THE EFFECT OF RTRACE]
[;; IF UNTRACE IS CALLED WITHOUT A LIST OF RELATION NAMES,
   IT UNTRACES ALL THE RELATIONS THAT HAVE BEEN SET]

(DF UNRTRACE (X) (COND (X (MAPC '(LAMBDA (X) (PUT X 'RTRACE NIL)) X))
              ((MAPC (FUNCTION (LAMBDA (X)
                           (MAPC (FUNCTION (LAMBDA (Y)
                                   (COND ((GET Y 'RTRACE)
                                          (PUT Y 'RTRACE NIL)))))
                                  X)))
                      OBLIST]

(DE SKIM (X N)
 (COND ((ATOM X) X)
       ((ZEROP N) '&)
       ((CONS (SKIM (CAR X) LENGTH) (SKIM (CDR X) (SUB1 N))))))

[;; ****************SETV* RELATION***************]

[;; SETV* IS A PREDICATE FUNCTION FOR ASSIGNING TO A VARIABLE
   THE VALUE OF AN ARBITRARY LISP EXPRESSION]
[;; THE FORMAT IS: (SETV* <VARIABLE> <LISP EXPRESSION>)]
[;; IF THE LISP EXPRESSION CONTAINS LOGIC PROGRAM VARIABLES, THEY
WILL BE REPLACED BY THEIR VALUES BEFORE THE EXPRESSION IS EVALUATED]

(AXIOMS '((((SETV* X Y) < (SETV Z Y) (EQ X Z) /)))
(DF SETV (Z)
 (PROG (Y)
  (SETQ Y (EVAL (CADR Z)))
  (COND ((OR(NOT (ATOM (CAR Z)))(NUMBERP (CAR Z))) NIL)
        ((GET (CAR Z) 'VARIABLE)

Sec. A.10 Selected Readings

```
            (SETQ SAVE (CONS (CDAR X) SAVE))
            (RPLACA (CDAR X) (CONS (CONS (CAR Z)
                                         (CONS Y (LIST NIL)))
                                   (CADAR X)))
            (RETURN T)))))))

(PUT 'SETV 'FN T)

[;; ***************ASSERT RELATION***************]

[;; ASSERTS NEW AXIOMS]
[;; THE FORMAT IS (ASSERT <FORMULA1> <FORMULA2> --- <FORMUALN> )]
[;; IF ONLY <FORMULA1> IS PRESENT, IT STORES THE AXIOM
   ( <FORMULA1> ) ]
[;; OTHERWISE IT STORES THE AXIOM
   ( <FORMULA1> <FORMULA2> --- <FORMULAN> ) ]
[;; NORMALLY <FORMULA2> SHOULD BE THE SYMBOL < BUT ANY EXPRESSION IS
ALLOWED; THIS EXPRESSION CAN BE USED TO DISTINGUISH CONTEXTS IF
DESIRED]

(DF ASSERT (X)
(PROGN (MAKEVARIABLES X)
       (CAR (PUT(INDEX (CAAR X) '(NIL)) 'AXIOMS
                      (CONS X (GET(INDEX (CAAR X) '(NIL)) 'AXIOMS]

(PUT 'ASSERT 'FN T)

(DE RELATIONS ()
(MAPCAN (F:L (X) (MAPCAN (F:L (X)
                               (COND ((GET X 'AXIOMS) (LIST X))))
                         X))
         OBLIST]

[;; ***************PREFIX FOR LOGIC VARIABLES**********]

[;; A VARIABLE MAY BEGIN WITH UNDERSCORE ]
[;; SUCH A VARIABLE DOES NOT HAVE TO BE DECLARED PROVIDED IT IS
   IN A QUESTION OR AN AXIOM ENTERED BY AXIOMS OR ASSERT]

(AXIOMS '(
((EQ X X))
((NEQ* X Y) < (UNLESS (EQ X Y)))
((RREAD X) < (SETV* X (READ)))
( / )
((UNLESS X) < X / (FAIL))
((UNLESS X))
))

(SETQ QFLAG NIL)

(DEXPR *RANDOM NIL
 (SETQ RANDOM* (BOOLE 1 (PLUS (TIMES RANDOM* 3473.) 1121.) 1048575.)))
```

(DEFPROP RAND* T FN)

[;; ***************RAND* RELATION**************]

[;; RAND* IS THE RANDOM SELECTION FUNCTION]
[;; WITHOUT AN ARGUMENT IT CHOOSES BETWEEN T AND NIL]
[;; OTHERWISE IT RETURNS ONE OF ITS ARGUMENTS]
[;; IN THIS CASE RAND* SHOULD BE USED WITH SETV* EG
    (SETV* X (RAND* . Y)) WHERE Y WILL BE BOUND TO A LIST]

(DFEXPR RAND* (X) (COND ((NULL X) (ZEROP (RANDOM 2)))
                       ((CAR X) (CAR (NTH (CAR X) (ADD1 (RANDOM
                                       (LENGTH (CAR X]

(DEXPR RANDOM (N) (FIX (TIMES N (*QUO (*RANDOM) 1048576.0))))

(DEFV RANDOM* 5243.)

[;; ***************CLEAR FUNCTION AND RELATION**********]

[;; CLEAR REMOVES AXIOMS THAT HAVE BEEN ADDED BY ASSERT]
[;; THE ARGUMENT OF CLEAR SHOULD BE THE CONTEXT EXPRESSION
(THE SECOND ELEMENT IN THE AXIOM) THAT IDENTIFIES WHICH AXIOMS
TO REMOVE FROM ALL RELATIONS]
[;; IF CLEAR HAS NO ARGUMENT, ALL AXIOMS WITH CONTEXT OTHER THAN
< AND AXIOMS OF THE FORM (<FORMULA> <) ARE REMOVED]
[;; (CLEAR <) REMOVES ONLY AXIOMS OF THE FORM (<FORMULA> <)]

(DFEXPR CLEAR (Z)
 (PROG (Y)
       (MAPC (FUNCTION (LAMBDA (X)
              (MAPC (FUNCTION (LAMBDA (X)
                     (COND [(SETQ Y (GET X 'AXIOMS))
                            (PUT X 'AXIOMS (CLEANAX Z Y))])))
                    X)))
             OBLIST)))

(DEXPR CLEANAX (Z Y)
 (COND [(NULL Y) NIL]
       [(OR (NULL (CDAR Y))
            (AND (CDDAR Y) (EQ (CADAR Y) '<))
            (AND Z (NOT (EQ (CAR Z) (CADAR Y)))))
        (CONS (CAR Y) (CLEANAX Z (CDR Y))]
       [(CLEANAX Z (CDR Y))]]

[;; ***************ATOM* RELATION**************]

[;; ATOM* DETERMINES WHETHER ITS ARGUMENT IS AN ATOM]

(DEFPROP ATOM* T FN)

(DFEXPR ATOM* (PR) (ATOM (CAR PR)))

Sec. A.10   Selected Readings

[;; *************VAR* RELATION**************]

[;; VAR* DETERMINES IF ITS ARGUMENT IS A LOGIC PROGRAM VARIABLE]

(DEFPROP VAR* T FN)

(DFEXPR VAR* (X) (AND (ATOM (CAR X))
(NOT(NUMBERP (CAR X)))
(GET (CAR X) 'VARIABLE)))
(PUT 'RTERPRI 'FN T)

[;; ***************RTERPRI RELATION********************]

[;; RTERPRI IS A RELATION (NO ARGUMENTS) THAT DOES A <CRLF>]

(DE RTERPRI () (TERPRI) T)

(PUT 'RPRINT 'FN T)

[;; ******************RPRINT RELATION****************]

[;; RPRINT IS A RELATION THAT PRINTS EACH OF ITS ARGUMENTS ON A SEPARATE LINE; THE NUMBER OF ARGUMENTS IS NOT FIXED]

(DF RPRINT (X) (MAPC (FUNCTION (LAMBDA (X) (PRINT X))) X) T]

[;; ***************AFLAG VARIABLE****************]

[;; SETTING AFLAG TO T CAUSES THE AXIOMS TO BE TRACED AS THEY ARE APPLIED]

(SETQ AFLAG NIL)
(SETQ RTIME '(0 SECS))

[;; =============AUGMENTATIONS===========================]

[;; THE FOLLOWING PROCEDURES FURTHER AUGMENT THE 1980 VERSION OF HCPRVR AND ARE USED FREQUENTLY IN THE EXAMPLES IN THE TEXT]

[;; LSTALL IS CALLED TO CLEAR AXIOMS FROM SPECIAL CONTEXTS AND TO PRODUCE A DSKOUT LISTING OF ALL FUNCTIONS, AXIOMS, AND VARIABLES]

(DFEXPR LSTALL (FILE)
  (PROG (TEMP)
      (CLEAR)
      (SETQ TEMP
        (MAPCAN
         '[LAMBDA (Z)
           (MAPCAN '[LAMBDA (X)
                    (COND [(OR [GET X 'EXPR]
                              [GET X 'FEXPR]

```
                              [GET X 'VARIABLE]
                              [GET X 'AXIOMS])
                         (LIST X)])]
                Z)]
        OBLIST))
       (MAPC '[LAMBDA (X)
               (COND [(NOT (MEMBER X PRETTYPROPS))
                      (SETQ PRETTYPROPS (CONS X PRETTYPROPS))])]
             '[FN VARIABLE AXIOMS])
       (SETQ TEMP (SORT TEMP))
       (EVAL (LIST 'DSKOUT (CAR FILE) 'TEMP))))
```

[;; YAK ELIMINATES THE NEED TO USE <?(THEOREM)>, WHEN THE SYSTEM
IS STARTED OR RESTARTED AFTER A BREAK (YAK) MUST BE CALLED TO
GIVE THIS CAPABILITY, IF A CONTROL C IS GIVEN TO ESCAPE AND
REENTER, THE CALL TO YAK MUST BE REPEATED OR THE ? MUST BE
USED]

```
(DEXPR YAK NIL
   (PROG (M*M*)
      A (SETQ M*M* (READ))
        (COND [(EQUAL M*M* 'YAK) (RETURN 'OK)]
              [(AND [NOT (ATOM M*M*)] [GET(INDEX (CAR M*M*) '(NIL)) 'AXIOMS])
               (PRINT (TRY M*M*))]
              [T (SETQ M*M* (ERRSET (EVAL M*M*)))
                 (COND [M*M* (PRINT (CAR M*M*))])])
        (TERPRI)
        (GO A)))
```

[;; D* IS THE DELETE FUNCTION THAT RETURNS TRUE IF IT SUCCEEDS IN
DELETING ITS SINGLE AXIOM ARGUMENT, NIL OTHERWISE]

[;; CORRESPONDING TO D*, A* IS OFTEN DEFINED
   ((A* X) < (ASSERT X))]

(DEFPROP D* T FN)

```
(DFEXPR D* (X)
   (PROG (J)
        (RETURN (COND [(SETQ J (GET (INDEX (CAAR X) '(NIL)) 'AXIOMS))
                       (PUT(INDEX (CAAR X) '(NIL)) 'AXIOMS (DEL (CAR X) J))
                       T]))))

(DEXPR DEL (X J)
   (COND [(NULL J) NIL]
         [(VEQ X (CAAR J)) (DEL X (CDR J))]
         [T (CONS (CAR J) (DEL X (CDR J)))]))

(DEXPR VEQ (Q F)
   (COND [(EQ Q F)]
         [(ATOM Q) (OR [VAR Q] [VAR F])]
         [(ATOM F) (VAR F)]
```

Sec. A.10   Selected Readings   **271**

```
              [(VEQ (CAR Q) (CAR F)) (VEQ (CDR Q) (CDR F))]))

(DEXPR VAR (X)
 (AND (ATOM X)(NOT(NUMBERP X))(GET X 'VARIABLE)))

[;; THE FOLLOWING IS A CONVENIENT LIST OF VARIABLES USED IN ALL
PROGRAMS IN THE TEXT, (EVAL (CONS 'VARIABLES VARS)) WILL DECLARE
THE SET]

(DEFV VARS '(M M1 M2 M3 M4 N N1 N2 N3 N4 O O1 O2 O3 O4 P P1 P2 P3
P4 Q Q1 Q2 Q3 Q4 R R1 R2 R3 R4 S S1 S2 S3 S4 T T1 T2 T3 T4 U U1 U2
U3 U4 V V1 V2 V3 V4 W W1 W2 W3 W4 X X1 X2 X3 X4 Y Y1 Y2 Y3 Y4 Z Z1
Z2 Z3 Z4))
```

B

FURTHER ANALYSIS OF THE ROCKET STORY OF CHAPTER 8

B.1 A GRAMMAR FOR THE ROCKET STORY

Each set of axioms is preceded by a call to the LISP function, DEFPROP, which creates a property list structure of the form [<NAME> AXIOMS <AXIOMS>]. The LISP procedure (GET <NAME> AXIOMS) returns that list of axioms. The grammar is the one originally written to analyze the rocket story, augmented with rules to translate the questions studied in Chapter 9.

```
(DEFPROP ADJ
  (((ADJ *2400))
   ((ADJ FORTY))
   ((ADJ NEWMEXICO))
   ((ADJ EIGHT))
   ((ADJ LIQUID))
   ((ADJ FIVE))
   ((ADJ EMPTY))
   ((ADJ READY))
   ((ADJ TWO))
   ((ADJ RED))
   ((ADJ EARTH))
   ((ADJ GREAT))
   ((ADJ BLACK))
   ((ADJ YELLOW))
```

Sec. B.1 A Grammar for the Rocket Story

```
  ((ADJ V-2))
  ((ADJ FORTY-SIX))
  ((ADJ LONG))
  ((ADJ GIANT))
  ((ADJ SIXTY))
  ((ADJ FEW))
  ((ADJ HIGH))
  ((ADJ THREE-THOUSAND))
  ((ADJ MUCH))
  ((ADJ PRESENT))
  ((ADJ THERE))
  ((ADJ MANY))
  ((ADJ FAST)))
 AXIOMS)

(DEFPROP ADJP
 ((((ADJP (X Y . Z) (X W V1) R)
      < (CONJ Y) (ADJ X) (ADJP Z V1 R) (FEAT Y W))
  ((ADJP (X . Y) (X W V1) R)
      < (ADJ X) (INFVP Y V1 R) (ARCNAME X V1 W))
  ((ADJP (X . Y) (X) Y) < (ADJ X)))
 AXIOMS)

(DEFPROP ADV
 ((((ADV BEHIND))
  ((ADV SLOWLY))
  ((ADV THEN))
  ((ADV FASTER))
  ((ADV SOON))
  ((ADV TOO))
  ((ADV UPWARD))
  ((ADV AFTER)))
 AXIOMS)

(DEFPROP ADVPH
 ((((ADVPH (X Y Z . X1) (X *THEN V1) R)
   <
   (ADV X)
   (CONJ Y)
   (ADV Z)
   (FEAT Z TI)
   (ADVPH X1 V1 R))
  ((ADVPH (X Y . Z) (X W V1) R)
      < (ADV X) (CONJ Y) (ADVPH Z V1 R) (FEAT Y W))
  ((ADVPH (X . Y) (V1 W X . Q) R)
      < (ADV X) (ADVPH Y (V1 . Q) R) (FEAT V1 W))
  ((ADVPH (X . Y) (V1 W X . Q) R)
      < (ADV X) (ADJP Y (V1 . Q) R) (FEAT X W))
  ((ADVPH (X . Y) X Y) < (ADV X)))
 AXIOMS)

(DEFPROP ARCNAME
 ((((ARCNAME X Y Z) < (FEAT X X1) (FEAT Y Y1) (ARCVAL X1 Y1 Z)))
```

AXIOMS)

(DEFPROP ARCVAL
 (((ARCVAL MOVE POBJ INSTR))
  ((ARCVAL POBJ MOVE INSTR))
  ((ARCVAL POBJ TPC AE))
  ((ARCVAL ACT HUMAN AGT))
  ((ARCVAL ST LGTH AE))
  ((ARCVAL ST PU AE))
  ((ARCVAL ST HUMAN AE))
  ((ARCVAL HUMAN ST AE))
  ((ARCVAL ST LOC LOC))
  ((ARCVAL ST COLOR AE))
  ((ARCVAL POBJ PLACE LOC))
  ((ARCVAL ST SIZE SIZE))
  ((ARCVAL ST POBJ AE))
  ((ARCVAL SEE MOVE AE))
  ((ARCVAL LOC ACT LOC))
  ((ARCVAL SEE HUMAN AGT))
  ((ARCVAL DEVICE SEE INSTR*))
  ((ARCVAL SEE POBJ AE))
  ((ARCVAL POBJ ACT AE))
  ((ARCVAL POBJ POBJ TYPE))
  ((ARCVAL SEE TI TI))
  ((ARCVAL TI TI TI))
  ((ARCVAL TI ACT EVT))
  ((ARCVAL SEE ACT AE))
  ((ARCVAL ACT LOC LOC))
  ((ARCVAL ACTT MSR MSR))
  ((ARCVAL ST MSR MSR))
  ((ARCVAL ST ST ST))
  ((ARCVAL ST HT HT))
  ((ARCVAL HT SEE RESULT))
  ((ARCVAL SYMB ACT PU))
  ((ARCVAL MOVE POBJ AE))
  ((ARCVAL MOVE HUMAN AGT))
  ((ARCVAL MOVE LOC LOC))
  ((ARCVAL HUMAN MOVE AGT))
  ((ARCVAL ACTT SUBST AE))
  ((ARCVAL ACT POBJ AE))
  ((ARCVAL SEE DEVICE INSTR))
  ((ARCVAL AP SUBST AE))
  ((ARCVAL ACT TI EVT))
  ((ARCVAL ACTT POBJ INSTR))
  ((ARCVAL ACTT HUMAN AGT))
  ((ARCVAL ACTT LOC LOC))
  ((ARCVAL ST DEVICE INSTR))
  ((ARCVAL ST TI TI))
  ((ARCVAL MOVE MSR LOC)))
AXIOMS)

(DEFPROP ART (((ART SOME)) ((ART A)) ((ART THE))) AXIOMS)

Sec. B.1 A Grammar for the Rocket Story

(DEFPROP AUX (((AUX DID (DO TNS PAST)))) AXIOMS)

(DEFPROP COMP
 ((((COMP NIL V NIL NIL))
  ((COMP X V (W V1) R)
     < (FEAT V SEE) (S1 X V1 R) (ARCNAME V V1 W))
  ((COMP X V (W V1 . V2) R)
     < (NP X V1 R1) (COMP R1 V V2 R) (ARCNAME V V1 W))
  ((COMP X V (W V1 . V2) R)
     < (PP X V1 R1) (COMP R1 V V2 R) (PREPTEST V V1 W))
  ((COMP X V (W V1 . V2) R)
 < (ADVPH X V1 R1) (COMP R1 V V2 R) (FEAT V1 W))
  ((COMP (X . Y) V (W V1) R)
 < (CONJ X) (VP Y V1 R) (FEAT X W))
  ((COMP (X . Y) V (W V1) R)
 < (EQ X AS) (S1 Y V1 R) (FEAT X W))
  ((COMP (X . Y) V (W . V1) R)
 < (CONJ X) (S1 Y V1 R) (FEAT X W))
  ((COMP (X) V (W X) NIL) < (PREP X) (FEAT X W))
  ((COMP X V (W V1 . V2) R)
  < (ADJP X V1 R1) (COMP R1 V V2 R) (FEAT V1 W)))
 AXIOMS)

(DEFPROP CONJ ((((CONJ AND)) ((CONJ BUT))) AXIOMS)

(DEFPROP FEAT
 ((((FEAT SOON TI))
  ((FEAT TYPE TYPE))
  ((FEAT LENGTH LGTH))
  ((FEAT FLIGHT POBJ))
  ((FEAT FLY MOVE))
  ((FEAT FROM FROM))
  ((FEAT HIDE MOVE))
  ((FEAT PILOT HUMAN))
  ((FEAT SEE SEE))
  ((FEAT WATCH SEE))
  ((FEAT PLANE DEVICE))
  ((FEAT RETURN MOVE))
  ((FEAT AFTER TI))
  ((FEAT FEW QU))
  ((FEAT STAND ST))
  ((FEAT HE HUMAN))
  ((FEAT RETURN ACT))
  ((FEAT *2400 QU))
  ((FEAT PLUNGE MOVE))
  ((FEAT EARTH POBJ))
  ((FEAT ITS ASSOC))
  ((FEAT FORTY QU))
  ((FEAT START ACT))
  ((FEAT POINT LOC))
  ((FEAT NEWMEXICO LOC))
  ((FEAT DESERT LOC))
  ((FEAT BEHIND LOC))

((FEAT FUEL SUBST))
((FEAT IT POBJ))
((FEAT CARRY ACTT))
((FEAT EIGHT QU))
((FEAT TON MSR))
((FEAT OXYGEN SUBST))
((FEAT LIQUID ST))
((FEAT ALCOHOL SUBST))
((FEAT WEIGH ST))
((FEAT FIVE QU))
((FEAT EMPTY ST))
((FEAT EVERYTHING POBJ))
((FEAT BE ST))
((FEAT READY ST))
((FEAT TWO QU))
((FEAT RED COLOR))
((FEAT FLARE POBJ))
((FEAT RISE MOVE))
((FEAT SIGNAL SYMB))
((FEAT FIRE ACT))
((FEAT DISTANCE LOC))
((FEAT SCIENTIST HUMAN))
((FEAT GENERAL HUMAN))
((FEAT MOUND POBJ))
((FEAT WITHDRAW MOVE))
((FEAT CROUCH MOVE))
((FEAT EARTH SUBST))
((FEAT AND *AND))
((FEAT BUT OP))
((FEAT GREAT SIZE))
((FEAT BLACK COLOR))
((FEAT YELLOW COLOR))
((FEAT V-2 TYPE))
((FEAT ROCKET POBJ))
((FEAT FORTY-SIX QU))
((FEAT FOOT MSR))
((FEAT LONG LGTH))
((FEAT ROAR SOUND))
((FEAT BURST ACT))
((FEAT FLAME SUBST))
((FEAT GIANT SIZE))
((FEAT SLOWLY RATE))
((FEAT FASTER RATE))
((FEAT THEN TI))
((FEAT TRAIL ACTT))
((FEAT SIXTY QU))
((FEAT SOON TI))
((FEAT LOOK AP))
((FEAT STAR POBJ))
((FEAT FEW QU))
((FEAT SECOND TI))
((FEAT TOO INTENS))
((FEAT HIGH HT))

Sec. B.1　A Grammar for the Rocket Story

```
  ((FEAT RADAR DEVICE))
  ((FEAT AS DUR))
  ((FEAT TRACK SEE))
  ((FEAT SPEED MOVE))
  ((FEAT UPWARD DIR))
  ((FEAT THREE-THOUSAND QU))
  ((FEAT MPH RATE))
  ((FEAT MINUTE TI))
  ((FEAT MILE MSR))
  ((FEAT MUCH MSR))
  ((FEAT PRESENT LOC))
  ((FEAT THEY POBJ))
  ((FEAT PURPOSE PU))
  ((FEAT GO MOVE))
  ((FEAT UP LOC))
  ((FEAT KIND TYPE))
  ((FEAT VEHICLE POBJ))
  ((FEAT SUMMARIZE ACT))
  ((FEAT HAPPEN ACT))
  ((FEAT COLOR COLOR))
  ((FEAT USE ACT))
  ((FEAT STORY POBJ))
  ((FEAT ABOUT TPC))
  ((FEAT THERE LOC))
  ((FEAT MANY QU))
  ((FEAT FAST RATE))
  ((FEAT (X . Y) Z) < (FEAT X Z)))
AXIOMS)

(DEFPROP INFVP
 ((((INFVP (X . Y) (V1 INF X . Q) R) < (EQ X TO) (VP Y (V1 . Q) R)))
 AXIOMS)

(DEFPROP NCOMP
 ((((NCOMP N X (W . Y) R) < (PP X Y R) (PREPTEST N Y W))
  ((NCOMP N (X . Y) (W . V1) R)
 < (CONJ X) (NP Y V1 R) (FEAT X W))
  ((NCOMP N X (W . V1) R) < (POSTMOD X V1 R) (FEAT V1 W))
  ((NCOMP N X (WHCH V W N . V1) R)
 < (INFVP X (V . V1) R) (ARCNAME N V W))
  ((NCOMP N (X) (W X) NIL) < (PREP X) (FEAT X W)))
 AXIOMS)

(DEFPROP NOUN
 ((((NOUN TYPE (TYPE NBR SING)))
  ((NOUN PLUNGE (PLUNGE NBR SING)))
  ((NOUN FLARE (FLARE NBR SING)))
  ((NOUN GENERAL (GENERAL NBR SING)))
  ((NOUN ROCKETS (ROCKET NBR PL)))
  ((NOUN SCIENTIST (SCIENTIST NBR SING)))
  ((NOUN TON (TON NBR SING)))
  ((NOUN LENGTH (LENGTH NBR SING)))
  ((NOUN FLIGHT (FLIGHT NBR SING)))
```

```
((NOUN PILOT (PILOT NBR SING)))
((NOUN PLANE (PLANE NBR SING)))
((NOUN EARTH (EARTH NBR SING)))
((NOUN POINT (POINT NBR SING)))
((NOUN NEWMEXICO (NEWMEXICO NBR PR)))
((NOUN DESERT (DESERT NBR SING)))
((NOUN FUEL (FUEL NBR SING)))
((NOUN TONS (TON NBR PL)))
((NOUN OXYGEN (OXYGEN NBR SING)))
((NOUN ALCOHOL (ALCOHOL NBR SING)))
((NOUN FLARES (FLARE NBR PL)))
((NOUN SIGNAL (SIGNAL NBR SING)))
((NOUN DISTANCE (DISTANCE NBR SING)))
((NOUN SCIENTISTS (SCIENTIST NBR PL)))
((NOUN GENERALS (GENERAL NBR PL)))
((NOUN MOUNDS (MOUND NBR PL)))
((NOUN ROCKET (ROCKET NBR SING)))
((NOUN FEET (FOOT NBR PL)))
((NOUN ROAR (ROAR NBR SING)))
((NOUN BURST (BURST NBR SING)))
((NOUN FLAME (FLAME NBR SING)))
((NOUN STAR (STAR NBR SING)))
((NOUN SECONDS (SECOND NBR PL)))
((NOUN RADAR (RADAR NBR SING)))
((NOUN MPH (MPH NBR PL)))
((NOUN MINUTES (MINUTE NBR PL)))
((NOUN SPEED (SPEED NBR SING)))
((NOUN MILES (MILE NBR PL)))
((NOUN PURPOSE (PURPOSE NBR SING)))
((NOUN KIND (KIND NBR SING)))
((NOUN VEHICLE (VEHICLE NBR SING)))
((NOUN COLOR (COLOR NBR SING)))
((NOUN STORY (STORY NBR SING)))
((NOUN MILE (MILE NBR SING)))
((NOUN FLAMES (FLAME NBR PL)))
((NOUN FOOT (FOOT NBR SING))))
AXIOMS)

(DEFPROP NP
 (((NP (X . Y) (V1 DET X . V2) R)
   <
   (VAR* Y)
   (ART X)
   (PREPTF V (V1 . V2))
   (NP1 Y V R))
  ((NP X V1 R) < (VAR* X) (PREPTF V V1) (NP1 X V R))
  ((NP (X . Y) (V1 DET X . V2) R)
   <
   (VAR* V1)
   (ART X)
   (NP1 Y V R)
   (PREPTF V (V1 . V2)))
  ((NP X V1 R) < (VARBLE V1) (NP1 X V R) (PREPTF V V1)))
```

Sec. B.1   A Grammar for the Rocket Story   **279**

```
   AXIOMS)

(DEFPROP NP1
 ((((NP1 (X . Y) X1 Y) < (PRON X X1))
  ((NNP1 (X . Y) (Y1 TYPE X1 . Q) R)
 < (NOUN X X1) (NP1 Y (Y1 . Q) R))
  ((NP1 (X . Y) (X1 V V1 . Q) R)
 < (NOUN X (X1 . Q)) (NCOMP X1 Y (V . V1) R))
  ((NP1 (X . Y) X1 Y) < (NOUN X X1))
  ((NP1 X (V2 W V1 . Q) R)
 < (ADJP X V1 R1) (NP1 R1 (V2 . Q) R) (FEAT V1 W))
  ((NP1 (X . Y) (V1 W X1 . Q) R)
 < (POSPRON X X1) (NP1 Y (V1 . Q) R) (FEAT X W))
  ((NP1 (X . Y) (V1 W (X1 TNS U1) . Q) R)
  <
  (VV X (X1 TNS U1))
  (PARCPL U1)
  (NP1 Y (V1 . Q) R)
  (ARCNAME V1 X1 W))
  ((NP1 (X . Y) (V ASSOC X1 . V1) R)
 < (POSPRON X X1) (NP1 Y (V . V1) R)))
 AXIOMS)

(DEFPROP PARCPL (((PARCPL PRPRT)) ((PARCPL PAPRT))) AXIOMS)

(DEFPROP POSPRON
 (((POSPRON ITS (IT NBR SING)))
  ((POSPRON ITS (IT NBR POSING))))
 AXIOMS)

(DEFPROP POSTMOD
 ((((POSTMOD X (V2 W V1 . Q) R)
 < (NP1 X V1 R1) (ADJP R1 (V2 . Q) R) (FEAT V2 W))
  )
 AXIOMS)

(DEFPROP PP
 ((((PP (X . Y) (V1 PREP X . Q) R)
 < (PREP X) (NP Y (V1 . Q) R)))
 AXIOMS)

(DEFPROP PREP
 (((PREP AT))
  ((PREP INTO))
  ((PREP IN))
  ((PREP FOR))
  ((PREP BEHIND))
  ((PREP OF))
  ((PREP AS))
  ((PREP TO))
  ((PREP WITH))
  ((PREP LIKE))
  ((PREP FROM))
```

    ((PREP AFTER))
    ((PREP BEFORE))
    ((PREP UP))
    ((PREP ABOUT)))
   AXIOMS)

  (DEFPROP PREPARC
   (((PREPARC POBJ ABOUT POBJ AE))
    ((PREPARC POBJ FOR POBJ PU))
    ((PREPARC ST BEHIND POBJ LOC))
    ((PREPARC ACTT FOR SUBST PU))
    ((PREPARC ST IN LOC LOC))
    ((PREPARC POBJ IN LOC LOC))
    ((PREPARC HUMAN OF DEVICE AGT))
    ((PREPARC MOVE INTO POBJ *TO))
    ((PREPARC MOVE OF MSR MSR))
    ((PREPARC ACT FROM LOC *FROM))
    ((PREPARC LOC IN LOC LOC))
    ((PREPARC MSR OF POBJ QU))
    ((PREPARC AP LIKE POBJ AP))
    ((PREPARC ST IN TI TI))
    ((PREPARC MOVE TO LOC LOC))
    ((PREPARC MOVE AS SYMB PU))
    ((PREPARC MOVE WITH SOUND AC))
    ((PREPARC MOVE BEHIND POBJ LOC))
    ((PREPARC ACT OF SUBST SUBST))
    ((PREPARC ACT BEHIND POBJ AE))
    ((PREPARC MSR OF SUBST QU))
    ((PREPARC MOVE TO RATE RATE))
    ((PREPARC MOVE OF RATE RATE))
    ((PREPARC SUBST OF MSR MSR))
    ((PREPARC POBJ OF MSR MSR))
    ((PREPARC ACT AT RATE RATE))
    ((PREPARC ACT AT MOVE RATE))
    ((PREPARC MSR FROM LOC LOC))
    ((PREPARC MOVE FROM LOC LOC)))
   AXIOMS)

  (DEFPROP PREPTEST
   (((PREPTEST X (U PREP OF . Q) OF))
    ((PREPTEST X (U PREP V . Q) Z)
     < (FEAT X X1) (FEAT U U1) (PREPARC X1 V U1 Z)))
   AXIOMS)

  (DEFPROP PREPTF
   (((PREPTF (V . V3) (X W (V . V1) . Y))
     <
     (DEPAIR (OF (X . Y)) V3 V1)
     (FEAT X X1)
     (FEAT V V2)
     (PREPARC X1 OF V2 W))
    ((PREPTF V V)))
   AXIOMS)

Sec. B.1 A Grammar for the Rocket Story

```
(DEFPROP PRON
 (((PRON HE (HE NBR SING)))
  ((PRON IT (IT NBR SING)))
  ((PRON EVERYTHING (EVERYTHING NBR SING)))
  ((PRON THEY (THEY NBR PL))))
 AXIOMS)

(DEFPROP Q1
 (((Q1 (X . Y) V) < (VBE X X1) (VP (X . Y) V NIL))
  ((Q1 (X . Y) V) < (VAUX X) (S1 Y V NIL))
  ((Q1 X V) < (VP X V NIL)))
 AXIOMS)

(DEFPROP QS
 (((QS X (U QOBJ V . W)) < (QTERM X V R) (Q1 R (U . W)))
  ((QS X (V MOOD IMPER . W)) < (VP X (V . W) NIL)))
 AXIOMS)

(DEFPROP QTERM
 (((QTERM (X Y . Z) (Y1 . Z1) R)
   < (QWD X X1) (NP Z Z1 R) (ATT Y Y1))
  ((QTERM (X Y . Z) X1 (Y . Z)) < (QWD X X1) (VAUX Y))
  ((QTERM (X Y Z . W) Y1 (Z . W))
   < (QWD X X1) (ADJ Y) (FEAT Y Y1))
  ((QTERM (X Y . Z) Y1 Z) < (QWD X X1) (NOUN Y Y2) (ATT Y Y1))
  ((QTERM (X Y . Z) X1 (Y . Z)) < (QWD X X1) (VV Y V))
  ((QTERM (X . Y) TRUTH (X . Y)) < (VAUX X)))
 AXIOMS)

(DEFPROP QWD
 (((QWD WHAT AE))
  ((QWD WHAT INSTR))
  ((QWD WHERE LOC))
  ((QWD WHEN TIME))
  ((QWD WHY PU))
  ((QWD WHO AGT))
  ((QWD HOW HOW)))
 AXIOMS)

(DEFPROP S1
 (((S1 X (V2 W V1 . Q) R)
   < (NP X V1 R1) (VP R1 (V2 . Q) R) (ARCNAME V2 V1 W)))
 AXIOMS)

(DEFPROP SS
 (((SS (X . Y) (V2 W V1 . Q))
   <
   (ADV X)
   (ADVPH (X . Y) V1 R)
   (S1 R (V2 . Q) NIL)
   (FEAT V1 W))
  ((SS (X . Y) (V2 W V1 . Q))
   <
```

```
  (PREP X)
  (PP (X . Y) V1 R)
  (S1 R (V2 . Q) NIL)
  (PREPTEST V2 V1 W))
 ((SS X (V3 W1 (R W1 V1 W2 V2) . Q))
  <
  (NP X V1 (R . R1))
  (FEAT V1 TI)
  (ADV R)
  (S1 R1 V2 R2)
  (S1 R2 (V3 . Q) NIL)
  (ARCNAME R V1 W1)
  (ARCNAME V2 R W2)
  (ARCNAME V3 R W1))
 ((SS X Y) < (S1 X Y NIL)))
AXIOMS)

(DEFPROP VARBLE
 (((VARBLE X) < (VAR* X)) ((VARBLE (X . Y)) < (VAR* X)))
 AXIOMS)

(DEFPROP VAUX
 (((VAUX X) < (AUX X X1)) ((VAUX X) < (VBE X X1))) AXIOMS)

(DEFPROP VBE
 (((VBE IS (BE TNS PRES)))
  ((VBE WAS (BE TNS PAST)))
  ((VBE BE (BE TNS PRES)))
  ((VBE WERE (BE TNS PAST))))
 AXIOMS)

(DEFPROP VP
 (((VP (X . Y) (V1 W X . Q) R)
 < (ADV X) (VP Y (V1 . Q) R) (ARCNAME V1 X W))
  ((VP (X . Y) (V1 AUX X1 . Q) R)
 < (VBE X X1) (VP Y (V1 . Q) R))
  ((VP (X . Y) (V1 AUX X1 . Q) R)
 < (AUX X X1) (VP Y (V1 . Q) R))
  ((VP (X . Y) (X1 U W . V2) R)
 < (VV X (X1 U W)) (COMP Y X1 V2 R))
  ((VP (X . Y) (X1 U V W V1) R)
  <
  (VBE X (X1 U V))
  (ADJP Y V1 R)
  (ARCNAME X1 V1 W))
  ((VP (X . Y) (X1 U V . W) R)
 < (VBE X (X1 U V)) (COMP Y X1 W R))
  ((VP (X . Y) X1 Y) < (VBE X X1))
  ((VP (X . Y) X1 Y) < (VV X X1)))
AXIOMS)

(DEFPROP VV
 (((VV SEE (SEE TNS PRES)))
```

Sec. B.2   Complete Top-Down Flight Schema

```
      ((VV FLY (FLY TNS PRES)))
      ((VV CROUCH (CROUCH TNS PRES)))
      ((VV CARRY (CARRY TNS PRES)))
      ((VV FLOWN (FLY TNS PPAST)))
      ((VV WITHDRAW (WITHDRAW TNS PRES)))
      ((VV HIDE (HIDE TNS PRES)))
      ((VV STOOD (STAND TNS PAST)))
      ((VV WATCHING (WATCH TNS PRPRT)))
      ((VV RETURN (RETURN TNS PRES)))
      ((VV SAW (SEE TNS PAST)))
      ((VV PLUNGED (PLUNGE TNS PAST)))
      ((VV STARTING (START TNS PRPRT)))
      ((VV CARRIED (CARRY TNS PAST)))
      ((VV WEIGHED (WEIGH TNS PAST)))
      ((VV ROSE (RISE TNS PAST)))
      ((VV FIRE (FIRE TNS PRES)))
      ((VV WITHDREW (WITHDRAW TNS PAST)))
      ((VV CROUCHED (CROUCH TNS PAST)))
      ((VV TRAILED (TRAIL TNS PAST)))
      ((VV LOOKED (LOOK TNS PAST)))
      ((VV SEEN (SEE TNS PAST)))
      ((VV TRACKED (TRACK TNS PAST)))
      ((VV SPED (SPEED TNS PAST)))
      ((VV FIRED (FIRE TNS PAST)))
      ((VV WEIGH (WEIGH TNS PRES)))
      ((VV GO (GO TNS PRES)))
      ((VV RISE (RISE TNS PRES)))
      ((VV SUMMARIZE (SUMMARIZE TNS PRES)))
      ((VV HAPPEN (HAPPEN TNS PRES)))
      ((VV USE (USE TNS PRES)))
      ((VV TRACK (TRACK TNS PRES)))
      ((VV TRAIL (TRAIL TNS PRES)))
      ((VV PLUNGE (PLUNGE TNS PRES)))
      ((VV SPEED (SPEED TNS PRES)))
      ((VV STAND (STAND TNS PRES))))
AXIOMS)
```

B.2 COMPLETE TOP-DOWN FLIGHT SCHEMA

```
    (DEFPROP FLIGHT
     (((FLIGHT X (FLIGHT TPC X LOC U SETT T1 SEQ T2 OUTC Z) S)
       <
       (FLIGHTSYSTEM X U T1 S R)
       (ASCENT X U T2 R NIL)
       (LASTACT T2 Z)))
    AXIOMS)

    (DEFPROP FLIGHTSYSTEM
     (((FLIGHTSYSTEM X U (FLTSYSTEM EVT (T1 T2 T3)) S R)
       <
       (LOCAT X U T1 S R1)
```

```
   (WT X T2 R1 R2)
   (SUPPORT X T3 R2 R)))
 AXIOMS)

(DEFPROP ASCENT
 (((ASCENT X L (ASCEND TPC X FROM L SETT Y EVT Z SEQ W) S R)
   <
   (PREPAR X Y S R1)
   (ASCEND X Z R1 R2)
   (CRUISE X W R2 R)))
 AXIOMS)

(DEFPROP LASTACT
 (((LASTACT (Z . Z2) Z1)
  < (MEMPR (SEQ NIL) Z2) (MEMPR (EVT Z1) Z2))
  ((LASTACT (Z . Z1) W) < (MEMPR (SEQ U) Z1) (LASTACT U W))
  ((LASTACT X NIL)))
 AXIOMS)

(DEFPROP LOCAT
 (((LOCAT X Y (X POSIT U LOC Y . Q) ((U . W) . R) R)
   <
   (RELATE U POSITION)
   (MATCHPR (AE (X1 . Q) LOC Y) W W)
   (RELATE X X1)))
 AXIOMS)

(DEFPROP WT
 (((WT X (X WT Y . Q) ((U . W) . R) R)
   <
   (RELATE U WEIGH)
   (MATCHPR (AE (X1 . Q) MSR Y) W W)
   (RELATE X1 X)))
 AXIOMS)

(DEFPROP SUPPORT
 (((SUPPORT X (X CO (Z PU Y)) ((U . W) . R) R)
   <
   (RELATE U SUPPORT)
   (MATCHPR (AE X1 CO Z PU Y) W W)
   (RELATE X1 X)))
 AXIOMS)
(DEFPROP PREPAR
 (((PREPAR X (PREPARE EVT (T1 T2 T3)) S R)
   <
   (READY X T1 S R1)
   (WITHDRAW X T2 R1 R2)
   (SIGNAL X T3 R2 R)))
 AXIOMS)

(DEFPROP ASCEND
 (((ASCEND X ((U TPC X . W) . V) ((U . W) . R) R1)
   <
```

Sec. B.2   Complete Top-Down Flight Schema   **285**

```
   (RELATE U RISE)
   (MEMPR (AE X1) W)
   (RELATE X X1)
   (DESCRIP X V R R1)))
 AXIOMS)

(DEFPROP CRUISE
 ((((CRUISE X (CRUISE TPC X
                     SETT (OBSERVE EVT (V)) EVT (V1) SEQ W) S R)
   <
   (STATES X V S R1)
   (OBSERVE X V1 R1 R2)
   (DESCENT X W R2 R)))
 AXIOMS)

(DEFPROP RELATE
 (((RELATE X Y) < (SET X Y))
  ((RELATE (X . W) Y) < (RELATE X Y))
  ((RELATE X (Y . W)) < (RELATE X Y))
  ((RELATE X Y) < (EQ* X Y))
  ((RELATE X Y) < (X SUP Y))
  ((RELATE X Y) < (PROFORM X Y)))
 AXIOMS)

(DEFPROP DESCRIP
 ((((DESCRIP X ((U . W) . V) ((U . W) . R) R1)
    <
   (U SUP DESCRIP)
   (FOCUS W X1)
   (RELATE X1 X)
   (DESCRIP X2 V R R1))
  ((DESCRIP X NIL S S)))
 AXIOMS)

(DEFPROP STATES
 (((STATES X (U . W) ((U . W) . R) R)
   <
   (U SUP STATE)
   (MEMPR (AE X1) W)
   (RELATE X1 X)))
 AXIOMS)

(DEFPROP OBSERVE
 ((((OBSERVE X (U TPC X . W) ((U . W) . R) R)
    <
   (RELATE U OBSERVE)
   (MEMPR (AE X1) W)))
 AXIOMS)

(DEFPROP DESCENT
 ((((DESCENT X
       (DESCEND TPC X
                SETT (STATES EVT (Y)) LOC Z EVT (V) SEQ NIL)
```

```
    S
    NIL)
  <
  (OBSERVE X Y S R)
  (DESCEND X V R NIL)
  (LOCUS V Z)))
AXIOMS)

(DEFPROP OBSERVE
 (((OBSERVE X (U TPC X . W) ((U . W) . R) R)
  <
  (RELATE U OBSERVE)
  (MEMPR (AE X1) W)))
AXIOMS)

(DEFPROP DESCEND
 (((DESCEND X (U TPC X . W) ((U . W) . R) R)
  (RELATE U DESCEND)
  (MEMPR (INSTR X1) W)
  (RELATE X1 X)))
AXIOMS)

(DEFPROP LOCUS
 (((LOCUS (U . W) Z) < (MEMPR (LOC Z) W))
  ((LOCUS (U . W) Z) < (MEMPR (TO Z) W) (RELATE Z PLACE))
  ((LOCUS X NIL)))
AXIOMS)

(DEFPROP SIGNAL
 (((SIGNAL X (U . W) ((U . W) . R) R)
  <
  (RELATE U RISE)
  (MATCHPR (AE Y PU Z) W W)
  (RELATE Z SIGNAL)))
AXIOMS)

(DEFPROP TRACK (((TRACK SUP OBSERVE))) AXIOMS)

(DEFPROP LOOK (((LOOK SUP DESCRIP))) AXIOMS)

(DEFPROP CARRY (((CARRY SUP SUPPORT))) AXIOMS)
```

B.3 COMPLETE INSTANTIATION OF THE FLIGHT SCHEMA BY THE ROCKET STORY

```
(FLIGHT TPC ROCKET LOC (DESERT PREP IN DET A LOC (NEWMEXICO)
                                                  NBR SING)
        SETT (FLTSYSTEM
               EVT ((STAND AE (ROCKET DET A SIZE (GREAT)
                                      COLOR (BLACK *AND (YELLOW))
                                      TYPE (V-2)
```

Sec. B.3　Complete Instantiation of the Flight Schema by the Rocket Story　　287

```
                              LGTH (LONG MSR (FOOT QU (FORTY-SIX) NBR PL))
                                    NBR SING)
                                    TNS PAST
                                    LOC (DESERT PREP IN DET A
                                         LOC (NEWMEXICO) NBR SING))
                          (WEIGH AE (ROCKET ST (EMPTY) NBR SING)
                                 TNS PAST
                                 MSR (TON QU (FIVE) NBR PL))
                          (CARRY PU (FUEL PREP FOR NBR SING)
                                 INSTR (ROCKET NBR SING)
                                 TNS PAST
                                 AE (ALCOHOL MSR (TON QU (EIGHT)
                                                         NBR PL)
                                              PREP OF
                                              *AND (OXYGEN ST (LIQUID)
                                                           NBR SING)
                                              NBR SING))))
               SEQ (ASCEND TPC ROCKET
                           FROM (DESERT PREP IN DET A
                                        LOC (NEWMEXICO) NBR SING)
                           SETT (PREPARE EVT ((BE AE (ROCKET NBR SING)
                                                  TNS PAST
                                                  ST (READY))
                                             (WITHDRAW AGT (SCIENTIST
                                                           *AND (GENERAL NBR PL)
                                                           NBR PL)
                                                       TNS PAST
                                                       LOC (DISTANCE PREP TO
                                                                 DET SOME NBR SING)
                                              *AND (CROUCH TNS PAST
                                                         LOC (MOUND PREP BEHIND
                                                                    TYPE (EARTH NBR SING)
                                                                    NBR PL)))
                                             (RISE AE (FLARE QU (TWO)
                                                           COLOR (RED) NBR PL)
                                                   TNS PAST
                                                   PU (SIGNAL PREP AS DET A
                                                          WHCH (FIRE PU SIGNAL
                                                                     INF TO TNS PRES
                                                                     AE (ROCKET DET THE NBR SING))
                                                          NBR SING))))
                EVT ((RISE AC (ROAR PREP WITH DET A SIZE (GREAT)
                              *AND (BURST OF (FLAME PREP OF NBR SING)
                                         NBR SING)
                              NBR SING)
                         AE (ROCKET DET THE SIZE (GIANT) NBR SING)
                         TNS PAST
                         RATE (SLOWLY *THEN (FASTER *AND FASTER)))
                     (TRAIL LOC BEHIND INSTR (IT NBR SING)
                            TNS PAST
                            AE (FLAME MSR (FOOT QU (SIXTY) NBR PL)
                                     PREP OF COLOR (YELLOW) NBR SING))
                     (LOOK TI SOON AE (FLAME DET THE NBR SING)
```

                        TNS PAST
                        AP (STAR PREP LIKE DET A
                                COLOR (YELLOW) NBR SING)))
SEQ
   (CRUISE TPC ROCKET
            SETT (OBSERVE EVT
                    ((BE TI (SECOND PREP IN DET A QU (FEW) NBR PL)
                    AE (IT NBR SING) TNS PAST
                    HT (HIGH INTENS TOO
                    RESULT (SEE INF TO AUX (BE TNS PRES) TNS PAST)))))
            EVT ((TRACK INSTR (RADAR NBR SING) TNS PAST
                    AE (IT NBR SING)
                    DUR (SPEED AE (IT NBR SING) TNS PAST
                            DIR UPWARD
                            RATE (MPH PREP TO
                                    QU(THREE-THOUSAND) NBR PL))))
    SEQ (DESCEND TPC ROCKET SETT
            (STATES EVT ((SEE TI (AFTER TI (MINUTE DET A QU (FEW) NBR PL)
                                EVNT (FIRE AE (IT NBR SING)
                                        AUX (BE TNS PAST)
                                        TNS PAST))
                                AGT (PILOT DET THE
                                        OF (PLANE PREP OF DET A
                                                INSTR* (WATCH TNS PRPRT)
                                                NBR SING)
                                        NBR SING)
                                TNS PAST
                                AE (RETURN AE (IT NBR SING) TNS PRES))))
    EVT ((PLUNGE AE (ROCKET NBR SING) TNS PAST
            *TO (EARTH PREP INTO NBR SING)
                    LOC (MILE QU (FORTY) LOC (POINT PREP FROM DET THE
                                                LOC (START TNS PRPRT)
                                                NBR SING)
                    NBR PL)))
    SEQ NIL)))
OUTC (PLUNGE AE (ROCKET NBR SING) TNS PAST
            *TO (EARTH PREP INTO NBR SING)
                    LOC (MILE QU (FORTY) LOC (POINT PREP FROM DET THE
                                                LOC (START TNS PRPRT)
                                                NBR SING)
                    NBR PL))))

REFERENCES AND BIBLIOGRAPHY

Aho, A. and Ullman, J., *The Theory of Parsing, Translation, and Compiling,* Vol. 1, Prentice-Hall, N.J., 1972.

Allen, J. F., A Plan-Based Approach to Speech Act Recognition, Ph.D. dissertation, Dept. Comp. Sci., University of Toronto, 1979.

Allen, J. F., and Frisch, A. M., What's in a Semantic Network, *Proc. Assoc. Comp. Ling.,* pp. 19–27, Toronto, 1982.

Alterman, R., A System of Seven Coherence Relations for Organizing Event Concepts, Ph.D. dissertation, Dept. Comp. Sci., University of Texas, Austin, 1982.

Amsler, Robert A., A Taxonomy for English Nouns and Verbs, *Proc. Assoc. Comp. Ling.,* Stanford, Calif., 1981.

Anderson, J. R., A Theory of Language Acquisition Based on General Learning Principles, *Proc. 7th IJCAI,* Vancouver, B.C., 1981, pp. 97–103.

Barr, A., and Feigenbaum, E. A., *The Handbook of Artificial Intelligence,* Vol. 1., William Kaufmann, Los Altos, Calif., 1981.

Bartlett, F. C., *Remembering: A Study in Experimental and Social Psychology,* Cambridge University Press, Cambridge, England, 1932 (reprinted 1977).

Bates, M., and Ingria, R., Controlled Transformational Sentence Generation, *Proc. Assoc. Comp. Ling.,* Stanford, Calif., 1981.

Beaugrande, R. de, *Text, Discourse and Process,* Ablex, Norwood, N.J., 1980.

Beaugrande, R. de, Design Criteria for Process Models of Reading, *Reading Res. Q.,* Vol. 16, No. 2, pp. 261–315, 1981.

Black, F. S., A Deductive Question-Answering System, in M. Minsky (ed.), *Semantic Information Processing,* MIT Press, Cambridge, Mass., 1968.

Bobrow, D. G., and Fraser, B., An Augmented Transition State Network Analysis Procedure, *Proc. 1st IJCAI,* Washington, D.C., 1969, pp. 557–567.

Bobrow, D. G., and Winograd, T., An Overview of KRL, A Knowledge Representation Language, *Cognitiv. Sci.,* Vol. 1, No. 1, pp. 29–42, Jan. 1977.

Booth, A. D., *Machine Translation,* North-Holland, Amsterdam, 1967.

Borko, H., *Automated Language Processing,* Wiley, New York, 1967.

Boyer, R. S., and Moore, J. A., *A Computational Logic,* Academic Press, New York, 1979.

Brachman, R. J., On the Epistemological Status of Semantic Networks, in N. Findler (ed.), *Associative Networks,* Academic Press, New York, 1979.

Brown J. S., and Burton, R. R., Multiple Representations of Knowledge for Tutorial Reasoning, in D. G. Bobrow and A. Collins (eds.), *Representation and Understanding,* Academic Press, New York, 1975.

Bruce, B., Case Systems for Natural Language, *Artif. Intell.,* Vol. 6, pp. 327–360, 1975.

Bruce, B., and Newman, D., Interacting Plans, *Cognit. Sci.,* Vol. 2, No. 3, pp. 195–233, 1978.

Bruderer, H. E., *Handbuch der Mashinellen und maschinenunterstüzten Sprachubersetzung: Automatische Übersetzung natürlicher sprachen und mehrsprachige Terminologiedatenbanken,* Verlag Dokumentation, Munich, 1978.

Burton, R. R., *Semantic Grammar: An Engineering Technique for Constructing Natural Language Understanding Systems,* Bolt Beranek and Newman, Inc., Rep. 3453, Cambridge, Mass., 1976.

Bush, V., As We May Think, *Atlantic Monthly,* June 1955.

Carbonell, J. R., AI in CAI: An Artificial Intelligence Approach to Computer-Assisted Instruction, *IEEE Trans. Man–Mach. Syst.,* MMS-11, pp. 190–202, 1970.

Carbonell, J., Politics, in R. Schank and C. Riesbeck (eds.), *Inside Computer Understanding,* Lawrence Erlbaum Associates, Hillsdale, N.J., 1981.

Cherry, L., A Toolbox for Writers and Editors, *AFIPS Of. Automat. Conf.,* Houston, 1981, pp. 221–227.

Chester D., Using HCPRVR, Department of Computer Science, University of Texas, Austin, June 1980a.

Chester, D., HCPRVR: A Logic Program Interpreter in LISP, *Proc. AAAI 1980,* ms., Dept. Comp. Sci., University of Texas, Austin, 1980b.

Chomsky, N., *Aspects of the Theory of Syntax,* MIT Press, Cambridge, Mass., 1965.

Clancy, W. J., Shortliffe, E. H., and Buchanan, B. G., Intelligent Computer-Aided Instruction for Medical Diagnosis, *Proc. 3rd Symp. Comp. Appl. Med. Care,* 1979, pp. 175–183.

Clark, K. L., and McCabe, F., PROLOG: A Language for Implementing Expert Systems, in J. Hayes and D. J. Mitchie (eds.), *Machine Intelligence 10,* Ellis and Horwood, Edinburgh, 1982.

Clark, K. L., and Tarnlund, S., A First Order Theory of Data and Programs, *IFIPS 77,* North-Holland, Amsterdam, 1977, pp. 939–944.

Clark, K. L., and Tarnlund, S., *Logic Programming,* Academic Press, New York, 1982.

Coelho, H. M. F., A Program Conversing in Portuguese Providing a Library Service, Ph.D. dissertation, University of Edinburgh, Edinburgh, Dec. 1979.

Cohen, P.H., On Knowing What to Say: Planning Speech Acts, Ph.D. dissertation, Dept. Comp. Sci., University of Toronto, 1978.

Cohen, P., Perrault, C., and Allen, J., *Beyond Question Answering*, Bolt Beranek and Newman, Inc., Rep. 4644, Cambridge, Mass., 1981.

Colby, K. M., Simulations of Belief Systems, in R. Schank and K. Colby (eds.), *Computer Models of Thought and Language,* Freeman, San Francisco, 1973.

Colmerauer, A., Metamorphosis Grammars, in L. Bolc (ed.), *Natural Language Communication with Computers,* Springer-Verlag, New York, 1978.

Correira, A., Computing Story Trees, *Am. J. Comp. Ling.,* Vol. 6, Nos. 3–4, pp. 135–149, 1980.

Cullingford, R. E., Pattern-Matching and Inference in Story-Understanding, *Discourse Process.,* Vol. 2, pp. 319–334, 1979.

Dahl, V., Translating Spanish into Logic through Logic, *Am. J. Comp. Ling.,* Vol. 7, No. 3, pp. 149–164, 1981.

Darlington, J. L., Machine Methods for Proving Logical Arguments Expressed in English, *Mech. Transl. Comp. Ling.,* Vol. 8, pp. 41–67, Oct. 1965.

DeJong, G. F., Prediction and Substantiation: Two Processes That Comprise Understanding, *Proc. 6th IJCAI,* Vol. 1, pp. 217–222, Aug. 1979.

Dowty, D. R., Wall, R., and Peters, S., *An Introduction to Montague Semantics,* D. Reidel, Dordrecht, 1981.

Duda, R. O., and Gaschnig, J. G., Knowledge-Based Expert Systems Come of Age, *Byte,* pp. 238–281, Sept. 1981.

Duda, R. O., Hart, P. E., Konolige, K., and Reboh, R., A Computer-Based Consultant for Mineral Exploration, *SRI Tech. Rep., Menlo Park, Calif., May 1978.*

Fahlman, S. E., *NETL: A System for Representing and Using Real-World Knowledge,* MIT Press, Cambridge, Mass., 1979.

Feigenbaum, E. A., The Art of Artificial Intelligence, *IJCAI 77,* Cambridge, Mass., 1977, pp. 1014–1029.

Fillmore, C. J., The Case for Case, in E. Bach and T. Harms (eds.), *Universals in Linguistic Theory,* Holt, Rinehart and Winston, New York, 1968.

Findler, N. V. (ed.), *Associative Networks,* Academic Press, New York, 1979.

Futo, I., Darvas, F., and Szered, P., The Application of PROLOG To the Development of QA and DBM Systems, in H. Gallair and J. Minker (eds.), *Logic and Data Bases,* Plenum Press, New York, 1978.

Gallaire, H., and Minker, J., *Logic and Data Bases,* Plenum Press, New York, 1978.

Gazdar, G., Phrase Structure Grammar, in P. Jacobson and G. K. Pullum (eds.), *The Nature of Syntactic Representation,* D. Reidel, Dordrecht, 1981.

Goldman, N., Conceptual Generation, in R. C. Schank (ed.), *Conceptual Information Processing,* North-Holland, Amsterdam, 1975.

Green C., Application of Theorem Proving to Problem Solving, *Proc. IJCAI,* Washington, D.C., 1969, pp. 219–239.

Green, B. F., Wolf, A. K., Chomsky, C., and Laughery, K., Baseball, an Automatic

Question Answerer, in E. Feigenbaum and J. Feldman (eds.), *Computers and Thought,* McGraw-Hill, New York, 1963.

Green, L. E. S., Berkely, E. C., and Gotlieb, C., Conversations with a Computer, *Comp. Automat.,* Vol. 8, No. 10, pp. 9–11, 1959.

Grice, H. P., Logic and Conversation, in P. Cole and J. L. Morgan (eds.), *Syntax and Semantics,* Vol. 3, Academic Press, New York, 1975.

Grimes, J., *The Thread of Discourse,* Mouton, The Hague, 1975.

Grishman, R., and Hirshman, L., Question Answering from Natural Language Medical Data Bases, *Artif. Intell.,* Vol. 11, pp. 1–2, Aug. 1978.

Grosz, B., The Representation and Use of Focus in Dialogue Understanding, *SRI Tech. Note 151,* SRI, Menlo Park, Calif., 1977.

Halliday, M. A., and Hasan, R., *Cohesion in English,* Longman Press, London, 1976.

Hendrix, G. G., Partitioned Networks for the Mathematical Modelling of Natural Language Semantics, Ph.D. dissertation, Dept. Comp. Sci., University of Texas, Austin, 1975.

Hendrix, G. G., Sacerdoti, E. D., Sagalowicz, D., and Slocum, J., Developing a Natural Language Interface to Complex Data. *ACM Trans. Database Syst.,* Vol. 3, No. 2, June 1978, pp. 105–147.

Hewitt, C., Procedural Embedding of Knowledge in PLANNER, *Proc. 2nd IJCAI,* London, 1971, pp. 167–182.

Hirst, G., Discourse-Oriented Anaphora Resolution: A Review, *Am. J. Comp. Ling.,* Vol. 7, No. 2, pp. 85–98, 1981.

Hobbs, J. R., Coherence and Coreference, *Cognitive Science,* Vol. 3, No. 1, pp. 67–90, 1979.

Hobbs, J. R., Metaphor Interpretation as Selective Inferencing, *Proc. 7th IJCAI,* Vancouver, B.C., 1981, pp. 85–91.

Jorgenson, E., *Volkswagon Service-Repair Handbook,* Clymer Publications, Los Angeles, 1974.

Kaplan, R. M., A General Syntactic Processor, in R. Rustin (ed.), *Natural Language Processing,* Algorithmics Press, New York, 1971.

Kaplan, S. J., *Cooperative Responses from a Portable Natural Language Database Query System,* Stanford Heuristic Programming Project, HPP-79-19, Comp. Sci. Dept., Stanford University, Stanford, Calif., 1979.

Kay, M., The MIND System, in R. Rustin (ed.), *Natural Language Processing,* Algorithmics Press, New York, 1971.

Kellogg, C. H., A Natural Language Compiler for On-Line Data Management, *Proc. AFIPS,* Vol. 33, Thompson Book Co., Washington, D.C., 1968, pp. 473–493.

Klein, S., and Simmons, R. F., Syntactic Dependence and the Computer Generation of Coherent Discourse, *Mech. Trans. Comp. Ling.,* Vol. 7, pp. 50–61, 1963.

Komorowski, H. J., QLOG—The Software for Prolog and Logic Programming, Informatics Lab. Res. Rpt. LiTH-MAT-R- 1980-18, Linkoping University, Sweden, 1980.

Komorowski, H. J., QLOG—The Programming Environment for PROLOG in LISP, in K. L. Clark and S. A. Tarnlund (eds.), *Logic Programming,* Academic Press, New York, 1982.

Kowalski, R. A., Logic for Problem Solving, Memo 75, Dept. Comp. Logic, University of Edinburgh, Edinburgh, 1974.

Kowalski, R., *Logic for Problem Solving,* North-Holland, Amsterdam, 1979.

Kuno, S., and Oettinger, A., Multiple Path Syntactic Analyzer, in *Information Processing,* Proc. IFIP 77, C. M. Popplewell (ed.), North-Holland, Amsterdam, 1962.

Lakoff, G., and Johnson, M., *Metaphors We Live By,* University of Chicago Press, Chicago, 1980.

Lehmann, W. P., Pflueger, S., Hewitt, H., Amsler, R., and Smith, H., Linguistic Documentation of METAL System, Rome Air Development Center, RADC-TR-78-100, Griffis AFB, New York, 1978.

Lehnert, W., Human and Computational Question Answering, *Cognitive Science,* Vol. 1, No. 1, Jan. 1977.

Lehnert, W. C., *The Process of Question Answering: A Computer Simulation of Cognition,* Lawrence Erlbaum Associates, Hillsdale, N.J., 1978.

LeVine, Sharon, *Questioning English Text with Clausal Logic,* Thesis, Dept. Comp. Sci., University of Texas, Austin, 1980.

Lindsay, R. K., Inferential Memory as the Basis of Machines Which Understand Natural Thought, in E. Feigenbaum and J. Feldman (eds.), *Computers and Thought,* McGraw-Hill, New York, 1963.

Locke, W. N., and Booth, A. D. (eds.), *Machine Translation of Languages,* Wiley, New York, 1955.

Lockman, A. and Klappholz, A. D., Toward a Model of Contextual Reference Resolution, *Discourse Process.,* Vol. 3, No. 1, pp. 25–71, Jan. 1980.

Mann, W. C., Two Discourse Generators, *Proc. 19th Assoc. Comp. Ling.,* Stanford, Calif., 1981.

Marcus, M. P., *A Theory of Syntactic Recognition for Natural Languages,* MIT Press, Cambridge, Mass., 1980.

Markusz, Z., How to Design Variants of Flats Using Programming Language PROLOG Based on Mathematical Logic, *Proc. IFIP 77,* Toronto, 1977, pp. 885–890.

McCarthy, J., Recursive Functions of Symbolic Expressions and Their Computation by Machine, *Commun. ACM,* Vol. 7, No. 4, pp. 184–195, 1960.

McDermott, J., R1, The Formative Years, *AI Mag.,* pp. 21–29, Summer 1981.

Meehan, J., The Metanovel: Writing Stories by Computer, Ph.D. dissertation, Comp. Sci. Dept., Yale University, 1976.

Meehan, J., Tale-Spin, in R. Schank and C. Riesbeck, *Inside Computer Understanding,* Lawrence Erlbaum Associates, Hillsdale, N.J., 1981.

Miller, G. A., and Johnson-Laird, P., *Language and Perception,* Cambridge University Press, Cambridge, 1976.

Montague, R., Universal Grammar, in R. H. Thomason (ed.), *Formal Philosophy: Selected Papers of Richard Montague,* Yale University Press, New Haven, Conn., 1974.

Newell, A., The Knowledge Level, *AI Mag.,* Vol. 2, No. 2, pp. 1–20, 1981.

Norman, D. A., and Rumelhart, D. E., *Explorations in Cognition,* W. H. Freeman, San Francisco, 1975.

Novak, G. S., Representation of Knowledge in a Program for Solving Physics Problems, *Proc. 5th IJCAI*, 1977, pp. 286–291.

Nilsson, N. J., *Principles of Artificial Intelligence*, Tioga Press, Palo Alto, Calif., 1980.

Partee, B. H., *Montague Grammar*, Academic Press, New York, 1976.

Pereira, F. and Warren D., Definite Clause Grammars for Language Analysis—A Survey of the Formalism and a Comparison with Augmented Transition Networks, *Artif. Intell.*, Vol. 13, pp. 231–278, 1980.

Perrault, C. R., and Cohen, P. R., It's for Your Own Good: A Note on Inaccurate Reference, in A. Joshi, B. Webber, and I. Sag (eds.), *Elements of Discourse Understanding*, Cambridge University Press, New York, 1981.

Petrick, S. R., Transformational Analysis, in R. Rustin (ed.), *Natural Language Processing*, Algorithmics Press, New York, 1973.

Phillips, B., Topic Analysis, Ph.D. dissertation, Dept. Comp. Sci., State University of New York, Buffalo, 1975.

Pratt, V. R., Lingol—A Progress Report, *Proc. 4th IJCAI*, Tbilisi, USSR, 1975, pp. 422–428.

Propp, V., *Morphology of the Folktale*, (transl. L. Scott), University of Texas Press, Austin, 1968.

Quillian, M. R., Semantic Memory, in M. Minsky (ed.), *Semantic Information Processing*, MIT Press, Cambridge, Mass., 1968.

Raphael, B., SIR: A Computer Program for Semantic Information Retrieval, in M. Minsky (ed.), *Semantic Information Processing*, MIT Press, Cambridge, Mass., 1968.

Reddy, D. R., Speech Recognition by Machine: A Review, *Proc. IEEE*, Vol. 64, May 1976, pp. 501–531.

Reid, B. K., and Walker, J. H., *Scribe Introductory User's Manual*, Unilogic, Pittsburgh, Pa., 1980.

Riesbeck, C., An Expectation Driven Production System for Natural Language Understanding, in D. Waterman and F. Hayes-Roth (eds.), *Pattern-Directed Inference Systems*, Academic Press, New York, 1978.

Robinson, J. A., A Machine-Oriented Logic Based on the Resolution Principle, *J. ACM*, Vol. 12, pp. 23–41, 1965.

Robinson, J. A., Fundamentals of Machine-Oriented Deductive Logic, unpublished ms., Dept. Comp. Sci., Syracuse University, 1980.

Robinson, J. A., and Sibert, E. E., LOGLISP—An Alternative to PROLOG, School Inf. Comp. Sci., Syracuse University, Syracuse, N.Y., 1980.

Robinson, J. J., DIAGRAM: A Grammar for Dialogues, *Commun. ACM*, Vol. 25, No. 1, pp. 27–47, Jan. 1982.

Roussell, P., PROLOG: Manuel de Référence et Utilisation, Groupe d'Intelligence Artificielle, University of Marseille-Luminy, Sept. 1975.

Rumelhart, D. E., Notes on a Schema for Stories, in D. G. Bobrow and A. Collins (eds.), *Representation and Understanding*, Academic Press, New York, 1975, pp. 211–236.

Sacerdoti, E. D., *A Structure for Plans and Behavior*, Elsevier North-Holland, New York, 1977.

Sager, N., *Natural Language Information Processing*, Addison-Wesley, Reading,

Mass., 1981.

Satterthwaite, A. C., Sentence-for-Sentence Translation: An Example, *Mech. Transl. Comp. Ling.,* Vol. 8, No. 2, pp. 14–38, Feb. 1965.

Schank, R. C., *Conceptual Information Processing,* North-Holland, Amsterdam, 1975.

Schank, R. C., and Abelson, R. P., *Scripts Plans Goals and Understanding,* Lawrence Erlbaum Associates, Hillsdale, N.J., 1977.

Schank, R. and Riesbeck, C., *Inside Natural Language,* Lawrence Erlbaum Associates, Hillsdale, N.J., 1980.

Schubert, L. K., Extending the Expressive Power of Semantic Networks, *Artif. Intell.,* Vol. 7, pp. 163–198, 1976.

Schubert, L. K., and Pelletier, F. J., From English to Logic: Context-Free Computation of "Conventional" Logical Translations, *J. Assoc. Comp. Ling.,* 1981, in press.

Searle, J., *Speech Acts,* Cambridge University Press, Cambridge, 1969.

Shapiro, S. C., The SNEPS Semantic Network Processing System, in N. Findler (ed.), *Associative Networks,* Academic Press, New York, 1979.

Shortliffe, E. H., *Computer-Based Medical Consultations: MYCIN,* Elsevier North-Holland, New York, 1976.

Sidner, C. L., Towards a Computational Theory of Definite Anaphora Comprehension in English Discourse, Ph.D. dissertation, MIT, Tech. Rep. 537, Boston, 1979.

Silva, G., Montgomery, C., and Dwiggins, D., An Application of Automated Language Understanding Techniques to the Generation of Data Base Elements, *Proc. Assoc. Comp. Ling.,* San Diego, 1979.

Simmons, R. F., A Narrative Schema in Procedural Logic, in K. Clark and S. Tarnlund (eds.), *Logic Programming,* Academic Press, New York, 1982.

Simmons, R. F. and Burger, J. F., A Semantic Analyzer for English Sentences, *J. Mech. Transl. Comp. Ling.,* 1969.

Simmons, R. F., and Chester, D., Inferences in Quantified Semantic Networks, *Proc. 5th IJCAI,* pp. 267–273, Cambridge, Mass., 1977.

Simmons, R. F., and Chester, D., Relating Sentences and Semantic Networks with Clausal Logic, ms. Dept. Comp. Sci., University of Texas, Austin, 1980; *Commun. ACM,,* 1982, in press.

Simmons, R. F., and Correira, A., Rule Forms for Verse, Sentences and Story Trees, in N. Findler (ed.), *Associative Networks,* Academic Press, New York, 1979, pp. 363–392.

Simmons, R. F., and Slocum, J., Generating English Discourse from Semantic Networks, *Commun. ACM,* Vol. 15, pp. 891–905, 1972.

Simmons, R. F., Burger, J. F., and Schwarcz, R. M., A Computational Model of Verbal Understanding, *Proc. AFIP,* Thompson Book Co., Washington, D.C., Fall 1968, pp. 441–456.

Slocum, J., An Experiment in Machine Translation, *Proc. Assoc. Comp. Ling.,* Philadelphia, 1980, pp. 163–167.

Slocum, Jonathan, A Practical Comparison of Parsing Strategies for Machine Translation and Other Natural Language Processing Purposes, Ph.D. dissertation, Dept. Comp. Sci., University of Texas, Austin, 1981.

Smith, H. R., A System to Deduce a Semi-Syntactic Grammar from Sentences and Their Corresponding Deep Case Structures, Ph.D. dissertation, Dept. Comp. Sci., University of Texas, Austin, 1982.

Smith, M. K., Knowledge-Based Contextual Reference Resolution for Text Understanding, Ph.D. dissertation, Dept. Comp. Sci., University of Texas, Austin, 1981.

Tennant, H., *Natural Language Processing,* Petrocelli, Princeton, N.J., 1981.

Thompson, F. B., and Thompson B. H., Practical Natural Language Processing: The Rel System as Prototype, in M. Rubinoff and M. C. Yovits (eds.), *Advances in Computers 13,* Academic Press, New York, 1975.

Thorne, J. P., Bratley, P., and Dewar, H., The Syntactic Analysis of English by Machine, in D. Mitchie (ed.), *Machine Intelligence 3,* American Elsevier, New York, 1968.

TINLAP-1 (Schank, R., and Nash-Webber, B., eds.) *Theoretical Issues in Natural Language Processing,* MIT, Cambridge, Mass., 1975.

TINLAP-2 (Waltz, D., ed.) *Theoretical Issues in Natural Language Processing-2,* ACM, New York, 1978.

Tosh, W., *Syntactic Translation,* Mouton, The Hague, 1965.

Turing, A., Computing Machinery and Intelligence, in E. Feigenbaum and J. Feldman (eds.), *Computers and Thought,* McGraw-Hill, New York, 1963.

Usui, T., *An Experimental Grammar for Translating English to Japanese,* Dept. Comp. Sci., University of Texas, Tech. Rep. TR-201, Austin, 1982.

van Emden, M. H., Programming in Resolution Logic, in D. Mitchie (ed.), *Machine Intelligence 8,* University of Edinburgh, 1977, pp. 266–299.

Vauquois, B., Aspects of Mechanical Translation in 1979, Université Scientifique et Médicale de Grenoble, Groupe d'Etudes pour la Traduction Automatique, July 1979.

Waltz, D. L., and Goodman, B. A. Writing a Natural Language Data Base System, *Proc. 5th IJCAI,* 1977, pp. 144–150.

Warren, D. H. D., WARPLAN: A System for Generating Plans, DCL Memo 76, Dept. Artif. Intell., University of Edinburgh, Edinburgh, 1974.

Warren, D. H. D., Implementing PROLOG—Compiling Logic Programs, DAI Research Reps. 39, 40, University of Edinburgh, Edinburgh, 1977.

Warren, D. H. D., and Pereira, F. C. N., An Efficient Easily Adaptable System for Interpreting Natural Language Queries, *Am. J. Comp. Ling.,* 1982, in press.

Warren, D. H. D., Pereira, L. M., and Pereira, F. C. N., PROLOG—The Language and its Implementation Compared with LISP, *Proc. ACM Symp. Artif. Intell. Programming Languages, SIGPLAN Notices,* Vol. 12, p. 8/*SIGART Newsl.,* Vol. 64, pp. 109–115, Aug. 1977.

Weizenbaum, J., Eliza, *Commun. ACM,* Vol. 9, pp. 36–45, 1966.

Wilensky, R., Why John Married Mary: Understanding Stories Involving Recurring Goals, *Cognit. Sci.,* Vol. 2, No. 3, Yale Tech. Rep., 1978.

Wilensky, R., Understanding Complex Situations, *Proc. 6th IJCAI,* Vol. 2, Aug. 1979, pp. 954–959.

Wilensky, R., and Morgan, M., One Analyzer for Three Languages, Elect. Res. Lab.

Memo UCB/ERL M81/67, College of Engineering, University of California, Berkeley, 1981.

Wilks, Y., An Artificial Intelligence Approach to Machine Translation, in R. C. Schank and K. M. Colby, *Computer Models of Thought and Language,* W. H. Freeman, San Francisco, 1973.

Winograd, T., *Understanding Natural Language,* Academic Press, New York, 1972.

Woods, W. A., Procedural Semantics for a Question-Answering Machine, *Proc. AFIP,* Vol. 33, Thompson Book Co., Washington, D.C., Fall 1968, pp. 457–471.

Woods, W. A., What's in a Link: Foundations for Semantic Networks, in D. G. Bobrow and A. Collins (eds.), *Representation and Understanding,* Academic Press, New York, 1975.

Woods, W. A., Kaplan, R., and Nash-Webber, B., The Lunar Sciences Natural Language Information System: Final Report, BBN Rep. 2378, Bolt Beranek and Newman, Inc., Cambridge, Mass., 1972.

Young, R. L., Text Understanding: A Survey, *Am. J. Comp. Ling.,* Vol. 4, No. 4, Microfiche 70, 1977.

INDEX

A

Adjectival constructions, 137
Adjective:
   comparative, 65, 139
   contrast pairs, 65
   lexical form, 138
   superlative, 65, 108
Adverbials, 138, 139
Anaphora, 177, 237*ff*
Atomic clause, 36
Augmented p.s. grammar, 76*ff*
Automatic translation, 207 (*See also* Mechanical Translation and Translation.)

B

Backup problems, 108
Blocks world:
   blocks defined, 103
   commands, 100, 104
   lexicon, 106
   operation, 1
   robot, 99

Bottom-up control, 196
Bottom-up parsing, 77, 237*ff*

C

Case roles, 58
Case studies, 171, 175
Clausal form, 37
Clausal logic, 37
Clause, 54
Cocke-Kasami-Younger algorithm, 171
Coherence relations, 243
Communication, 19
Concept dependencies, 244
Concepts, 19
Concept strings, 27
Concept symbolization, 23
Conceptual dependencies, 152
Conceptualization, 21
Conceptual representation, 17, 29
Conceptual thought, 19
Conciseness, 96
Conjunction, 66
Connectives, 33
Consciousness, 14

Constituent:
  adjectival, 65
  adjective-noun, 88
  adverbial, 65
  binary, 55
  clausal, 62
  discontinuous, 55
  immediate, 55
  inflectional, 60
Context free grammar, 195
Control flow, complex, 206
Cooperative response, 122, 149
Cut symbol, 206

D

Data base:
  document, 123*ff*
  inferential, 225
  PROLOG, 225
  text, 175*ff*
Definite clause grammars, 48
Dependencies, clausal, 245
Dependency:
  analysis, 59
  rules, 56
  schema, 245
  structure, 56, 78
  tree, 56
Determiners, 66
Dialogue, 2
  politics, 235
  with expert mech, 232
Discourse:
  expository, 151
  narrative, 151
  outlines, 170, 227, 243–45
  representation, 151
  scripts, plans, 152
  semantic relations, 152
Document data-management, 119
Document relation, 123
Dominance, 56
Dualism, 15

E

Elision, 148, 241
Ellipsis, 177, 241
Expert knowledge system, 224*ff*
Expert mechanic, 225*ff*

F

Flow of control, 109
  bottom-up, 171*ff*
Formal data base, 120
Formal queries, 120
Formal query language, 128, 129
Frame problem, 100
Frames, 1
Functional arguments, 36
Functions, HCPRVR, 251, 256
Fuzzy matching, 175*ff*

G

Games, adventure, 234
Generation:
  answers, 187
  summaries, 188
Generator, 77
Grammar, 8
  ad hoc, 121
  augmented phrase structure, 76*ff*
  declarative, 198
  learning systems, 2
  in LISP, 82
  procedural logic, 84, 89, 253
  queries, 132, 133
  rocket story, 272*ff*
  transition net, 135

H

Harvard Predictive Analyzer, 194
HCPRVR, 40
HORN clauses, 10

I

Idiom, 53
Images, 19
Implication, 33
Index relations, 163*ff*
Inference, 34
Input-output HCPRVR, 258
Intelligence measures, 18
Intentions, 118, 236
Introspection, 20–23

K

Knowledge, 14
Knowledge representation, 17
Knowledge schemas, 239*ff*

L

Levels of structure, 53
Lexicon, English, 54
   assertions, 90
Linear resolution, 39
Literal, 36
Logic:
   plausible, 235*ff*
   predicate, 35
   probabilistic, 235
   propositional, 31
LOGLISP, 40
Lush resolution, 41

M

Meaning, 28, 29
   propositional, 31
Mechanical translation, 5*ff*
   (*See also* Translation.)
Menu-driven system, 123*ff*
MICROPLANNER, 7
Monism, 16
Morpheme, 54

N

Negation, 66
Noun phrase ambiguity, 111–12

O

Outline:
   hierarchic, 227
   of text, 170, 243–45
Paradigm:
   expert knowledge, 224
   knowledge, 246
   microworld, 224

P

Paraphrase, 57, 208*ff*
   fair, 209
   interpreter, 210–11
Paraphrased SSR, 212
Parse, alternate, 92
Parse tree, 84
Parsing, 194
   bottom-up, 200, 203
   chart, 202*ff*
   top-down, 201
   two-line, 199
Perceptual experience, 19
Pharmacological text, 8
Phenomenalism, 16
Phrase, 54
Plans, 118
Politics system, 235
Portability, 122
Postmodifiers, 135
Predicate logic, 35
Prefixes, 54
Print, 258
Procedural logic, 2, 39
Procedural semantics, 113–15
Programs:
   bottom-up control, 166–68
   candidates, 183

Programs (cont.)
  DOCQUERY, 126
  DOCREAD, 124
  expert knowledge, 231
  logic grammar, 136*ff*
  pronoun reference, 170
  query interpreter, 131
  summarize, 191
  member, 46
  merge, 48
  qsort, 48
  sort, 48
  subset, 46
  union, 47
  HCPRVR, 259
  (*See also* Parsing.)
PROLOG, 2, 10, 39
Proof tree, 50
Proving theorems, 38

Q

QLOG, 40
Quantification, explicit, 121
Quantifier-free forms, 39
Quantifiers, 37
Queries, complex, 179
  predicate logic, 175
Query context, 178
  extraction, 179
  term analysis, 180
Questions, 27, 60, 80
  and answers, 185*ff*
  context, 148
  document data base, 135
  how and why, 230
  natural language texts, 174
  politics, 235
  query and identifier, 177
  sublanguage, 177

R

Rationalization, 236
Read, 258

Reasoning, plausible, 235, 237
Relational data base, 123*ff*
Relational structure, 57
Relations, inverse, 182
  transitive, 182
Resolution proof, 34
Robots, 15
  intelligence, 118
  introspection, 118
  retrospection, 118
  shelf-manager, 119
Root forms, 60
Rules:
  as procedures, 81
  BNF for HCPRVR, 249
  if-then, 227
  possible fault, 229
  (*See also* Grammar.)

S

Schemas, 54
  bottom-up analysis, 162*ff*
  flight, 158*ff*
  flight instantiated, 286*ff*
  human memory, 155
  knowledge, 239
  parallel evaluation, 171
  top-down analysis, 153*ff*
  top-down flight, 283*ff*
SCHOLAR, 8
Scripts, 1
Semantic event forms, 79, 86, 137
Semantic features, 79, 86
Semantic networks, 7, 25, 28
Semantic parsing, 120
Semantic processing, 26
Semantic relations, 24, 60, 76*ff*
  logic of, 73
  quantifiers in, 75
  theory of, 72
Semantic rules, 79
Semantics, procedural, 99, 106
Semantic test, transformation, 93
Semantic translation, 85
  (*See also* Translation.)

Semantic well-formedness, 79
Sentences, 54
   analysis, rocket story, 156, 157
   embedded, 68
SHRDLU, 7
   (*See also* Blocks world.)
Simulation model, 154
Skolem constants, 74
Stories from problem solving, 153
Story grammars, 153, 157
Story trees, 158
Subschema, 54
Suffixes, 54
Summaries, 188*ff*
   computed, 192
Summary property, 56, 78–80, 96
Surface semantic relation, 76*ff*, 81, 86
Symmetry, 96, 187
Syntactic slots, 57
Syntactic subject, object, 78

T

Taxonomic hierarchy, 79
Taxonomic system, 148
Taxonomies, ad hoc, 181
Teaching programs, 225, 233–34
Text assertions, 175*ff*
Text grammar, PROLOG, 174
Theorem-proving, 9
Thoughts, 19
Top-down control, backup, 195
Top-down parsing, 77

Transfer rules, 209*ff*
   English-Japanese, 219
   symmetric, 222
   transformations, 55, 76*ff*
Translation:
   English-French, 214
   English-Japanese, 214*ff*
   paradigm, 207
   Spanish-English, 214
Truth functions, 33
Turing test, 15

U

Understanding text, 7
Unification, 39
Unification algorithm, 256

V

Variables, 32, 35
   global, HCPRVR, 251
   predicate logic, 35
   propositional, 32
Verbs, give, steal, 237*ff*
   have, 64
   to be, 64

W

Well-formed-formula, 36
Word, 53*ff*

AUTHOR INDEX

Abelson, R. P., 8, 9, 235, 295
Aho, A., 78, 207, 289
Allen, James F., 10, 75, 235, 236, 289, 291
Alterman, R., 243, 244, 245, 289
Amsler, Robert A., 181, 289, 293
Anderson, J. R., 289

Barr, A., 7, 13, 289
Bartlett, F. C., 155, 289
Bates, M., 289
Beaugrande, R. de, 10, 153, 289
Berkeley, E. C., 292
Black, F. S., 34, 258, 289
Bobrow, Daniel, 246, 290
Booth, A. D., 4, 6, 207, 290
Borko, H., 6, 290
Boyer, R. S., 39, 290
Brachman, R. J., 181, 246, 290
Bratley, P., 296
Bravo-Ahuja, Francisco, 214
Brown, F., 259
Brown, J. S., 9, 233, 290

Bruce, B., 75, 290
Bruderer, H. E., 6, 290
Buchanan, B. G., 290
Burger, J. F., 295
Burton, R. R., 233, 290
Bush, V., 4, 290

Carbonell, Jaime R., 9, 153, 235, 290
Cherry, L., 290
Chester, D., 12, 40, 75, 153, 215, 259, 290, 295
Chomsky, C., 291
Chomsky, N., 290
Clancy, W. J., 233, 290
Clark, K. L., 12, 225, 290
Coelho, H. M. F., 291
Cohn, P. H., 10, 291
Cohn, P. R., 291, 294
Colby, K. M., 172, 291
Colmerauer, A., 11, 39, 291
Correira, A., 153, 291, 295
Cullingford, R. E., 174, 291

Dahl, V., 121, 259, 291
Darlington, J. L., 291
Darvas, F., 291
deJong, G. F., 172, 174, 291
Dennett, D. C., 29
Dewar, H., 296
Dowty, D. R., 291
Duda, R. O., 224, 291
Dwiggins, D., 295

Fahlman, S. E., 181, 291
Feigenbaum, E. A., 7, 13, 224, 289, 291
Fillmore, C. J., 58, 291
Findler, N. V., 10, 13, 72, 291
Fraser, B., 290
Frisch, A. M., 75, 289
Futo, I., 225, 291

Gallaire, H., 12, 291
Gashnig, J. G., 224, 291
Gazdar, G., 291
Goldman, N., 291
Goodman, B. A., 296
Gotlieb, C., 292
Green, B. F., 291
Green, C., 291
Green, L. E. S., 292
Grice, H. P., 10, 292
Grimes, J., 152, 292
Grishman, Ralph, 9, 174, 292
Grosz, B., 152, 292

Halliday, M. A., 152, 292
Hart, P. E., 291
Hasan, R., 152, 292
Hendrix, G. G., 10, 120, 292
Hewitt, C., 292
Hewitt, H., 293
Hirshman, L., 174, 292
Hirst, G., 292
Hobbs, J. R., 152, 292

Ingria, R., 289

Johnson, M., 293
Johnson-Laird, P., 10, 238, 293
Jorgenson, E., 225, 292

Kaplan, Jerry, 122, 181, 292
Kaplan, R. M., 292, 296
Kay, Martin, 202, 292
Kellogg, C. H., 292
Klappholz, A. D., 152, 293
Klein, S., 153
Komorowski, H. J., 12, 40, 292
Konolige, K., 291
Kowalski, R. A., 11, 39, 40, 293
Kuno, S., 194, 293

Lakoff, G., 292
Laughery, K., 291
Lehmann, W. P., 207, 293
Lehnert, W. C., 13, 293
LeVine, Sharon, 175, 179, 293
Lindsay, R. K., 293
Locke, W. N., 4, 293
Lockman, A., 152, 293
Loveland, David, 250

Mann, W. C., 293
Marcus, M. P., 293
Markusz, Z., 225, 293
Mascaro, J., 29, 30
McCabe, F., 225, 290
McCarthy, J., 44, 293
McDermott, J., 225, 246, 293
Meehan, James, 153, 293
Miller, G. A., 10, 293
Minker, J., 12, 291
Montague, R., 293

Montgomery, C., 295
Morgan, M., 296
Moore, J. A., 39, 290

Nash-Webber, B., 296, 297
Newell, A., 246, 248, 293
Nilsson, N. J., 294
Norman, D. A., 10, 30, 290, 293
Novak, G. S., 154, 248, 294

Oettinger, A., 194, 293

Partee, B. H., 294
Pelletier, F. J., 295
Pereira, F. C. N., 11, 175, 259, 294, 296
Pereira, L. M., 11, 259, 296
Perrault, C. R., 291, 294
Petrick, S. R., 9, 121, 294
Pflueger, S., 293
Phillips, B., 152, 294
Pratt, V. R., 294
Propp, V., 153, 294

Quillian, M. R., 7, 294

Raphael, B., 294
Reboh, R., 291
Reddy, D. R., 294
Reid, B. K., 123, 294
Riesbeck, C., 9, 13, 207, 237, 294, 295
Robinson, J. Alan, 11, 12, 40, 41, 294
Robinson, Jane, 9, 121, 294
Roussell, P., 11, 39, 294
Rumelhart, D. E., 10, 153, 293, 294

Sacerdoti, E. D., 292, 294
Sagalowicz, D., 292
Sager, Naomi, 9, 13, 85, 121, 294
Satterthwaite, A. C., 207, 295
Schank, Roger, 8, 9, 13, 207, 235, 237, 295, 296
Schubert, L. K., 20, 295
Schwartz, R. M., 295
Schwind, C., 259
Searle, J., 10, 295
Shapiro, S. C., 10, 295
Shortliffe, E. H., 224, 290, 295
Sibert, E. E., 12, 40, 175, 294
Sidner, C. L., 152, 295
Silva, G., 174, 295
Simmons, R. F., 75, 153, 215, 259, 292, 295
Slocum, Jonathan, 172, 292, 295
Smith, H. R., 293, 296
Smith, M. K., 152, 296
Suzuki, S., 30
Szered, P., 291

Tarnlund, S., 12, 290
Tennant, H., 13, 296
Thompson, B. H., 120, 296
Thompson, F. B., 120, 296
Thorne, J. P., 296
Tosh, W., 207, 296
Turing, A., 4, 296

Ullman, J., 78, 289
Usui, T., 214, 215, 217, 296

van Emden, M. H., 39, 296
Vauquois, B., 6, 207, 296

Walker, J. H., 123, 294
Waltz, D. L., 296
Warren, D. H. D., 11, 39, 175, 259, 294, 296
Weizenbaum, J., 172, 296
Whitehead, A. N., 30
Wilensky, R., 296
Wilks, Y., 207, 297

Winograd, Terry, 13, 58, 99, 246, 290, 296
Wittgenstein, L., 30
Wolf, A. K., 291
Woods, W. A., 9, 10, 85, 120, 297

Young, R. L., 152, 297